The Twelve Years Truce (1609)

Legal History Library

VOLUME 13

Studies in the History of International Law

VOLUME 6

The titles published in this series are listed at *brill.com/shil*

The Twelve Years Truce (1609)

Peace, Truce, War and Law in the Low Countries at the Turn of the 17th Century

Edited by

Randall Lesaffer

BRILL
NIJHOFF

LEIDEN | BOSTON

Cover illustration: Official Dutch publication of the Truce of 1609. © National Archives, The Hague, Archives of the States General 1576–1796.

Library of Congress Cataloging-in-Publication Data

The Twelve Years' Truce (1609) : peace, truce, war, and law in the low countries at the turn of the 17th century / edited by Randall Lesaffer.
pages cm. -- (Legal history library ; v. 13)
ISBN 978-90-04-27491-4 (hardback: alk. paper) -- ISBN 978-90-04-27492-1 (e-book) 1. Spain. Treaties, etc. United Provinces of the Netherlands, 1609 Apr. 9. 2. Netherlands--History--Twelve Years' Truce, 1609-1621. 3. Spain. Treaties, etc. United Provinces of the Netherlands, 1648 January 30. 4. Netherlands--History--Eighty Years' War, 1568-1648. 5. Law--Benelux countries--History. I. Lesaffer, Randall, editor of compilation.

KZ1329.8.A58T84 2014
949.2'03--dc23

2014014503

This publication has been typeset in the multilingual "Brill" typeface. With over 5,100 characters covering Latin, IPA, Greek, and Cyrillic, this typeface is especially suitable for use in the humanities.
For more information, please see www.brill.com/brill-typeface.

ISSN 1874-1793
ISBN 978-90-04-27491-4 (hardback)
ISBN 978-90-04-27492-1 (e-book)

This book is printed on acid-free paper.

Contents

Note on Contributors

Peter Borschberg
is an associate professor in the Department of History at the National University of Singapore and a visiting professor in modern history at the University of Greifswald. He has published widely on the history of early modern trade from a global perspective, colonial Southeast Asia as well as on the origins of modern international law.

Erik-Jan Broers
is assistant professor of legal history at Tilburg Law School. He has widely published on the history of criminal law.

Paul Brood
is a legal historian and archivist at the National Archives of the Netherlands in The Hague.

Bram De Ridder
is a PhD fellow of the Research Foundation – Flanders (FWO) at the University of Leuven. He studied history in Leuven and International Relations at the University of Cambridge. His work focuses on early modern border issues and peace.

Alicia Esteban Estríngana
is professor of history at the University of Alcalá de Henares. She is a leading specialist on the Spanish Empire in the Early Modern Age.

Carlo Focarelli
is professor of international law at the University of Perugia and LUISS Guido Carli University of Rome where he has also taught history of international law. He is the author of *International Law as Social Construct* (Oxford, 2012) and *Introduzione storica al diritto internazionale* (Milan, 2012).

Beatrix C.M. Jacobs
is professor of Dutch legal history at Tilburg Law School. She published especially on the history of the administration of justice, procedural law and constitutional law.

Randall Lesaffer
is professor of legal history at Tilburg Law School and part-time professor of international and European legal history at the University of Leuven. Most of his work relates to the law of nations in Early-Modern Europe.

Bernd Klesmann
is research assistant at Cologne University (Historisches Institut). His primary areas of interest are international, especially French history of the 17th and 18th centuries and the history of journalism.

Georges Martyn
is professor of legal history at the University of Ghent. His main fields of research are the history of the legal professions, legal iconography and early modern private and public law.

Tim Piceu
is a historian and an assistant at the University of Leuven campus Kortrijk. He currently works on the historiography of the Southern Netherlands between 1500 and 1830.

Violet Soen
is professor of Early Modern History at the University of Leuven. Her work focuses on war, peace and reconciliation during the Dutch Revolt.

Werner Thomas
is professor of Spanish and Latin American history at the University of Leuven. He has focused his research on the Low Countries as a part of the Spanish monarchy, and has published on the history of the Spanish inquisition, Protestantism in Spain, and the government of the Archdukes in the Southern Netherlands.

Olaf van Nimwegen
is a research fellow at the University of Utrecht. He is a specialist in the military history of the Dutch Republic.

Johanna Waelkens
studied classics as well as law and is now a PhD fellow at the Faculty of Law of the University of Leuven. She writes a thesis in the field of contract law.

Alain Wijffels
teaches at the universities of Leiden, Leuven and Louvain-la-Neuve. His main subjects are legal history and comparative law. He is also a research fellow of the French CNRS (UMR 8025, Lille).

Introduction

Randall Lesaffer

On 9 April 1609, the representatives of the States General of the Republic of the United Provinces of the Northern Netherlands and the representatives of the Archdukes Albert and Isabelle, sovereign lords of the Southern Netherlands, signed a truce for twelve years at Antwerp. On 7 July, the Spanish King Philip III ratified the Treaty at Madrid, putting his signature under a text that implied the, albeit temporary, recognition of the United Provinces as free states. The Treaty suspended the hostilities between the rebellious Northern Netherlands and the Spanish Monarchy that had first erupted in 1567 and which had grown into a major, full scale war and spilled over into the Indies. After the expiration of the truce in 1621, war resumed until the final peace settlement at Munster of 30 January 1648 put an end to what has become known as the Eighty Years War (1567–1648).

The Twelve Years Truce is a major event in the national political and constitutional history of the Netherlands. Although formally speaking, the recognition of its freedom by Spain was temporary, it was a crucial step in the birth of the Republic as a sovereign power. The Peace Treaty of Munster would add little to that, except for the definite acquiescence by Spain to a reality that had by then existed and had hardly been seriously contested for almost four decades. The text of the Peace Treaty itself was largely copied from the Twelve Years Truce.

The scope of this book is not limited to the significance of the Twelve Years Truce in Dutch national history. The Antwerp Treaty is rather looked upon as an event through which to study the turmoil and upheaval that marked the international order of Europe and the law of nations at the time. The period running from the early 16th to the midst of the 17th century saw a fundamental transition of the international order of Europe. At its beginning stood the late-medieval order of the *respublica christiana*, a conglomerate of a myriad of diverse political entities which all enjoyed a measure of autonomy but at the same time formed a certain political and legal unity under the supreme, if highly theoretical overlordship of the pope and the emperor. Under this system, the law regulating inter-power relations, the *jus gentium,* did not as yet form an autonomous body of law but was part and parcel of the law at large. At its end stood the modern states system and its classical law of nations – the *jus publicum Europaeum* – as an autonomous body of law. This new order and law became established in the decades that followed the Westphalian Peace Treaties (1648).

 | DOI 10.1163/9789004274921_002

This transition was overshadowed by great unrest and upheaval. Three major factors drove the change. First, there was the Reformation which brought an end to the religious unity of the Latin West and collapsed the authority of canon law and papal jurisdiction upon which the fabric of European political and legal order ultimately rested. What had been the foundation of European unity now became a factor of division. Second, the 16th century saw the rise of dynastic power-complexes which liberated themselves from the final vestiges of the 'universal' authority of emperor and pope and started the drawn-out process of internal centralisation and state formation, breaking the mould of the complex mixture of hierarchy and freedom that was the hallmark of late-medieval order. Third, the discoveries, trade and conquests by European power in Asia, Africa and America set new questions on the agenda of international relations and law to which the old medieval *jus gentium* did not have ready answers.

Halfway through the 16th century, the old European order was in shambles. What followed was a long period of destabilisation at the heart and fringes of the old Latin West, with internal political strife, religious war and endemic international war, culminating in the greatest conflict of all, the Thirty Years War (1618–1648). These were hardly the conditions for a new consent on the political and legal order of Europe to arise. For this, one had to await the midst of the 17th century when the Westphalia Peace Treaties put an end to the Thirty and Eighty Years Wars.

Although the century running from the midst of the 16th to the midst of the 17th century failed to bring consent on a new stable order, it was a period in which the order of Europe and the law of nations stood high on the agenda and which in the end proved very productive and inspirational for the new order that was to be articulated after 1648. As it is widely recognised in the historiography of international law, it was the period in which the law of nations started to emerge as an autonomous intellectual discipline with its own literature through the endeavours of both theologians and jurists, chiefly among whom stands the Dutch humanist Hugo Grotius (1583–1645). But also diplomatic practice was rife with changes and experiments in the ways 'international' relations and transactions were legally organised. Whereas many old customs and practices from the late Middle Ages were rehearsed and recycled, they often had to be adapted to the changing context of state formation, religious diversity, the expansion of Europe and the shifting nature of war and trade. Many of the changes and innovations of the late 16th and early 17th centuries would later find their way into the classical law of nations.

The Twelve Years Truce offers a uniquely fascinating prism through which to look at the colours and shades of the turmoil and change of the international order of Europe at the turn of the 17th century. The Antwerp Truce was a major diplomatic event in Europe. It brought a temporary end to a long-lasting and large-scale conflict which had deeply wounded the leading power of the time, the Spanish Monarchy, and sucked in other powers, including the French and English. The Treaty itself did not only involve the Republic, the Archdukes and Spain but also the French and English kings, whose representatives acted as mediators. But even more to the point, the conflict which was suspended by the Antwerp Truce reflected in every respect the turmoil of the age. The conflict between the Netherlands and the Spanish Monarchy was an example, only rare in its extent and success, of local elites resisting the policies of centralisation of the prince. It also rapidly turned into a religious war, with time seeing the borderlines drawn between a catholic south loyal to the Spanish King and a rebellious north dominated by Calvinists. Already from its earlier stages, the war in the Low Countries expanded into a major international conflict as the enemies of the Spanish Monarchy intervened on the side of the northern rebels and the conflict became a new nucleus for anti-Habsburg coalitions. The break with Spain also brought the merchants and navigators from the rebellious provinces to venture on their own into the Indies and mount a successful challenge to the Portuguese and Spanish claims to monopoly of trade and navigation there.

But the Antwerp Truce itself is also of a more direct relevance to the historiography of international law. First, there was the involvement of Grotius, whose treatise *Mare Liberum* was published in the context of the negotiations of the Truce.[1] Second, the Antwerp Treaty forms an interesting document from the perspective of the growth of the tradition of modern European peace treaties. Although it was not a definite peace but a truce, the Antwerp Treaty was an extremely elaborate legal instrument, containing many detailed regulations about the suspension of the state of war and the restoration of normal peaceful relations, thus being highly informative for the laws of war and peace of the period. To some extent, it was also constitutive to the laws of war and peace of the later 17th and 18th centuries as the Antwerp Truce and its additional, interpretative treaties of 1610 served as the textual basis for the Peace Treaty of Munster.[2] Through the central role Dutch diplomacy played in the

1 Grotius' involvement is not covered in this book. For a recent study, see Martine van Ittersum, *Profit and Principle: Hugo Grotius, Natural Rights Theories and the Rise of Dutch Power in the East Indies (1595–1615)* (Leyden/Boston, 2006).

2 Randall Lesaffer, 'La Tregua de los Doce Años y la formación del Derecho de Naciones clásico' in Bernardo J. García García (ed.), *Tiempo de Paces 1609–2009. La Pax Hispanica y la Tregua de los Doce Años* (Madrid, 2009), 177–191.

peacemaking efforts of the later 17th and early 18th centuries, some of the Antwerp Truce would thus find its way into the lore of great European peace treaties of the classical law of nations.[3]

The essays collected in this volume fall into three groups. Part I: 'Truce and Peace' consists of four essays. The first, introductory chapter by Paul Brood places the Antwerp Truce in the line of great constitutional texts of the Dutch Republic, highlighting its relation to the Munster Peace Treaty. The contributions by Alicia Esteban Estríngana, by Bram de Ridder and Violet Soen and by Alain Wijffels delve into three phases of the diplomatic pre-history of the Antwerp Truce negotiations. They cover the drawn-out process of efforts by Madrid to disentangle from war in the north but with ultimately failed to secure a lasting peace.

Part II: 'Truce and War' collects three essays dealing with matters of war and alliance. Peter Borschberg addresses the consequences of the Truce for the Dutch prior war-time alliance with the Kingdom of Johor in the East Indies. Olaf van Nimwegen covers tactical military reforms in the Dutch army in the period before and under the truce while Tim Piceu offers an in-depth-study of the Antwerp settlement in relation to contributions.

Part III: 'Truce and Law' turns to the legal context and implications of the truce, both constitutional as well as international. Beatrix C.M. Jacobs tries to assess the legal implications of the recognition of the United Provinces as free states while Georges Martyn discusses the position of the Archdukes as sovereign princes of the Southern Netherlands. Carlo Focarelli offers a general outline of the role of the early modern jurisprudence of the law of nations in the transition from to modernity, focussing on the subject of diplomatic immunity. Randall Lesaffer, Johanna Waelkens and Erik-Jan Broers use the unique history of the Antwerp Truce and the Munster Peace Treaty and their close interrelation to try to assess the character and implications of a truce under the laws of war and peace. Bernd Klesmann discusses the reference to peace and truce agreements for the justification of new wars. Finally, Werner Thomas's essay discusses the consequences of the 1604 English-Spanish Peace Treaty and the Antwerp Truce for religious policy and relevant law in the Netherlands and the Spanish Monarchy.

3 Randall Lesaffer and Erik-Jan Broers, 'Private Property in the Dutch-Spanish Peace Treaty of Münster (30 January 1648)' in Michael Jucker, Martin Kintzinger and Rainer Christoph Schwinges (eds.), *Rechtsformen internationaler Politik. Theorie, Norms und Praxis vom 12. bis 18. Jahrhundert* (Zeitschrift für Historische Forschung, Beihefte 45; Berlin, 2011), 165–195.

PART 1

Truce and Peace

CHAPTER 1

The Twelve Years Truce

Textual Explanations

Paul Brood

Introduction

The treaty and the ratification of The Twelve Years Truce (1609) are documents which should be reckoned among the monuments of Dutch constitutional history. Although the Twelve Years Truce has long remained underexposed, its significance is comparable with the Utrecht Union of 1579 and the Peace Treaty of Munster of 1648. In the Dutch National Archives, these constitutional documents form the backbone of the collection.

The Utrecht Union of 1579 was a union between seven autonomous provinces in the Northern Netherlands with one goal: war against Spain. The provinces retained their sovereignty. They would only act together if their common interest dictated so; the union pertained chiefly to foreign relations, defence and war. But the Utrecht Union actually became and remained the closest thing to a constitution the Dutch Republic had for more than two centuries. The Truce of 1609 marked the factual recognition of the Dutch Republic as an independent power. It was a moment of tremendous significance and would serve to some extent as an inspiration of the Founding Fathers of the American republic for the Declaration of Independence in 1776.[1] In the Westphalian Peace Treaty of 1648, Spain confirmed the independence of the Dutch provinces from the Spanish Monarchy.[2]

In the Introduction, it was indicated that the Twelve Years Truce formed the foundation for the text of the Munster Peace Treaty. This chapter explains to what extent this was the case. Furthermore, it addresses what the textual influence of the older constitutional texts, the Union of Utrecht and the Act of Abjuration (1581), on the 1609 Truce was. Finally, some light is shed on the question who the main penholder to the Truce was.

1 J.P.A Coopmans, 'Het Plakkaat van Verlatinge (1581) en de Declaration of Independence (1776)', *Bijdragen en Mededelingen betreffende de geschiedenis der Nederlanden*, 8 (1983) 540–567.

2 Its legal position in relation to the Holy Roman Empire has been covered by Robert Feenstra, 'A quelle époque, les Provinces-Unies sont elles-devenues indépendentes en droit à l'égard du Saint-Empire?', *Legal History Review*, (20) 1952. See also Johannes Arndt, *Das Heilige Römisches Reich und die Niederlande 1566 bis 1648* (Cologne/Weimar/Vienna, 1998).

 | DOI 10.1163/9789004274921_003

Constitutional Monuments

The commemoration of the Twelve Years Truce in 2009 offered the occasion for the Dutch National Archives to edit a book containing 21 constitutional monuments which form part of its collection and which highlight the major steps in Dutch constitutional history.[3] The oldest document in the collection is the so-called *Groot Privilege* from 1477. This privilege brought more uniformity to the apparatus of government in the Burgundian Netherlands. The most recent document is the general constitutional amendment of 1983. At that moment, a new first article was inserted into the Dutch constitution: the injunction of discrimination.

Among these 21 highlights of Dutch history, the Utrecht Union of 1579, the Westphalian Peace of Munster of 1648 and the Constitution of 1814 can be found. Each has played a significant role in Dutch history. The Utrecht Union of 1579 was considered more or less to be the constitution of the Republic of the Netherlands for more than two centuries. The Constitution of 1814 still forms the foundation of the current constitution, although it went through important amendments in 1848, 1917 and 1983. From a very different order are three treaties of separation edited in this book: in 1839 with Belgium, in 1949 with Indonesia and in 1975 with Suriname.

From the period between 1648 and 1798, a period of exactly 150 years, not a single document was reproduced. Although the Republic went through important changes, the old 'fundamental laws' as they were entitled in old editions of laws and placards, apparently still sufficed.

In the lineage of constitutional monuments, The Twelve Years Truce holds its place. The significance of the Twelve Years Truce has always been underexposed. The Quattrocentenary of the Truce in 2009 was therefore a welcome occasion to change that.

At the beginning of the 17th century, Spain and the Dutch provinces had reached a stalemate in the war that had been raging since 1567 and would eventually become known in history as the Eighty Years War. The government in Brussels began to consider the idea of peace talks. However, King Philip III (1598–1621) was not easily convinced, in spite of the enormous financial concerns of Spain. In the Republic of the Netherlands, the opinions differed greatly on the matter. The agricultural provinces, such as Groningen, Overijssel and Gelderland, which had often found themselves at the frontline of the war and had suffered most from it, were in favour of peace. The merchant class of

3 Martin Berendse and Paul Brood, *In 21 stappen vrij onverveerd. Constitutionele topstukken van het Nationaal Archief* (Hilversum, 2009).

Holland agreed. But Zeeland, which took great advantage of its privateering against Spanish shipping, preferred to continue this profitable business. Slowly, the supporters and opponents of continuing the war found their respective leaders in the persons of Prince Maurits of Nassau (1567–1625), Stadholder and Captain- and Admiral-General of the Union and the Pensionary of Holland, Johan van Oldenbarnevelt (1547–1619).

Since 1606, Spain and the Republic had been negotiating about an end to the war. For the Dutch chief negotiator Oldenbarnevelt, the recognition of the United Provinces as free and independent states was a strict condition. In October 1607, King Philip III agreed to a ceasefire, under condition that the Catholic people in the North could practise their religion. The States General of the Republic accepted the King's demand, but found at the same time that their freedom included control over religious issues. The peace talks that followed came to a standstill in 1608 because of two demands of the King: freedom of religion for the Catholics and no free trade in the East Indies. The States General decided to break off the negotiations. To the French diplomate Pierre Jeannin (1540–1622) falls the merit of having revived the talks. Together with the other French and English diplomats (and in the beginning also Danish and Germans ambassadors), in their role as mediators, he was able to broker a long-term truce.

On 9 April 1609, the representatives agreed in Antwerp on a final treaty text. The hostilities would stop for twelve years and during that time the 'freedom' of the Republic would be recognised. Officially, the sea-going trade outside Europe needed the approval of Philip III, but this approval was rendered to the Dutch in a separate, 'secret' article.

Textual Analysis

The Antwerp Truce of 1609 consists of 38 articles. The five first articles concern the points that form the backbone of the agreement: 1) The Archdukes Albert and Isabella, sovereign rulers of the Southern Netherlands, entered into a truce with the United Provinces as being free states; 2) for a period of twelve years all acts of hostility would be stopped; 3) both sides would hold on to the territories as they possessed them at the time of the agreement (the status quo); 4) the parties guaranteed free movement and the right to trade within Europe, while they would ask the King for permission for the Dutch to trade in the Indies and 5) the Truce would be announced everywhere within the year. The two final articles concern the ratification. Article 37 stipulated that the treaty would be ratified by the Archdukes and the States General within four days and by the King within three months, whereas in Article 38 it was stated that the text of the Truce would be published forthwith.

The other 31 articles can be divided into two categories: first, matters of private interest and second, the implementation of the ceasefire. Among the articles relating to matters of private interest, we find articles on the equal taxation of inhabitants in both territories, the equal treatment of merchants, the restitution of property seized during the war and the like. The Treaty contains some particular stipulations concerning the inheritance of William the Silent (1531–1584). Ecclesiastical property in the north had to be returned as well. The Antwerp Treaty also contained articles pertaining to the cessation of hostilities, such as the promise not to arrest merchants and the agreement not to admit warships in the harbours. Whoever had moved abroad during the war could benefit from the truce and freely choose a place of residence. Building new fortresses was forbidden. All prisoners of war were released and both sides promised to free the seas of pirates and do nothing that conflicted with the Truce. Last but not least, the parties stipulated the freedom of sea-going trade.

After twelve years the truce indeed ended and, in 1621, hostilities were resumed. But in the long run, Spain tired of the war. Piet Hein (1577–1629) took the Spanish silver fleet in 1628 while Maarten Tromp (1598–1653) destroyed a Spanish Armada in 1639 at the Battle of the Downs. As from 1635, The Republic's main ally France was at war with Spain, while from 1640 onwards revolts raged in Portugal and Catalonia. All this induced the Spanish King to make the Republic an advantageous offer to end the war.

In 1644, a peace conference was opened in the German towns of Munster and Osnabruck. Participants were the Emperor and many of the estates of the Holy Roman Empire, Spain, France and Sweden. After two years, in 1646, the Republic of the Netherlands acceded to this Westphalian conference. The most important Dutch negotiators were Adriaan Pauw (1622–1697) and Johan de Knuyt (1587–1654). The negotiators signed a ceasefire on 30 January 1646. This ceasefire would last for twenty years and included the recognition of Dutch sovereignty. On 8 January 1647, a provisional treaty was made, in which the status quo in the East and West Indies was recognised and the charters for the Dutch East Indies Company and the West Indies Company accepted. After a third round of negotiations the Spanish and Dutch negotiators agreed on the text of a peace treaty and signed it at Munster on 30 January 1648.

This Munster Peace Treaty contains 79 articles. Its essence lies in the first three articles:

> Article 1: Philip IV recognises the United Provinces as free and sovereign states. The peace will last for ever.

Article 2: All hostilities, on land or on sea, will end.
Article 3: The status quo is applied in relation to territorial matters. The Republic may keep the occupied parts of Flanders, Brabant and Limburg. Disputes on territories will be brought before the Chambre mi-parti.

Furthermore, a few articles concern the ratification and publication of the Treaty:

Article 7: Because of the great distance the Peace will only enter into force in the East Indies after one year; in the West Indies after half a year.
Article 77: Within two months, ratifications must be exchanged.
Article 78: Until then, amendments to the status quo are not allowed.
Article 79: The text of the Treaty will be published immediately upon ratification.

Just as with the Twelve Years Truce, the articles of the Munster Peace Treaty can be divided into two categories: the implementation of peace and matters of private interest. Under the first category we see articles like:

Article 4: Subjects on both sides may travel and trade freely in the other party's lands.
Article 5: Sea-going trade on the East and West Indies is to remain as it is at that time of the agreement.
Article 11: Traffic and trade among subjects of the signatories will not be impeded.
Article 14: The Republic may continue the (qualified) 'closure' of the River Scheldt.
Article 19: Subjects from both sides should be discrete in the practice of their religion in the other party's lands.
Article 20: Merchants and sailors will not be arrested nor their goods seized in case of war or for other reasons.
Article 21: A Chambre mi-parti will be installed to pass judgment on disputes relating to the execution of the Peace Treaty.
Article 63: All prisoners of war will be released.

The Munster Peace Treaty also held many stipulations on matters of private interest:

Article 8: Subjects on both sides will pay equal taxes on trade. Taxation imposed during the Twelve Years Truce is no longer valid.

Article 9: Both sides will not impose taxes on transit trade through their lands.
Article 24: Former owners may repossess of all the property which was seized during the war without any judicial sentence.
Article 25: Prince William the Silent's heirs will enjoy the same advantages.

It is clear that the articles of the Antwerp Truce directly inspired the Munster Peace Treaty. The Dutch draft of the Munster Treaty, which served as basis for the treaty text, took the majority of its 71 articles literally from the Twelve Years Truce and the two treaties of interpretation of 7 January 1610 and 24 June 1610. One regulation expressly refers to the Antwerp Truce. Article 66 from the Munster Treaty states that Article 15 of the Antwerp Truce and Article 10 of the Treaty of 7 January 1610 amending the Truce would remain valid. These articles pertain to the compensation for confiscated property. Many wordings and sentences in other articles are literally the same. The Articles 3 of both the 1609 Truce and the Westphalian Peace Treaty are a significant example:

Een yegelick sal behouden ende datelick gebruycken die lantschappen, steden, plaetsen, landen ende heerlijckheyden die hij tegenwoordich houdt ende besidt, sonder daerinne getroubleert ofte belet te worden.

[Everyone will retain and actually use the lands, towns, places, manors and domains which one possesses nowadays, without any prevention or refusal.]

Some Additional Considerations

Most interesting in international treaties often are the considerations about why a treaty was made, often to be found in the preamble. The preamble to the 1609 Truce opens by offering a kind of historical review of past events. Several short term-ceasefires were reached in the last years, but an agreement for peace had not been possible. Even now both sides wanted to stop hostilities, a long term ceasefire was hard to reach, but the special efforts of the ambassadors finally brought the wonderful result of a truce.

In the 1648 Peace Treaty, the preamble sets out that for many years, bloody wars have oppressed the people and countries under obedience of the King of Spain and the States General of the Republic. Now they desire to end this dreadful situation for the prosperity and peace of the people and to restore all the damage. The text invokes the help of God. Whereas the preamble to the 1609 Truce went more into historical detail, the preamble of 1648 almost makes us hear the parties moan: 'Thanks God it is over.'

The similarities between the 1609 Truce and the 1648 Peace Treaty are many and clear. But did the drafters of these treaties also use other constitutional documents, such as the Act of Abjuration and the Utrecht Union?

The comparison of these documents gives us a negative answer. The Utrecht Union of 1579 is a union between the principalities Gelre and Zutphen, the counties and provinces of Holland, Zeeland, Utrecht and the Frisian Ommelanden, agreeing to confirm the Union that was made at Ghent. The most important of the 26 articles is the commitment to help each other defend their lands against foreign powers and to pay for the common defence from common taxes. So, the Union was an agreement to cooperate against a common enemy.

In the Act of Abjuration of 1581, a fascinating argument is set out on the obligations of a king to protect his subjects and not to oppress them. In case the prince acts tyrannically, his subjects have a right to suspend their allegiance to their king and choose another sovereign.[4] Moreover, the Act gives a broad survey of the misdemeanours of King Philip II (1556–1598). The logical conclusion is that the States General renounce him as their prince.

The Act of Abjuration did not inspire the texts of 1609 and 1648, but it looks like it has served for the American Declaration of Independence in 1776. It is generally accepted that the Act of Abjuration, which has also been called 'the Dutch Declaration of Independence,' was well known among the drafters of the American Declaration. It is quite likely that copies of the Dutch text were circulating in the Continental Congress. The precedent of an abjuration of a sovereign because of his failure to be a good king was very important for the law-minded drafters of the Declaration of Independence. For the first time in modern history, a king was successfully renounced by the people. A close comparison between both texts shows that some of ideas in the Declaration of Independence indeed came from the Dutch text.[5]

Who wrote the text of the Twelve Years Truce?

Was the Dutch statesman Johan van Oldenbarnevelt the author of the 1609 Truce, as many people think? Or was it someone else? It is quite certain that

4 Paul Brood and Raymond Kubben (eds.), *The Act of Abjuration. Inspired and Inspirational. Twelve Authors on One of the Highlights of the Nationaal Archief of the Netherlands* (Nijmegen, 2011).

5 Stephen E. Lucas, 'The Act of Abjuration as a Model for the Declaration of Independence: Thomas Jefferson and the Art of Imitation' in Brood and Kubben, *Act of Abjuration*, 173–189, and literature there.

the Act of Abjuration of 1581 is written by the audiencer (the registrar) of the central government, Jan van Asseliers. For the text of the Twelve Years Truce it is not possible to point out one author. It is plausible that several diplomats had a hand in the drafting of the text.

Van Eysinga elaborated on the matter in a study in 1959.[6] He read the most fascinating *Négociations diplomatiques et politiques du Président Jeannin*, written down in 1598–1620, and he reconstructed the diplomatic genesis of the Truce.[7] This allowed him to indicate who played a pivotal role in the text's genesis.

From the perusal of Jeannin's correspondence and its confrontation with the resolutions of the Sates General, we can see that on 27 August 1608, the French negotiator Pierre Jeannin, on behalf of the ambassadors of all mediating powers, made an important proposition. Jeannin proposed that as peace had proved unattainable, the belligerents should try to make a long-term truce between themselves. The United Provinces would be recognised as free states, trade in the Indies and all Spanish territories should be free. Everyone would keep what he possessed at the commencement of the Antwerp Truce.

This proposition gave the States General everything they wanted and the Dutch negotiator Johan van Oldenbarnevelt understood that its acceptance was urgent. Nevertheless, it would take until 13 January 1609 for the States General to open negotiations on the basis of the proposition and text of 27 August.

The express role of Jeannin in the year before the Twelve Years Truce is a convincing argument for the presumption that he was the main responsible for its text. Other negotiators have surely made their contributions to the text. Among them Johan van Oldenbarnevelt surely figured among the foremost, as it is shown by his notes from his personal papers.

---

6 W.J.M. van Eysinga, *De wording van het twaalfjarig bestand van 9 April 1609* (Verhandelingen der Koninklijke Nederlandse Akademie van Wetenschappen, afdeling Letterkunde N.S. 66.3; Amsterdam, 1959).

7 J.A.C. Buchon (ed.), *Négotiations diplomatiques et politiques du Président Pierre Jeannin (1598–1620)* (Paris, 1875).

CHAPTER 2

Preparing the Ground

*The Cession of the Netherlands' Sovereignty in 1598 and the Failure of its Peace-Making Objective (1607–1609)**

Alicia Esteban Estríngana

Introduction

In December 1608, the Dominican friar Iñigo de Brizuela, confessor to Archduke Albert of Austria, travelled to Madrid to persuade Philip III to arrange a lengthy truce with the United Provinces that would include the terms of the initial agreement of the eight-month ceasefire concluded in The Hague in the spring of 1607. This agreement took the form of a declaration of wills dated 24 April 1607,[1] which the Archdukes and Philip III had ratified that same year.

Unlike the Archdukes, the monarch did not issue his ratification immediately. He did so on 18 September 1607,[2] once the ceasefire – originally applicable only on land – had been extended to cover the sea (namely, the waters of the North Sea, the English Channel and the Iberian Peninsula) in a second joint declaration dated in The Hague on 1 June 1607.[3] However, the cessation of hostilities at sea was not the greatest impediment that Philip III encountered when Brussels asked him to confirm the first declaration. The fact that, at the beginning of the declaration, the Archdukes should proclaim that they were 'content to negotiate with the States General of the United Provinces in their capacity as, and holding them to be, free countries, provinces and States over which Their Highnesses make no claims, whether by means of a perpetual peace, a truce or suspension of arms for twelve, fifteen or twenty

* Study carried out within the framework of a research contract in the MICINN's Ramón y Cajal subprogram, attached to the University of Alcalá, and an R&D project (same ministry, same university): HAR 2009-12963-C03-02/HIS. This is a shorter modified version of my article: 'La Tregua de los Doce Años: fracaso del principio de reunión pactada de los Países Bajos bajo el dominio de los Archiduques', *Pedralbes. Revista d'Història Moderna*, 29 (2009), 99–158, translated to English by Janet Dawson.

1 Papel nº 5 'Cessación de armas para ocho meses', Brussels and The Hague, 24 April, 1607, Biblioteca Nacional de España (hereafter BNE), Manuscript (MS) 11.187, fols. 8r–v.

2 Papel nº 9 'Segunda ratificación de S. M. sobre la cessaçión de armas', Madrid, 18 September, 1607, BNE, MS 11.187, fols. 17r–19v.

3 Papel nº 6 'Cessación de las armas por la mar', The Hague, 1 June 1607, BNE, MS 11.187, fols. 9r–10r.

 | DOI 10.1163/9789004274921_004

years, whichever the said states choose',[4] was the cause of extreme displeasure among the royal entourage. Moreover, the delay of close to five months was evidence of how little those who had the King's ear agreed with its approval.

The States General of the Republic turned this proclamation into a precondition of the ceasefire and of the negotiations that were to pave the way to the main peace treaty or long truce that was to complement the accessory ceasefire agreement. Philip III also had to end his declaration of ratification by proclaiming that he was 'content that in our name and on our behalf the said States [General] be negotiated with in their capacity as and holding them to be countries, provinces and free states over which we make no claims'. Nonetheless, the monarch added a clause that had not been foreseen. The addition ran as follows: 'If the main peace treaty or long truce of many years, in which the claims of both parties are to be proposed and resolved (both in matters of religion and everything else) were not to reach a conclusion, this ratification will be regarded as null and void, as if it had never been made'.[5] With this clause, Philip III make it possible for his own ratification to be annulled or rescinded by establishing the need to legalise it through a subsequent confirmation that was to be included in the main treaty. If the treaty was not concluded and that confirmation was not forthcoming, the declaration would be deprived of all legal effects by the unilateral will of the monarch.

Philip III's ratification was delivered to the States General of the United Provinces on 29 November 1607 and, although the addition was not well received by the deputies, it was finally accepted by the assembly.[6] This enabled the negotiating process of the main treaty to be set in motion in early 1608. Fray Iñigo de Brizuela's journey to Spain was suggested after eight months of intense negotiation in The Hague between February and September 1608. It was a negotiation plagued with delays and interruptions in which the two interlocutors tried to avoid committing themselves on two matters of vital importance: complete freedom of public worship for Catholics within the Republic and freedom of trade with the East and West Indies not subject to the control of Philip III for the inhabitants of the Republic.[7]

4 BNE, MS 11.187, fol. 17r.

5 BNE, MS 11.187, fols. 18v–19r.

6 The reasons for this are given in a speech by the Grand Pensionary of the province of Holland, Johan van Oldenbarnevelt, reproduced by the papal nuncio in Brussels (1607–1615), Guido Bentivoglio, 'Relación del Tratado de la Tregua de Flandes', in *Relaciones del cardenal Bentivollo* (Madrid, 1638), fols. 102v–104v.

7 Paul C. Allen, *Philip III and the Pax Hispanica, 1598–1621: The Failure of Grand Strategy* (New Haven, 2000), 199–227; Bernardo J. García García, *La Pax Hispanica: Política exterior del*

For the Republic, yielding on religious matters implied giving way on questions of a strictly internal political nature and for Philip III, yielding on commercial matters meant agreeing to the loss of the inherited monopoly of sailing to the Indies. By the end of 1608, it was obvious that the United Provinces were not going to accept the imposition of freedom of worship for Catholics, nor were they prepared to give up their aspirations with regard to overseas trade. So, none of Philip III's objectives could be satisfactorily achieved in a possible treaty as far as he was concerned, and in accordance with the royal ratification of 18 September 1607, this implied the breakdown of negotiations and a return to the starting point: to the moment prior to the declaration of 24 April 1607, rendered null and void by the clause the monarch had inserted in his ratification.

According to many contemporaries, that declaration was tantamount to recognising the independence of the United Provinces, in other words, granting them freedom and, consequently, granting them sovereignty over the territory.[8] Such an interpretation was not entirely unreasonable. If freedom was to be understood as the absence of subjection or submission to a higher authority, it was obvious that in their ratifications of the ceasefire agreement of 1607, the Archdukes and Philip III were declaring that they laid no claim to any jurisdiction over the United Provinces, either because they no longer had it – jurisdiction having lapsed because it had not been exercised – or because they were renouncing it at that time through force of circumstance. The result was that the United Provinces were exempt from any jurisdictional obligation towards the Archdukes and Philip III by virtue of the ratifications.

The purpose of Fray Iñigo de Brizuela's journey was to convince Philip III's entourage not to break off negotiations. Continuing to negotiate meant agreeing to include the first part of the declaration of 24 April 1607 as the initial clause in the possible treaty and to be less demanding in religious and commercial matters. On the face of it, this meant submitting to the United Provinces' claims for sovereignty without receiving any reasonable concessions on religion and trade in return: it was the equivalent of giving up sovereignty in exchange for nothing. However, Brizuela's task was to reveal the deception behind the appearance: to demonstrate that there was no such cession and to inject a dose of realism into the court in Madrid. The Royal

---

duque de Lerma (Leuven, 1999), 62–69. On the question of the Indies see Juan E. Gelabert, 'El artículo IV de la Tregua de los Doce Años (1607–1609)', in Manuel R. García Hurtado, Domingo L. González Lopo and Enrique Martínez Rodríguez (eds.), *El mar en los siglos modernos: O mar nos séculos modernos* (Santiago de Compostela, 2009), vol. 2, 187–208.

8 Allen, *Philip III and the Pax Hispanica*, 242–316 provides documentary evidence.

Exchequer would not be in a position to send the necessary resources to the Archducal Netherlands to sustain a new offensive war, as was clear from the decree issued on 6 November 1607 suspending payments. By setting up the *Diputación del Medio General* on 14 May 1608, the financial position had improved,[9] but the structural problems of the Crown's system of credit had not been resolved. From then on, it was imperative to maintain the defensive war to hold on to the possessions along the Flemish front, as the correspondence arriving from Madrid in the second half of 1608 openly admitted.[10] Yet a defensive war would not improve the negotiating position of the Archdukes and Philip III with a view to the future. Such a position might or might not be maintained; that is, it could deteriorate over time and that would have fatal consequences for the common interests of both Courts, as the recent past had shown. The earlier attempts at negotiation in 1607 had failed for military reasons and only the financial and war effort carried out during the 1605 and 1606 campaigns had borne fruit, leading the two warring sides to start talks early in 1607, as Brizuela himself explained to the monarch during his stay in Madrid (December 1608–January 1609) in a brief report entitled 'Peace Treaties of Different Times'.[11]

Brizuela's report referred to earlier attempts to reach a diplomatic settlement to the conflict with the rebels, going back even as far as the failed Breda conference of March–November 1575, mediated by the Emperor Maximilian II. He also emphasised the crucial influence that the enterprise against England in 1588 had had on the political future of the Netherlands. Rumours of the arrival of a Great Armada on the shores of England had prompted Elizabeth I to reach a negotiated settlement of the Dutch problem; she sent her own representatives to treat for peace with the commissioners of the rebel States General and the Duke of Parma at the conference in Bourbourg (an enclave between Gravelines and Dunkirk), which was also a failure, during the spring and early summer of 1588, and later recalled the English troops who were backing the United Provinces (Treaty of Nonsuch, 1585) to defend England.[12] This situation compromised the position of the rebel provinces, by then

9 Carlos J. De Carlos Morales, 'Política y Finanzas', in José Martínez Millán and Mª Antonietta Visceglia (eds.), *La Monarquía de Felipe III: La Corte* (Madrid, 2008), vol. 3, 749–865, esp. 792–814.

10 Allen, *Philip III and the Pax Hispanica*, 226.

11 'Los tratados de paces de diferentes tiempos', BNE, MS 11.187, fols. 129r–132v.

12 Simon Adams, 'The Decision to Intervene: England and the United Provinces, 1584–1585', in José Martínez Millán (ed.), *Felipe II, 1527–1598: Europa y la Monarquía Católica* (Madrid, 1999), vol. 1, 19–31.

weakened by Alessandro Farnese's successful, systematic military advance between 1581 and 1587. But, 'because of the unfortunate outcome' of the 'Spanish Armada against England' in the summer of 1588, and 'the French war that suddenly broke out [1590 campaign], the Islands [rebel provinces] became more powerful and insolent than ever before, refusing to enter into peace talks at all, even though they were exhorted and admonished to do so on various occasions' during the early 1590s.[13]

Because of the failure of the Great Armada and the intervention of the Army of Flanders in France, the rebels seized the stronghold of Breda in 1590. That victory marked the beginning of an extremely significant military advance for the United Provinces in the central and eastern strips of the Netherlands. That progress did not stop until 1599, but the capture of Groningen (situated in the extreme northeast of the territory) in 1594 anticipated something: a two-pronged attack from the south and the northeast would not be able to stifle the resistance of the United Provinces. The rebels, with this notable improvement in their military as well as their negotiating position, made an offer to negotiate with the Brussels government in 1595:

> In the year 1595, when the count of Fuentes was governor, the Islands [rebel provinces] made a show (*motu proprio*) of wanting to treat, but with the premise of treating only with the States and lords of the obedient provinces, without the direct or indirect intervention of the name or authority of His Majesty or his ministers, and so the talks were called off.[14]

The improvement in the military position of the Republic had two important political consequences. On the one hand, the rebels restated their refusal to hold peace talks with Philip II and his representatives in Brussels. Their refusal had been clear from the time of the failed Cologne peace conference of May–November 1579, held on the initiative of Emperor Rudolph II and mediated by him, and after which, all offers of negotiation emanating from Brussels were turned down.[15] After 1588, their refusal to hold peace talks gathered new strength. On the other hand, the rebels offered to negotiate only with the States General or Provincial of the loyalist provinces, guaranteeing that peace would return to the Netherlands only if they shook off Philip II's tutelage. It was an interesting change of attitude. The United Provinces

13 BNE, MS 11.187, fols. 129v–130r.

14 BNE, MS 11.187, fol. 130r.

15 BNE, MS 11.187, fol. 129v.

admitted that they were ready to negotiate peace and made it clear with whom they would negotiate.

This intransigent attitude obliged Philip II to continue to depend on the pressure of war to force negotiations. Nevertheless, the monarch did not discard the 'soft approach' – of clemency, forgiveness and reconciliation – as much in evidence in his Flemish policy from almost the beginning of the revolt as the 'hard approach' – of punishment, repression and military rigour – even though this has received less attention from scholars.[16] As a matter of fact, in that very year of 1595, Philip II had already worked out his own general strategy for pacifying the Netherlands, imbued with one basic principle: a negotiated union of the obedient and rebel provinces under the rule of new sovereigns residing in Brussels, and with whom, *a priori*, the rebels had no reason to refuse negotiations. This strategy required the cession of the territory's sovereignty, dismembered from the hereditary prince's territorial patrimony. The future dismemberment of the Netherlands was officially accepted by Philip II in the thirty-first clause of his will, dated 7 March 1594. According to this clause, rule over this patrimonial territory would be transferred to the Infanta Isabella Clara Eugenia (1566–1633) for her future marriage to Archduke Ernest of Austria, who had been invested as governor in Brussels in February 1594.[17]

The Cession of the Netherlands' Sovereignty and its Peace-Making Purpose (1597–1599)

The cession of sovereignty fitted perfectly into the dynastic logic, which was at one with the patrimonial concept of sovereignty, and according to that logic, it was not possible to dissociate dismemberment from marriage. The peace-making purpose behind the cession, as clarified by Philip II in a codicil to his will dated 24 August 1597, may also be considered dynastic. This addition proved apposite, since Ernest's death in February 1595 obliged the monarch to deal with this contingency and decide what steps were needed to effect the dismemberment. Ernest's younger brother, the Cardinal-Archduke Albert (1559–1621), who had been governing in the Southern Netherlands since his arrival at Brussels on 11 February 1596, would marry Isabella, and the bride

16 Violet Soen, 'Estrategias tempranas de pacificación de los Países Bajos', in Bernardo J. García García (ed.), *Tiempo de Paces: La Pax Hispanica y la Tregua de los Doce Años* (Madrid, 2009), 61–75.

17 *Testamento de Felipe II*, facsimile edition with introduction, Manuel Fernández Álvarez (Madrid, 1982), 41.

would take as her dowry the Low Countries and the Franche-Comté of Burgundy to 'the relief of these my kingdoms and the better governance of them and of the Low States themselves'. The dismemberment was being put into effect with the aim of benefiting both the whole – all the territories that the future Philip III would inherit – and the part, the Netherlands themselves. In a paper attached to the codicil, Philip II described the legal formula and instruments that would be used to cede dominion of the territory: enfeoffment and dowry.[18]

Enfeoffment was chosen because in this case dismemberment would not mean the complete loss of territorial links. The Netherlands would become a fief of the holder of the Crown of Castile, into which it had originally been incorporated upon the death of Isabella the Catholic in 1504 (no formal links had been maintained with the Crown of Aragon until the death of her husband, King Ferdinand the Catholic in 1516). As the grantor of the fief, the holder of the Crown would limit the faculties of *dominium*, or ownership, of the fief holders (that is, Isabella and her future husband), by imposing upon them obligations and burdens that they would admit when accepting the fief. The limitation would be put into effect by applying the principle of reserving faculties. The grantor would reserve for himself the faculty of fixing the married couple's religious policy and controlling their succession, including their matrimonial policy and that of their successors, as well as their foreign policy. The fief holders' authority to form leagues, alliances and sign peace treaties would be supervised by the grantor and be subject to the convenience of the grantor, although the latter undertook not to damage the fief holders' interests with any of the leagues, alliances or peace treaties that he might enter into on his own account.[19] Moreover, the grantor would keep a certain number of strongholds in the Southern Netherlands (designating and financing the garrison troops) for an indefinite period. Non-compliance with the agreed impositions would enable the patrimonial cession to be revoked and the fief reclaimed. In this way, the addition to the will in 1597 assigned the condition of direct lord of the fief to the grantor and underlined his determination to cede the *dominium utile* (that is, sovereignty, although incomplete) and to retain the *dominium eminens* (that is, the suzerainty) of the territorial patrimony of

18 The codicil and attached paper in *Testamento de Felipe II*, 73–76 and 99–103.

19 'That between these kingdoms [of the Crown of Castile] and those states [of Flanders] there be a perpetual league and confederation and that they be friends of friends and enemies of enemies, and that in any other league or confederation that be made by each of the parts with other princes or potentates, this league with the principal inviolable one should always be safeguarded', *Testamento de Felipe II*, 101.

Burgundy. Nonetheless, Philip II ignored the fact that this patrimony was an imperial fief and that the condition of subinfeudation of the anticipated dismemberment would therefore place an intermediate authority (the holder of the Crown of Castile) between its new holders and the Emperor. As a result, the grantor would cede the only thing that he could, sovereignty but not suzerainty, but in an imperfect way, with the aim of preserving a clear jurisdictional superiority over the fief holders.

The dowry element was important because the dismemberment was linked to a marriage and it was necessary to regulate the patrimonial relations of the married couple. The dowry enabled their patrimonies to be kept separate. By keeping the Low Countries and the Franche-Comté as Isabella's independent, inalienable patrimony (she would be the holder of the *dominium* but would cede its management to Albert), it would guarantee its immediate, integral restitution to the holder of the Crown of Castile if she or her husband died without issue.

This addition to the will can be considered the first step in the process of ceding the sovereignty of Flanders,[20] which was initiated in 1597 when hostilities with France had ceased and the negotiations that would culminate in the Peace of Vervins on 2 May 1598 were in progress. The second step was to publicise – in the Southern Netherlands – the purpose of ceding the Low Countries to Isabella for her future marriage to Albert, as well as the political principle that inspired the cession: the creation of a new government framework aimed at bringing peace to the territory and uniting the provinces. The success of both objectives was predicated on a negotiated reconciliation between the rebels and the new resident sovereigns. The purpose and principle were made public by circulars dispatched via the Supreme Council of Flanders in Madrid and dated 10 September 1597, and directed by the King and his heir at the principal Flemish institutions and political figures, including the various provincial states.[21]

In 1598, the *corpus juris* that underpinned the cession was drawn up. It consisted of five notarial deeds executed in Madrid between 4 and 8 May. The date shows the importance of each one for the juridical act that they were seeking to perfect.

20 Reconstructed in Alicia Esteban Estríngana, 'Los estados de Flandes: Reversión territorial de las provincias leales, 1598–1623', in Martínez Millán and Visceglia, *La Monarquía de Felipe III*, vol. 4, 593–640; Alicia Esteban Estríngana, 'Haciendo rostro a la fortuna: Guerra, paz y soberanía en los Países Bajos, 1590–1621', in García García, *Tiempo de paces*, 85–91.

21 Victor Brants (ed.), *Recueil des ordonnances des Pays-Bas: Deuxième Série 1506–1700: Règne d'Albert et Isabelle, 1598–1621* (Brussels, 1909), vol. 1, 1–5.

The deed dated 4 May was executed by Prince Philip – the future Philip III – to declare that the cession of the territorial patrimony of Burgundy proposed by his father was being implemented with his knowledge and voluntary consent. Both elements had to coincide in the act because Philip II was aiming to alienate a territory that was part of the indivisible and inalienable primogeniture of his heir and that should be passed on to him in its entirety. The monarch was not at liberty to do as he liked with that primogeniture, because he could neither arbitrarily jeopardise the present rights of his successor nor the future rights of Prince Philip's successors, which were recognised by the law of succession. For that reason, without the declaration of will by the prince, the alienation could not be put into effect or rather it would remain open to annulment or rescission. So, this deed acted as a deed of confirmation of the patrimonial cession and, in it, Philip renounced – in his own name and that of his successors – his right to bring actions of annulment in the future and his right to *restitutio in integrum* which the law granted to him and his heirs for suffering an undeserved wrong.[22] In fact, the deed revealed in practice what royalist political theory at the time maintained with respect to sovereignty: the validity of the principle of inalienability.[23] To a certain extent, the cession was a legal fiction; the Burgundian patrimony could remain dismembered from the territorial patrimony of the future Philip III and his successors, if they so wished and for as long as they wished.

Two of the three deeds dated 6 May were executed by Philip II. The first was a public deed of donation by reason of marriage; this was the dowry, with the idiosyncrasy already commented upon. It contained a main introductory clause and a further thirteen accessory clauses. The main one set out the cession of the *dominium* of the Low Countries and the Franche-Comté to the Infanta Isabella in anticipation of her marriage and under the conditions stipulated in the thirteen accessory clauses, which had been agreed by the donor, Philip II, with the approval of Prince Philip and the Infanta Isabella.

The first clause determined Isabella's obligation to contract marriage with Albert, indicated the territories that Isabella would bring to the marriage as her marriage portion and established the ineffectiveness of the cession (the cessation of its effects) if the marriage would not take place. It introduced, in this

22 Brants, *Recueil des ordonnances*, vol. 1, 11–12; Esteban Estríngana, 'Los estados de Flandes', 624–625.

23 Laura Manzano Baena, *Conflicting Words: The Peace Treaty of Münster (1648) and the Political Culture of the Dutch Republic and the Spanish Monarchy* (Leuven, 2011), 182–186; idem, 'Negotiating Sovereignty: The Peace Treaty of Münster, 1648', *History of Political Thought*, 28 (2007), 627–628 and 636–638.

way, a voluntary legal distortion. In donations by reason of marriage, the bond of matrimony was a suspending condition to the donation, which was left 'in suspense' until the marriage took place; here the bond acted as a condition to the donation, which would be undone if the *vinculum matrimonii* was not made. The second, sixth and seventh clauses laid down the obligation to respect the rules of succession established by the donor, and the obligation of Isabella's successors to submit to the matrimonial policy defined by him and his descendants. The third and fourth clauses affirmed the reversion of the donation in favour of the donor and his descendants should Isabella have no issue. The fifth established the inalienability of the *dominium* that was the object of the cession, forbidding Isabella and her successors to alienate it without the consent of the donor and his successors. The eighth prohibited the inhabitants of the Low Countries and the Franche-Comté from trading in any way whatsoever with the East and West Indies. The ninth stipulated how the Burgundian patrimony would be governed if its holder, Isabella, were to die leaving descendants; the widower would act as beneficial holder of the sovereign government and would retain it for his lifetime. The tenth established the obligation to swear on oath to maintain the Catholic faith, that is, obedience to Rome, for the heirs of the marriage and the revocation of the donation if they incurred in heresy. The eleventh stated it was obligatory to confirm and ratify the content of the deed for all Isabella's descendants at the moment of succession. The twelfth established non-compliance with the agreed conditions as a reason for revoking the donation, which the donor and his successors could exercise at any time. It also assigned the condition of enfeoffment to the donation and that of fief and retro-fief to the territorial patrimony of Burgundy, more to reflect its condition as an indirect imperial fief than to highlight the jurisdictional subordination of the fief holders. It further obliged future spouses to observe the content of the 1549 Pragmatic Sanction, which regulated the common succession of the Burgundian patrimony and established its indivisibility (its parts could not be alienated separately). Finally, the thirteenth clause established the obligation of satisfying all the charges that weighed on the patrimonial income of the Low Countries and the Franche-Comté for Isabella and her future husband; moreover, it confirmed the retention of the sovereignty of the Order of the Golden Fleece, which was attached to the title of the Duke of Burgundy and which both spouses could use with that limitation.[24]

This first deed executed by Philip II on 6 May 1598 stipulated Isabella's dowry. The second deed the monarch executed that day was a private deed of

24 Brants, *Recueil des ordonnances*, vol. 1, 7–11; Esteban Estríngana, 'Los estados de Flandes', 621–624.

donation, the content of which was not to be made public in the Southern Netherlands. For this reason, and unlike the others, it was not written in French, but in Spanish. Its execution was suggested by Archduke Albert; he had advised early in 1598 that all limitations of the *dominium* to be ceded to Isabella should be included in a secret deed so as to expedite her swearing in as the new sovereign by the States General of Brussels. Albert, Isabella's proxy, was to be charged with the task of taking the oath on behalf of his betrothed and was afraid that the assembly might raise objections and seek clarifications that would delay taking possession of the territory. Objections were foreseeable, since the States could refuse to take the oath of allegiance before the wedding was held and Philip II had reasons for demanding she would be sworn in before the marriage. The wedding did not guarantee her being sworn in and it could place Isabella in an irreversible position. Moreover, the oath had to be sworn before the death of the monarch, who had been seriously ill since 1597, otherwise the process of cession would have to be suspended and restarted in the name of his successor, Philip III. Even so, only three limitations were included in the private deed: 1) the retention of the strongholds, some of which were deliberately vague (the castles of Antwerp, Ghent and Cambrai 'and another two or three strongholds that are conquered and taken from the rebels, those which seem the best'), which would be garrisoned 'by soldiers of the nation that we choose' (foreigners and Spaniards), paid 'with money from these kingdoms' (the Crown of Castile and not with funds from the Low Countries, which would be beyond the control of the holder of the said Crown); 2) the obligation under oath of the future spouses to actively persecute heresy; and 3) a ban on having in their service any servants or personnel of the household and court 'who are not very good Catholics', which ensured that the holder of the Crown of Castile had the faculty of overseeing the policy of patronage of the new sovereigns.[25]

The third deed dated 6 May was executed by Isabella. It was a deed of acceptance of the donation made in her favour in the terms contained in the public deed, which Isabella pledged not to contradict or oppose in her own name or in that of her successors. It has not been located, but is alluded to in contemporary documents – for example, in the procuration in which Isabella authorised Albert to exchange the obligatory oath of fealty and take possession of her new territorial patrimony[26] – and by the imperial ambassador to the

25 Brants, *Recueil des ordonnances*, vol. 1, 12–13; Esteban Estríngana, 'Los estados de Flandes', 626–628; Esteban Estríngana, 'Haciendo rostro a la fortuna', 85–86.

26 Brants, *Recueil des ordonnances*, vol. 1, 14–15; Esteban Estríngana, 'Los estados de Flandes', 625–626.

Courts of Madrid and Valladolid, Hans Khevenhüller (1574–1606), who reproduced it in his diary.[27]

The marriage articles, agreed by Albert's mother, the Dowager Empress Maria on behalf of her son, and by Philip II, Prince Philip and the Infanta Isabella, date from 8 May. The bride-to-be brought to the covenant the three deeds that enabled her to bring her dowry to the marriage: the public deed of donation executed by her father, the deed of consent and renunciation executed by her brother and the deed of acceptance of the dowry executed by herself. Once these contributions were made, nine clauses were agreed. The first concerned the obligation to formalise the betrothal and the celebration of the wedding, which would take place 'as quickly as possible'. The second concerned the restricted nature of the *dominium* that the couple would enjoy, with emphasis on the agreed contractual nature of the cession of patrimony. The third was about increasing that patrimony by obliging Albert to endeavour to recover and subjugate 'the part of those states that have strayed from obedience to the Holy Roman Apostolic See and their natural lord'. Furthermore, he was to ensure that it was to be added to the obedient Catholic part by accession, thus guaranteeing that the obedient and rebel provinces would form a union under the *dominium* of Isabella. This union would then become the primogeniture of her successors while Albert and his Austrian heirs would be explicitly deprived of rights over the Low Countries. The fourth dealt with patrimonial increase, stipulating that this would also rebound to the exclusive benefit of Isabella and her descendants and be added to the primogeniture. The fifth stated that should Albert die childless, any possessions he left in the Low Countries would be inherited by his widow. The sixth concerned 100,000 ducats assigned to each of the spouses 'from the money and income of these kingdoms' (of Castile) to be freely disposed of by them in their bequests. The seventh made plain Isabella's authority to take part in the management of her patrimony, safeguarded by establishing that all government dispatches would be issued in the name of the couple and would be signed by both. If they were in different places, dispatches issued in the name of the spouses could be signed by only one of them; Albert, however, could only sign in his own name whenever he was not in the same place as Isabella; on the other hand, she could issue dispatches with full authority even when she was not accompanied by her husband. The eighth dealt with the coinage minted in the patrimonial territories, which would carry the insignia and inscriptions of both rulers. Finally, the ninth clause recorded Isabella's renunciation of any

---

27 *Diario de Hans Khevenhüller, embajador imperial en la Corte de Felipe II*, transcription and eds. Sara Veronelli and Félix Labrador Arroyo (Madrid, 2001), 478–479.

further inheritance from her paternal line and the maternal dowry, which she was to ratify after her marriage with the consent of her husband.[28]

The process of the cession of sovereignty was completed with two ceremonies once the titles, that is, the set of deeds that made the transfer of patrimony possible, had been issued. The first was the swearing in of Isabella as the new sovereign before the States General of Brussels, which represented the effective transfer of the legal possession of that patrimony (the tradition or handing over of the same) and took place on 22 August 1598. The second, her marriage to Albert, upon which the survival of the patrimonial dismemberment depended, was held by proxy in Ferrara on 15 November 1598, while the marriage proper took place in Valencia on 14 April 1599.[29]

Isabella's swearing in brought about a fundamental change in the political situation of the Netherlands, because it installed a new sovereign and gave rise to a proposal to negotiate with the rebel provinces, which had received neither an official notification of the patrimonial dismemberment nor a formal summons to swear an oath of allegiance to the new sovereign.[30] Realising that the time was propitious to set up a meeting, the States General of Brussels wrote a letter in late August 1598 to their opposite numbers at The Hague:

> (...) par la cessation de plusieurs empeschemens l'ayant retardé jusques ores, puisque maintenant sommes réduictz en dessoubz l'obéissance de la dicte sérénissime princesse, laquelle, avecq Sadicte Altèze [Alberto], tenant sa continuelle résidence en ce pays, n'aurat aultre soing ny charge que de nous et le pays maintenir en paix et union, sans diversión d'ailleurs, comme ce poinct et plusieurs aultres raisons se pourroyent explicquer, moyennant que veuillez, avecque nous ou nous députez, venir en conférence au lieu que l'on trouvera convenir, lorsque du mesme nous serions contens de nous y trouver aussy, avecq le sceu et consentement de Sadicte Altèze.[31]

28 'Copia de las capitulaciones de la Sra. Infanta Doña Isavel con el Archiduque Alberto', Madrid, 8 May, 1598, Archivo General de Simancas [hereafter AGS], E, Negociación de Flandes [hereafter NF], legajo [hereafter leg.] 2224/1, 3; Esteban Estríngana, 'Los estados de Flandes', 619–621.

29 Esteban Estríngana, 'Los estados de Flandes', 631–640.

30 Despite the fact that, at the ceremony, their deputies had been reserved benches which remained empty, in Esteban Estríngana, 'Haciendo rostro a la fortuna', 85 and 87–88.

31 'Lettre des États Généraux assemblés à Bruxelles aux États Généraux des Provinces-Unies', Brussels, 28 and 29 August 1598, in Louis Prosper Gachard (ed.), *Actes des États Généraux de 1600* (Brussels, 1849), CXXXVI–CXXXVII.

The disposition of the rebels to negotiate only with the obedient States General or provincial states, which they made clear in 1595, conditioned this first attempt at negotiation, which came from the assembly but was endorsed by Archduke Albert. An emissary of the States General, Guillaume Maes, a member of the deputation of the States of Brabant, handed the letter into The Hague in early October 1598. Upon his return, he stated that the Grand Pensionary of the province of Holland, Johan van Oldenbarnevelt, and other principal members of the rebel States General had declared:

> (…) qu'il n'y avoit apparence aulcune de traicter avecq Sadicte Altèze, ou aultre en son nom, disans qu'ilz avoyent leur Estat entier et libre, et qu'ilz le povoyent aisément maintenir contre tous ceulx quy les vouldroyent offencer, et qu'ilz avoyent acquis leur liberté par armes et avecq juste cause, comme ilz disoyent; laquelle liberté ilz ne vouloyent perdre par ung tel prétendu accord. Et, en cas que cy-après ilz se trouvoyent en nécessité, qu'ilz estoyent libres pour choisir ung prince et protecteur, quy les embrasseroit volontiers pour defender leus corps, biens, priviléges et libertez: dont ilz disoyent desjà estre asseurez.[32]

The rebels' confidence in their own forces was amply justified by the territorial gains they had accumulated between 1590 and 1597: 18 strongholds in all within the Netherlands and in areas adjacent to the Rhine and the Ems.[33] So, their official reply to the letter, issued on 22 March 1599, was an invitation to the obedient States General to take up arms with them against the common enemy – the Spanish – to liberate all the provinces and so as to arrange matters of government and religion among themselves.[34] This intransigent attitude also conditioned later attempts at negotiation on the part of Brussels, once the Archdukes had arrived in late August 1599, and once the new Court was established at the beginning of March 1600, after a succession of Joyous Entries which took place throughout the territories to renew the oaths of allegiance to

32 'Verbal de Guillaume Maes, sur son voyage en Hollande', n.d. in Gachard, *Actes des États Généraux*, Gachard, CXXXVIII–CXLI, quotation, CXL.

33 For the sequence of captured strongholds and date of capture, see Esteban Estríngana, 'Haciendo rostro a la fortuna', 77–78.

34 'Reponse des États Généraux des Provinces-Unies à la lettre des États Généraux assemblés à Bruxelles', The Hague, 22 March, 1599, in Gachard, *Actes des États Généraux*, CXLII–CXLIII; the Spanish interpretation of the response is in 'Los tratados de paces de diferentes tiempos', BNE, MS 11.187, fol. 130v; Esteban Estríngana, 'Haciendo rostro a la fortuna', 89.

Isabella and establish personal contact with the city communities (November 1599–February 1600).[35]

The ephemeral architectures and decorations produced for the occasion of these ceremonial entries are testimony to the high expectations of peace that the new sovereignty brought with it. At the Entry into Antwerp on 10 December 1599, the expectation of uniting the Low Countries was represented by a *pegma* dedicated to Hercules Gallicus. His figure appeared dressed in a lion's skin, clutching his club upside down in his right hand and with a ring in his mouth, from which hung chains that linked together seventeen shields without tension or strain, held by seventeen maidens sitting peacefully next to him and who personified the seventeen provinces of the Netherlands. The *pegma* bore the inscription 'Non Armis Opus' to denote that concord, peace and the unity of the provinces would be achieved by means other than force of arms.[36] Since 1568, the same seventeen maidens had been represented, sitting on their knees and bound or tightly chained, to the Duke of Alba's throne in versions of the well-known composition *The Tyranny of Alva*.[37] The Hercules that held them in 1599 was taken from Andrea Alciato's *Emblematum Liber* (1531). This was an allegorical representation typical of Rhetoric and Eloquence and, as such, had been included in the frescoes of the Seven Liberal Arts which covered the vault of the library in the monastery of the Escorial.[38]

35 On these Entries, see commentary and bibliography cited in Esteban Estríngana, 'Haciendo rostro a la fortuna', 89–91; also, François Zanatta, 'Pour une relecture du serment public entre le prince et les communautés d'habitants: l'exemple des joyeuses entrées des Archiducs', *Revue du Nord*, 90 (2008) 729–748.

36 Vincent van Zuilen, 'The Politics of Dividing the Nation? News Pamphlets as a Vehicle of Ideology and National Consciousness in the Habsburg Netherlands, 1585–1609', in Joop W. Koopmans (ed.), *News and Politics in Early Modern Europe, 1500–1800* (Leuven, 2005), 77; Margit Thøfner, *A Common Art: Urban Ceremonial in Antwerp and Brussels During and After the Dutch Revolt* (Zwolle, 2007), 219.

37 Andrew C. Sawyer, 'The *Tyranny of Alva*: The Creation and Development of a Dutch Patriotic Image', *De zeventiende eeuw: cultuur in de Nederlanden in interdisciplinair perspectief*, 19 (2003) 181–211; Cristina Fontcuberta, 'La iconografía contra el III duque de Alba: Sobre usos y recursos de las imágenes de oposición en la época moderna', in Joan Lluis Palos and Diana Carrío-Invernizzi (eds.), *La Historia imaginada: Construcciones visuales del pasado en la Edad Moderna* (Madrid, 2008), 207–234.

38 For emblem 180 'Eloquentia fortitudine praestantior', see Andrea Alciato, *Emblemas* (1531, ed. Santiago Sebastián, Madrid, 1993), 243–244; Diego López, *Declaración magistral sobre las emblemas de Andrés Alciato. Con todas las Historias, Antigüedades, Moralidad y Doctrina tocante a las buenas costumbres* (1615, edn. Valencia, 1670) 613–616; Juan López Gajate, 'Los frescos de la Biblioteca escurialense: la Retórica', *Ciudad de Dios*, 201 (1988)

In his description of the iconographic motif Hercules Gallicus, Fray José de Sigüenza confessed 'that no better enigma or symbol could be invented to show the impact that speaking with art and beauty has upon the hearts of men;' Sebastián de Covarrubias alluded to this very same Hercules – who attracted people with his eloquence and chained men together with his reason – when defining the word *chain* and also *love* 'which means binding with chains those who love each other well'.[39] With his auspicious discourse, Hercules Gallicus won over and united the hearts of men, and the same ability to have a beneficial effect on human hearts was attributed to the art of Rhetoric and Eloquence. The intention was to persuade and convince, that is, 'reduce' with effective reasoning, so as to modify opinions, cause attitudes to be abandoned and change harmful behaviour. At that time, the word 'reduce' combined this sense with two others pertinent to the case: 'to bring back to a previous state' and 'to subject to obedience or rule those who had broken away from it'. Return and subjection through love and not force; the kindness (clemency and tenderness) of Albert (the personification of Hercules Gallicus) would win the love and affection of the seventeen provinces and succeed in safely pacifying and uniting Isabella's patrimony.[40] Albert was encouraged to use the 'soft approach' in attempting to unite the patrimony by one of the memoranda ('Des deux voyes: Amour et force') presented to the Archdukes and attributed to the count of Solre, Philippe de Croÿ, shortly after they arrived in Brussels.[41] It was an approach that had, in fact, already

637–677; Carmen García-Frías Checa, *La pintura mural y de caballete de la Biblioteca del Real Monasterio de El Escorial* (Madrid, 1991), 114–116.

39 'Que no se pudo inventar mejor enigma o símbolo para mostrar la fuerza que tiene el hablar con arte y hermosamente en los corazones de los hombres', Fray José de Sigüenza, *La Fundación del Monasterio de El Escorial* (1605, edn. Madrid, 1988), 289; 'El amor dicen atar con cadenas a los que se quieren bien', Sebastián de Covarrubias Orozco, *Tesoro de la lengua castellana o española* (1611, edn. Madrid, 1995), 229.

40 The doctrinal referent is from Justo Lipsio, *Políticas* (eds. Javier Peña Echevarría and Modesto Santos López, Madrid, 1997), 54–56; the 'Definición de la clemencia encomendándola al príncipe y mostrando hacerle ser amado, glorioso y con seguridad' found in Book 2, Chapter 12.

41 The Spanish version of the set of memoranda is in BNE, MS 2346, fols. 271–295, reproduced in *Colección de documentos inéditos para la Historia de España* [hereafter CODOIN] (Madrid, 1863), vol. 42, 242–276; the French version is in Brussels, Archives Générales du Royaume [hereafter AGR], Conseil Privé Espagnol [hereafter CPE], register 1586, pp. 493–540; an analysis of the memorandum is quoted in Bernardo J. García García, '"Ganar los corazones y obligar los vecinos": Estrategias de pacificación de los Países Bajos, 1604–1610', in Ana Crespo Solana and Manuel Herrero Sánchez (coords.), *España y las 17 provincias de los Países Bajos: Una revisión historiográfica, XVI–XVIII* (Cordoba, 2002), vol. 1, 137–165.

proved its effectiveness in the pacification of the neighbouring Kingdom of France during the 1590s.[42]

In essence, the *pegma* of Hercules Gallicus and Solre's memorandum revealed the desire for peace and a negotiated union of all the provinces that the obedient subjects of the Southern Netherlands shared with the new sovereigns. Peace and union did not seem mutually exclusive at the time and, once the moment had arrived, the negotiations with the rebels would ensure that they would be achieved.

Failed Negotiation Attempts of the Archducal Period (1600–1606)

In order to negotiate, it was necessary to compromise the security of the rebels and to undermine their confidence. Military successes might make a fresh attempt to negotiate viable, but the Archdukes, consistent with the 'soft approach', made an offer without having achieved any military success. The new session of the States General in Brussels, convened for fiscal purposes in April 1600, offered another opportunity to enter into communication with the States General of The Hague; the Archdukes authorised a three-delegate embassy (from Brabant, Guelders and Flanders) to propose a bilateral conference. In June, the delegates undertook the journey via Antwerp but were refused passports for entry into rebel territory. The defeat of Albert's army at the Battle of Nieuwpoort (The Dunes, 2 July 1600) induced the States General of The Hague to accept the meeting. On 21 July, they agreed to send deputies to the rebel city of Bergen-op-Zoom, even though their attitude had not changed according to reports of the obedient delegates upon their return to Brussels on 28 July. Oldenbarnevelt, on behalf of his delegation, had reproached them for having wasted the opportunity to remedy the problems that were afflicting the territory:

> (...) lorsqu'il a esté question d'advouer ou désadvouer la donnation et transport de ces pays, faict au prouffict de Leurs Altèzes, avecq conditions si estranges et serviles, inicques et domageables au pays, lesquelz ilz disoyent estre par là plus assubjectis et esclaves à l'Espaigne, qu'ilz ne furent oncques, selon que clairement ilz eussent démonstré, si y fussiont esté lors appellez avecq les aultres: ce que mesdicts Sieurs Estatz [of Brussels] debvoyent avoir procuré [...] et, pour obvier à tout ce que dessus, ils

42 Michel de Waele, 'Clémence royale et fidélités françaises à la fin des Guerres de Religion', *Historical Reflection/Réflexions Historiques*, 24 (1998) 231–252.

> aviont, de leur part, prins les armes, et faict ce que jusques ores ilz ont faict: le tout pour le bien du pays [...] et que Dieu aussy, à ce regard, auroit de sa grâce bénit leurs actions, selon qu'on avoyt peu veoir mesmement par la belle victoire par eulx obtenue les jours passez [at Nieuwpoort]: par moyen de quoy, et le bon establissement de leur Estat, ilz espéroyent asseurer leurs affaires. Aussy disoyent que les Estatz de par deçà, ayans laissé perdre une belle ocasion pour la liberté du pays, après la mort du roy d'Espaigne, ne debvroyent laisser escouller ung aultre.[43]

Another opportunity arose in 1600, but the States General of Brussels did not have the authority to sue for peace in their own name, nor would they while they were under the government and tutelage of the Archdukes. If the States General of The Hague agreed to treat with them, they would be negotiating with the Archdukes, and therefore with the King of Spain, since the Archdukes were subordinate and bound to him. They had no intention of submitting to the King of Spain, as they had shown in the past. For this reason, there was no chance of peace talks. In fact, the rebel delegation insisted that the obedient delegation should break away from the new sovereigns and set up formal negotiations in their own name, suggesting they should do so there and then, at a time when the Spanish troops were depleted and weakened by the defeat.[44] Their attitude was just as intransigent as it had been in 1595 as their confidence was still intact and remained so in the following years, while the Archdukes' military campaigns were not particularly successful.

In the summer of 1601, the Archdukes lost the strategic Rhineland stronghold of Rheinberg and laid siege to Ostend. Once the siege had begun, they made unofficial soundings to find out if the rebels were willing to negotiate some kind of agreement. According to a communiqué from Don Baltasar de Zúñiga, Philip III's ambassador to the court of the Archdukes, the soundings were coordinated by the President of the Private Council of Brussels, Jean Richardot. With the latter's knowledge, a nobleman of the Duchy of Guelders with good connections in Holland, a certain Britanorst (Wittenhorst?), had travelled to the province and later confirmed the rebels' interest in knowing Albert's attitude on four key questions: religion; the departure of foreign troops; the form of government; and what reassurance he was able to offer

43 'Relation de ce que le conte de Bassigni, le sieur de Bicht et Henry de Codt [...], comme députez de messeigneurs les Estaz Généraulx, ont besoingné avecq les députez d'Hollande, Zélande et aultres associez', Brussels, 28 July 1600, in Gachard, *Actes des États Généraux*, 777–782, quotation on 779–780.

44 Gachard, *Actes des États Généraux*, 780.

about fulfilling a hypothetical agreement that covered all the points. These were matters of enormous importance the negotiation on which would involve difficulties and require time. For this reason, Zúñiga suggested to Albert that he should first agree a suspension of arms and postpone the peace treaty, an option that Philip III's entourage openly supported at that date to 'give the Exchequer a rest' and which Albert at that time rejected out of hand, alleging 'that to make the suspension was to remain perpetually at war'.[45]

For his part, the Admiral of Aragon, Don Francisco de Mendoza – cavalry general and lord steward to the Archdukes, captured at Nieuwpoort and held prisoner in Holland in the company of more than 300 officers and men – decided to put forward a peace proposal when negotiating the ransom of the captives in the course of 1601. On 30 April, he sought accreditation from Albert to undertake it officially in The Hague. At the end of November, he received a letter of credence (predated 8 January), together with a commission to take charge of the negotiations until delegates were appointed (predated 27 April). He also received a letter from Albert (predated 25 June) stating what he could offer the rebel States General. These dispatches enabled Mendoza to make a 'firm, secure and general' offer of peace between 22 and 24 December 1601, which he handed over in writing and the preamble of which specified the following:

> That Their Highnesses will make peace if the United Provinces receive them and take an oath of allegiance to them as their princes and lords, each province according to its privileges and ancient customs, as the rest of the provinces of the Low Country have received them.

The Admiral decided to include it on his own initiative in his document because in the course of the first of the three interviews held with a deputation of the States headed by Oldenbarnevelt, the latter had asked him 'what the Archduke was seeking by means of this peace and if he would be happy to leave the United Provinces as they were, as a republic, with good mutual relations with His Highness'. Mendoza's response was 'that in no way would he be happy for them to remain a republic and outside his rule, because that would not be making peace, but divesting himself of what was his and renouncing his own ancient patrimony, which was something that could be neither asked for nor conceded and nor was it to be admitted as a proposal in the talks'.[46]

45 D. Baltasar de Zúñiga to Philip III, From the field of Ostend, 15 September 1601, AGS, E, NF, leg. 2288; Esteban Estríngana, 'Los estados de Flandes', 645–647.

46 For the final paragraphs, see 'Relaçión de lo que passó en el tratado de la paz las provinçias desobedientes de los estados bajos que se llaman unidas quando el almirante de

It appears that the strongly worded preamble thwarted the attempt at negotiation, formally rejected by the States on 6 January 1602.

It has been stated that the United Provinces offered to negotiate the suspension of arms with the Admiral[47] and one of the charges brought against him on his return to Spain in 1603[48] was 'not having accepted the suspension of arms offered to him by the enemy when he was a prisoner on the Islands [rebel provinces]'. In his defence, Mendoza admitted having received a dispatch from Albert at the end of February 1602 and dated the previous 23 January, ordering him to secure a suspension of arms, but the States General asked him to refrain from negotiating the matter with them, assuring him that 'it was being dealt with in another part of the peace process by order of Their Highnesses'. As a result, the suspension did not prosper, not through any fault or negligence of his own, but because 'Their Highnesses were persuaded to allow this negotiation to be dealt with at the same time by others who [...] sabotaged and delayed the discussions, and because different people were involved, the authority of the commissioners of each negotiation was undermined and the matter became suspect'. According to the Admiral's argument, avenues of negotiation parallel to his own weakened his authority before the States General, because 'those treating for peace elsewhere, offered them greater advantages'[49] – they agreed to negotiate under less rigorous conditions – and it was this multiplicity of avenues that ended up thwarting the attempted negotiation in its entirety.

The consistency of the argument is confirmed by several letters sent from Brussels in the early months of 1602. According to these, Albert consented to negotiating a suspension of arms in mid-January 1602 and agreed to attempt it via three different channels. The Admiral was one of these, another was Richardot's agents and the third was England, whose mediating role was to be

Aragón trató este negoçio por orden y poder que tuvo de Sus Altezas estando prisionero en Olanda', BNE, MS 2394, fols. 173r–201v. The quotations are from fols.198v and 199r.

47 Hugo de Schepper, 'Los Países Bajos y la Monarquía Hispánica: Intentos de reconciliación hasta la Tregua de los Doce Años, 1574–1609', in Crespo Solana and Herrero Sánchez, *España y las 17 provincias*, vol. 1, 347.

48 On the career of this prominent figure, see Antonio Rodríguez Villa, 'Don Francisco de Mendoza, almirante de Aragón, 1547–1623', in J. Valera (ed.), *Homenaje a Menéndez y Pelayo en el año vigésimo de su profesorado: Estudios de Erudición española* (Madrid, 1899), vol. 2, 486–610.

49 'Relaçión de los cargos y descargos del Almirante de Aragón' and 'Descargo de la culpa que se pone al almirante de Aragón en el negoçio de la suspensión de las armas en la guerra del Pays Bajo', BNE, MS 2394, fols. 233r. and 240v–245r. Quotations from fols. 243r. and 244r–v.

obtained by a certain confidant dispatched to London. Having proposed very hard conditions at the outset, Don Francisco de Mendoza received the order to speak 'more softly' in order to prolong the dialogue,[50] but the rebels, realising that other interlocutors were available, decided to ignore him. However, before Mendoza sent off his written peace offer to the States General of The Hague in December 1601, Oldenbarnevelt would have had time to declare that 'to come to talk of peace, a suspension of arms was necessary', and the Admiral might well have replied that 'there was no reason for that, but that each one should do what he could in war until peace was made', in the full knowledge that Albert 'at that time did not look kindly upon this means of suspension'. Zúñiga suspected as much in May 1602, when he confirmed that the Archduke, 'wary of this Ostend enterprise', had been perfectly willing for four or five months to accept the suspension of arms.[51]

The military reverses soon cast a shadow over any possibility of negotiating it; the siege of Ostend made no progress and the Grave stronghold surrendered to Maurice of Nassau in late September 1602. In the wake of this loss, Zúñiga showed he was utterly sceptical of the negotiations, but confirmed that Albert would accept the suspension without the shadow of a doubt if the rebels were in agreement with it.[52] In October, some provincial states, in particular those in Brabant, urged the Archduke to convene the States General to deal with 'the means of pacification', in other words, to design actions aimed at achieving it at that difficult juncture. Albert refused to convene the States General and decided to allow delegates from the provincial assemblies to be sent to some frontier location if it turned out to be necessary to reassure the provinces. They would be able to convey the viability of negotiation, although not negotiate; they would only go 'with instructions to persuade them to look for means with their princes to reach an agreement, endeavouring in the first place to set suspension on the right path'.[53] To get round the predictable refusal of the rebels to enter into negotiations with the Archdukes, the assemblies demanded that delegates be sent with the power 'to negotiate as States with States' with explicit limitations: the Archdukes would designate and arbitrate the terms of the negotiation. Zúñiga thought the initiative put them in an

---

50 Zúñiga to Philip III, Nieuwpoort, 20 January 1602 and 6 March 1602, AGS, E, NF, leg. 620, 27 and 128. Also, in the same legajo, D. Fernando Carrillo to Philip III, Nieuwpoort, 20 January 1602 and 23 April 1602, 248 and 259.

51 Zúñiga to Philip III and Carrillo to Philip III, From the field of Ostend, 24 May 1602, AGS, E, NF, leg. 620, 10 and 7.

52 Zúñiga to Philip III, Maastricht, 29 September 1602, AGS, E, NF, leg. 620, 139.

53 Zúñiga to Philip III, Ghent, 28 October 1602, AGS, E, NF, leg. 620, 127.

awkward position, but understood that they had to resort to any channel if no significant military advance were achieved in the next campaign.[54]

The obedient delegates did not manage to travel in 1602 because the rebels, knowing full well that the assemblies were pushing in that direction, 'wrote and had printed a letter to all the obedient States exhorting them to endeavour to ensure that Their Highnesses should be content to leave the country, because then it would not be a difficult thing to make the Spaniards and other foreigners follow and to organise the States among themselves'.[55] In this way, the negotiations reached a worrisome deadlock which lasted all of 1603. Throughout that year, Ostend remained impregnable, but at least Maurice of Nassau's attempt to besiege the northern Brabant stronghold of Bois-le-Duc ('s-Hertogenbosch) in September was foiled. The success of the relief caused the States of Brabant to call for the dispatch of their own delegates to rebel territory. Two were deputised, but their entry was not permitted and they were invited to send their proposal in writing. This was not answered until 12 May 1605, when the States General of The Hague 'flatly refused to meet saying that since the obedient States could not negotiate freely with them, but with the authority and commission of Their Highnesses, that there was no reason to weary themselves, but wait for the end and outcome of the war'.[56]

The uncompromising response of 1605 is easy to explain. Even though the Archdukes managed to take Ostend at the beginning of September 1604, the rebels had occupied the nearby stronghold of Sluys a few weeks earlier. Its conquest compensated for the loss of Ostend and that loss did not threaten the security of the Republic because both cities were on the Flanders coast, not in rebel territory. Also the Republic made the most of the opportunity to destabilise the southern provinces by stirring up trouble between the obedient subjects and their sovereigns. With the object of persuading them that the Republic was ready and willing to negotiate, the rebels addressed a letter to the magistrates of some Flemish and Brabant towns, implying that if negotiations were not taking place it was because of the obstinate refusal of the Archdukes. In the face of the pressure received from the States of Flanders and Brabant to convene the States General, Albert authorised those of Brabant to reply to the letter, showing the same disposition to negotiate, and speaking on their own behalf without mentioning the sovereigns. Foreseeing that the contents of this letter would not take long to be known in Valladolid, Albert wrote to the Count of Solre, Philippe de Croÿ, in extraordinary embassy at the monarch's court to

54 Zúñiga to Philip III, Ghent, 22 November 1602, AGS, E, NF, leg. 620, 232.

55 BNE, MS 11.187, fol. 131r.

56 BNE, MS 11.187, fol. 131r.

expound the strategy defined for the 1605 offensive campaign, the 'first Frisian campaign'.[57] He made clear to his ambassador what explanation he should give if he were called upon to do so by Philip III's entourage:

> Because [the letter in reply] speaks in general terms, it could appear that, if those of Brabant were able to come together in a meeting with the rebels, they would wish to negotiate and conclude a peace without our [the Archdukes'] involvement, because we are not named in it (which would be for them to assume too much authority and which the world would consider strange). But their intention is very different from all of this, since their making no mention of us is to draw the Dutch into joining in more easily and then have a closer insight into their inclinations and to demonstrate to them that this body cannot be without a head and that, therefore, we [the Archdukes], or someone acting on our behalf, should be involved in the peace-making process, expecting those of Brabant to lay before them [the rebels] reasons of such import that make them [the rebels] agree to the peace treaty being negotiated and finalised in the presence of our delegates. And on the other hand, by speaking of us or wishing to follow our orders, the rebels would withdraw and would use this excuse to cover themselves with their people. We believed this consideration to be to the point and with the certainty that we have that they will not do anything without our order and that the intention is not to negotiate but only to induce the other party to enter into communication.[58]

Albert's clarification proves that the Archdukes had not abandoned the idea of uniting the obedient and rebel provinces by means of negotiation on the eve of the great military offensive, launched by Brussels against rebel territory in 1605 and 1606. They were still determined to pursue this objective and although the response issued by the States General of the Hague in the spring of 1605 ruled out negotiation, the panorama was changed by the favourable balance of the 1605 and 1606 campaigns led by the new *maestre de campo general* [≈ Field Marshal] of the Army of Flanders, the wealthy marquis Ambrosio Spinola. His progress in the area of the Rhine, Ems and Ijssel (the capture and recovery

57 On the first and second Frisian campaigns, conducted in 1605 and 1606, see Eduardo De Mesa Gallego, *La pacificación de Flandes: Spínola y las campañas de Frisia, 1604–1609* (Madrid, 2009).

58 Albert to the Count of Solre, Brussels, 15 December, 1604, AGS, E, Negocios de partes, leg. 1851. On this same letter, see García García, 'Ganar los corazones', 156.

of 8 strongholds in all) and the victory won in the field against Maurice of Nassau's army at the battle of Mülheim – referred to in Spanish sources as 'el encuentro de Brouck' – between the rivers Rhine and Roer, demonstrated two things: first, that the Republic was vulnerable if it was attacked systematically along the eastern strip of the Netherlands; second, that the States General of The Hague could not afford a defence of such magnitude in the medium or long term since they were forced to rely on their allies' financial assistance.[59] Consequently, Richardot's agents – the nobleman from Guelders, Walraven van Wittenhorst, and the lawyer Johan Gevaerts, from the Brabant town of Turnhout – received an offer on behalf of the States General of The Hague in December 1606: the Republic was ready to discuss a suspension of arms of three or four years. At the beginning of January 1607, the two agents travelled to The Hague to explain the Archdukes' negotiation proposal.[60]

The Illusion of a United Territory: 1607–1609

The rebel States General rejected the proposal on 27 January 1607; they refused to deal with anyone claiming to have any jurisdiction over them.[61] They implicitly required the Archdukes to renounce this right – to *not* claim it, that is, to abandon it – and thus invalidated the principle of a negotiated union of the provinces under archducal sovereignty. They made it explicit to two of the Archdukes' new agents, the Dutch tradesman, Werner Cruwel, and the vicar general of the Franciscans, Jan Neyen who travelled to The Hague in the month of February to confirm the Archdukes' willingness to negotiate. This willingness was understandable because their military position had never been so good and could not get any better, since they knew that Philip III was unable to finance a new offensive campaign in 1607. So, the States prepared the draft of a written declaration by means of which the Archdukes released or exempted the United Provinces from jurisdictional obligations towards them and

59 For a synthesis and assessment of the 1605 and 1606 campaigns, see Esteban Estríngana, 'Haciendo rostro a la fortuna', 106 and 292–293; the Republic's vulnerability is also stressed in Olaf Van Nimwegen, 'The Quest for Security: the Case of the Dutch Republic', in Michael Burgess and Hans Vollaard (eds.), *State, territoriality and European integration* (London/New York, 2006), 19.

60 Albert to the Duke of Lerma, Brussels, 21 December 1606, CODOIN, vol. 43, pp. 27–31; Spinola to Philip III, Brussels, 22 December 1606, AGS, E, NF, leg. 2289, 170; Allen, *Philip III and the Pax Hispanica*, 169–171 and 173–174.

61 'Copia de la respuesta que los Estados Unidos han dado a Mos. de Wyttenhorst y a Mes. Juan Gevaerts', The Hague, 27 January 1607, BNE, MS 11.187, fols. 3r–4r, see also fol. 131v.

demanded that the written draft of the declaration be accepted by the Brussels government. The acceptance of their demand made the suspension of arms which both the United Provinces and the Archdukes desired, a reality. It gave rise to the eight-month ceasefire treaty, which was finalised at the end of March, dated 24 April 1607, and quickly ratified by the Archdukes. The suspension was to serve to negotiate an agreement of broader scope, a peace or a long truce. Philip III had to authorise its negotiation by ratifying the previous ceasefire agreement.

The content of this prior agreement caused surprise in royal circles, since it was made 'in prejudice of the *dominium directum*' that Philip III 'reserved for himself in the consent that he gave for the cession that the king, our lord [Philip II], made of the States of Flanders to the Infanta'. For that reason, it was not acceptable to ratify it 'unless it was by way of enfeoffment and the Islands making some recognition each year for reasons of seigniory'. In other words, the Archdukes might well have renounced their rights – deriving from *dominium utile* – which they exercised temporarily; Philip III, however, had no reason to forgo his own, deriving from *dominium directum* or *eminens* (anticipating the recovery of *dominium utile*, since it was now taken for granted that the Archdukes would remain childless). Even so, the possibility of renouncing them was admitted if the rebels granted the Catholics the 'freedom to appear what they are',[62] since there was no money to pursue an offensive war. In such circumstances, one had to 'choose the lesser of two evils, and that was to cut off a limb to set the whole body free'.[63] In this way, the convenience of waiving the Crown's rights to the rebel provinces in order to protect and preserve all the other territories under Philip III's sovereignty was made explicit. Setting free the body was equivalent to not breaking off the negotiations in view of the Crown's financial difficulties, although some of the King's counsellors were opposed to going ahead with them if it involved exempting the rebels from the sovereignty and direct seigniory of the monarch. Above all, because it meant that:

> Your Majesty's giving just title to the Dutch rebellion and unjust [title] to the war that such zealous and Catholic princes have waged against them for so many years could have the dreadful consequence of the vassals of other kingdoms and seigniories of Your Majesty claiming the same thing

62 The expression equates to freedom of worship for Catholics and comes from a letter addressed to Philip III by the marquis of Guadaleste, the monarch's ambassador in Brussels between 1607 and 1616, Brussels, 20 September 1608, AGS, E, NF, leg. 625, 119.

63 Council of State, n.p. 13 May 1607, AGS, E, NF, leg. 2138, 79.

> [that is, exemption from the sovereignty and direct seigniory of the monarch], especially the obedient states of the Low Countries, whose sovereignty would be severely damaged and I base it on this: it is not being proposed to Your Majesty that the rebels should be released from the obedience that they owe, for this, although very wrong, would not be so wrong, but that you should declare that you are not claiming such a right from them. This declaration is as much in favour of one group of states as the other, because the actions and authority that one has over them is the same. I would very much fear that, following the example of and envying their neighbours, those who are now silent would speak up and try to use the same decree with a good deal more reason than those of Holland have for exemption. I would add that Your Majesty cannot dispose of the kingdoms of which God made you their lord without very just cause and the consent of your successors, and this consent cannot be given by the Prince at his present age.[64]

This view confirmed several things. First of all, Philip III could not freely dispose of his sovereignty in 1607 as he was being asked to do; he had to take into account the consent of his successor, Prince Philip – the future Philip IV, born in 1605 – just as Philip II had had to take into account his own when he was the prince in 1598. Second, the rebels did not ask to be released from an obligation that was owed (obedience); such a request implied recognising their debt or duty towards the sovereign and admitting their prior disobedience. The rebels expressly requested the power of subjection that the sovereign possessed over his subjects to be given up, that is, the repudiation of full *dominium* (*utile* and *directum*) and, as a result, the repudiation of any claim to exercise the rights that such *dominium* attributed to their holder. Third, acceding to the rebel demands would set a bad legal precedent, which the obedient subjects of the Netherlands could invoke when it suited them to be exempt from the same sovereignty, and which the subjects of the remaining

64 Ruling of the constable of Castile, n.d. addressed to Andrés de Prada, who requested it in a note in Madrid, 21 June 1607; for the report of the Council of State, n.p. 21 June 1607, all in AGS, E, NF, leg. 2138, 77 and 76–78, respectively. It coincides with Albert's feelings when he learned of the content of the declaration drawn up by the States General in The Hague to formalise the ceasefire: 'He thought it would be almost a confession of having waged an unjust war, by declaring those peoples who had been treated as rebels to be free now and [...] how dangerous it would be to cause their freedom to serve as a reward for rebellion, since an example so much in favour of the provinces that had rebelled would be like an opportunity for the obedient also to do the same one day', Bentivoglio, 'Relación del Tratado de la Tregua', fols. 93v–94r.

dominions of Philip III's monarchy could emulate when they considered it opportune to claim exemption from such obedience.

Despite the contraindications, the monarch ratified the ceasefire, subordinating its legal efficacy in the matter of sovereignty to the conclusion of the peace agreement or long truce that was to satisfy his demands in religious matters and trade, as mentioned at the beginning of this study. Once the ratification was signed on 18 September 1607 but before it was presented to the States General of The Hague on 29 November 1607, Emperor Rudolph II addressed a letter, dated in Prague on 9 October 1607, to the three parties involved: Philip III, the Archdukes and the rebel States General. In the letter, he reproached each of them for exceeding their authority by negotiating an agreement of such a nature without the Emperor's knowledge or approval.

The United Provinces exceeded their authority by attempting to be declared a 'free republic', since the Low Countries were an imperial fief, a member of the Holy Roman Empire, and formed one of its circles (the Burgundian Circle). According to the Empire's statutes, nothing that affected the nature and ownership of its dependencies could be altered without the consent of the Emperor and the confirmation of the Imperial Diet. Therefore, whatever the States General agreed with the Archdukes and the King of Spain without that consent would be ineffective and could be made legally null and void.[65] The Archdukes had exceeded their authority by accepting that claim, knowing full well that they could not 'dispose of such principal fiefs of the Empire nor of their possessions without our knowledge and consent, as the sovereign feudal lord'. So, Rudolph II exhorted them to refrain from negotiating further without his authorisation and not to agree anything 'that might later redound one day to the detriment of us and the Holy Empire, also of our Most Serene House of Austria and Your own self respect', in reference to declaring the United Provinces free and exempt from sovereignty.[66] And Philip III had exceeded his powers for the same reason; therefore, the Emperor also exhorted him not to treat or agree anything 'without our will and consent, being as we are the supreme head and superior feudal lord'.[67]

In the letters addressed to the Archdukes and Philip III, Rudolph II made plain his displeasure at having been excluded from the 1607 negotiations. The Emperor had acquired the status of recognised mediator in the Netherlands'

65 The contents of the letter are reproduced in English in Edward Grimeston, *A Generall Historie of the Netherlands* (London, 1608), 1386–1387.

66 'Copia sacada y traduçida de alemán alto de una carta que el emperador ha escritto a Sus Alteças Serenísimas en 9 de ottubre de 1607', AGS, E, NF, leg. 2289, 243.

67 'El emperador, de 9 de octubre, traduzida de alemán', AGS, E, NF, leg. 2138, 63.

conflict during Maximilian II's reign and Rudolph II had tried without success to fill the role in the 1590s. Above all, after the arrival of Archduke Ernest of Austria in Brussels in 1594, when the Diet of Ratisbon decided 'that the need for the peace treaty should be intimated to all parties and that if there was any one of them that did not wish to accept it, the Empire should join with the other party to make them obey'.[68] The Diet resolution was never executed, despite the insistence of Philip II's ambassador to the Imperial Court. But Rudolph II took the initiative again to mediate in the conflict in 1597, announcing his intention to send imperial delegates to The Hague, who were rejected by the States General.[69] In Philip III's view, both examples demonstrated the scant commitment the Emperor and the Empire had towards the pacification of the Netherlands and, in his response to the imperial communication, explicitly reproached him for his past negligence. Just as Philip had done, the Archdukes alluded to the Transaction of Augsburg of 1548 to remind Rudolph II 'that the lords of these provinces have always held themselves to be sovereigns knowing no other superior than God and that the Emperor Charles V [...], in the Treaty of Augusta of the year 48 never tried to subjugate them (as they had not been in the past), but to reassure them more and jointly fortify the Empire',[70] by establishing new quotas of contribution from their circles to the imperial subsidies for the common security of the whole and the individual security of each member, including the Low Countries, which had received so little by way of consideration from the Empire after 1548. The political primacy of the holders of the *dominium* (*utile* and *directum* in 1607) of the Low Countries was not an issue to be discussed; they had no obligation or need to account to the Emperor for their negotiating initiatives, although Albert agreed that, once the negotiations with the rebels were concluded, he would communicate the outcome to Rudolph II and ask for his opinion.

Before he received both replies, the Emperor had proposed the pacification of the Low Countries as a specific point for discussion at the Diet of Ratisbon, held in January 1608, where he reiterated his concern about the course of the

68 Council of State, Madrid, 6 December 1607. 'Sobre lo que advierte don Guillén de San Clemente [Philip III's ambassador in Prague] açerca de los puntos que contiene la carta del emperador en lo de las cosas de Flandes', AGS, E, Negociación de Alemania (hereafter NA), leg. 2323, 23. The draft is in AGS, E, NF, leg. 625, 54.

69 BNE, MS 11.187, fols. 130r–131v.

70 'Copia de carta de Su Alteça para el emperador', n.d. sent to Madrid with Albert's letter to Philip III, Vintz, 8 November, 1607, AGS, E, NF, leg. 2289, 242 and 241. The meaning of Philip III's reply is in Council of State, Madrid, 6 December 1607 and 13 December 1607, AGS, E, NA, leg. 2323, 23 and 24.

negotiations and requested an assessment of whether it was worthwhile exhorting the parties again in the same way as before.[71] However, Albert's reply reached Prague in the second fortnight of February 1608 and reassured, or at least silenced Rudolph II, who showed no further sign of trying to interfere in the negotiating process.[72]

By then, as a result of Philip III's ratification of the ceasefire, the negotiations had entered a new phase. These began in February 1608, after the delegation backing the interests of the Archdukes and authorised by Philip III had transferred to The Hague. The following September, it became obvious that the United Provinces would not satisfy the religious and commercial demands of the monarch[73] and were insisting upon, as the first clause of the hypothetical truce treaty, a recognition of freedom – understood as a declaration of exemption from sovereignty – similar to that which already figured in the 1607 ceasefire treaty. The Archdukes were not confident that Philip III would agree to ratify it and so the freedom clause was drawn up in three ways, each one committing the monarch to a different extent. The first draft – identical to the declaration that had brought about the suspension of arms in 1607 – was put to the rebel delegation in September of the same year but was rejected by the rebel States General shortly before the conference was cut short and the Archdukes' delegation returned to Brussels on 1 October 1608. Next, the Archdukes sent the chief clerk of the Secretary of State and War of the captaincy-general of the Army in Flanders, Mateo de Urquina, to Madrid.[74]

---

71 'Sumario de lo que se propuso en nombre del emperador en la Dieta de Ratisbona, a 12 de henero 1608', with a letter from Guillén de San Clemente to Philip III, Prague, 16 February 1608, AGS, E, NA, leg. 2494, 23–24. The third point of the summary is commented upon and reproduced in García García, *La Pax Hispanica*, 62–63 and 292.

72 Guillén de San Clemente to Philip III, Prague, end of February 1608, 'Since the point about the pacification of Flanders has now quietened down, I shall not move on these talks until I see what results from the Meeting in The Hague [...], since the Emperor no longer talks about it and the lord Archduke Albert [...] has responded to him and very well on this point', AGS, E, NA, leg. 2494, 13. Once the replies had been received from Albert, Philip III and the United Provinces, 'as negotiations progressed, even in the most heated moments, there were no further reports of the Emperor using any means to insist upon being included [in the discussions]', Bentivoglio, 'Relación del Tratado de la Tregua', fols. 97v–98r.

73 In the matter of trade, Philip III could only decide if the rebels' freedom to sail to the Indies not controlled by himself would be 'with or without hostility', in other words, whether the war would also be interrupted on the oceans and non-European seas, Guadaleste to Philip III, Brussels, 20 September 1608, AGS, E, NF, leg. 625, 119.

74 Albert to Philip III, Brussels, 7 October 1608, CODOIN, vol. 43, 134–135.

Urquina he took with him an account containing the three different drafts.[75] The purpose of the trip was to secure Philip III's authorisation to conclude the treaty with either of the other two and, in a letter handed to Urquina, Spinola himself asked for the monarch's authorisation, with arguments as to why he should grant it:

> The first [draft] is point for point the same as the eight-month suspension of arms, in which it says that Their Highnesses are negotiating with the States General in their capacity as free states, and holding the United Provinces to be free states over which Their Highnesses make no claims, and in short, it promises that Your Majesty will make a similar declaration; the second is the same, but with Your Majesty's name added, and the third changes the odd word.[76] That His Highness will agree on what might be done about this, bearing in mind that while there are no words of renunciation nor is it expressly stated that he holds them to be free for ever, these being words used in a truce, it is to be understood that it shall have its effect for as long as the truce lasts and, in the ratification that Your Majesty will have to make, you will be able (if you think fit) to limit the conditions, as you did in the eight-month suspension of arms.[77]

The United Provinces were seeking to avoid what had happened with the suspension of arms agreement in 1607. At that time, a declaration was issued in the name of the Archdukes, who promised to deliver Philip III's confirmation by a certain date. This forced a second declaration to be issued in the name of the monarch, adding an unforeseen clause which was awkward for the Republic. If the treaty of truce, including the initial freedom clause, was drawn

75 'Relación de las tres formas de palabras que han platicado los embaxadores que se huviessen de poner en la tregua açerca el punto de libres', BNE, MS 11.187, fols. 46r. and 49v. (written in French and Spanish).

76 Ibid. First: 'Que Leurs Altezes traitten avecq les Estats en qualité et comme les tenans estats libres sur lesqueles Leurs Altezes ne pretendent riens, y en fin promete que S.M. hará semejante declaración'. Second: 'Les Archiducqz tant en leur nom que du Roy consentent et se contenten traiter avecq les ditz Estats en qualité et come les tenans estats libres et sur lesqueles Sa Majesté et Leurs Altezes ne pretendent rien, y en fin promete la ratificación'. Third: 'Que Leurs Altezes tant en leur nom que du Roy tenans et recognoisans ces estats libres et sur lesqueles Sa Majesté et Leurs Altezes ne pretendent rien, y en fin promete la ratificación de S.M'.

77 Council of State, Madrid, 27 October 1608, 'Sobre lo que contienen los despachos de Flandes que traxo Matheo de Urquina', BNE, MS 11.124, fols. 124r–139v, reference from fol. 125r.

up in the name of the Archdukes and Philip III, it better safeguarded the purpose of the States General of The Hague, because the monarch's ratification would only require the stamp of the royal rubric and seal on the text of the agreement itself. This reduced the opportunities for 'limiting the conditions', as Spinola had suggested, in imitation of what had been done in the ratification of the 1607 ceasefire treaty. Spinola, however, had not been mistaken in stating that, because it was a truce and not a final peace treaty – a temporary and not perpetual cessation of hostilities – the abandonment of seigniorial rights was temporary rather than permanent, being limited to the years that the treaty stipulated, and that temporary abandonment did not entail a renunciation of rights but the postponement of their 'replevin;' because, after the term fixed in the treaty had lapsed, the opponents would be able to resume their claims and to resort to force once more to defend them.[78]

Spinola's reasoning did not extract from Philip III the authorisation Brussels wanted and Mateo de Urquina returned from Madrid empty-handed in November 1608. During his absence, Albert had suggested a second rewording of the freedom clause using the ambassadors in The Hague who had been commissioned by different European kings and princes for the purpose of advising on, furthering and supervising the negotiations. At the beginning of December, he sent his confessor Fray Iñigo de Brizuela to Madrid 'so that he might persuade His Majesty to agree upon this form of truce without there following on from it the drawbacks that had been represented to His Majesty, and on account of which he in no way wanted to accept the aforementioned truce'.[79]

Brizuela's mission was to convince Philip III's entourage that a treaty could be concluded which would include the second draft of the freedom clause without loss of seigniorial rights (sovereignty), and that he could, in any case, add another clause to his ratification which would make explicit that his will was to retain them, and not cede or set the United Provinces free from their obligation of obedience forever, but only temporarily for the duration of the truce. If it was decided to add it, the States General of The Hague would not accept the ratification, but it was not necessary.[80] The rebels also knew that the

78 For legal differences between peace and truce, see Randall Lesaffer, 'La Tregua de los Doce Años y la formación del Derecho de Naciones clásico', in García García, *Tiempo de paces*, 177–191 as well as Chapter 12 in this volume.

79 BNE, MS 11.187, fol. 47v; Albert to Lerma, Brussels, 29 November 1608 and 30 November 1608; Isabella to Lerma, Brussels, 1 December 1608, CODOIN, vol. 43, 144, 146–147; Antonio Rodríguez Villa, *Correspondencia de la Infanta-Archiduquesa doña Isabel Clara Eugenia de Austria con el duque de Lerma y otros personajes* (Madrid, 1906), 200–201.

80 'Fray Iñigo de Brizuela. Copia de un papel que di a S. M. en 29 de mayo 1609', BNE, MS 11.187, fols. 67r–68r.

United Provinces would not achieve sovereignty 'with the words of free states' that figured in the second draft; this was demonstrated in an anonymous pamphlet printed and circulated in Holland in October and November 1608 by sections hostile to the truce to persuade compatriots of the legal inconsistency of the freedom clause, which Brizuela brought in Spanish.[81]

The friar's reasoning was solid. The negotiating process of 1607–1608 and the negotiation attempts before 1607 had been overshadowed by a longstanding problem: the acquisition and loss of *dominium*. The rebels alleged that they had acquired *dominium* (sovereignty) of the United Provinces because they had possessed and been publicly exercising the rights intrinsic to it with international recognition, in their capacity as holders, through just cause (the tyranny of the legitimate holder), and in good faith (the defence of the ancient privileges and freedoms of the territory) for a very long time. Although the legitimate holder of these rights – the 'King of Spain'-Duke of Burgundy and also the Archdukes since 1598 – had exercised the corresponding action of 'replevin' (the use of force to secure restitution) over a prolonged period, he had lost them because he had not exercised them; his sovereignty had expired. However, *dominium* was protected by an action of 'replevin', which was not subject to prescription. For this reason, the rebels sought to guarantee sovereignty through a complementary legal channel, voluntary loss of sovereignty, in other words, the voluntary abandonment or renunciation of rights by the titleholder. However, neither did this channel serve their liberating purpose for various reasons: first, inheritance rights could not be waived, because it infringed the interests of the successors, hence the impossibility of alienating (renouncing and ceding) sovereignty (its inalienability); second, waiving a right implied being dispossessed of it, whereas attributing it to another, that is transferring or ceding it, required an explicit declaration of will in that sense because a waiver had extinctive, but not translative effects. For this reason, Fray Iñigo de Brizuela's argument and the pamphlet's comment on the second draft of the freedom clause were indisputable in legal terms. If a waiver existed, it was only temporary since the action of 'replevin' was interrupted only transitorily, was only valid for Philip III, not for the future Philip IV, and cession was not contemplated at all. Consequently the rebels, who possessed the *de facto* seigniory of the United Provinces, would not be able to acquire the *de jure* seigniory of those provinces by virtue of the truce, nor could the Archdukes and Philip III lose it.

81 'Copia de un papel que han estampado en Olanda los contrarios de la Tregua para persuadir a las Islas que no vengan en ella, mostrando que con estas palabras de libres no alcanzan la soberanidad', BNE, MS 11.187, fol. 58r–v.

Brizuela was successful in his mission[82] and when he arrived in Brussels with Philip III's authorisation at the beginning of February 1609, the States General of The Hague had already given their approval, in mid January, to the second draft of the freedom clause and to the truce itself. So, the treaty was quickly formalised in Antwerp (not The Hague) to where the delegations of the Archdukes and the rebel States General journeyed. It was drawn up during the months of March and April and signed on 9 April 1609 for a period of twelve years. The Archdukes and the States General of the Republic ratified it on 13 April and its public proclamation, in Antwerp, on 14 April, and The Hague on 21 April, was celebrated with great solemnity. In May, the Treaty was taken to Madrid by Brizuela himself,[83] commissioned to obtain Philip III's ratification. The friar deployed the same arguments as he had on his earlier trip and his commission was a success. Philip III ratified the Treaty on 7 July, 1609,[84] because the description of free provinces granted to the rebel provinces

> (...) had to be understood always in a figurative sense [...], as if they were free, and not with the meaning of true and legitimate freedom; for they had never been able, by means of their rebellion, either to acquire it justly or possess it with any good reason; and so, this being so manifest, the King and the Archdukes were not agreeing to the loss of any right that they first had over the United Provinces.[85]

---

82 Luis Cabrera de Córdoba, *Relación de las cosas sucedidas en la corte de España desde 1599 hasta 1614* (intro. R. García Cárcel, Salamanca, 1997), 360–361.

83 Rodríguez Villa, *Correspondencia de la Infanta-Archiduquesa*, 207–208.

84 Allen, *Philip III and the Pax Hispanica*, 233.

85 Bentivoglio, 'Relación del Tratado de la Tregua', fol. 94r.

CHAPTER 3

The Act of Cession, the 1598 and 1600 States General in Brussels and the Peace Negotiations during the Dutch Revolt

Bram De Ridder and Violet Soen

Introduction

On 10 September 1597, Philip II wrote a short letter to the loyal Estates, councils and nobles in the Low Countries, wherein he announced 'la benigne resolution qu'avons prise pour vostre propre bien'.[1] Without any prior consultation, the Habsburg King informed his subjects that he would cede the Low Countries to his daughter Isabella and her prospective husband Albert of Austria, the then serving Governor General in Brussels. The idea of a cession was certainly not new, the possibility of seceding the territories in the Netherlands had already been formulated under Emperor Charles V.[2] During the reign of Philip II, however, it was the first time that concrete steps towards an implementation were carried out: Isabella would receive the Low Countries and the Franche-Comté of Burgundy as a dowry. Amongst other things, the aim was to appease the rebellious United Provinces by meeting one of their most important complaints, namely the removal of Philip II himself. Still, in the end, the main goal was to restore Habsburg rule over the totality of the Seventeen Provinces.[3]

1 Philip II to the loyal Estates, Councils and Nobles, 10 September 1598: Victor Brants (ed.), *Recueil des Ordonnances des Pays-Bas: deuxième série, 1506–1700: Règne d'Albert et d'Isabelle, 1598–1621* (Brussels, 1909), vol. 9, 4–5.

2 Rafael Valladares, 'Decid adiós a Flandes. La Monarquía Hispánica y el problema de los Países Bajos', in Werner Thomas and Luc Duerloo (eds.), *Albert & Isabella 1598–1621, Essays* (Turnhout, 1998), 48–50; Jochen A. Fühner, *Die Kirchen- und die antireformatorische Religionspolitik Kaiser Karls V. in den siebzehn Provinzen der Niederlande 1515–1555* (Brill's Series in Church History 23; Leyden/Boston, 2004), 47–54.

3 Valladares, 'Decid', 48–51; Alicia Esteban Estríngana, 'Haciendo rostro a la fortuna. Guerra, paz y soberanía en los Países Bajos', in Bernardo J. García García (ed.), *Tiempo de Paces. La Pax Hispanica y la Tregua de los Doce Años* (Madrid, 2009), 82–84 and her contribution to this volume; Paul Allen, *Philip III and the Pax Hispanica, 1598–1621: The Failure of Grand Strategy* (New Haven/London, 2000), 17–18; Violet Soen, 'Philip II's Quest. The Appointment of Governors General during the Dutch Revolt (1559–1598)', *Bijdragen en Mededelingen betreffende de Geschiedenis der Nederlanden*, 126 (2011) 15–16.

 | DOI 10.1163/9789004274921_005

Within this context, it is not so surprising that the Act of Cession provided a new stimulus for peace negotiations with the rebellious provinces. Time and again during the Dutch Revolt, contacts between Brussels and The Hague were made in order to proceed to more formal peace negotiations. What might come more to a surprise then, is that the Act of Cession led twice to the convocation of a States General in Brussels, once in 1598 and again in 1600. This was after all the same Spanish Habsburg Monarchy which had opposed time and again such convocation throughout the preceding conflict. Hence, this chapter ponders why this double gathering happened in a short time span of two years, and how this affected the peace negotiations during the Dutch Revolt.[4] As will become clear, the developments within the 1598–1600 peace process decisively configured the political context for the conclusion of the Twelve Years Truce in 1609.

Convoking a States General?

To understand why the States General were convoked twice in 1598 and 1600, it is important to return to the medieval origins of this institution. The first States General in the Burgundian lands are traditionally considered to have been held on 9 January 1464, at the instigation of Duke Philip the Good (1419–1467). These first States General relied upon on an even older and wider parliamentary tradition of a representation of the governed, consisting of delegations by the provincial Estates, each organised in three groups comprehending the nobility, clergymen and commoners. This new institution enabled the Duke of Burgundy to negotiate directly with all of the provinces in his *pays par deça*, turning these States General into a centralising institution as well. Only the Duke of Burgundy had the right to convoke a meeting, but the Great Privilege issued by Mary of Burgundy in 1477 extended this prerogative to the provincial states. In practice though, the subsequent rulers never allowed this to happen.[5]

---

4 Hugo De Schepper, 'Los Países Bajos y la Monarquía Hispánica. Intentos de reconciliación hasta la tregua de los Doce años (1574–1609)', in Ana Crespo Solana and Manuel Herrero Sánchez (eds.), *España y las 17 provincias de los Países Bajos. Una revisión historiográfica (XVI–XVIII)* (Cordoba, 2002), 329–330; Violet Soen, 'Estrategias tempranas de pacificación de los Países Bajos (1570–1598)', in García Garcia, *Tiempo de Paces*, 75.

5 Marc Boone, '"In den beginne was het woord". De vroege groei van "parlementen" in de middeleeuwse vorstendommen der Nederlanden', *Bijdragen en Mededelingen betreffende de Geschiedenis der Nederlanden*, 120 (2005) 338–361; Hugo De Schepper, 'Staatsgezag en macht

The States General soon turned into a crucial institution in the Burgundian-Habsburg Low Countries. They provided the provincial delegations with the opportunity to discuss fiscal and political issues with their ruler. In theory, the assembly had little formal power, but as the States General had to consent to the subsidies (*beden*) demanded by the ruler, they were nevertheless in a position to exert considerable influence. As these taxes usually served to pay for war, their say in external affairs was not insignificant. Hence, until the reign of Philip II, the States General were frequently consulted to deliberate on matters of war and peace, even becoming crucial to the ratification of peace treaties.[6] Moreover, they could and did intervene directly in attempts at making peace during governmental crises. In addition to their role in fiscal and foreign policies, the States General played an essential role in the acknowledgment of new rulers. New princes swore their oaths before the assembly, in return receiving the allegiance from their new subjects. Helmut Koenigsberger has identified these evolutions in the political government of the Low Countries as a *dominium politicum et regale*. This term – originally codified in *The Governance of England* written by Sir John Fortescue in the 1470s – described a form of constitutional monarchy based upon a sharing of power between rulers and representative institutions.[7]

in de Nederlanden. Verworvenheden en beperkingen in het Bourgondisch-Habsburgse systeem', in Jac Geurts and Hugo De Schepper (eds.), *Staatsvorming onder Bourgondiërs en Habsburgers. Theorie en Praktijk. Handelingen van het 7de Colloquium van de Werkgroep 'Internationale Verhoudingen, 1350–1800' gehouden aan de Katholieke Universiteit Nijmegen, 2 November 2001* (Maastricht, 2006), 35–36; Robert Wellens, 'Staten-Generaal', in Erik Aerts et al. (eds.), *De centrale overheidsinstellingen van de Habsburgse Nederlanden (1482–1795)* (Algemeen Rijksarchief en Rijksarchief in de Provinciën, Studia 55; Brussels, 1994), vol. 1, 65–67, 69; Robert Wellens, *Les États-Généraux des Pays-Bas des origines à la fin du règne de Philippe le Beau (1464–1506)* (Standen en Landen 64; Heule, 1974), 92–97, 285–286; John Gilissen, 'Les États Généraux des pays de par deçà, 1464–1632', *Standen en Landen*, 33 (1965) 263–321.

6 Randall Lesaffer, 'Peace Treaties from Lodi to Westphalia' in Randall Lesaffer (ed.), *Peace Treaties and International Law in European History: From the End of the Middle Ages to World War One* (Cambridge, 2004), 19–21.

7 Koenigsberger has used the term as an analytical tool to coin evolutions in the relationship between rulers and parliamentary institutions in the Low Countries, and it is in this perspective that the concept will appear in this contribution too. Helmut G. Koenigsberger, 'Monarchies and Parliaments in Early Modern Europe. Dominium Regale or Dominium politicum et Regale?', *Theory and Society*, 5 (1978) 191–217; idem, *Monarchies, States Generals and Parliaments. The Netherlands in the Fifteenth and Sixteenth Centuries* (Cambridge, 2001), 25, 220–340.

With the abdication of Charles V in Brussels in 1555, Philip II also started his rule over the Seventeen Provinces during a session of the States General.[8] The relation between prince and provinces would soon turn problematic: already the prolonged States General between 1557 and 1559 was a clear political showdown, demonstrating once again that the deputies of the Estates could seriously impede royal policies. During the Dutch Revolt, this troubled relation took a turn for the worst, especially when the insurgents organised themselves from 1572 onwards through a 'Free Estates'.[9] Despite the continued veto against a States General from Madrid – out of fear for religious change – local peace-making attempts often included parliamentary-like meetings. This tactic fitted into the overall strategy of 'ganar los corazones', as opposed to more violent approaches of subduing the rebellion.[10] On the eve of the Iconoclastic Fury for example, Governess General Margaret of Parma convoked several provincial Estates separately for a consultation on a mitigated anti-heresy law.[11] Also in June 1574, Governor General Luis de Requesens appealed to the pacifying potential of the States General by convoking all fifteen 'loyal provinces' in Brussels and announcing them a new and broad general pardon.[12]

Things changed considerably when in the vacuum following the death of Governor Requesens, the States of Brabant convoked a States General on their own initiative in September 1576, extending the invitation to the 'Free Estates' of Holland and Zeeland. Later on, this initiative would be endorsed by the

8 Violet Soen, 'De troonsafstand van Karel V: Achter de schermen van een ceremonie' in *Keizer Karel en Eeklo. Verslag van een colloquium over Keizer Karel, Eeklo, 24 September 2005* (Eeklo, 2006), 67–76.

9 James Tracy, *The founding of the Dutch Republic: War, Finance, and Politics in Holland, 1572–1588* (Oxford, 2008).

10 Bernardo J. García García, '"Ganar los corazones y obligar los vecinos". Estrategias de pacificación de los Países Bajos (1604–1610)', in Crespo Solana and Herrero Sanchez, *España y las 17 provincias*, 137–166.

11 Violet Soen, 'Between Dissent and Peacemaking. The Dutch Nobility on the Eve of the Revolt (1564–1567)', *Belgisch Tijdschrift voor Filologie en Geschiedenis*, 86 (2008) 745–746.

12 See in particular: Guido Marnef, 'Resistance and the Celebration of Privileges in Sixteenth-Century Brabant', in Judith Pollmann and Andrew Spicer (eds.), *Public Opinion and Changing Identities in the Early Modern Netherlands. Essays in Honour of Alastair Duke* (Leyden, 2007), 125–140; Violet Soen, *Geen pardon zonder paus! Studie over de complementariteit van het koninklijk en pauselijk generaal pardon (1570–1574) en over inquisiteur-generaal Michael Baius (1560–1576)* (Verhandelingen Koninklijke Vlaamse Academie van België voor Wetenschappen en Kunsten, New Series 14; Brussels, 2007), 257–273.

Council of State, which was at that time serving as interim Governor General.[13] The ensuing Pacification of Ghent of 8 November 1576 somehow conferred the political authority to this States General, especially when relations with the new Governor General Don Juan did neither normalise nor stabilise.[14] Almost five years later, on 26 July 1581, the States General formally and famously abjured Philip II, even if they continued to seek for an appropriate substitute as ruler.[15] Even so, these States General did no longer represent the former Seventeen Provinces brought together under the Emperor. Luxembourg had remained loyal, while Namur would forcefully follow after the seizure of its citadel by Don Juan in the summer of 1577. With the Treaty of Arras in May 1579 also Artois, Hainaut and Walloon-Flanders reconciled with Philip II.[16] Likewise, the ensuing military campaigns of the new Governor Alexander Farnese reduced the territory over which the States General exerted power.[17] After several failures to offer sovereignty to a new ruler, around 1588, the then insurgent 'seven provinces' considered themselves capable enough to maintain their powers and organised themselves in the Republic of the United Netherlands. For Koenigsberger, they continued the legacy of the *dominium politicum*, while leaving behind former monarchical tendencies.[18]

13 Gustaaf Janssens, *Brabant in het verweer. Loyale oppositie tegen Spanje's bewind in de Nederlanden van Alva tot Farnese 1567–1578* (Standen en Landen 89; Kortrijk/Heule, 1989), 292–314.

14 Michel Baelde and Paul Van Peteghem, 'De Pacificatie van Gent', in *Opstand en pacificatie in de lage landen. Bijdrage tot de studie van de pacificatie van Gent. Verslagboek van het Tweedaags Colloquium bij de vierhonderdste verjaring van de Pacificatie van Gent* (Ghent, 1976), 16–17.

15 Paul Brood and Raymond Kubben (eds.), *The Act of Abjuration. Inspired and Inspirational. Twelve Authors on One of the Highlights of the Nationaal Archief of the Netherlands* (Nijmegen, 2011).

16 Gustaaf Janssens, 'Van de komst van Alva tot de Unies', in Michel Cloet et al. (eds.), *Algemene Geschiedenis der Nederlanden 6. Nieuwe Tijd* (Haarlem, 1979), 230–243; De Schepper, 'Intentos de reconciliación', 330–333; Violet Soen, 'Les Malcontents au sein des États Généraux aux Pays-Bas (1578–1581): Défense du pouvoir de la noblesse ou défense de l'orthodoxie?', in Ariane Boltanski and Frank Mercier (eds.), *La noblesse et la défense de l'orthodoxie XIII-XVIIIme siècles* (Rennes, 2011), 135–149.

17 Krista de Jonge et al. (eds.), *Alexander Farnese and the Low Countries* (Turnhout, forthcoming); Violet Soen, 'Reconquista and Reconciliation in the Dutch Revolt. The campaign of Alexander Farnese in the Dutch Revolt (1578–1592)', *Journal of Early Modern History*, 16 (2012) 1–22. For a broader interpretation, see: Marjolein 't Hart, 'De democratische paradox en de Opstand in Vlaanderen, Brabant en Holland', in Mario Damen en Louis Sicking (eds.), *Bourgondië voorbij. De Nederlanden 1250–1650* (Hilversum, 2010), 375–388.

18 Koenigsberger, *Monarchies*, 311–315.

Meanwhile, in the loyal provinces, the principle of monarchical rule was reiterated, although it was not the immediate emergence of the strong and univocal *dominium regale* ignoring the parliamentary tradition, as Koenigsberger has alleged.[19] Due to the renewed war with England and France, there was a lot of discontent in border provinces like Artois and Hainaut. Still in 1595, some form of parliamentary representation was tried as a means to pacify the loyal provinces: Governor General Ernst of Austria then convoked a special *junta* of Bishops, Knights of the Golden Fleece and provincial states to find remedies for the ongoing troubles.[20] In the tense atmosphere of the last decade of the 16th century, a one-sided move like the Act of Cession could thus alienate the loyal provinces already in distress. Moreover, the abdication of a ruling sovereign had already been considered unusual in 1555, when Charles V had ceded Spain and the Low Countries to his son, but in 1598 both the King and his successor gave up their hereditary rights on conditions.[21] Hence, it seemed that the cession Philip II intended would definitely benefit from the traditional legitimacy that a States General could offer. After all, the practice of convoking the States General was still considered to be the normal procedure for a transfer of power.[22] By embodying the embattled *dominium politicum et regale*, these States General could moreover appeal to conciliation. It is therefore no surprise that Marc de Hertoghe, member of the Council of Flanders, stated after the announcement of the King's intention to cede the Low Countries that exactly the convocation of the States General would be a 'unicque remede pour pacifier ces troubles'.[23]

---

19 Ibid., 315–321, 336.

20 'Avis donné à l'Archiduc Ernest, gouverneur des Pays-Bas, les 18 et 19 janvier 1595, par les archevêques, évêques, chevaliers de l'Ordre, gouverneurs des provinces, et par le conseil d'État, sur les mesures à prendre pour le rétablissement des affaires du pays, avec les apostilles de Phillipe II, en date du 18 février 1596': Louis P. Gachard (ed.), *Les États Généraux de 1600* (Brussels, 1849), 415–450.

21 Philip II and his son never gave up all their rights. In order to preserve the Netherlands under all possible circumstances the public and secret clauses of the Act of Cession guaranteed a clear connection between these territories and the Spanish Habsburgs: See Werner Thomas, 'Andromeda Unbound. The Reign of Albert & Isabella in the Southern Netherlands, 1598–1621', in Werner Thomas and Luc Duerloo (eds.), *Albert & Isabella 1598–1621. Essays* (Turnhout, 1998), 1–14. See also Chapters 2 and 10 in this volume.

22 Karin Van Honacker, 'The Archdukes and Their Subjects: The Political Culture of the Citizens in the Netherlands', in Thomas and Duerloo, *Albert & Isabella,* 241.

23 Victor Brants, 'Avis sur les remèdes à la situation de Flandre adressé à l'Archiduc Albert en 1598 par Marc de Hertoghe, membre du Conseil de Flandre', *Bulletin de la Commission Royale d'Histoire,* 81 (1912) 335–338. Marc de Hertoghe: Knight, born in a noble family

The Short States General of 1598

On 26 July 1598, Albert informed all provincial states of the Act of Cession. The official text argued that the transfer of power was meant to serve 'le bien et repos de nosdicts pays d'embas'. It clearly supported the dynastic and monarchical goals linked to a *dominium regale*, but the states were told that the whole plan would serve their interests more than those of the Spanish King. According to Philip II, the Cession would solve the old sore of royal absence by awarding the provinces the honour of 'se trouver régy et gouverné à la veue et par la présence de son prince et seigneur naturel'. Furthermore, the Act reminded the states to the fact that in their first responses to the planned cession they had voiced no clear objections against the decision or against the proposed new rulership.[24] Albert now invited all states to send delegates to Brussels on 14 August. Hence, this new States General was intended to serve as the formal inauguration of Isabella as sovereign, making it an expression of the old contract between rulers and subjects.[25]

In order to quell any protest against the Act of Cession, the *mise-en-scène* of the States General contained numerous ceremonial references to its 1555 counterpart of the Abdication of Charles V. The meetings were held in the same place, the great hall of the Coudenberg Palace, and the delegates' sitting places and the phrasing of the harangues all echoed the time of the Abdication.[26] As the imperial rule was increasingly seen as a foregone 'Golden Age' in the loyal provinces, these references created the impression that the cession would

---

living in the region of Waasland and married with Lucie de Tengnagel. He was member of the Council of Flanders and became president of this institution in 1617.

24 The Act of Cession, 6 May 1598: Brants, *Règne*, vol. 9, 7–13; The Estates of Brabant to Philip II, 5 December 1597: Brants, *Règne*, vol. 9, 6–7; Different Estates to Philip II, 8 December 1597 to 3 February 1598: Brussels, Archives Générales du Royaume de Belgique (hereinafter AGR), *Audiëntie*, nr. 619, f. 103–125. On the problem of the absence of the King: Soen, 'The Quest', *passim*.

25 Pieter Geyl, *The Revolt of the Netherlands, 1555–1609* (London/New York, 1958), 241; Paul Janssens, 'De Spaanse en Oostenrijkse Nederlanden (1579–1780)', in Johannes C.H. Blom and Emiel Lamberts (eds.), *Geschiedenis van de Nederlanden* (Baarn, 1993), 181.

26 Albert to Philip II, 17 February 1598: Joseph Lefèvre (ed.), *Correspondance de Philippe II sur les affaires des Pays-Bas* (Académie royale de Belgique, Commission royale d'histoire, Collection de chroniques belges inédites 50; Brussels, 1940–1960), vol. 4, 450; *Relation des particularitez et ceremoins passées a Bruxelles lors de la publication des patentes royalles e la cession des pays bas, au prouffit de la ser(enisi)me Infante, et de l'acceptation que les estatz g(e)n(er)aulx ont fait d'icelle, ensemble de la presta(ti)on des sermens hinc inde ensuyviz les xxi et xxiie d'aoust 1598*: AGR, *Audiëntie*, nr. 1191/21, (1), f. 2–8.

not only grant its supporters the benign return of the peace and prosperity of this past age, but that it would also revive the *dominium politicum et regale*, considered to be a core aspect of the Emperor's rule.[27] During the actual debates the message of expected compliance between rulers and subjects was voiced by Jean Richardot, President of the Secret Council and Albert's upcoming right hand.[28] His rhetorical style was intended to appeal both to emotional and rational reasoning: Richardot referred to the fatherlike nature of the Habsburg King and reminded his audience of the important financial, material, and above all personal efforts Charles V and his son had taken to guarantee the peace in the whole Netherlands. The King now even gave them 'la plus chere perle qui soit en ses tresors:' the fully qualified Infanta, who had aided her father in affairs of government and was 'la princesse la plus religieuse de monde, sainctement nourrie en la maison du roy'. Furthermore, according to Richardot the government would further improve due to the Act, since instead of one ruler (the King of Spain) they now would have two rulers (the King of Spain and his daughter). For Richardot, the Netherlands were indebted to the Spanish-Habsburg dynasty, a debt which had to be repaid by agreeing to the cession.[29]

Still, this convocation, although foreseen, took place sooner than expected: the peace with France signed in Vervins on 2 May 1598 had created a positive momentum, one which Philip II wanted to use to push through his plans for the cession. The sudden acceleration meant that not everything was fully prepared yet. Most importantly, the wedding around which the cession revolved had not yet taken place and the Infanta herself still resided in Spain. This situation generated an extra juridical complexity: Isabella sent her future husband

27 Helmut G. Koenigsberger, 'Republicanism, monarchism and liberty', in Robert Oresko et al. (eds.), *Royal and Republican Sovereingty in Early Modern Europe. Essays in memory of Ragnhild Hatton* (Cambridge, 1997), 65.

28 Jean Grusset or Richardot (1540–1609): Born in Champlite as son of Willem Grusset and Margaretha Richardot. He was a cousin of François Richardot, who later adopted him. As protégé of Cardinal Granvelle, he studied in Leuven, Rome, Milan and Padua and he became doctor in law in 1565. In 1568 he was appointed in the Great Council and in 1575 in the Privy Council. After his support for the States General in 1576–1577, he reconciled with Farnese in 1579. From then onwards, he built his further career in Habsburg service as a diplomat and member of the Council of State, ultimately becoming president of the Privy Council under Albert. He is best known for his central role in the Peace Treaties of Vervins (1598) and London (1604) and his involvement in the Twelve Year's Truce. Hugo de Schepper, 'Richardot', in *Nationaal Biografisch Woordenboek* (Brussels, 1964), vol. 1, 762–775.

29 *Relation des particularitez et ceremoins*: AGR, *Audiëntie*, nr. 1191/21, (1), f. 9–18, 31–3.

a letter which named him the proxy through which she would receive and give the necessary oaths during the States General. Simultaneously, she appointed him as Governor General in her name until she would have arrived.[30] This upcoming wedding would turn into a matter of great concern for the gathered States General. Philip II demanded that the ceremony would take place in Spain, which implied that Albert would have to leave the Low Countries and that yet another Governor General would be appointed *ad interim*.[31] These objections were understandable, because Albert's leave would oblige the appointment of a new Governor General for the fourth time in less than ten years. Due to a range of difficulties (not in the least the deaths of his appointees), Philip II had not been able to form a stable government in Brussels.[32] Hence, the spokesman of the States General, the Brabant Pensionary Philip Maes,[33] asked the Archduke not to leave or alternatively to return with his bride within a year. The Habsburg party responded that the voyage was demanded for by the King, and as such the Archduke, being a royal subject, had to comply.[34]

Even so, the upcoming wedding in Spain was in fact the only worry expressed by the States General. The contrast between the 1557–1559 and 1598 assemblies could not be bigger: during the former it took the provinces two years to reach an agreement with the King, whilst the latter only lasted four days of which two were spent on elaborate meals and a mass.[35] Given these facts, it is not so surprising that both Robert Wellens and Helmut Koenigsberger have stated that from 1598 onwards the States General had lost all their political power to the ruler.[36] The compliant behaviour of the loyal provinces and their acceptance of the shaky juridical construction at first sight suggest that the

30 Esteban Estríngana, 'Haciendo', 87; Isabella to Albert, 31 May 1598: Brants, *Règne*, vol. 9, 14–15.

31 *Relation des particularitez et ceremoins*: AGR, *Audiëntie*, nr. 1191/21, (1): f.1–5; Robert Wellens, 'Les États généraux de Bruxelles en 1598 et la cession des Pays-Bas aux Archiducs Albert et Isabelle', *Cahiers bruxellois*, 23 (1978) 24–25.

32 Soen, 'Quest', 3–29.

33 Philip Maes: son of Jacobus Maes and Alyde de Tassis and brother of the well-known Engelbert Maes, president of the Privy Council. He acted as *audiencier* for the Estates of Brabant and for the 1598 and 1600 States Generals. Gisela Jongbloet-Van Houtte (ed.), *Brieven en andere bescheiden betreffende Daniel Van der Meulen 1584–1600. Deel 1, augustus 1584–September 1585* (The Hague, 1986), 146, note 8.

34 'Relation des particularitez et ceremoins': AGR, *Audiëntie*, nr. 1191/21, (1), f. 25–6, 31–3.

35 'Relation des particularitez et ceremoins': AGR, *Audiëntie*, nr. 1191/21, (1), f. 42–5; Wellens, 'Cession', 28–29.

36 Wellens, 'Staten-Generaal', 68; Koenigsberger, *Monarchies*, 317–321.

harmonious collaboration behind the *dominium politicum et regale* had weakened significantly. Nevertheless, most likely, the states never really intended to make major political demands at this time. First and foremost, there was Albert's promise to organise a second States General upon his return, where more elaborate talks could be held. This also explains why the assembly demanded that the Governor General *ad interim* should not be allowed to issue new policies. In this way, the States General wanted to avoid further political manoeuvring before the next assembly gathered.[37] Second, there was the fact that one had to await Isabella's arrival before real decisions could be taken. Delaying Albert's departure would therefore only prolong the confused politico-juridical situation. Hence, both the Archduke and the loyal provinces realised the necessity of a speedy transfer of power, while sharing the same goal of stabilising policy rather than disrupting it. This danger, combined with Albert's guarantee, induced the States General to keep a low profile in expressing their concerns and objections, for other and better opportunities would arise. So despite the Habsburg emphasis on monarchical rule in speech and act, it is not clear from the events in 1598 whether or not the tradition of the *dominium politicum et regale* had already been replaced by a *dominium regale*, as Koenigsberger contended.

Peace Talks in 1598

The Act of Cession not only presented a new incentive to convoke a States General in Brussels, but also to revive contacts with the Dutch Republic in the hope of a reunification.[38] In January 1598, long before the States General gathered, preliminary talks with this aim were held in Brussels with the merchant Daniel Van der Meulen, based in Leyden but a former member of the Antwerp magistrate.[39] For the first time in a long while, proposals were made to solve

37 Commentary on the demands of the States General, 27 August 1598: AGR, *Audiëntie*, nr. 1191/21, (1); 'Extraict des poincts et articles remonstres par messieurs les etatz generaulx des pays bas a son Alteze': AGR, *Audiëntie*, nr. 619, f.469–84; Conditions of Brabant for the inauguration: AGR, *Audiëntie*, nr. 1191/21, (3); 'Relation des particularitez et ceremoins': AGR, *Audiëntie*, nr. 1191/21, (1), f. 28–9.

38 On earlier mediation attempts around 1592–1595, see: Violet Soen, 'Naturales del país o Espaignolizés? Agentes de la Corte como negociadores de paz durante la guerra de Flandes (1577–1595)', in René Vermeir, Maurits Ebben and Raymond Fagel (eds.), *Agentes y Identidades en movimiento. España y los Países Bajos, siglos XVI–XVIII* (Madrid, 2011), 171–193.

39 Daniel Van der Meulen (1554–1600): son of the Antwerp Merchant Jan Van der Meulen the younger and Elizabeth Zeghers. He was sent to Cologne in 1572 because of the upcoming

religious disputes as well, although on a very moderate level. Still, Van der Meulen remained very pessimistic on the conditions offered within the context of the cession. By the time the States General were convoked in July, these first mediation attempts had failed.[40] During the opening speeches of the States General, then, the Pensionary of Brabant Philip Maes referred to a possible reunification, yet the Archduke kept the means of achieving this under tight control. He permitted the States General to draft a letter which would be sent to the United Provinces, but only after he had reviewed it himself. By postponing his review, the Estates were sidelined in the peace process.[41]

Still, the Archduke again explored the possibility of peace talks just before his departure for Spain. He now delegated Marie de Brimeu, Duchess of Aarschot, in his name to The Hague. She could act as a perfect go-between, as she was a Calvinist noblewoman who lived in Republic, while officially she was still married to her Catholic husband living in the loyal provinces.[42] On 2 September 1598, she delivered to Oldenbarnevelt a package of letters, written by Albert and some of the most important loyal noblemen. Oldenbarnevelt brought the letters before the Dutch States General, who opened them but subsequently refused to write a reply. The United Netherlands considered the Archduke to be part of the faction of King Philip II, with whom they had sworn never to negotiate again.[43]

---

revolt, but participated in his family's trading company from 1576 onwards. After the peace negotiations in Cologne, he returned in 1579 to Antwerp, where he became enrolled in the city government. In 1584 he participated in the States General and married around this time with the merchant daughter Hester de la Faille. After the fall of Antwerp he moved to Hamburg, Bremen and Leyden. Jongbloet-Van Houtte, *Daniel Van der Meulen*, 15–35, 62–83.

40 'Verbael oft journael van t'gepaseerde in Brabant anno 1598': Johannes H. Kernkamp (ed.), 'Vredehandel met Spanje in 1598', *Bijdragen en Mededelingen van het Historisch Genootschap, gevestigd te Utrecht*, 57 (1936) 341–382; also Thomas, 'Andromeda Unbound', 2–4.

41 Commentary on the demands of the States General, 27 August 1598: AGR, *Audiëntie*, nr. 1191/21, (1); 'Relation des particularitez et ceremoins': AGR, *Audiëntie*, nr. 1191/21, (1), f. 37–38.

42 Marie de Brimeu (ca. 1550–1605): daughter of George de Brimeu and Anna von Walthausen. She married in 1572 with Lancelot of Berlaymont, and remarried after his death with Charles of Croÿ, Prince of Chimay and later Duke of Aarschot. Converted to Calvinism and supported the Revolt. In 1584, Charles of Croÿ reconciled with Philip II, after which he and the Duchess lived separately. She was also a regular guest in the salon of Daniel Van der Meulen. (www.biografischportaal.nl/persoon/71498005).

43 Secret resolution, 3 September 1598: Nicolas Japikse (ed.), *Resolutiën der Staten Generaal van 1576 tot 1609, tiende deel, 1598–1599* (Rijksgeschiedskundige Publicatiën 71; The Hague, 1930), 41–42; 'Verbael oft journael': Kernkamp, 'Vredehandel', 358.

Due to this diplomatic silence, Albert sought an alternative in the letter promised to the already finished States General in Brussels, mentioned above. This tactic had the advantage that he seemingly adhered to the old peace- and policy-making function of the parliamentary institution, a major demand from The Hague.[44] Hence, at the beginning of October, William Maes arrived in the Republic, carrying a letter from the States General from Brussels anti-dated on 28 and 29 August.[45] The letter asserted that the Act of Cession offered a unique opportunity to end the disastrous war, claimed that the United Netherlands owed their allegiance to Isabella, and promised that Albert would be a residing ruler whose sole occupation would be the well-being of the Netherlands. It was signed by the States General in Brussels and the mentioned dates suggested that the letter had been written just after the end of the assembly. Still, the text was neither compiled before 11 September (after Albert had received the negative reply from The Hague), nor was it written by the loyal provinces. The proposition might have been drafted by the States General in Brussels, but it is almost certain that Richardot composed the final message.[46] By resorting to a false or falsified letter, the Archduke tried to compromise between the demand of the States General in The Hague to negotiate with its counterpart in Brussels and the veto of Philip II to these plans.[47]

This time the States General in The Hague indeed responded to the letter of their 'colleagues', yet only after half a year: they acknowledged the need for peace, but they were also convinced that this would only be possible after the forceful removal of every Spaniard from the Low Countries. They therefore requested the loyal states to join them with arms; whatever the response they surely would continue the war themselves. They would, however, keep their military actions as moderate as possible, to avoid collateral damage.[48] In a way, it was

44 'Verbael oft journael': Kernkamp, 'Vredehandel', 380.

45 It is not known who this person exactly was. Presumably he was an Antwerp merchant with connections to Daniel Van der Meulen, for there are documents referring to a certain Willem Maes who was at the time managing certain properties for the Van der Meulen family in Antwerp. Neither is it known whether or not he was related to the mentioned Philip Maes. See Hugo De Schepper, *De Kollaterale Raden in de katholieke Nederlanden van 1579 tot 1609* (Unpublished doctoral dissertation, University of Leuven, 1972), 1061–1064; Jongbloet-Van Houtte, *Daniel Van der Meulen*, 17, note 17.

46 The States General in Brussels to the States General in The Hague, 28–29 August 1598: Gachard, *Les États Généraux*, cxxxvi–cxxxvii; Resolution of the Estates of Brabant, 11 September 1598: AGR, *Audiëntie*, nr. 1191/21, (1).

47 Philip II to Albert, 1 April 1597: Lefèvre, *Correspondance*, 405–406.

48 The States General in The Hague to the States General in Brussels, 22 March 1598: Gachard, *Les États Généraux*, cxlii–cxliii.

only natural for the United Provinces to portray the Habsburgs as violent oppressors. Their young State had been formed during a war with a dynasty whose powers were supposed to have derived from God.[49] Any evidence of the maliciousness of Habsburgs would therefore legitimate the war and consequentially their state. Simultaneously, they also gave in print some pamphlets denouncing the supposedly sincere character of the Act of Cession. As the envoy Maes reported upon his return: the United Provinces alleged to have fought for their freedom and were not prepared to give this up for 'ung tel prétendu accord'.[50] Jonathan Israel interpreted the attitude of the early Republic as contributing to its own internal stability, and Laura Manzano Baena contended that this refusal was in fact an articulation of its own principles of future government.[51]

The response of the States General in The Hague to the supposed letter of their counterparts in Brussels bore witness to an increasing divide between the two centres of government. Now formally, the United Netherlands considered the loyal Netherlands to be occupied territory, tightly held in check by the 'devious' and 'forfeited' Habsburgs. They suspected that the Estates were weakened and silenced by their rulers, otherwise they already would have expressed their support for their countrymen in the United Provinces.[52] They had found proof for their reasoning in the fact that the letter supposedly written by the States General in Brussels was vague, and that the envoy carrying it did not deliver a secret message. Therefore, the Republic concluded that the Habsburgs still remained oppressive tyrants, who showed their disregard for parliamentary deliberation by keeping the other provinces 'les bras et jambes lies'.[53] The States General of 1598 had thus not created common ground for peace talks, rather the contrary.

---

49 Koenigsberger, 'Republicanism', 58; Hugh Dunthorne, 'Resisting monarchy: the Netherlands as Britain's school of revolution in the late sixteenth and seventeenth centuries', in Oresko, *Royal and Republican Sovereingty*, 126; Laura Manzano Baena, 'Inventando al enemigo: Imágenes de "España" en las Provincias Unidas', in Crespo Solana and Herrero Sanchez, *España y las 17 provincias de los Países Bajos*, 788; Simon Groenveld, *Het Twaalfjarig Bestand, 1609–1621. De jongelingsjaren van de Republiek der Verenigde Nederlanden* (The Hague, 2009), 74–75.

50 Report of Willem Maes: Gachard, *Les États Généraux*, cxl–cxli.

51 Jonathan I. Israel, *The Dutch Republic. Its Rise, Greatness, and Fall 1477–1806* (Oxford, 1998), 254–256; Laura Manzano Baena, *Conflicting Words. The Peace Treaty of Münster (1648) and the Political Culture of the Dutch Republic and the Spanish Monarchy* (Leuven, 2011), 13; Manzano Baena, 'Imágines', 786.

52 The States General in The Hague to the States General in Brussels, 22 March 1598: Gachard, *Les États Généraux*, cxlii–cxliii.

53 Report of Willem Maes: Gachard, *Les États Généraux*, cxxxix.

The 1600 States General

As promised by Albert in 1598, a new States General was held in Brussels from April to November 1600. This was to be the long awaited forum to talk about war and peace with the Republic. In the previous months, the Joyous Entries of Albert and Isabella in the provinces had made clear that their new subjects had not yet given up the hope for an agreement with the uprising provinces: the decorations and festivities clearly referred to peace and reunification.[54] By letting the invitation letters hint at possible peace negotiations, the Habsburgs again provided lip service to the *dominium politicum et regale*. Nevertheless, the new States General were mainly intended to raise new taxes in time of war. As in 1598, Richardot defended the Habsburg strategy. On 28 April 1600, he opened the assembly with the declaration that the States were convoked to find a solution for the war and that they should try to restore peace and unity to the whole Low Countries. At the same time, he declared his confidence in the ability of the Spanish-Habsburg army to do so, yet it would not be funded by Philip III alone: payments from the provinces were expected for reaching final peace.[55]

On 12 May, every province was asked to give their opinion on the matter of war and peace.[56] At this instance, the States General split over two issues, which demonstrated that even within the same Brussels assembly different opinions survived about the ideal relationship to the ruler. The first apple of discord concerned the means to achieve peace. Brabant, Hainaut, Lille, Douai and Orchies, Gelre, Limburg and Tournaisis were adherents of the 'soft approach' (traditionally described as the *voie de douceur*). The States General could organise peace talks, whilst the Archdukes could help with measures

54 Albert to different provincial governors, 31 March 1600: Gachard, *Les États Généraux*, 8–9; 'Première relation, rédigée par Nicolas Du Bois, conseiller pensionnaire des états du Tournaisis': Gachard, *Les États Généraux*, 215; 'Voyage de l'archiduc Albert en Espagne, en 1598': Louis P. Gachard et al. (eds.), *Collection des Voyages de Souverains des Pays-Bas* (Brussels, 1847–1882), vol. 4, 536–556; Margit Thøfner, 'Domina & Princeps proprietaria. The Ideal of Sovereignty in the Joyous Entries of the Archduke Albert and the Infanta Isabella', in Thomas and Duerloo, *Albert & Isabella*, 57–65; Margit Thøfner, 'Marrying the City, Mothering the Country: Gender and Visual Conventions in Johannes Bochius's Account of the Joyous Entry of the Archduke Albert and the Infanta Isabella into Antwerp', *Oxford Art Journal*, 22 (1999) 20–21; Inge Van Bamis, *Een nieuw begin? Gratieverlening naar aanleiding van de Blijde Intrede van Albrecht en Isabella* (Ghent, 2012).

55 Proposition made by Richardot, 28 April 1600: Gachard, *Les États-Généraux*, 385–388.

56 Report of the States General of 1600: Gachard, *Les États Généraux*, 111–119; 'Mémoire de ce qui est passé aux Estatz Généraulx': Ibid., 191.

such as providing information, restructuring the government or re-allowing trade with the United Provinces. Yet Artois, Valenciennes, Luxemburg and Tournai were opposed to this soft tactic. They had benefitted from the peace with France and therefore could take an offensive stance in opting for war and a reorganisation of the army. Furthermore, they considered war and peace a prerogative of the sovereign, so the Archdukes should take the initiative, not the States General.[57]

The second dispute arose over the question whether a long or a short truce should be approved, an idea that already circulated in 1598.[58] This time, Brabant and Hainaut wanted that a six to twelve years truce should be negotiated, if peace was unachievable. This proposal met with the likely opposition from Artois, Tournai and Valenciennes. As could be expected from provinces which already opposed to possible peace talks, they declared that the States General had no mandate to discuss a truce. More significantly, some of the 'doves' joined their ranks for political reasons: they feared that once the Republic learned that a truce would be offered upon a failure of negotiations, it would never accept a permanent peace. For these provinces, only a truce of maximum one year was acceptable, that is, when it was meant to facilitate negotiations and not to prepare new war manoeuvres.[59]

As the discussions dragged on, the States General decided to ask the advice of the Archdukes themselves. Time and again, Albert had reminded the delegations that any decision concerning the peace had to be taken in consultation with him.[60] In any case, he was more interested in his own negotiations: in order to raise pressure on the Republic he had sent Richardot to Boulogne to negotiate a peace with Elizabeth I, the last major ally of the United Provinces. Until as late as May 1600 these talks seemed an alternative for the attempt to negotiate through the States General in Brussels.[61] The division in the assembly

57 Opinion of the Estates of Hainaut, 12 May 1600: Gachard, *Les États Généraux*, 397; Summary of opinions of the different delegations, 12, 13, 15 May 1600: Ibid., 399–402; Report of the States General of 1600: Ibid., 121–122; 'Mémoire de ce qui est passé aux Estatz Généraulx': Ibid., 197–198, 200–202.

58 'Poinctz et articles pour redresser l'estat': Brants, 'Remèdes', 338.

59 'Première relation, rédigée par Nicolas Du Bois': Gachard, *Les États Généraux*, 222; Opinion of Michel d'Esne, deputy of Tournaisis, 15 May 1600: Ibid., 403–404.

60 'Première relation, rédigée par Nicolas Du Bois': Gachard, *Les États Généraux*, 221; Report of the States General of 1600: Ibid. 149–150, 178–183, 675–676; Hugo De Schepper, 'De Nederlanden, 1560–1604: oppositie, opstand, oorlog', in Werner Thomas (ed.), *De val van het Nieuwe Troje. Het beleg van Oostende, 1601–1604* (Leuven, 2004), 30.

61 Report of the States General of 1600: Gachard, *Les États Généraux*, 124–125; 'Mémoire de ce qui est passé aux Estatz Généraulx': Ibid., 199–200; Allen, *Pax Hispanica*, 42.

in Brussels thus suited Albert very well. In his final answer of 25 May to their request, he authorised the States to discuss a truce but did not say whether it should be short or long, and he allowed them to send an invitation to The Hague. At the same time, Albert declared that the enemy had never been further away from reconciliation. This answer was thus a carefully drafted compromise, and certainly not a *carte blanche* for negotiations.[62]

Renewed Talks

As such, the Habsburg strategy for the States General in 1600 failed to some extent. The Archdukes were impatient over war and finances, while the States General persistently deliberated on the possibility of peace talks. In the end the Archdukes felt obliged to consent that the assembly took concrete diplomatic steps in that direction. Almost immediately, the States General delegated the Baron of Bassigny,[63] Pensionary Codt[64] and Colonel Bentinck[65] to the United Provinces, allowing them to start negotiations if possible.[66] Their invitation letter argued that the newly gathered assembly in Brussels demonstrated that the old form of *dominium politicum et regale* was restored, and that under these circumstances The Hague could not any longer remain adverse to peace talks. Even if the negotiation offer was modelled after the 1598 communications, it now called upon the rebellious provinces to forget past events by an 'eternal silence'.[67]

In turn, the States General in The Hague debated a whole day on the question whether or not to open the letter because they believed it to be addressed

62 Act of the Archdukes allowing the States General in Brussels to contact the States General in the Hague, 24 May 1600: Gachard, *Les États Généraux*, 453–454.

63 Gerard of Hoorn, baron of Bassigny: A rather unknown figure, he was the brother of Maximilian of Hoorn and reconciled in 1578 with Philip II (www.biografischportaal.nl/persoon/63102201).

64 Henri de Codt (1529–1606): Born in Ypres, where he started his career. He was awarded the symbolic title of 'Royal councillor for life' by Farnese, and participated later in both the 1598 and the 1600 States General. Jacques J.J. Vereecke, 'Codt (Henri de)', in *Biographie Nationale* (Brussels, 1866–1986), vol. 4, 247–251.

65 Philip of Bentinck, Lord of Obbicht and Papenhoven (died 1610/1611): son of Charles, Lord of Berrinckhuizen, and Catherine of Hakfort. In 1579 he was Governor of Stralen and in 1586 he became Governor of Venlo. (www.biografischportaal.nl/persoon/85090384).

66 Report of the States General of 1600: Gachard, *Les États Généraux*, 121–122, 126–133.

67 'd'beste te wesen allen voirleden saecken ende misverstanden te vergeten by een eeuwich geswygh'. The States General in Brussels to the States General in the Hague, 5 June 1600: Gachard, *Les États Généraux*, 757–759.

incorrectly. Compared to the six months delay in 1598–1599 though, they would respond relatively swiftly. They now declared to be rejoiced because the States in the loyal provinces were again able to witness the restoration of their state. Still, they hoped that this recovery would soon enable them to oppose the Spanish tyrants. In their opinion, peace talks were impossible because Albert still dominated the States (to name but one example, the mandates of the envoys were issued in his name).[68] So, in contrast to the States General in Brussels, the States General in The Hague equalled Albrecht and Isabella with their 'tyrannical' predecessor. On 23 June, Bassigny returned with this answer to Brussels, where a deputy noted that the text resembled the response from 1599 and was so filled with self-complacency 'que l'air en pue'. The content would not be dispersed beyond the assembly, but the feeling that the Republic behaved unreasonable was widely shared.[69]

Nevertheless, the communications were not suspended. Lobbying from the deputies of Brabant made that the envoys could continue their mission in their own name and had to appease the Republic by starting talks about the *brandschattingen* by Habsburg troops and the presence of foreigners in the government.[70] Moreover, a coastal invasion and the subsequent victory of Nieuwpoort by Maurits of Nassau (2 July 1600) enhanced the urgency of diplomatic action.[71] Even if in these circumstances the delegations in Brussels accorded some parts of the undecided tax grants in order to strike back, they also insisted on negotiations with the Republic. Provinces like Hainaut still believed in the potential

68 Secret resolution, 12 June 1600: Nicolas Japikse (ed.), *Resolutiën der Staten Generaal van 1576 tot 1609, elfde deel 1600–1601* (Rijksgeschiedskundige Publicatiën 85; The Hague, 1941), 79; The States General in the Hague to the States General in Brussels, 17 June 1600: Gachard, *Les États Généraux*, 763–765; 'Première relation, rédigée par Nicolas Du Bois': Ibid., 230–231.

69 The deputies of Tournaisis to the Estates of Tournaisis, 23 June 1600: Gachard, *Les États Généraux*, 305–308; *Beclach ende doleancie van den Pays* (Brussels, 1600): Willem P.C. Knuttel, *Catalogus van de pamfletten-verzameling berustende in de Koninklijke Bibliotheek* (Utrecht, 1978), nr. 454/The Early Modern Pamphlets Online, nr. 1103 (tempo.idcpublishers.info/search.php).

70 'Mémoire de ce qui est passé aux Estatz Généraulx': Gachard, *Les États Généraux*, 210; 'Avis des États Généraux assemblés à Bruxelles, sur la réponse à faire aux États Généraux des Provinces-Unies': Ibid., 768–769.

71 Report of the States General of 1600: Gachard, *Les États Généraux*, 149–150, 153; Project lettre of the Brussels States General to Philip III, 13–14 October 1600: Ibid., 677–688; Albert to the Council of State, 4 July 1600: Ibid., 561–562; 'Mémoire de ce qui est passé aux Estatz Généraulx': Ibid., 212–213; Ronald De Graaf, *Oorlog, mijn arme schapen. Een andere kijk op de Tachtigjarige Oorlog 1565–1648* (Franeker, 2004), 336–338; Leen Dorsman, *1600: slag bij*

success of the diplomatic efforts and refused to start discussions on new taxes before the peace 'tombera par terre'.[72] After the Nieuwpoort battle, Bassigny, Codt and Bentinck had received word that Oldenbarnevelt, who was still in Bergen-op Zoom, approved to hold a small peace conference. Albert reluctantly agreed, while requiring that the three envoys would not remain in Bergen-op-Zoom for too long, as this would only give the impression that he was seriously weakened and desperately needed peace.[73]

As a result, new negotiations started in Bergen-op-Zoom on 20 July 1600. Hiding the annoyance expressed in Brussels over the past few months, the Habsburg envoys thanked Oldenbarnevelt and the other representatives for the 'always' constructive attitude of the Republic. Nevertheless, the delegation from the United Netherlands again criticised the misbehaviour of the Habsburgs, the loyalty of the 'Hispanicised' States General to Philip III and some of the clauses integrated in the Act of Cession. They alleged that a possible acceptance of the Act of Cession had been seriously deliberated in The Hague, but that the four-day States General in 1598 in Brussels had shown decisively that the Habsburg dynasty would not restore their vision of the desired *dominium politicum et regale*.[74] Most likely, Oldenbarnevelt only accepted the talks because the expected support for his military campaign in the loyal provinces never materialised, so he personally wanted to convince these provinces to join in arms.[75] He stated that the loyal provinces had missed a great opportunity to dispose of the Habsburg dynasty at the moment of Philip II's death, but with Albert weakened after the battle they should try once again: by joining forces the Archdukes would have no other option than to accept the demands they would make. But just like two years earlier, the Habsburg States refused and continued to support the dynasty's claims of rightful government.

Nieuwpoort (Verloren Verleden. Gedenkwaardige momenten en figuren uit de vaderlandse geschiedenis 10; Hilversum, 2000); Vibeke Roeper en Wilfried Uitterhoeve (eds.), *De slag bij Nieuwpoort. Journaal van de tocht naar Vlaanderen in 1600* (Nijmegen, 2000).

72 'Avis des députés du Hainaut sur la dernière déclaration des Archiducs', 3 July 1600: Gachard, *Les États Généraux*, 545–547.

73 The States General in Brussels to the States General in the Hague, July 1600: Gachard, *Les États Généraux*, 770–771; The States General in The Hague to the States General in Brussels, 16 July 1600:Ibid., 772–773; Report of the States General of 1600: Ibid., 149–150, 157–158; The deputies of Tournaisis to the Estates of Tournaisis, 19 July 1600: Ibid., 327–328.

74 Report of the conference held in Bergen-op-Zoom: Gachard, *Les États Généraux*, 778–780.

75 Oldenbarnevelt to Willem-Lodewijk of Nassau, 19 July 1600: Sikko P. Haak (ed.), *Johan van Oldenbarnevelt: bescheiden betreffende zijn staatkundig beleid en zijn familie, eerste deel 1570–1601* (Rijksgeschiedkundige publicatiën 80; The Hague, 1934), 562–563.

Bassigny, Codt and Bentinck could do nothing more than to ask the United Provinces to forget their past quarrels with the Habsburgs according with the projected 'eternal silence', but no breakthrough was made.[76]

In the end, the talks in Bergen-op-Zoom ended the peace attempts in both of the States General of the formerly Seventeen Provinces.[77] A last proposal to resume contacts was rejected by Albert: he declared that the United Provinces knew very well what their obligations were, and that a new letter would only increase their self-complacency.[78] For some loyal observers, the peace talks 'ne semble avoir apportée autre effect, hors qu'elle servira de justification a tout le monde de la bonne volonté de noz princes et des Etatz généraux, leurs subjects, au bien de la paix'. The only positive aspect of the failure was that they now could start thinking about themselves.[79] Hence, the Brussels deputies resumed their gatherings over new tax grants after a break of one and a halve month, intended to have some feedback from their respective provincial Estates. With their failure to achieve some success in the peace talks of Bergen-op-Zoom and in the renewed theatre of war, the States General in Brussels depended on the money and troops of the Habsburg dynasty. The assembly tried to obtain some compensations in return for the acceptation of new taxes, but internal discord and external pressure rendered these attempts rather futile. The Archdukes received the money they originally demanded, without giving any serious compensation.[80] So the long awaited States General on peace and war turned out to be an anti-climax on both a political and diplomatic level. The assembly in Brussels had not convinced its counterpart in The Hague and the peace talks were aborted prematurely. Moreover, the subsidies to the Archdukes had made the necessity of new States General redundant. In the Habsburg realm, they would not be organised again until 1632.

---

76 Report of the conference held in Bergen-op-Zoom: Gachard, *Les États Généraux*, 779–780.

77 The in Nieuwpoort captured military commander Mendoza would still be used to mediate, but these talks were managed by the Habsburg dynasty themselves and not by the States General. See De Schepper, 'De Nederlanden, 1560–1604', 31 and Chapter 2 in this volume.

78 Report of the States General of 1600: Gachard, *Les États Généraux*, 149–150, 168–170; 'Deuxième relation, rédigée par Nicolas Du Bois': Ibid., 253–255.

79 The deputies of Tournaisis to the Estates of Tournaisis, 28 July 1600: Gachard, *Les États Généraux*, 331–334.

80 Koenigsberger, *Monarchies*, 319–320; Report of the States General of 1600: Gachard, *Les États Généraux*, 149–150, 161–168, 178–185.

A Prelude to 1609

To conclude, then, the peace talks in the context of the Act of Cession in fact contributed to the growing divergence between the Habsburg Netherlands and the Dutch Republic. In the end, it were precisely the States General held in Brussels in 1598 and 1600 which served as a catalyst for this increasing separation in political culture. With these double States General, the loyal provinces eventually linked themselves even more closely to the Habsburg dynasty and acted in accord with the policy set out by the Archdukes and the Spanish-Habsburg King. They claimed that they were the real defenders of order and stability, because at least they still had sovereigns, which were even ostensibly prepared to revive the practice of gathering the States General. For their part, the United Provinces asserted that they were opposing 'Spanish tyrants' who had nothing but contempt for provincial representation and privileges, as the assemblies in Brussels in 1598 and 1600 had demonstrated once more. They considered themselves the last line of defence against the Habsburg centralising government, fighting for the survival of old privileges, the practices of shared power and freedom. This renewed conviction resulted in new military campaigns in order to liberate the loyal Low Countries. So by 1600, both negotiating parties could claim that they were the true supporters of the traditional 'good' form of government. Similar parliamentary institutions, born out of the same tradition of a *dominium politicum et regale*, now embodied different political theories.[81]

Hence, the same clash of political cultures returned during the negotiations leading to the Twelve Years Truce some nine years later.[82] The demands made by the Republic in 1607–1609 on sovereignty and republicanism and the subsequent objections phrased by the Habsburg party were not so different from those in 1600: only had the above discussed peace process clarified once again the differences in state building, allowing the positions taken in 1607–1609 to be more explicit. By then, the discussions on sovereignty also extended to the religious realm, which stands in contrast to the peace talks on the Act of Cession, where religious issues were only very briefly addressed in January 1598.[83] However, through the Act of Cession, it became clear that even

81 See also M. Van Gelderen, 'Contested Kingship. Conceptions of Monarchy and Civil Power in Spanish and Dutch Political Thought, 1555–1598', in José Martínez Millán (ed.), *Felipe II (1527–1598). Europa y la Monarquía Católica* (Madrid, 1998), 365–377.

82 Groenveld, *jongelingsjaren*, 15–20, 59–60.

83 Vincent van Zuilen has also noted this fact for the ensuing period 1600–1604. See Vincent Van Zuilen, 'Bronnen van identiteit. Het algemeen Nederlands samenhorigheidsgevoel in

reciprocal talks between the States General in The Hague and in Brussels forced no breakthrough in the peace process, despite the longstanding platitude that such negotiations would be able to finally end the conflict. The brief conference in Bergen-op-Zoom in 1600 made this painfully clear. From this point of view, the 1598 and 1600 States Generals and the ensuing peace talks were both a demonstration and a reinforcement of the different political theories which accounted for the problems of the Antwerp Truce in 1609 and which would be only solved by the Treaty of Munster in 1648. Nevertheless, until that time the myth survived that as soon as the States General of the Republic and those of the loyal provinces would negotiate without delegates of the Habsburg dynasty, a peace and a reunification of the Low Countries would take place.

---

enkele pamfletten over de Nederlandse Opstand', José De Kruif et al. (eds.), *Het lange leven van het pamflet. Boekhistorische, iconografische, literaire en politieke aspecten van pamfletten 1600–1900* (Hilversum, 2006), 79.

CHAPTER 4

The Anglo-Spanish Peace Treaty of 1604

A Rehearsal for Belgian Diplomats?

Alain Wijffels

During the decade which preceded the Twelve Years Truce, the statesmen of the Southern Netherlands who were in office under the Archdukes' regime had had several opportunities to sharpen their diplomatic skills. The conference leading to the Treaty of Vervins,[1] the unsuccessful negotiations of 1600 at Boulogne,[2] the 1604 Somerset House Conference[3] and its sequels, the negotiations towards a provisional truce – to mention but a few major international meetings – had involved directly or indirectly the major actors of Western European international relations at a time when the apparently accelerated

1 'Traité de la Paix entre Henri IV. Roi de France Philippe II. Roi d'Espagne et Charles-Emanuel Duc de Savoie. Fait à Vervin le 2. Mai 1598', in *Recueil des traitez de la paix, de trêve, de neutralité, de suspension d'armes, de confédération, d'alliance, de commerce, de garantie, et d'autres actes publics, comme contracts de mariage, testaments, manifestes, declarations de guerre, etc.* [...], (A Amsterdam, Chez Henry et la veuve de T. Boom, A La Haye, Chez Adrian Moetjens, Henry van Bulderen, 1700), vol. 2, 616–623. Jean-François Labourdette, Jean-Pierre Poussou, Marie-Catherine Vignal (eds.), *Le Traité de Vervins* (Paris, 2000), esp. (on Spanish-English relations), the contributions by Philippe Loupès, 'L'Irlande celtique, enjeu de l'affrontement Hispano-Anglais à la fin du XVIe siècle', 233–236 and Jean-Pierre Poussou, 'La politique extérieure d'Elisabeth Ière et la paix de Vervins', 247–263, and also (on the Belgian ambassadors) Jean Houssiau, 'Les ambassadeurs des Pays-Bas à Vervins', 267–283; C. Vidal et F. Pilleboue (eds.), *La paix de Vervins 1598* (Société archéologique et historique de Vervins et de la Thiérache – Fédération des Société d'Histoire et d'archéologie de l'Aisne, s.l. 1998). The involvement of diplomats from the Southern Netherlands in the negociations is documented in *Mémoire historique concernant la négociation de la paix traitée à Vervins l'an 1598 entrre Henry IV, roi de France et de Navarre, par Messieurs de Bellièvre et de Sillery; Philippes II, roy d'Espagne, par les sieurs Richardot, Taxis et Verreyken; et Charles Emmanuel, duc de Savoye, par le sieur marquis de Lullin* [...] (Paris, Chez Charles de Sercy, 1667, 2 vols.).

2 E.-Th. Hamy, 'Conférence pour la paix entre l'Angleterre et l'Espagne, tenue à Boulogne en 1600. Étude historique suivie d'un choix de lettres relatives à cet événement', *Bulletin de la Société académique de Boulogne sur-Mer*, 8 (1907) 434–460 [I consulted an offprint, 27 pp.].

3 In 2004, an exhibition and a conference in London commemorated the Peace Treaty of 1604: *1604: An exhibition of books from the Foyle special collections library*, and *Talking Peace 1604: The Somerset House Conference Paintings* (Gilbert Collection 20th May 2004–20th July 2004: see King's College, London, News archive 2004, on the website www.kcl.ac.uk/newsevents/news/news-archive/2004/may/Talking-Peace-Somerset-House-1604.aspx, and

 | DOI 10.1163/9789004274921_006

decline of Spain in the general balance of power forced those actors to reconsider their foreign policy strategies. For the Southern Netherlands – for which I shall use the somewhat anachronistic designation 'Belgium' –, the political position granted by Madrid to the Archdukes had ambivalent effects. On the one hand, it gave the Spanish Crown a degree of greater diplomatic flexibility regarding the Dutch Question in so far as the Belgian sovereigns were given some autonomy in their international affairs. On the other hand, the Belgian government's dependence on Madrid also complicated Western European diplomacy, because at the end of the day, Belgian autonomy could not be exercised so as to be incompatible with what Spain saw as its essential interests – both geo-political and ideological – on European and extra-European issues.

FIGURE 4.1 *The Somerset House Conference, 19 August 1604* (© NATIONAL MARITIME MUSEUM, GREENWICH, LONDON)

web.archive.org/web/20041210230602/www.gilbert-collection.org.uk/previous_exhibitions/1604/index.html (both retrieved on 25 Feb. 2014). For a short and general publication by one of the participants: Pauline Croft, 'England and the Peace with Spain, 1604', *History Review* (2004) 18–23; and by the same author: *King James* (Basingstoke/New York, 2003), in particular Chapter 2.

A brief glance at the famous painting of the Somerset House Conference[4] which led to the Anglo-Spanish Peace Treaty of London in 1604 reminds us that Belgian diplomacy took a significant place at the negotiation table (Figure 4.1).

To the right (from the viewer's perspective), one recognises the English delegates (going up the order of precedence, i.e. starting from the sitter closest to the viewer to the furthest one, near the window – an order which does not reflect the part taken by the respective delegates during the negotiations) –: the Secretary of State Robert Cecil,[5] Henry Howard (Earl of Northampton),[6] Charles Blount (Earl of Devonshire),[7] Charles Howard

4 London, National Portrait Gallery, NPG 665, http://www.npg.org.uk/collections. See also the copy at the National Maritime Museum, Greenwich, Repro ID BHC2787, http://collections.rmg.co.uk/collections/objects/14260.html (retrieved on 25 Feb. 2014). The picture is to some extent a fictional representation, yet a rare contemporary artistic construction of a major peace conference.

5 *Oxford Dictionary of National Biography*, vol. 10, s.v. 'Cecil, Robert, first earl of Salisbury (1563–1612)', 746–759. Cecil had been acquainted with diplomacy and ambassadors from his childhood onwards at his father's (Lord Burghley) home. In 1588, he accompanied an English embassy in the Low Countries, where he was introduced to the Duke of Parma. From 1593 onwards, he was much involved in foreign affairs as a Privy Councilor, and from 1596 onwards, as Secretary of State, in all major diplomatic negotiations and in shaping England's foreign policy. In the conflict which opposed him to Essex, he represented the supporters of a peace policy in England's interest. During the Anglo-Spanish peace negotiations, he was the most active member of the English delegation (Ibid., 751). See also Pauline Croft, 'Brussels and London: the Archdukes, Robert Cecil and James I', in Werner Thomas and Luc Duerloo (eds.), *Albert and Isabella 1598–1621. Essays* (Brussels/Leuven/Turnhout, 1999), 79–86.

6 *Oxford Dictionary of National Biography*, vol. 28, s.v. 'Howard, Henry, earl of Northampton (1540–1614)', 366–374. Although from a family linked to Roman Catholicism and several times suspected of disloyalty during the 1580s, when he was repeatedly imprisoned and occasionally an informant of the Spanish ambassador, Howard rose in the Elizabethan court under the patronage of Essex, an association which allowed him to gain the lasting confidence of James VI already during the late 1590s. Critical of Essex's policies, he became closer to Cecil's faction from 1598 onwards. In 1603, he was appointed a Privy Councilor. During the Anglo-Spanish peace negotiations, he intervened on behalf of the English merchants' claims to trade in the Indies. As the Lord Warden of the Cinque Ports, he successfully welcomed the Constable of Castille on his arrival in England. He was educated at Cambridge, where he is said to have been the only nobleman of the Tudor age who ever held a teaching position, and his learning was widely recognised.

7 *Oxford Dictionary of National Biography*, vol. 6, s.v. 'Blount, Charles, eighth Baron Mountjoy and earl of Devonshire' (1563–1606)', 290–294. Blount made a name as a military commander, especially in Ireland during the years 1600–1602, after crushing the Spanish invasion in Kilsale and the Tyrone insurrection. In the 1580s, he served in military campaigns in the Low Countries; he also fought at the time of the Armada expedition and participated to Essex's

(First Earl of Nottingham),[8] and Thomas Sackville (First Earl of Dorset);[9] on the left, six members of the Spanish-Belgian (or, as it was sometimes referred to: Spanish-Burgundian) delegation (starting from the closest to the window, and thus with the most prominent sitter): Juan de Velasco, Constable of Castille, Juan de Tassis (Count of Villa Mediana), Alessandro Rovida (a jurist, Milanese senator),[10] Charles de Ligne (Count of Arenberg),[11] Jean Richardot

---

expedition to the Azores in 1597. His military abilities earned him the Governorship of Portsmouth in 1594. His association with Essex in the 1590s brought him in contact with James VI, who, upon his accession in England in 1603, made him a Privy Councilor.

8 *Oxford Dictionary of National Biography*, vol. 28, s.v. 'Howard, Charles, second Baron Howard of Effingham and first earl of Nottingham (1536–1624)', 318–322: Lord Admiral of England since 1585, Howard had successfully been in charge of the defence and counter-attack against the Armada and the war against Spain, notably as supreme naval commander during the 1596 Cadiz expedition. In his earlier years, he had lived in France and been entrusted with a few diplomatic missions; in 1559, he had accompanied his father at the negotiations of the Treaty of Câteau-Cambrésis. In 1604, he led the English embassy to Spain in order to obtain the formal ratification of the Anglo-Spanish Peace Treaty.

9 *Oxford Dictionary of National Biography*, vol. 48, s.v. 'Sackville, Thomas, first Baron Buckhurst and first earl of Dorset (c. 1536–1608)', 542–548. Appointed Lord Treasurer by James I, he was both a financial expert and a Privy Councilor with diplomatic experience, especially with regard to the Low Countries (where he had spent several months in 1587 in order to assess the English involvement; later, he was regularly directly involved in Anglo-Dutch negotiations, e.g. with Oldebarnevelt in 1598); he had also been on missions in Italy and France.

10 Credited with a 'Oratio habita per senatorem Rovidium Londini die XXXa. Maii respondens Comiti de Hortanton in prima conferentia Tractatus Pacis', London, Robinson Trust, Phillips Collection, Ms. 25553, ff. 373–7 ('Hortanton' stands presumably for Northampton), cf. Paul Oskar Kristeller, *Iter italicum: A Finding list of the uncatalogued or incompletely catalogued humanistic Mss.*, vol. IV, *Alia itinera*, II, *Great-Britain to Spain* (Leyden, 1989), 236, possibly also printed in Milan in 1604, cf. Argelati, Philippus, *Bibliotheca scriptorum Mediolanensium, seu acta, et elogia virorum omnigena eruditione illustrium, qui in metropoli insubriae, oppidisque circumjacentibus orti sunt* [...] (Mediolani In Aedibus Palatinis, 1745; reprint Farnborough, 1966, vol. 2, col. 1246–7: Mediolani, denuoque Novarriae, apud Hieronymum Sesallum, 1604). See also: *Discorso circa il punto della religione cattolica in Inghilterra notato mentre fu in quel regno a trattar le paci tra Spagna e Inhilterra*, Milan, Biblioteca Pinacoteca Accademia Ambrosiana, Ms. S 18 inf. (which I have not been able to see). Ken MacMillan, *Sovereignty and Possession in the English New World: The Legal Foundations of Empire, 1576–1640* (Cambridge, 2006), 182, mentions Rovida's interventions on behalf of Iberian interests in the Indies (referring to the 'Diary of the conferences and proceedings in the Treaty of London 1604', London, BL Sloane Ms 1851 and Add. Mss. 14033; and Simancas Estado Ingliterra, 840–842).

11 L.-P. Gachard, s.v. 'Arenberg (Charles, comte d')', *Biographie Nationale de Belgique* (Brussels, 1866), vol. 1, col. 380–8; Hugo de Schepper (with the assistance of Willem Schrickx), s.v.

(President of the State Council),[12] and Louis Vereycken (*audiencier* in Brussels).[13] Three of the six Spanish-Belgian delegates came thus from the Archdukes' dominions. They were involved in several diplomatic ventures during those years and the last two also appear in the final treaty of the truce. Arenberg had been entrusted from a comparatively young age onwards (mainly due to his family connections) with some mainly ceremonial embassies, for example after the Treaty of Vervins to France and to England on the occasion of James I's coronation. Richardot was an old hand with extensive experience of difficult negotiations: for example with Flemish and Brabant cities in the early 1580s on behalf of Farnese, with England in 1587, or at Vervins in 1597–1598. Verreycken was also present at Vervins and in 1600 he had been sent to England. All three Belgian delegates had therefore acquired previous experience in major negotiations involving the English, and all three had already visited England before 1604. The biographies of Arenberg and Richardot also suggest that, at an earlier stage of their life or career, they may have entertained doubts as to where their interests and loyalties lay in the turmoil of civil and religious unrest which afflicted the Habsburg Netherlands from the late 1560s onwards. Both, however, had eventually preferred to link their fate to the royal authority, Spanish rule, and thus the Catholic side.

The strong presence of the Archdukes' representatives in London is not surprising. Although the Treaty of London is often referred to as an Anglo-Spanish peace treaty, it was formally concluded between King James of England and Scotland, King Philip of Spain, and the Archdukes. A substantial part of the Treaty deals specifically with provisions relating to the rights and duties of the parties to the convention in the Southern Netherlands. Indeed, the situation in the Low Countries appears in the 1604 Treaty as one of the most important issues on which various explicit agreements had been reached.[14]

'Arenberg, prins en graaf Karel van', *Nationaal biografisch woordenboek* (Brussels, 1990), vol. 13, col. 47–53.

12 Victor Brants, s.v. 'Richardot (Jean Grusset, dit)', *Biographie Nationale de Belgique* (Brussels, 1907), vol. 19, col. 274–80.

13 Em. Dony, s.v. 'Verreycken (Louis)', *Biographie Nationale de Belgique* (Brussels, 1938), vol. 26, col. 682–5.

14 Joseph Cuvelier, 'Les préliminaires du traité de Londres (29 août 1604)', *Revue belge de philologie et d'histoire*, 2 (1923) 279–304 and 485–508, was written shortly after the author had published (with Henri Lonchay and Joseph Lefèvre) the first volume of correspondence of the Spanish Court relating to the Low Countries, on which the article draws to supplement previously published materials and studies. Cuvelier's contribution centres on the policy of the Archdukes and the role of their senior delegate at the London conference, Richardot. His main thesis, which has to be placed in the Belgian historiographic

The purpose of the present paper is to offer a brief analysis of the Treaty of London in the context of early-modern treaty-making around 1600. Randall Lesaffer has already pointed out, building on the work of earlier historians of international relations and international law, that by the latter half of the 16th century, peace treaties tended to be drafted according to a set proto-typology of issues.[15] In a recent paper, he illustrated that tentative typology, which reflected the diplomatic practice as it had gradually developed at the time, by comparing the Treaty of Vervins (1598) and the 1604 Treaty of London.[16] In the following pages, that general typology will be taken as a starting point for further analysis, and a preliminary comparison of the latter treaty with the Twelve Years Truce.[17]

---

context of the 1920s, was that the Archdukes strove towards a more independent foreign policy from Spain, less inspired by religious motives, but more strongly concerned with their country's economic and commercial interests (cf. 288, 507).

15 Treaty-making around 1600 (and the Twelve Years' Truce in particular) also inspired a renewal of doctrinal works, such as the treatise by the Louvain law professor Petrus Gudelinus *De jure pacis commentarius* (*ed.pr.* 1620), see Randall Lesaffer, 'An Early Treatise on Peace Treaties: Petrus Gudelinus between Roman Law and Modern Practice', *The Journal of Legal History*, 23 (2002) 223–252.

16 Randall Lesaffer, 'Gentili's *ius post bellum* and Early Modern Peace Treaties', in Benedict Kingsbury and Benjamin Straumann (eds.), *The Roman Foundations of the Law of Nations: Alberico Gentili and the Justice of Empire* (Oxford, 2010), 210–240.

17 Quotations of the Treaty of London in this paper's main text are made in the present contribution from a quasi-contemporary unofficial English translation: *Articles of the Peace, Entercourse, and Commerce, London 1605*, (original edition: Imprinted at London, Robert Barker, Printer to the Kings most Excellent Maiestie, 1605; reprint: Amsterdam/ New York, 1971 [The English Experience 378]). The original version to be used for any technical reference and citation would of course be the authentic original version in Latin. One will also be aware of contemporary pamphlets (in different imprints) offering a Dutch translation of the Treaty: e.g. *De Artijckelen van den Peys, ghemaeckt tusschen den zeer doorluchtighen Coninck van Engelant, Schotlant etc. ter eender zijde: Ende den alder doorluchtichsten Coninck van Spangien, ende den Aertshertoge ter ander: Gesonden uut Engelant den 25. Augusti Stylo Angliae, 1604. Ghetranslateert uuten Engelsche, in onse Nederlantsche sprake* (s.l.n.d.); *De Artijckelen van den peys, gemaeckt tusschen den seer doorluchtighen Coninck van Enghelant, Schotlant, etc. ter eender zijde. Ende den alder doorluchtichsten Coninck vanSpaengien, ende den Ertz-hertoghe ter ander: Gesonden uyt Engelant den vijfentwintichsten Aug. Ouden stijl xvi^e vier* (s.l.n.d., Ghetranslateert uyt het Enghels in onser Nederlandtsche tale); *Articulen van het Contract ende Accoort ghemaeckt tusschen Jacobus den eersten van dien Name, Coninck van Enghelandt ter eenre, ende Philips den derden van dien Name, Coninck van Spaengnien: midtsgaders de Eerts-hertoghen Albertus ende Isabella Clara Eugenia. Gemaect ende geconcludeert den xviii^en. der Maent Augusti duysent ses-hondert en viere, near den ouden stijl. Uut het Enghels in het*

A general caveat to remember when reading such treaties is that, particularly when they bridge the religious divide between Catholic and Protestant rulers, they do not necessarily express long-term political aims.[18] Specific terms upon which the parties reached an agreement or settlement only partly reflect their general geo-political strategies.[19] This was particularly true as regards the calculations with regard to the Low Countries. Strategically, it remained essential for England's security that the Northern Netherlands would not fall back under Spanish rule, however diminished Spanish power may have appeared as compared to the first years of Elizabeth's reign.[20] And already, English diplomacy could perceive the threat of the United Provinces becoming too dependent on France. For France, the diminishing threat of Spanish power meant that French diplomacy could start looking more seriously beyond a policy aimed at avoiding the country's 16th-century Habsburg encirclement, but

---

Neder-duytsch overgeset (s.d., Nae de Copie. Ghedruckt tot London, Robert Barker. Met Privelegie). For a French version: *Articles du traicté faict en Angleterre entre les Rois de France et d'Espagne, et les Archiducs de Flandres, pour la restauration du commerce* (A Lyon, Guichard Iullieron, 1604); for a Spanish version, see the reference given by Porfirio Sanz Camañes, 'España ante las paces del Norte a comienzos del siglo XVII. Del Tratado de Londres a la Tregua de Amberes', *Cuadernos de historia de España*, 81 (2007), note 62 [I have consulted the journal's electronic version]. An easily accessible Latin version can be found in Rymer, cf. Thomas Rymer, *Foedera, conventiones, literae, Et cujuscunque generis acta publica, inter reges Angliae, Et alios quosvis imperatores, reges, pontifices, principes, vel communitates, ab Ineunte saeculo duodecimo, viz. ab Anno 1101. Ad nostra usque tempora, habita aut tractata* [...] (Hagae Comitatus Apud Joannem Neaulme, 1742; reprint Farnborough, 1967), see vol. 7, Pars 2, 114–115 (*De Communicando et Tractando cum Ambassiatoribus Hispaniae et Burgundiae*), and pp. 117–121 (*Confirmatio Tractatus Hispaniae et Burgundiae*). See also: *Articuli pacis et confederationis perpetuo duraturae inter serenissimos regem Hispaniarum etc. et archiduces Austriae etc. ex una. Et serenissimum regem Angliae etc. ex altera partibus, eorumque heredes et successores, Anno Domini 1604* (Bruxellae, Ex Officina Rutgeri Velpii, Typog. Iur. anno Domini 1604).

18 Albert J. Loomie, *Toleration and Diplomacy. The Religious Issue in Anglo-Spanish Relations 1603–1605* (Transactions of the American Philosophical Society, New Series, vol. 53, Pt. 6; Philadelphia, 1963); idem, 'Spanish Secret Diplomacy at the Court of James I', in Malcolm R. Thorp and Arthur J. Slavin (eds.), *Politics, Religion and Diplomacy in Early Modern Europe, Essays in Honor of De Lamar Jensen* (Sixteenth Century Essays and Studies 27; Kirksville, Missouri, 1994), 231–244.

19 Paul E.J. Hammer, *Elizabeth's Wars. War, Government and Society in Tudor England, 1544–1604*, (Basingstoke/ New York, 2003), 229–235.

20 The 'war party' in England opposed a peace which would not secure both English and Dutch interests, cf. Andrew Thrush, 'The Parliamentary Opposition to Peace with Spain in 1604: A Speech of Sir Edward Hoby', *Parliamentary History*, 23 (2004) 301–315.

French might was not such that it could envisage bringing the Northern Netherlands in its political ambit merely on its own political or military strength. The United Provinces realised that their continuing independence would still require the support of, preferably, both England and France, while their own strength depended primarily on their capacity to pursue the development of their maritime trade, whether the country was at war or not. A reunification of the Burgundian Netherlands – North and South – was not necessarily, in the context of the other powers' rivalries, the most attractive prospect for securing the territorial security of its Protestant heartlands. Spain faced the spiralling costs of the Flemish wars while its claims in its overseas empire were increasingly being challenged by English and Dutch trade.[21] At best, it could hope to retain a dynastic foothold in the Low Countries which could be used in the somewhat unlikely event of a collapse of the Protestant regime in Holland. The personal union between England and Scotland and Spain's failure to acquire a decisive leverage in Ireland effectively prevented it to counter the English privateers' threat to its supplies from the Indies and the New World.[22] All this left relatively little leeway for any Belgian diplomacy, especially since its commercial and financial position remained substantially reduced by Antwerp's loss of direct maritime trade.[23]

Against that general background, the explicit 1604 settlement (i.e. not taking into account the so-called 'secret' articles)[24] only appears to have cleared

21 K.R. Andrews, 'Caribbean Rivalry and the Anglo-Spanish Peace of 1604', *History, The Journal of The Historical Association*, 59 (1974) 1–17; idem, 'English Voyages to the Caribbean, 1596 to 1604: An Annotated List', *The William and Mary Quarterly*, 31 (174) 234–254. On the applicability of the Peace outside Europe: G. Mattingly, 'No Peace Beyond What Line?', *Transactions of the Royal Historical Society*, Fifth Series, 13 (1963) 145–162 at 159. On the Dutch involvement in the East Indies, see in this volume Chapter 6 by Peter Borschberg, who kindly let me read an earlier draft.

22 For the Spanish perspective and its long-term geo-political strategy, Paul C. Allen, *Philip III and the Pax Hispanica, 1598–1621. The Failure of the Grand Strategy* (New Haven/London, 2000), which should of course be read as a sequel in its own right to Geoffrey Parker, *The Grand Strategy of Philip II* (New Haven/London, 1998); also: Bernardo J. García García, *La Pax Hispanica. politica exterior del duque de Lerma* (Louvain, 1996), esp. on the peace with England 45–47, and on tentative considerations of a foreign policy based on a concept of 'balance of powers', *viz.* between the 'Catholic monarchy' and France, 89–96.

23 Cuvelier, 'Préliminaires', *passim*, esp. 283, 286, 297–298, 507 on the perceived threat of Spanish hegemony.

24 On the 'secret articles', see in this volume Chapter 5 by Werner Thomas, who also discusses the incidents in Spain when an English delegation was sent in order to attend the ratification of the Treaty by the Spanish king. They are included at the end of the English publication of the 1604 Peace Treaty (*o.c.*): *Three Articles concerning a*

comparatively minor and short-term issues. Even so, its provisions were at least partly phrased in general legal terms which belonged to an established tradition of drafting a general peace settlement.

Not too much is to be read into the expressions 'amity, league and peace' (*amicitia, confoederatio, pax*) for styling the effects of the Treaty, in spite of the ambiguities of the phrase league/*confoederatio*, especially when associated with several discriminatory terms against the United Provinces restricting England's trade and dealings with those provinces. However, those discriminatory terms should be seen against the background of Spain's continuing state of war against the Dutch: for Spain, one of the main purposes of the peace with England consisted in ensuring the latter's relative neutrality in the conflict.

More relevant for an analysis of the Treaty's text is the way the signatories are styled. It is noteworthy that the signatories bind not only themselves as rulers and sovereigns, but also their heirs and successors, and their realms and subjects, while their 'vassals' are still mentioned as a separate category. The formula already reflected an advanced stage of state-formation, allowing the sovereigns to bind directly their territory and population as a whole. The formula should be seen in connection with the system of sanctions adopted throughout the Treaty. Most provisions impose an obligation on some or all the signatories. As sovereigns, however, they cannot be subjected to any form of penalty in case they would breach a term of the treaty. On the other hand, many of the provisions state that in case of a breach of the peace terms by a subject, the sovereign commits himself to punish the author of the infringement. The most general provision in that respect appears to be Article 27:

> Item, it is accorded, that if during this Peace and Amitie, any thing happens to be attempted, committed or done, against the force and effect thereof, by land, sea, or fresh waters, either by any of the said Princes, their Heires and Successors, their Vassals, Subiects, or Allies comprehended in this League, or of any the Heires or Successours of those Allies, their Subiects, or Vassals, yet notwithstanding this Peace and Amitie shal remaine in his strength and virtue, and the attempters, and such as doe offend therein onely, and no other, shall bee punished for their attempts.

---

moderation to be had in the proceedings of the Inquisition, toward the Kings Maiesties Subiects, in Spaine. The 1609 Truce explicitly referred to these secret articles (Art. 7). Thomas also recalls that after the Anglo-Spanish war of 1624–1630, the application of the secret articles was re-established.

The text is perhaps in so far surprising because, taken literally, it would also apply to a sovereign (to whom the phrase 'Prince' refers). That, however, would not make any sense, since the sovereign was by definition not subjected to any human jurisdiction – or, as the contemporary international lawyer Alberico Gentili (1552–1608), who taught at Oxford, put it: in the law of nations, the prince is the judge. The clause should therefore be construed as a commitment by the princes to secure punishment of any subject who would act in breach of the treaty. That is also the mechanism applied in several special provisions of the treaty: an infringement or injury caused by a subject will be punished, although how that punishment has to be meted out – in terms of procedural or substantive law – is left to the sovereigns to decide and to work out in their domestic order. For at least one issue one has an example of how that mechanism was implemented.[25] Already at the time when the peace negotiations were afoot, English investors were scheming to continue their lucrative privateering business under Dutch commissions. Shortly after the Peace Treaty, one such case was brought, perhaps as a test-case, before the High Court of Admiralty, and it offered the Spanish ambassador an opportunity to exert pressure on the English government. The Spaniards could argue that if Iberian shipping continued to be attacked by English privateers acting under Dutch commissions, an essential reason for their acceptance to the peace settlement was frustrated. Accordingly, the King issued a proclamation forbidding henceforth all English mariners to seek employment on foreign ships.[26] Arguably, the prohibition to English subjects of entering foreign service against Spain, even though it would have been admissible by the prevailing standards of the law of nations, was already implicitly entailed in the general clause forbidding any subjects of one of the signatories to cause harm to the subjects of one of the other signatories, in particular Article 6:

> Item, it is agreed and accorded, that the said most renowned Kings, and Archdukes, shall take care, that their Subiects shall from henceforth abstaine from all force, and wrong doing, and that they likewise shall revoke all Commissions, and Letters of Reprisall, and Mar[k], or otherwise conteining Licence to take Prizes, of what condition, or kinde soever

---

25 The case is set out in: A. Wijffels, *Alberico Gentili and Thomas Crompton. An Encounter between an Academic Jurist and a Forensic Practitioner* (Studia Forensia Historica 1; Leyden, 1992).

26 'A Proclamation for revocation of Mariners from forreine Services (1 March 1605)', in James F. Larkin and Paul L. Hughes (eds.), *Stuart Royal Proclamations*, vol. 1, *Royal Proclamations of King James I 1603–1625* (Oxford, 1973), No. 50, 108–111.

> they are, being to the preiudice of the one, or other of the said Princes, or of their Subiects, whether the same have beene given, or graunted by them unto Subiects, or Inhabitants, or unto Strangers, and shall declare the same to bee void, and of no force, as by this Treatie of Peace they are declared so to be; And whosoever shall do any thing to the contrary, he shall be punished not only criminally according to the merit of his offence, but shall also be compelled to make restitution, and satisfaction for the losses to the parties damnified, requiring the same.

Such a provision would seem to reinforce the general call to the signatories' subjects to 'favour' each other, 'and to use one another with all kind and friendly offices' (Article 1). However, a strict construction of the clause and the Treaty may have left some doubt as to whether English subjects would be prohibited to enter the legitimate service of a foreign power. The King's proclamation is an indication that, in law, the government saw it as a safer course to make sure that a special prohibition stating criminal penalties would clarify the issue. It was also a clear message to the Spanish authorities, during the early months of the peace, that the political will of the English government was to maintain its undertakings on the essentials of the settlement that had been reached.

The sanction system of the Treaty can thus be summarised as follows: the sovereigns' own infringements (or failure to comply with an obligation under the Treaty) could not be punished in any way. Breaches of the Treaty by subjects were to be punished by their own sovereigns (i.e. when the subjects were within their own sovereign's jurisdiction); the punishment could be, depending on the nature of the infringement, a criminal penalty,[27] a confiscation[28] or a civil sanction (restitution, damages, or the application of a higher tax rate).[29] In some cases, reprisals or prizes could be exacted.[30] One clause of the Treaty relating to the application of pre-war treaties referred future disputes to a form of arbitration (Article 20).[31]

---

27 See Arts. 6, 10, 11, 15, 18, 22, 27.

28 Arts. 11, 14, 22.

29 Arts. 2 (restitution, damages), 6 (restitution,), 13 (rate).

30 Art. 16.

31 'But as concerning the ancient Treatises of entercourse and Commerce, whereof divers are extant, betwixt the Kingdomes of England, Scotland, and Ireland, and the Dominions of the Dukes of Burgundie, and Princes of the Low Countreyes, which notwithstanding during the late troubles have beene intermitted, and peradventure in some parts impaired; it is agreed by way of provision, That they shall retaine and have their auncient force and authoritie, and that they shall bee used on both parts, as they were before the Warres: And if it happen that either by both partes or any one part any breach thereof be alleadged,

The individual provisions of the Treaty fall into different categories. First, the Treaty contains a number of general provisions which, sometimes apart from a few specifications, would be expected in any peace treaty. A second category is more closely linked to the direct concerns of the negotiators, *viz.* the restoration of trade between the signatories' territories, which included inevitably several arrangements regarding maritime trade.[32] Thirdly, some of the general, but especially some of the trade provisions are also expressed in a series of articles which deal specifically with Belgium, i.e. the Archdukes' dominions. Within each category, specific articles or part of articles also deal in more detail with special concerns, whether from the English or the Spanish perspective, regarding the United Provinces. These different categories only appear partly in the sequence of articles followed in the Treaty.

Within the general category, some clauses aim at resolving difficulties arising from the past state of war (and in the case of the Anglo-Spanish conflict, it should be remembered that the hostilities had dragged on for some twenty years), others seek to restore the peaceful post-bellum relations.

Among its most general provisions, the Treaty includes an amnesty clause regarding past injuries and damage (Article 2),[33] which considers retrospectively

---

or that the Subiects shall complaine that the Conventions are not observed, or that more grievous burdens then were accustomed are imposed on them, there shall bee Deputies appointed on either part which may meete, and calling unto them (if neede be) Merchants experienced in such matters, may friendly Treate, and equally renew, and restore such things, as shal bee founde either to have slipped out of course, or to have beene changed by the iniurie of time, or by corrupt custome and use'.

32 The importance of Iberian trade for a substantial segment of English merchants had been an important factor in favour of restoring peace: Pauline Croft, 'English Commerce with Spain and the Armada War, 1558–1603', in M.J. Rodriguez-Salgado and Simon Adams (eds.), *England, Spain and the Gran Armada 1585–1604. Essays from the Anglo-Spanish Conferences London and Madrid 1988* (Edinburgh, 1991), 236–263.

33 'And that from henceforth all Hostilitie, and enmitie shall cease, and all offences, iniuries or damages which either part (in time of the troubles) hath susteined by the other, shalbe taken away and forgotten, in such sort, as that hereafter neither partie against other, for, or upon occasion of any damages, offences, depredations or spoyles past, may pretend any matter, but that there shall be a perfect abolition of all and every of them untill this present day: and that all actions for the same shall be held and reputed to be extinguished, excepting onely such depredations as have beene committed since the xxiiij. of April 1603 (because of these an account is to be made:) And each partie shall hereafter abstaine from all depredations, offences, and spoiles as well by Sea and Land, and fresh waters, in whatsoever the Kingdomes, Dominions, Places, or Governments of the other: neither shal the aforesaid Princes consent, that any of the grievances before mentioned, be done by any of their Vassals, Inhabitants, or Subiects; and they shall also cause restitution to be made of

a much earlier date as its date of reference (*viz.* 24 April 1603), a clause excluding the *droit d'aubaine* (Article 23), the restoration of old grants and privileges (Article 24), a (qualified) forbearance of seizing each other's ships for war purposes (Article 26), the release of prisoners of war (arranging, however, for the payment of legitimate ransoms and costs of maintenance, Article 28), the resumption of civil actions (the period of limitations deemed to have been suspended during wartime, Article 29). The general clause with respect to breaches of the peace has already been mentioned (Article 27);[34] it is supplemented by a clause through which the signatories commit themselves to ensure that the Treaty will be ratified, published and observed (Article 34), and by two articles enumerating the signatories alleged *adhaerentes* and friends (Articles 32–3), which expresses the signatories' wish to see the effects of their peace acknowledged by a wider international community.[35]

---

all depredations and spoiles which hereafter shall be committed, and of the damages growing by meanes thereof'.

34 'Item, it is accorded, that if during this Peace and Amitie, any thing happen to be attempted, committed or done, against the force and effect thereof, by land, sea, or fresh waters, either by any of the said Princes their Heires and Successors, their Vassals, Subiects, or Allies comprehended in this League, or of any the Heires or Successours of those Allies their Subiects, or Vassals, yet notwithstanding this Peace and Amitie, shal remaine in his strength and vertue, and the attempters, and such as doe offend therein onely, and no other, shall bee punished for their attempts'.

35 Art. 32 lists on behalf of the King of England: 'Rodulphe Romane Emperour, with the Archdukes of Austrice, and the Electors of the Empire, together with the States, and Cities of the Empire, the Duke of Lorrain, the duke of Savoy, the dukes of Brunswicke, Lunenburg, Meckleburg, Wirtemberg, the Landgrave of Hesse, the Marquesse of Baden, the duke of Pomerane, the Prince of Anhalt, the Earle of East-freisland, the Cantons of Helvetia, and the Grisons, the Haunse-cities; the French King, the King of Poland, and Swethland, the King of Denmarke, the duke and state of Venice, the duke of Holst, the duke of Florence'. On behalf of the King of Spain and the Archdukes the following article mentions: 'Rodulphe Romane Emperour, and his Brethren, and other Princes, Archdukes of Austrice, Princes of the Empire, the Electors, Cities, and States subiect to the Empire, the French King, the King of Poland and Swethland, the King of Denmarke, the duke and State of Venice, the duke of Savoy, the duke of Bavire, the duke of Cleve, the duke of Holstein, the duke of Lorraine, the duke of Parma and Placentia, with his Brother, the Cardinall, the Bishop and Province of Liege, the duke of Florence, the duke of Mantua, and Regium, the duke of Urbine, the Confederats and Cantons of the Helvetians, and Grisons, the Cities of the Haunse, the Earles of East-friesland (without notwithstanding any preiudice of the right by the King of Spaine, and Archdukes pretended for their States) the duke and Common wealth of Genua, the Common wealth of Lukes, the Principall of the House of Columna, the Prince of Oria, the Principall of the house of Ursine, the duke of Serrmoneta,

Several articles deal more in detail with the forbearance of afflicting any harm to the subjects of the other signatories. In general terms, the principle is expressed in the same article as the amnesty clause (Article 2). It is supplemented by commitments that no harm will be caused either by the sovereigns or by their subjects: the sovereigns promise to inflict no harm to each other by military, diplomatic or political means, nor to assist each other's enemies (and the addition of the term 'rebels' makes it clear that England's assistance to the United Provinces is to be ended, Articles 3–4);[36] they also promise to end any existing treaties or undertakings which would be contrary to their present commitment (Article 5). Article 6, already quoted, extends their commitment to any action by their subjects.

The commitment to end previous undertakings suffers an exception in Article 7: the King of England is allowed, because of the arrangements made under his predecessor, to retain the cities and strongholds kept as securities, although he promises that he will enter negotiations with the United Provinces about the status of those places and will avoid any decision regarding those places which would offend the cosignatories to the present Treaty. In addition, the continuing presence of English troops in those places will not be used to assist or provide military equipment to the Spanish and Belgian sovereigns' enemies, the 'Hollanders' being here explicitly mentioned; conversely, the Spanish and Belgian sovereigns undertake not to take any action against the English garrisons (Article 8).

The second category of provisions tends to restore free trade between the signatories' countries according to the conditions which prevailed before

the Lord of Monacho, the Earle of Mirandula, the Marques of Massa, the Earle of Sala, the Earle of Colorno'.

36 'III. Item, that none of the forenamed Princes, their Heires, or Successors whosoever, by himselfe or by any others, shall doe, treat, or attempt any thing against the other, or against their Kingdomes, Lands or Dominions whatsoever in any place, on Land or Sea, or in the Ports, or fresh waters, by pretence of any cause, or upon any occasion; neither any of them shall give assistance or consent unto any Warre, Counsell, Attempt, or Treaties, had, made, or to be made in the preiudice of either, or against the other. IIII. Item, that neither of the former parties, shall themselves give, or shall consent to be given, by any of their Vassals, Subiects, or Inhabitants, aide favour, or counsell, directly or indirectly, on Land, Sea, or fresh waters: nor shall supply and minister, nor consent to be supplyed and ministred, by their said Vassals, Inhabitants and Subiects, unto the Enemies or Rebels of either part, of what nature or condition soever they be, (whether they shall invade the Countreys and Dominions of either of them, or withdraw themselves from their obedience and subiection) any Souldiers, provision of Victuals, Monies, Instruments of Warre, Munitions, or whatsoever other aide else to maintaine Warre'.

the war (a well-known formula which allowed negotiators and signatories to bypass the possibly controversial issues regarding the pre-war position). The free trade clause (Article 9) is strengthened by a clause guaranteeing free access to each other's ships (including, with some qualifications, warships, provided the trade is not on behalf of the host country's enemy, Article 10) – the purport of the latter provision is made explicit in a separate article (Article 11), according to which King James promises to prohibit any trade carried out by his subjects on behalf of the Dutch towards Spain and Belgium. Other provisions supplementing free trade and equal treatment (cf. Article 10) ensure the application of ordinary tax rates for British exports to Spain and for exports by Britons from Spain (Articles 12–4, including some safeguards in Articles 13 and 15).[37]

Some of these provisions (both general and commercial) are substantially repeated in a third category of clauses dealing specifically with the relations between Britain and Belgium (Articles 16–20). They include clauses on free trade between the two countries (except on behalf of the United Provinces), mutual access to each other's ports and territories (including a restricted access for war-ships), equal treatment for business, ordinary tax rates, forbearance (also by subjects) to provide military assistance to enemies, the restoration of pre-war treatises and agreements, while the English king committed himself to contribute to a peace settlement between Belgium and the United Provinces (Article 31).[38]

In the Twelve Years Truce,[39] one recognises a similar typology, but also quite different concerns. Article 1, which entails an explicit willingness from the Spanish-Belgian side to recognise and accept the United Provinces as a party with whom they could conclude a treaty is in that respect perhaps one of the

37 See also, in supplement to the publication of the Treaty, the 'Articles concerning Merchandize of high Germanie to be transported into Spaine, free of the Imposition of 30. in the 100' (English translation of the 1604 Treaty, *loc. cit.*, in the appendix).

38 'Item, that if the Hollanders and other confederate States, will accept of conditions of pacification with the most renowned Archdukes, or their Successors, through the meanes of the most renowned king of England &c. the sayd Archdukes and their Successors, will allwayes willingly hearken unto that which shal be proposed therein, and will desire that by the helpe of the sayd most renowned King of England, &c. they may bee brought to embrace equall conditions, wherin they shal wel understand, how much the said Archdukes doe attribute unto the authority of the most renowned King of England &c. their loving brother'.

39 Simon Groenveld, *Unie – Bestand – Vrede. Drie fundamentele wetten van de Republiek der Verenigde Nederlanden* (Hilversum, 2009), was only available to me after this paper was written.

most notorious terms.[40] But a closer reading of the 1609 Truce Treaty shows a much more detailed concern to deal with the effects on private property (and to some extent the estates of some public figures and families, *viz.* the Orange and the Nassau:[41] Articles 14 and 30; conversely, Article 20 deals specifically with church property)[42] affected by the long-standing war and military operations. Most of the Articles 13 to 35 of the 1609 Truce – a substantial part of the whole agreement – endeavour to determine or restrict the effects of seizures, confiscations, auctions, the use of private land for defence works, obligations, legal proceedings, inheritance, restitution and compensation.

Apart from that significant cluster of provisions on private interests, the more general clauses of the treaty are to some extent more conventional when compared to other treaties from the same period. Noteworthy is that the provisions here are far less frequently buttressed by a sanction than in the 1604 Peace Treaty.[43] There is probably no reason to believe that the terms of a truce would per se be seen to be less in need of a sanction than the provisions of a firm and permanent peace, but perhaps the drafters of the 1609 Truce were more aware that its implementation would even more strongly depend on the continuing commitment of the parties to keep the peace as long as it served their interest.[44] In that respect, the United Provinces' commitment could be expected to be less inspired by immediate opportunism, as they still faced the

40 This was also an issue which was extensively discussed by the major actors who were involved in the negotiations leading to the truce, as may be established (e.g.) from many passages in the records of the Dutch States-General, H.H.P. Rijperman (ed.), *Resolutiën der Staten-Generaal van, 1576 tot 1609*, vol. 14, *1607–1609* (Rijks geschiedkundige publicatiën, Grote Serie 131; The Hague, 1970), *passim*, and esp. 341–2, 348–3, 458–60, or from the correspondence and documents collected by Pierre Jeannin, for which I am referring to the edition: J.A.C. Buchon (ed.), *Choix de chroniques et mémoires sur l'histoire de France, Négociations du Président Jeannin* (Paris, 1838); I have also consulted the *ed.pr.*: *Les negociations de Monsieur le President Ieannin* (Paris, Chez Pierre le Petit, 1656); on the Spanish position, see Allen, *Philip III and the Pax Hispanica, o.c., passim*, and esp. 176 (in 1607). The issues of freedom of religion in the United Provinces and of trade in the Indies were possibly raised by the King of Spain in order to scupper the negotiations even at an advanced stage, cf. W.J.M. van Eysinga, *De wording van het Twaalfjarig Bestand van 9 april 1609* (Verhandelingen der Koninklijke Nederlandse Akademie van Wetenschappen, afd. Letterkunde, Nieuwe Reeks 66.3, Amsterdam, 1959), 122; the issue of the Indies remained controversial until the very last discussions, Ibid., 146–147.

41 *Resolutiën der Staten-Generaal, o.c.*, 415–416, 654–655, 659–662, 678 ff..

42 Ibid., 427–429, 697 ff.

43 Arts. 35 (in order to repress acts of piracy), 36 (against infringements of the truce).

44 On the opportunistic considerations of Spanish foreign policy in pursuing the 1604 Peace and the 1609 Truce: Sanz Camañes, 'España ante las paces', Conclusión; and the

need to prove their credibility as a new, but nevertheless reliable actor of the European international community.[45]

The more conventional clauses, for which some equivalent may be found in the comparison with the Treaty of London, include formal terms regarding the commencement of the treaty (Article 5), its ratification (Article 37) and publication (Article 38). The more general provisions regard the ending of hostilities (Article 2), the forbearance of causing any harm during the truce (Article 3), the peaceful intercourse between the subjects of the signatories (Article 4), the intermittence of periods of limitations for legal actions (Article 27: for the period from 1567 to 1609), the liberation of prisoners of war (Article 34), breaches of the truce (Article 31) or the punishment of infringements (Article 36). The more striking post-bellum provisions (in so far as the phrase may be used for a truce) are concerned with taxation (Articles 6 and 9), the restrictions on privateering and reprisals (Article 11), the restricted access of warships to the other signatories' harbours (Article 12). The *travaux préparatoires* of the 1609 Truce show that, on the vexed issue of trade with Spain, Spanish dominions outside Europe and in the Indies, the negotiators took their cue from previous treaties, in particular Vervins and London.[46]

---

underlying perception of England (partly as a 'rogue state', cf. 138), Bernardo J. García García, 'Peace with England, from Convenience to Necessity, 1596–1604', in Anne J. Cruz (ed.), *Material and Symbolic Circulation between Spain and England, 1554–1604* (Aldershot, 2007), 136–149.

45 Even after the conclusion of the Antwerp Truce, the United Provinces had to face the continuing efforts of the French King to influence their domestic state system and to subject them to some form of overlordship, cf. J.C.H. de Pater, *Maurits en Oldenbarnevelt in den strijd om het Twaalfjarig Bestand* (Amsterdam, 1940), 134–137.

46 Cf. in the *Négociations* of Jeannin (1838 edn.), 620 (letter from Jeannin and Russy to the King, 8 March 1608), where Jeannin explains that no articles in the draft of the Truce refer to the Indies, but that two articles are relevant to the issue: (italics added by me in the following quotation): '... l'un, par lequel la trève est générale, partout, et sans distinction de lieux ni de personnes; l'autre, par lequel le commerce est général par tous les royaumes, pays, terres et seigneuries du roi d'Espagne, des archiducs et des États entre tous leurs sujets; et ensemble inféroient que la trève étoit aussi bien aux Indes qu'ailleurs, n'y ayant aucune restriction au commerce qui s'étendoit de même partout. Or, cette interprétation pouvoit être sujette à grande dispute, car, *encore que par les traités faits entre la France et l'Espagne,* le commerce soit général, et *de même ès traités entre l'Angleterre et l'Espagne,* si est-il certain que les Espagnols n'ont jamais entendu que les sujets de Vos Majestés eussent ledit commerce aux Indes, et, s'ils y vont, que c'est à leurs périls et fortunes, sans que la paix soit rompue ailleurs. Ainsi ils eussent pu donner la même interprétation à cet article; mais quand les députés des archiducs le voulurent restreindre aux

Conclusion

The period ca. 1598–1609 is particularly interesting from the viewpoint of early-modern treaty-making because it witnessed a series of treaties aiming at reaching a piece-meal adjustment of the new balance of powers in a still shifting era, although some of the major new tendencies had already become apparent. The focus, in several negotiations and agreements reached, on the Low Countries, in which both Spain, France and England had substantial stakes, also means that several other minor treaties of that period are nevertheless significant pieces of evidence of treaty-making on particularly international trade and tax issues: such as (e.g.) the Treaty of 12 October 1604 between France, Spain and Belgium regarding the re-establishment of trade,[47] of the Treaty of 26 May 1606 between France and England regarding trade between the two countries.[48] The recurrent pattern, for some types of clauses, is certainly relevant for assessing a set format of reference within the growing body of international law peace settlements. In a way, the very recurrence was also creating a degree of international customary law, particularly with regard to those clauses which were routinely included and did not reflect particular controversial issues. At the same time, this very mechanism also shows the limitations of treaties as a source of regulation of international relations, for it omitted to express the areas of disagreements, or issues with respect to fundamental conflicts of interests which a peace settlement could not solve. Both the analysis of individual treaties as well as a structural analysis of treaty practice over a period of reference will therefore continue to have to take into account the wider historical context of international relations, and particularly international economic relations.

lieux et limites désignés par ledit article, et hors iceux exclure les États des lieux, ports et havres appartenant au roi d'Espagne, on leur demanda un consentement exprès pour le commerce desdits pays ès lieux et ports qui n'étoient de l'obéissance du roi d'Espagne, et que durant la trève on promît aussi de ne faire la guerre aux alliés que les États ont esdits pays: et ce fut lors qu'il y eut grande contention continuée par trois conférences, et jusque sur le point de notre départ, que nous fûmes comme contraints d'accepter l'article aux conditions ci-dessus mentionnées, non autrement; en quoi nous estimons avoir bien fait, et donné un grand avancement en cette affaire, sans nous obliger néanmoins à ne pouvoir demander mieux, au cas que les États fassent refus de s'en contenter'. The correspondence also testifies that both the French and English delegates could argue vis-à-vis the States General that the latter could not expect the former to back a more favourable treatment of the Dutch in the Indies than what the former peace treaties had granted to the subjects of their kings.

47 *Recueil des traitez...* (Amsterdam, 1700), *o.c.*, *l.c.*, 18–19.

48 Ibid., 30–33.

PART 2

Truce and War

CHAPTER 5

Left 'Holding the Bag'

The Johor-VOC Alliance and the Twelve Years Truce (1606–1613)

Peter Borschberg

Introduction

In the context of early modern history, the Twelve Years Truce arguably represent one of the first – if not the first – European agreements to exert verifiably an impact of a truly global nature.[1] This was certainly not the underlying intention of the Treaty, but the effects became global because of the nature, geographic expanse and agendas of the signatory powers: on the one side the Spanish Empire in union with Portugal, and on the other the Dutch Republic and the desire of its merchant elites to conduct trade beyond the shores of Europe. Modern accounts touching on the forging, ratification and implementation of the Twelve Years Truce focus almost exclusively on the Treaty within the European theatre. Among the notable exceptions exploring its effects on the East Indies – and beyond – are the learned exposés of Jonathan Israel, as well as the expansive biography on the Land's Advocate of Holland, Johan van Oldenbarnevelt, published in the 1960s and early 1970s by Jan den Tex.[2] References to the East Indies are not uncommon in extant publications, such as notably, a chapter contained in the dissertation of Jan Somers[3] – but references are generally marginal in nature and these authors clearly remain intent on observing developments predominantly from a European perspective. To the best of my knowledge, no author has published a focused study touching on the reception and (initial) implementation of the truce in Southeast Asia. The present study hopes to make a first contribution to filling this lacuna by drawing attention to one of the Dutch East India Company's (VOC) earliest allies in the Malay world, namely the Kingdom of Johor. In selecting the title

1 This paper in part incorporates some evidence previously presented at a public lecture to the Malaysian Branch of the Royal Asiatic Society on 13 December 2008, at the premises of the Badan Warisan Malaysia in Kuala Lumpur.

2 Jonathan I. Israel, *Dutch Primacy in World Trade, 1585–1740* (Oxford, 1989); idem, *The Dutch Republic and the Hispanic World, 1606–1661* (Oxford, 1982); idem, *The Dutch Republic. Its Rise, Greatness and Fall* (Oxford, 1995); also J. den Tex, *Oldenbarnevelt* (Haarlem/Groningen, 1960–72, 5 vols.). An abridged English translation in 2 volumes of this Dutch language biography was published by Cambridge University Press in 1973.

3 J.A. Somers, *De VOC als volkenrichtelijke actor* (Deventer, 2001), 75–90.

 | DOI 10.1163/9789004274921_007

'Left Holding the Bag', I seek to present the case chiefly from the vantage point of this polity. I shall concentrate on two factions which, according to period materials of largely European provenance, broadly shaped decision-making at the royal court. Raja Bongsu, (the sibling of Johor's ruler Alauddin Riayat Shah III) who chiefly handled Johor's foreign relations and other affairs of state was 'saddened' by the conclusion of the truce and the cessation of hostilities with the Iberian powers it entailed. As a result, he and his faction at the court felt abandoned by their Dutch allies, especially in their on-going hostilities with Portuguese Melaka. By October 1610, Raja Bongsu had lost power to, and was marginalised by, the so-called pro-Portuguese or Lusophile faction headed by none other than their own sibling and half-brother, Raja Siak. These developments within the Johor royal court also form the immediate historical backdrop to the genesis and revision of the *Sejarah Melayu* or 'Malay Annals' (Ms. Raffles 18) around 1612–15.

General Observations on the Evolution of Early VOC Policy in Southeast Asia: Front-Line Alliances

Before turning to explore the reception of the Twelve Years Truce in the specific case of Johor, I shall furnish the reader with a synopsis of the early Dutch alliance policy in Asia at large, particularly with reference to forging formal ties and alliances with what I shall call front-line polities. What is meant by the term front-line polity? In employing this expression, I refer to the perceived 'front line' or 'front lines' in Asia in the war between the Dutch Republic (and its plenipotentiary proxy east of the Cape of Good Hope, the VOC) on the one side and the united Spanish and Portuguese empires on the other. The expression front line has nothing to do with local Asian concepts of power or authority, or even with varying ideas of boundaries and borderlands. The front line consists of zones or regions perceived or imagined by the VOC, its directors in Europe, and especially its officers on the ground in various outposts across maritime Asia. Polities located in this zone tended to be small or politically weak. The VOC feared that these would be drawn into the political and commercial sphere dominated by one of the Iberian crowns.

Spain and Portugal were (unhappily) united for about six decades in the so-called Union of the Two Crowns (1581–1640). The focal point of this union was the monarch who ruled as the king of both Spain and Portugal. Below this personal union the two empires continued to function more or less as they had before 1581, namely as fierce rivals and competitors, especially in the East Indies. There was minimal co-ordination – if any – between the two. They even faced considerable difficulties in joining forces in Asia to combat their common enemies from Europe. The Treaty of Zaragoza (Saragossa) of 22 April 1529 was stubbornly upheld, as a result of which Spain was legally compelled to access its colonies in the Philippine archipelago via the Pacific from Mexico and at one stage also Peru. Trade between Spanish Manila and Portuguese Macao technically remained prohibited, but actually flourished. Goa and Mexico City were far removed from the two ports in the South China Sea, and the courts of Lisbon and Madrid were even further removed, literally half-way around the globe. As a result, they remained largely aloof from many aspects of official control. Also, the Spanish and the Portuguese elites were deeply suspicious of each other, especially in Europe, but on the ground in Southeast Asia, the practicalities of daily life regularly clashed with the maze of regulations, laws and instructions that were successively issued by the monarchs and viceroys. These generally aimed at protecting markets, marketplaces and merchants in Europe. However, when it came to generating profits and tax revenues in the colonies across Asia and beyond, everyone, especially the crown officials, benignly looked away. The Church too acquiesced. It was just poor business sense to let God get in the way of making money. The various orders of the Roman Catholic Church certainly had a hand in creaming off profits generated in the trade with so-called 'pagans' and 'unbelievers' in Asia. High-minded religious ideals were either abandoned completely, and in the Southeast Asian context at best took a back seat.

For sure, the Union of the Two Crowns was not a union of partners, let alone equals. The Spanish regarded the Portuguese *Estado da Índia* (the 'State of India') as politically, financially and militarily weak, and sometimes considered it to be a serious financial and strategic liability. The VOC was well aware of the tension between the two Iberian powers in Asia, and recognised the Portuguese as the soft, vulnerable underbelly of the 'Spanish' empire that truly spanned the globe.

A range of excellent studies touching on the early VOC have shown that the Dutch company served as the Asian arm of the Dutch Republic's protracted war against the Iberian powers. Shortly after its formation in 1602, the VOC began to identify and single out a number of regions in South and Southeast Asia that in the context of the present paper shall be called front-line regions or front-line polities.[4] With this expression I collectively refer to polities that

4 The term 'state' in the context of early modern Southeast Asia is deliberately avoided here, as the nature of political power in the Malay world differed substantially from the situation in Europe. The choice of the term 'polity' is in line with established and contemporary discourses on political structures and institutions in early modern Southeast Asia.

the VOC deemed important from the perspective of commerce and/or hegemony, but were politically weakened or even considered unstable by the Dutch. These regions were not static, but changed over time with local developments and the evolving strategic priorities of the VOC. Polities seen positioned at the front line were therefore regarded by the Dutch company in danger of being subsumed into the political, commercial and strategic spheres of the Iberian empires. We need to bear in mind that, while the *Estado da Índia* was financially and militarily weakened, it certainly remained a diplomatic force to be reckoned with, as the Dutch soon came to learn, and as the case of Johor will also evidences in this exposé.[5] With reference to insular as well as mainland Southeast Asia, there were several front-line regions closely monitored by the early VOC: the Malay Peninsula is certainly one area, and in the early 17th century there were also the Maluku and Banda island groups situated in present-day Indonesia. The Dutch company quickly set out to forge military alliances and treaties of friendship with the rulers of these polities situated at the front line, often concluded in conjunction with agreements to supply spices and rare commodities exclusively to the Dutch. The rulers of polities situated at the front line were either already in armed conflict with the Spanish and the Portuguese, or had been co-opted by the VOC to fight these Iberian powers. The Dutch were well aware that not all rulers at the front line required, let alone desired, their assistance. As a rule, therefore, the VOC did not meddle in the affairs of expansive, land-based, agriculturally rich and militarily strong polities such as Aceh (which at the time covered much of north and central Sumatra), Pegu (which covered much of eastern and northern Myanmar and present-day northern Thailand), Siam and then of course China.

As a memorial concerning the draft truce articles of 11 April 1608, and later also details of the Treaty of Antwerp (April, 1609) arrived in Southeast Asia between February and December 1609, rulers at the front line, who had signed treaties with the Dutch, were left proverbially 'holding the bag', that is to say carrying the war effort against the Iberian powers on their own. The memorial of April 1608 and the articles of the Treaty of April 1609 unleashed a great deal of confusion. It took some time for details of the actual text of the 1609 Treaty,

5 The Twelve Years Truce, once implemented, shifted attention of the Luso-Dutch conflict in the East Indies from battling one another directly at sea to destabilising each others' Asian treaty partners. Concerning Portuguese efforts to this effect, see for example P.A. Tiele and J.E. Heeres (eds.), *Bouwstoffen voor de Geschiedenis der Nederlanders in den Maleischen Archipel* (The Hague, 1886–1895), vol. 1, 109, letter of Governor General Reynst to his brother-in-law J. Nequet in Amsterdam, 26 October 1615.

specific instructions from home governments, and also assessments of the wider implications for colonies and commercial operations in Asia to filter down to the various settlements, factories and outposts. But in some cases, such as Johor, the weeks of confusion and wrangling proved enough to have far-reaching political and economic consequences. Generally, there was deep dissatisfaction among the Dutch treaty partners across Southeast Asia, unhappiness that quickly spilled over into disappointment, frustration, resentment and in some cases restrained anger. Diplomatically – and arguably also commercially – the memorial of 11 April 1608 together with the Treaty of April 1609 inflicted a great deal of damage to the VOC. Although in practice the Truce seriously dented the Dutch company's credibility among rulers across Southeast Asia, especially among those who were formally tied by alliance or treaty to the Dutch company, it must be said in defence of the Dutch States General that they negotiated with the Spanish for an inclusion of Southeast Asian allies and treaty partners into the truce arrangement, and specifically singled out Siam, Banten, Johor, Aceh, Pahang, Kedah, Makassar, Banda and Ternate in this context.[6]

The Twelve Years Truce in Asia

What can be said about the Twelve Years Truce in relation to its applicability in the Asian theatre? As is known from surviving accounts of the negotiations leading up to the conclusion of the 1609 Truce, the Spanish were willing to concede full sovereignty to the Dutch Republic in return for a complete withdrawal of the Dutch from trading activities in the Indies.[7] This condition was not acceptable among the Dutch political and commercial elites whose interests in any case were tightly intermeshed. Like the memorial of April 1608, the agreement of April 1609 acquiesced to Dutch trade in the Indies, but only in such locations where the Iberian powers held no permanent foothold. Technically this rendered all of the Americas off limits, but the East Indies presented a different story. The Spanish only claimed the Philippine archipelago which can hardly be seen as the jewel in the crown of its colonial possessions. What rendered the Philippines – and specifically the island of Luzon – a desirable possession was the trade conducted by the Chinese in Manila. Goods

6 H.P. Rijperman (ed.), *Resolutiën der Staten-Generaal van 1576 tot 1609, veertiende deel, 1607–1609* (Rijks Geschiedkundige Publicatiën, Grote Serie 131; The Hague, 1970), 658.

7 Israel, *The Dutch Republic*, 8; E. van Veen, *Decay or Defeat: An Inquiry into the Portuguese Decline in Asia, 1580–1645* (Leiden, 2000), 187–188.

were subsequently transhipped across the Pacific to the Americas. As for the Portuguese, the *Estado da Índia* was not a land-based colonial enterprise, but rather consisted of a string of forts, factories and ports of differing and uneven legal status tenuously linked to the political and financial umbilical cord in Goa. Intra-Asian trade was far more important than the trade with Europe as the VOC would quickly learn, and thus there was tremendous scope and opportunity for expansion. In Asia, the Twelve Years Truce was to take effect one year after its ratification in Europe (that is to say April 1610) but in the words of the historian Jonathan Israel, Johan van 'Oldenbarnevelt must have known his sincere desire to see the Truce observed in Asian waters was scarcely more than pious hope'.[8] Still the twelve month delay in implementing the truce outside the European theatre was intended to give sufficient time to the signatory powers to inform their officials in Asia and issue them with fresh instructions.

As soon as the memorial of 11 April 1608 arrived in Banten sometime around February 1609,[9] the Asian-based servants of the VOC rushed to consolidate positions vis-à-vis the Iberians across the region. This was in line with express instructions received from the VOC directors in Europe.[10] They did so by signing a flurry of treaties with relevant rulers whose polities were situated at or near the front line, with the Maluku (Moluccas) and Banda island groups (the so-called Spice Islands) as well as Solor and Timor specifically singled out by the directors in Europe as the top priority for the Dutch company.[11] Where possible, the VOC was to entrench its treaties and alliances with local rulers by gaining concessions to construct fortifications on their territory.[12] At the same time, the VOC sought to pluck or grab as much as possible from the Portuguese and Spanish before hostilities were to formally cease outside

8 Israel, *The Dutch Republic*, 14.

9 J.K.J. de Jonge, *Opkomst van het Nederlandsch gezag in Oost-Indië. Verzameling van onuitgegeven stukken uit het oud-coloniaal archief* (The Hague, 1866–1909, 16 vols.), esp. vol. 3, 309; M.E. van Opstall (ed.), *De reis van de vloot van Pieter Willemszoon Verhoeff naar Azië, 1607–1612* (The Hague, 1972), vol. 2, 255. See also J.E. Heeres (ed.), 'Corpus Diplomaticum Neërlando-Indicum. Verzameling van politieke contracten en verdere verdragen door de Nederlanders in het Oosten gesloten, van privilegiebrieven, aan hen verleend, enz.', eerste deel (1596–1650), *Bijdragen van het Koninklijk Instituut voor Land-, Taal-, en Volkenkunde*, 57 (1907) 56.

10 De Jonge, *Opkomst*, vol. 3, esp. 310, 311.

11 For the list and specific provisions of these treaties, see Heeres, 'Corpus Diplomaticum', 56–85. Solor was an important island and port in the trade with white sandalwood from Timor.

12 De Jonge, *Opkomst*, vol. 3, 310.

the European theatre by 1 September, 1609 – at least this was the deadline stipulated in the memorial of 11 April 1608.[13] It is against the backdrop of this latter context that we need to understand especially the attacks by Admiral Pieter Willemsz Verhoeff, and on his death by his designated successor, Vice-Admiral François Wittert, on hard and soft Spanish targets around the Malukus and later that year notably in Manila Bay.[14] After a five month blockade of Manila, Wittert was unceremoniously defeated by the *armada* of Spanish Philippine Governor Juan de Silva in April 1610. Even after the one year delay in the implementation of the Twelve Years Truce had lapsed, the Treaty had little hope of being observed as unfolding events in the Malukus, Bandas and in 1613 also Solor can easily evidence.

Back in Europe, peace in Asia was also not on the agenda of politicians and diplomats. In the presence of English and French envoys, the truce was appended by secret clauses shortly after its proclamation in April 1609 and an explanation of Article 4, that effectively paved the ground for the continuation of conflict outside the European theatre.[15] Admittedly, these secret clauses were almost certainly not communicated to agents and VOC servants on the ground in Asia, other than perhaps the Governor General Pieter Both, who was issued comprehensive and detailed instructions in December 1609 and took up residence in Southeast Asia in 1610.[16] These instructions charged the new Dutch Governor General with collecting as much information as possible about rulers and polities across Southeast Asia, especially of those who were allied to the Portuguese.[17] As the implementation of the truce was to take effect around the time when Pieter Both took up residence in Asia, it would appear that the directors in Europe wanted to temporarily shift attention away from attacking Portuguese and Spanish targets (which had been the

13 De Jonge, *Opkomst*, vol. 3, 309.

14 De Jonge, *Opkomst*, vol. 3, 93–94. Portuguese positions in Solor were attacked and taken over by the VOC in 1613 at a time when observance the truce had virtually ceased in Asia.

15 See Appendix 7 as well as H. Nellen, *Hugo de Groot: Een leven in strijd om de vrede, 1583–1648* (Amsterdam, 2007), 92.

16 P.J.A.N. Rietbergen, *De Eerste Landvoogd Pieter Both (1568–1615): Gouverneur-Generaal van Nederlands-Indië* (Zutphen, 1987, 2 vols.). The instructions issued to Governor-General Both can be found in vol. 2, 212–227.

17 Rietbergen, *De eerste*, vol. 2, 214–215. – Developments on the Portuguese side broadly mirror the web of treaties and contracts signed by the VOC with regional Asian rulers. For the full collection of extant agreements signed by the viceroy in Goa, see J.F. Judice Biker, *Collecção de tratados e concertos de pazes que o Estado da Índia Portugeza fez com os reis e senhores com quem teve relações nas partes da Ásia e Africa Oriente, desde o princípio da conquista até ao fin do século XVIII* (Lisbon, 1881–87, 10 vols.).

company's clear priority until then) to targeting the Asian trading and treaty partners of the Iberian powers.

The Malay Peninsula as a Front-line Region: The Case of Johor

One of the front-line regions identified by the Dutch company in the first decade of the 17th century was the Malay Peninsula. This land mass is defined by two important arteries of early modern seaborne trade, namely the Melaka Strait to the west, and the Singapore Strait to the south. To the east, it is bordered by the South China Sea and the Gulf of Thailand. In the north, the Isthmus of Kra (situated in present-day southern Thailand) forms the narrow link with the Eurasian land mass. In the late 16th and early 17th centuries, the Peninsula was the home of several polities of varying population size and marketplaces of scale, including the large land-based Kingdom Siam-Ayutthaya. In this period the various polities of the Peninsula were torn in a tussle between Johor and Aceh, mainly in their domestic dispute over primacy in the Malay world. In this jockeying for supremacy, Portuguese Melaka sometimes sided with Johor, but generally opposed Aceh. With the arrival of the first Dutch ships in the waters of the Singapore and Melaka Straits, and especially after the forging of a formal alliance of war between Johor and the VOC in May 1606,[18] the balance of power on the Peninsula tipped in favour of Johor, a situation which admittedly lasted for only a few years. It ended at the very latest with the 1613 Acehnese attack on Johor, in the course of which the towns of Singapura and Batu Sawar were burnt to the ground. During the relatively narrow time frame under review, namely the years 1606–13, Johor 'bordered' (if this term is even applicable in the context of describing a pre-modern Malay *negeri* or polity) the region controlled, or at least claimed, by Portuguese Melaka in the north and northwest. Reports and maps (of specifically Portuguese origin) draw a 'border' around the Muar River estuary, among other locations, but the fact is people, settlements and waterways were the chief concern of Malay rulers of this era, and not the sparsely populated lands that were subsumed by thick and almost impenetrable jungle. By all accounts, Johor was a front-line polity identified by, and allied to, the VOC. Its ruler commanded the loyalty of subjects across much of the southern region of the Malay Peninsula (broadly coinciding with the present-day Malaysian State of Johor, but not to be

18 The Dutch text version of this Treaty (together with the second Treaty of September 1606) can be found Heeres, 'Corpus Diplomaticum', 42–47.

confused with it), as well as the provinces of Riau and Kepulauan Riau in modern Indonesia. Loyal to Johor were also the inhabitants of some island clusters in the South China Sea located between the Peninsular mainland and the great island of Borneo, such as specifically the Tambelan, Anambas, and Natuna groups. Within Johor's orbit were also peoples on the great island of Borneo, specifically around the Sambas River in the present-day Malaysian State of Sarawak.[19] Johor was historically closely associated with Indragiri, Kampar and Aru in eastern Sumatra;[20] Pahang on the Malay Peninsula; and according to some European reports also Champa in the south of present-day Vietnam. In terms of geographic expanse, the Johor ruler's authority doubtlessly had a reach comparable, or even greater than, the nascent states in Western Europe at the time.

Factions at the Johor Court

Given the complexity and impressive geographic reach of the Johor Kingdom at the dawn of the 17th century, it should not surprise to find the political agenda of the royal court riddled with factionalism. In the period under review, the king and his court were based in Batu Sawar. Later the king as well as many high ranking nobles, such as the *bendahara*,[21] transferred their residence to a newly constructed settlement located further upstream known as Pasar Raja.

19 The King of Sambas, who is generally seen by the Dutch as a 'vassal' of the King of Johor, was a rival to the ruler of Sukadana. Both the rulers of Sambas and Sukadana controlled riverine networks where gemstones and also gold were panned. The two Borneo polities count among the most important diamond-producing regions in Asia during the early modern period.

20 The situation with Aru during this period appears somewhat murky. For the period preceding roughly the middle of the 16th century, Aru is described as a serious competitor and rival of Melaka and the nascent polity of Johor. See A.C. Milner, *The Malays* (Oxford, 2008), 50. According to the late French historian and Sumatra expert Denys Lombard, however, Aru had been taken in war by the King (Sultan) of Aceh in 1564, but cites a period English source that 'Aru holdeth with the king of Ior and refuseth subjection'. Aru was again attacked (together with Johor) in 1613, and finally submitted to Acehnese domination. See D. Lombard, *Le Sultanat d'Atjéh au temps d'Iskandar Muda 1607–1636* (Paris, 1967), 37, 83 and 92. With reference Aru in general, see also A.C. Milner, E. Edwards McKinnon and Tengku Luckman Sinar, 'Aru and Kota Cina', *Indonesia*, 26 (1978) 1–42.

21 Commonly identified in many sources as the minister of interior and later also the chief of police. Importantly, the *bendahara* also served as master of ceremonies who legitimised royal activity through ritual.

Raja Bongsu, however, continued to reside at Kota Seberang which was located across the river from Batu Sawar. Surviving reports of European provenance describe Batu Sawar as a sizeable town. It was located on the banks of the Johor River in the vicinity of present-day town of Kota Tinggi. The divisions at the Johor royal court(s) can be identified and tentatively reconstructed from period materials of mainly Dutch and sometimes also Portuguese provenance. Surviving Dutch materials inform us of deep rifts at (and between) the Johor royal court that had formed around the four surviving sons of Raja Ali Jalla bin Abdul Jalil and their respective followers among the Malay nobility. The four sons are Alauddin Riayat Shah III (who formally held the title of Yang di Pertuan, that is 'King'), Raja Bongsu (alias Raja Seberang, Raja di Ilir), Raja Siak and finally Raja Laut.

Alauddin Riayat Shah is described as a man of about 40 years, weak and inept, which in turn also serves to explain why he heavily leaned on his younger half-brother, Raja Bongsu, to attend to many facets of political business, and especially issues relating to external alliances and foreign affairs. It is insufficiently clear from VOC materials which of the Malay nobles actually supported Raja Bongsu's faction and foreign policy agenda, and whether his brother, King Alauddin, deferred to his choice of treaty partner. Carl-Alexander Gibson-Hill suggested that King Alauddin in fact leaned toward the Portuguese.[22] It was Raja Bongsu who had entered into an alliance with Dutch Admiral Jakob van Heemskerk (at the time when he took the Portuguese carrack *Santa Catarina* in the Singapore Straits in February 1603), dispatched a diplomatic mission to the Dutch Republic, and later also signed a formal alliance with Dutch Admiral Cornelis Matelieff de Jonge in May 1606. Raja Bongsu was a man with a vision for reviving the flagging political fortunes of Johor, and judging by the surviving descriptions of him, also an individual endowed with an almost spell-binding charisma. Like his late father Raja Ali Jalla,[23] he had a dream of reviving the Melaka sultanate, from whose last ruler the Raja and his brothers descended. He invoked the name and legacy of the fallen Melaka sultanate and

22 Gibson-Hill wants King Alauddin to hedge Portuguese sympathies, but I have not found any evidence in the source materials consulted to corroborate this view. Given Alauddin's supposed minor interest in affairs of state, he was probably indifferent to either party and that would not exactly render him a Portuguese sympathiser. See C.-A. Gibson-Hill, 'The Alleged Death of Sultan'Ala'udin of Johor at Acheh in 1613', *Journal of the Malayan Branch of the Royal Asiatic Society*, 29.1 (1956) 130, 138.

23 P. Borschberg, 'Jacques de Coutre as a Source for the Early Seventeenth-Century History of Singapore, the Johor River and the Straits', *Journal of the Malaysian Branch of the Royal Asiatic Society*, 81.2 (2008) 90.

referred to himself variously as the legitimate successor of Melaka's prestige and 'lands' in several communications with the Dutch.[24]

To rally his subjects behind this dream and this cause, he probably commissioned the revision of a work around or after 1612 which today is widely known as the *Sejarah Melayu* or 'Malay Annals'.[25] Pining for the lost, great days of the Melaka Sultanate, the *Sejarah Melayu* plots the legendary founding of the sultanate and its conquest by the Portuguese. The *Sejarah Melayu*, however, is more than a look into an ostensibly glorified and idealised past. It is significantly also a glimpse into Johor court politics in Raja Bongsu's own day.[26] In sharp contrast to his three male siblings, Raja Bongsu is described in overwhelmingly positive and flattering terms, at least in certain Dutch and German language source materials that survive.[27] His charm and personality

24 See for example Van Opstall, (ed.), *De reis*, vol. 1, 252–253, entry for 19 January 1609.

25 C.C. Brown (tr. and an.), *Sĕjarah Mĕlayu or Malay Annals*, with an introduction by R. Roolvink (Kuala Lumpur/Singapore, 1970) xxv–xxvi. The original list of kings was believed to have been written around 1536. The work was subsequently edited and reworked by the Johor *bendahara*, Tun Mohamad Sri Lanang or Tun Sri Lanang in or around 1612–13. The Dutch academic Gerrit Pieter Rouffaer in an article published in 1921, denies that 1612 is the proper date for the *Sejarah Melayu*, and revises this to 1615 instead. See G.P. Rouffaer, 'Was Malaka Emporium vóór 1400 AD. genaamd Malajoer? En waar lag Woerawari, Ma-Hasin, Langka, Batoesawar?', *Bijdragen van het Koninklijk Instituut voor Land-, Taal-, en Volkenkunde*, 77 (1921) 1–174 and 359–604. The revision of the date of completion of the *Sejarah Melayu* is found in Rouffaer, 'Was Malaka', 437. On the identity of Tun Sri Lanang, who also held the title of Paduka Raja, see Rouffaer, 'Was Malaka', 442.

26 The date of commissioning and later completing the *Sejarah Melayu* (Ms. Raffles 18) roughly corresponds to the time when Raja Bongsu lost out to the pro-Portuguese faction at the court.

27 A detailed description of Raja Bongsu can be found in the travelogue of the German VOC servant Johann Verken, 'Molukkenreise 1607–1612', in S.P. l'Honoré Naber (ed.), *Reisebeschreibungen von Deutschen Beamten und Kriegsleuten im Dienst der Niederländisch West- und Ost-Indischen Kompanien, 1602–1797* (The Hague, 1930), 58–59, 'As for the King of Johor, however, who is also known as Raja Bongsu, he is still a young man in his thirties. When he came aboard our ship, he was wearing a white cotton shirt, which reached down to knee level. Around his body he wore a beautifully colored, striped cotton cloth, which reached halfway down to his feet. Otherwise, he was bare on his body and legs. He wore on his feet a pair of black felt slippers, and around his head he had wrapped a black headpiece of silk. Around his neck he wore three gold chains, which were completely inlayed with gemstones. Around his left arm he wore two thick golden rings, and around his right arm [another] one. On his fingers he wore six precious rings. He also had a dagger at his side which is made in a very strange manner, and which they [the Malays] call "kris". The handle and the blade were made of pure, clear wrought gold, and were studded with

certainly helped sell his idea of a 'New Melaka' to the Dutch, and they evidently bought into it.

Raja Bongsu's rival for power was his half-brother, known from both Dutch as well as Portuguese source materials as Raja Siak, and from Chapter 38 of the *Sejarah Melayu* (Malay Annals) as his (half-) brother Hasan. Apart from the testimony given in Admiral Matelieff's travelogue, very little is known about this man from European sources. He was born of Ali Jalla Abdul Jalil's third wife and in any case from a different mother than either King Alauddin or Raja Bongsu.[28] Raja Siak was also married to a daughter of the Queen of Patani, Raja Hijau, whom he wed in either late 1602 or early 1603. Dutch sources such as the log of Admiral Matelieff paint him in a very negative light, describing him as a drunkard, and generally an evil, conniving person. At the royal court in Batu Sawar and later also at Pasar Raja, the Raja Siak was supported by the *bendahara*,[29] Sri Raja Negara the *shahbandar* (port master) of Singapura,[30] as well as the *laksamana* (admiral). Reference to the latter may also be taken as an indication that the fourth male sibling, known as Raja Laut ('King' or 'Prince of the Sea'), was also sympathetic to the Portuguese – or at least so we are told by Dutch source materials. Still, this cannot be taken for certain, nor is it clear whether the *laksamana* and the Raja Laut were not possibly one and the same individual. This question surrounding their precise identity was importantly

diamonds, rubies and sapphires.... [Raja Bongsu] was in his appearance and body a well-proportioned person, rather tall, softly spoken, and fair skinned both on his body and his face'. (My translation).

28 Anon., 'Historische Verhael Vande treffelijcke Reyse, gedaen naer de Oost-Indien ende China...door... Cornelis Matelief de Ionge', in Isaac Commelin, *Begin ende Voortgang Vande Vereenigde Neerlandsche Geoctroyeerde Oost-Indische Compagnie* (Amsterdam, 1967), vol. 3, 11; E. Netscher, *De Nederlanders in Djohor en Siak* (Batavia, 1870), 11. See also Borschberg, 'Jacques de Coutre', 88, citing De Coutre's brief 'Information about Building some forts and Castles in the Straits of Singapore, etc.': 'This land used to belong to the king of Johor, and the island of Sumatra features a kingdom that was governed by the Raja Siak, who was a brother of the said king of Johor. Siak is situated at the entrance of the Strait of Sabam [today: Kundur Strait], and the raja controlled more than 60 *leguas* [more than 300 kms] of [Sumatran] coastline. The sultan of Aceh has now occupied all of it'. (My translation).

29 Admiral Matelieff's travelogue suggests that the officer known as the *Stadt-houder van den coningh*, that is the *bendahara*, was more inclined toward the Portuguese than toward the Dutch, a point that is importantly also noted by Rouffaer. See 'Historische Verhael', 18, and Rouffaer, 'Was Malaka', 447, 452.

30 Netscher, *De Nederlanders*, 9; Rouffaer, 'Was Malaka', 402–403; C.G. Kwa, 'Records and Notices of Early Singapore', in J.N. Miksic (ed.), *Archeological Research on the 'Forbidden Hill' in Singapore* (Singapore, 1985), 121.

also raised by Rouffaer.[31] Almost nothing is known about the Raja Laut, and what sparse information survives about him is very negative indeed. Matelieff met him at the court in Batu Sawar around August or September 1606, and in the following testimony is unambiguously disdainful toward him:[32]

> From his third wife the old King of Johor [Raja Ali Jalla Abdul Jalil] had another son named Raja Laut, that is the 'King of the Sea,' a man qualified for nothing. He only drinks *arak*,[33] and chews tobacco and betel. Verily, [he] is worthy to be bound by his hands and feet and cast into the sea; a great drunkard, manslayer, and womaniser who knows all that there is to know about these three things.'

The Johor-Dutch Alliance of 1606

These were the principal persons and personalities who acted as power brokers at the Johor royal court in the period between 1606 and 1610.

In the following sections, I turn to examine how news of the ratification of the Twelve Years Truce was received at the Johor royal court and what course of events flowed therefrom. In order to provide some important contextual information, I proceed in my account with the agreement signed in May 1606 between Admiral Matelieff and the Johor co-rulers, Raja Bongsu and King Alauddin.[34]

Judging by the text and also from the skeletal historical accounts of the negotiations aboard the VOC ship *Orangie*, the Dutch-Johor agreement of May 1606[35] was clearly *ad hoc* in nature and intention and focused primarily on the division of spoils in the event that Melaka be successfully wrested from Portuguese control (Article 1). The Dutch were to receive the walled city as a 'payment' or 'reward' for their participation in the joint military offensive

31 Rouffaer, 'Was Malaka', 488, note 1.

32 Anon., 'Historische Verhael', 11; Netscher, *De Nederlanders*, 11, and Rouffaer, 'Was Malaka', 446, note 2. (My translation).

33 An alcoholic beverage.

34 King Alauddin and Raja Bongsu presented themselves to the Dutch as (joint) rulers at the ratification of the May 1606 Johor-Dutch Treaty. Their oath reads: '*We, the Yang di Pertuan and Raja Seberang, the kings of Johor*, swear herewith to sustain the abovewritten agreement in all of its points and articles and not to undertake anything to breach it, so help us God'. See Heeres, 'Corpus Diplomaticum', 50. (My translation and italics).

35 Heeres, 'Corpus Diplomaticum', 41–45. A summary of the principal points is found in Netscher, *De Nederlanders*, 13–15.

(Article 1).[36] Johor was to receive the lands controlled by the Portuguese as well as all pieces of artillery that might be found in the fort' A Famosa (Article 6). The Dutch were to enjoy a tax exemption on trade (Articles 1 and 3), receive limited trading privileges for the future Dutch residents of Melaka (Article 8), and be granted rights to fell trees and harvest wood (Article 2). There are also provisions for extradition, jurisdiction over criminals and the hearing of grievances (Articles 11–3). The agreement further stipulated that the royal court of Johor should be transferred (from Batu Sawar) to Kampung Kling, providing such a move was both possible and feasible (Article 5).[37] There are two provisions that merit express reference in the present context. These are featured in the Dutch-Johor agreement of May 1606 as Articles 9 and 10:[38]

> Art. 9. Both parties shall assist each other to the best of their ability to sever all contacts with the Portuguese and the Spanish, who are their mutual enemies. Should either party enter into war with a party other than the Portuguese and the Spanish, then the one party shall not be bound to lend assistance to the other, lest it only be for defensive purposes.
> Art. 10. Neither party shall enter into peace with the King of Spain without the consent of the other.

According to a surviving but virtually unknown Portuguese account, the 1606 assault on Melaka involved 1,400 Dutch soldiers, 16,000 Javanese troops, and the armed assistance of seven neighbouring rulers.[39] As is known, this show

36 Heeres, 'Corpus Diplomaticum', 43, and especially also the explanation of this clause found on Heeres, 'Corpus Diplomaticum', 44, 'In concluding these articles, Raja Seberang [alias Raja Bongsu] desired that since everything around the city had largely been burnt to the ground [by the Portuguese], and should the city be subsequently conquered, then the Admiral would obtain space within this city for housing and lodging, leaving the fortress for the King [of Johor]' (My translation). It transpires that during the negotiations for the treaty between Admiral Matelieff de Jonge and Raja Bongsu, the Johor co-ruler neither intended to cede the whole walled city of Melaka to the Dutch (but only space within it), nor did the Johorean side originally intend for the Dutch to obtain control of the A Famosa fortress.

37 Heeres, 'Corpus Diplomaticum', 42, Art. 5, 'His Majesty, however, shall [be able to] repopulate and rule in the suburb Kampung Kling, which has been burnt down, without any interference from the States [General]. If possible, he shall assume his residence here…' (My translation).

38 Heeres, 'Corpus Diplomaticum', 43. (My translation).

39 P.J. de Sousa Pinto, *Portugueses e Malaios: Malaca e os Sultanatos de Johor e Achém, 1575–1619* (Lisbon, 1997), appendix 16, 'Relação do sucesso que teve a armada do viso-rei

of force would not yield the expected results, and the Portuguese were not dislodged from Melaka. Raja Bongsu (who appears to have mainly been responsible for external relations) and the *bendahara* (who was responsible for internal Johorean affairs) were both becoming increasingly nervous. The articles ratified in May were only meant to act as a recorded agreement for the division of the spoils of war and also thwart future disagreements at large. Raja Bongsu ostensibly feared heavy-handed retaliation by the Portuguese, which indeed followed in 1607 with fresh attacks on Johor's riverine settlements, including Batu Sawar.[40] He succumbed to sense of urgency to bind the VOC more permanently to the interests of Johor, lest the Dutch may be lured away by a neighbouring ruler. Raja Bongsu was aware that Dutch support for his cause at the Batu Sawar court, and indeed VOC support against the Portuguese at large, had tipped the balance of power in his favour. With the aim of tying Dutch interests to Johor and also consolidating the Dutch presence in this front-line polity, Raja Bongsu (evidently with the approval of the *bendahara*) consented to the ratification of a new treaty.[41] This second treaty was hammered out in September 1606, and the short text reads as follows:[42]

> As it is also necessary that the States [General] establish a safe and permanent base for the benefit of their subjects and for the promotion of trade of the said East Indies, that they may collect and store their goods, merchandise, ammunition, equipment and other such things, and, if need be, also bring craftsmen and servants from their homeland, His Majesty, the King of Johor shall concede to the States [General] such a

Dom Martim Afonso', 294. This Portuguese account sharply contrasts with the testimony in many period Dutch sources as well as secondary literature according to which the Johoreans were reluctant to engage the Portuguese in battle. They supposedly left the Dutch to fight the battle on their own. The joint attacks on Portuguese Melaka allegedly failed because the Dutch attacked from the sea and Johorean troops, responsible for the assault on land, left the overland trails open to bring in supplies.

40 Anon., 'Historische Verhael', 131, reports the Portuguese had attacked Batu Sawar around 1607, forcing Raja Bongsu to flee to Lingga.

41 Anon., 'Historische Verhael', 31. Some contemporary historians call it a 'supplemental treaty' and do not treat it as a separate agreement by its own right, see for example D. de Witt, *A History of the Dutch in Malaysia* (Petaling Jaya, 2008), 49–50.

42 Heeres, 'Corpus Diplomaticum', 47–48, 'Second agreement concluded between Admiral Cornelis Matelieff de Jonge in the name and on behalf of the High Mighty Gentlemen, the States General of the United Provinces, on the one side and the great and manly King of Johor on the other, [on] this day the 23 of September in the year of our Lord Jesus Christ 1606 in the city of Batu Sawar'. The article in the main text is taken from Heeres, 'Corpus Diplomaticum', 48. (My translation).

> place as [they] desire. [This may] be located here on the [Peninsular] mainland, or on one of the islands falling under the authority of His Majesty,[43] be it as large or as small as the States [General] or their captain may deem fit. *[They shall be entitled] to construct houses and living quarters, and to own these as they [would] in Melaka.*[44] *The States [General] and their subjects shall also be bound to fulfil the articles added to the agreement made at Melaka.*[45]

The Dutch-Johor Treaty of 23 September 1606 evidences that the original *ad hoc* arrangement to reward the VOC for participating in a successful campaign against Portuguese Melaka was now transformed into a standing agreement, as a result of which the Dutch company would take a permanent stake in the political stability and economic future of Johor. The arrangement paved the way for establishing a Dutch presence either on the Peninsula near the Johor River estuary, or on one of the islands situated to the south of the Singapore Straits in Indonesia's present-day province Kepulauan Riau. Although the VOC had singled out the Peninsula and the Straits as a front-line zone, it is important to bear in mind that it was Raja Bongsu who originally mustered the support of the Dutch in 1603, dispatched a diplomatic mission to the Netherlands in the same year, and also forged two treaties with the VOC in 1606. It was Raja Bongsu who mobilised the VOC in support of his cause, and thus hoped to strengthen the factional balance of power at the Johor court in his favour. The prospect of a permanent Dutch presence in Johor was intended not only to thwart future Portuguese military attacks on this front-line polity, but also to stabilise the political scene at the court and the Johor Kingdom.

News of the Twelve Years Truce Arrives at the Johor Royal Court

Sources indicate that once Raja Bongsu and the *bendahara* had promised the Dutch a location to 'set up shop' and construct warehouses for ammunition, provisions and commercial goods, the Raja found it increasingly difficult to

---

43 Specific locations raised during the discussions between Admiral Matelieff, Raja Bongsu and the Johor *bendahara* included a location around the Johor River estuary, Bintan, Lingga and Karimun Besar.

44 This is presumably a reference to Art. 1 of the May 1606 alliance, which, if implemented, would have granted full possession of the walled city of Melaka to the Dutch.

45 My italics.

fulfil this commitment in practice. At the time of Admiral Pieter Willemsz Verhoeff's visit to Batu Sawar in January 1609 (which also coincided with the end of the fasting month of Ramadan), talks between Raja Bongsu and the Admiral focused on a fresh joint attack on Portuguese Melaka. Verhoeff had been earlier furnished with information by the resident Dutch factor at Batu Sawar, Abraham van den Broek,[46] that the Portuguese colony and fortress were well provisioned and defended by 500 local Portuguese *casados* together with their household slaves, by an unspecified number of Malays and Kelings (South Indians, probably Tamils) as well as by soldiers from other 'nations' that are not listed by name.[47] On the basis of this information and intelligence, the Admiral ascertained that an attack on Melaka was unlikely to be successful.

A careful dissection of Raja Bongsu's conversations with Admiral Verhoeff of January 1609 are indicative of two sets of problems at the Batu Sawar court. The first concerns the war against Portugal. The Raja intimated to Verhoeff that the Johoreans did not fear the Portuguese as much as their Dutch guests generally surmised, as it was possible during a Portuguese attack to flee farther upstream where one would be beyond the reach of artillery fire launched from marine and large riverine craft. Was this a subtle hint – confirming widespread rumours circulating at the time – that a peace deal between Portuguese Melaka and Johor was in the works? The second was a sense of disappointment expressed in different contexts that it was evidently not within the grasp and power of the Dutch to restore by war and conquest the 'Empire of Melaka'.[48] Is this, at least from Raja Bongsu's perspective, a reference to the evident unwillingness of Verhoeff to engage Melaka in a fresh siege of the port and city?

If the unwillingness to confront the Portuguese in battle was one sore point, arguments about the wording and validity of the two 1606 Treaties was certainly another. An acrimonious verbal exchange between Verhoeff and Raja Bongsu emerged from the Admiral's request for permission to construct a Dutch fortification on 'Johorean soil'.[49]

Some additional background information is warranted in the present context. Admiral Matelieff had already admonished Raja Bongsu to beef up existing fortifications in Batu Sawar and Kota Seberang (sometimes also

46 Abraham van den Broek served as chief merchant (*opperkoopman*, factor) at Batu Sawar between 1606 and 1609 (that is from the time of Admiral Matelieff's visit until shortly after the departure of Admiral Verhoeff from Batu Sawar). Van den Broek is also described as having served as the personal secretary to Admiral Matelieff. See Rouffaer, 'Was Malaka', 444, note 2.

47 Van Opstall, *De reis*, vol. 2, 248.

48 Ibid., 252.

49 Netscher, *De Nederlanders*, 21.

Sabrang in the older spelling) in order to repel future Portuguese attacks. But any of these recommended enhancements and improvements would have clearly left the fortification under complete Johorean control. Incidentally, security issues also surfaced during the negotiations for the terms of the May 1606 Treaty. Whilst Raja Bongsu was willing to cede at least parts of the walled town of Melaka to the Dutch as a residential area, he did not want to relinquish the whole city in perpetuity, and clearly resisted the idea of relinquishing control of the fort to the VOC. Raja Bongsu is on record to have protested at this provision set down in Article 1, wondering aloud why he would want to drive out the Portuguese from Melaka only to replace them with the Dutch.[50] These objections are also evidenced by period materials published or cited by Netscher in the late 19th and Heeres in the early 20th century. Admiral Matelieff appears to have skilfully dodged all of Raja Bongsu's objections in this matter, partially with an evasive and non-commital 'let us see how things go', and partially by mollifying his royal counterpart with the promise that all artillery captured from the Portuguese would rightfully become Johorean property. This latter arrangement is confirmed by Article 6 of the May 1606 Treaty. As the unfolding of historical events would show, however, Melaka was not conquered during the joint attack, and consequently, the arrangement governing the division of spoils was not implemented.

The second agreement signed between Admiral Matelieff and Raja Bongsu in September 1606 – at least from the vantage point of the Dutch – pursued two distinct objectives. First, it confirmed the validity of the May 1606 Treaty, transforming this from an *ad hoc* arrangement to a blueprint for future collaboration and co-operation. Second, it promised the VOC a plot of land on which it would be able to construct residences, depots and warehouses. Also, during his discussions with Admiral Verhoeff in January 1609, Raja Bongsu insisted that the treaty struck on 23 September 1606 with Admiral Matelieff did not extend the earlier agreement of May 1606, but represented a second, separate treaty in its own right. The objective of the latter was not to defeat the Portuguese, seize the town of Melaka and divide the spoils of war, but rather to give the Dutch a place to proverbially 'set up shop'. Permanent Dutch presence in Johor was to ensure the safety of Batu Sawar and commerce of (and between) the Johor River towns.[51]

Now I return to Verhoeff's request to construct a fortress on 'Johorean soil'. Sources indicate that Raja Bongsu was surprised and indeed taken aback by this and further requests that were made by Admiral Verhoeff and his *breede*

50 Netscher, *De Nederlanders*, 12.

51 Netscher, *De Nederlanders*, 21–22.

raad in writing.[52] In their remonstrance or petition to the Johor monarch,[53] the Dutch officers proposed a range of articles that sought to ensure for the VOC free trade and exemptions from taxes and imposts in Johor and the co-operation of the Johor royals in collecting debt from Batu Sawar merchants. Importantly, the Dutch officers wanted to thwart an unexpected, back-handed deal between Johor and the Portuguese. The draft articles contained in the petition states that the monarch would have to consult with the Dutch on any future agreement to secure peace or a truce with either Iberian power.[54] All of the proposed articles were rejected. The Raja swiftly retorted that the Treaty of September 1606 said nothing about a fortification, but only mentioned residences, depots and warehouses for the VOC and its employees, as well as housing for craftsmen and their servants. In his conversations with Admiral Verhoeff, Raja Bongsu also insisted that his personal Malay language copy of the September 1606 Treaty said nothing about confirming the May 1606 articles.[55] He offered to have a copy of the Malay text made and sent to the Netherlands for scrutiny.[56] Since the Malay language text no longer survives, it would be little more than speculation to question the veracity of this claim. Still, one cannot help but wonder whether Raja Bongsu was now getting cold feet about his close co-operation with the Dutch, a policy he had so vigorously pursued until that point in time.

Against the backdrop of these conversations, arguments, deliberations and disagreements we need to understand why Raja Bongsu decided to dispatch a formal letter of complaint to the Dutch States General and Stadholder Prince Maurice of Orange. This bears the date 6 February 1609 and incidentally also

---

52 The *breede raad* (broad council) is an institution of the VOC. It was comprised of the commanding officers of each of the vessels in the admiral's fleet as well as designated 'factors'. The council fulfilled the function as an advisory body to the admiral and also assumed collective responsibility for certain key decisions.

53 See the 'Oost-Indische Voyagie onder den Admirael Pieter W. Verhoeven' in Commelin, *Begin ende Voortgang*, vol. 3, 207–208. The written reply of Alauddin and Raja Bongsu is printed in Commelin, *Begin ende Voortgang*, vol. 3, 208–209.

54 Netscher, *De Nederlanders*, 22–25.

55 Concerning Raja Bongsu's claim that his Malay text version of the treaty did not contain the disputed sentence, see Netscher, *De Nederlanders*, 21. The opening lines of the second Johor-Dutch treaty reads from the Dutch text as follows: 'First, herewith are confirmed all articles included in the agreement concluded between the parties made on the 17th of May of this year aboard the ship *Orangie* at anchor in the roadstead of Melaka'. (My translation). Raja Bongsu claimed that his version of the treaty did not contain this clause. For the Dutch text, see Heeres, 'Corpus Diplomaticum', 47.

56 Netscher, *De Nederlanders*, 22.

marks the day when Admiral Verhoeff weighed anchor and set sail from Johorean waters.[57] The acrimony and sense of frustration brought to paper in this letter focus on the supposedly inconsistent or wavering commitments of the Dutch to Johor, their trade with polities and ports hostile to the Kingdom, and the nit-picking of VOC officers over the wording and nature of the two 1606 Treaties.[58]

Raja Bongsu was 'saddened' by (read: disappointed by, probably unhappy with) the rapidly deteriorating state of Dutch-Johor relations. News of the Twelve Years Truce in late November or early December 1609 only added fuel into the fire. To vent his profound disappointment and deep dissatisfaction the Raja dispatched yet another formal letter of complaint to the Stadholder, Prince Maurice.

In response to a letter by the Stadholder (which Raja Bongsu had received in the summer of 1609) beseeching the Johor ruler to amplify or amend existing treaty arrangements with the VOC, Raja Bongsu wrote:[59]

> ... [O]ur brother [Prince Maurice] asks us in his letter to renew or amplify the existing treaty. Why should this be changed or renewed? It is our desire that our brother send us hither a person of respect and bestowed with plenipotentiary powers and authority so that a treaty may be concluded which cannot be broken and will last until the Day of Judgement. Twenty or thirty admirals could come here without changing it....; Currently an admiral comes with whom we strike one good agreement, and then comes another and changes it. Like this, there is no end to making treaties.

Raja Bongsu was particularly 'saddened' that the 'King of Holland' (as Prince Maurice was often called by Asian rulers to whom the concept of a republic was something almost inconceivable) had signed an agreement that for the foreseeable future effectively made peace with Spain and Portugal. He may very well have heard rumours about an impending deal, and it is possible he had seen, or even been briefed about the memorial of 11 April 1608.[60] It is

57 Netscher, *De Nederlanders*, 17–20; Van Opstall, *De reis*, vol. 2, 255. For the actual text, see De Jonge, *Opkomst*, vol. 3, 307, 'Memorie en instructie aangebragt in Indië met het jagt, de *Goede Hoop*, op den 4.den Mei, 1609'.

58 Netscher, *De Nederlanders*, 18, letter by Raja Bongsu, dated 6 February 1609 (and later passed to Admiral van Caerden).

59 Netscher, *De Nederlanders*, 27, letter by Raja Bongsu, 8 December 1609. (My translation).

60 De Jonge, *Opkomst*, vol. 3, 307–312, instructs visiting admirals and factors across Asia only to discuss the ongoing truce negotiations in Europe with great caution and discretion as the situation requires, See esp. De Jonge, *Opkomst*, vol. 3, 307.

questionable whether he had received any particulars about the truce before December 1609, but he was eventually briefed by a letter from The Hague dated 16 September 1609.

On 4 May 1609, a sloop arrived in Johor bearing instructions from Banten (Bantam) destined for VOC company servants to carefully prepare the Asian treaty partners on the impending news of the truce.[61] On 10 May, less than one week later, the two resident factors in Batu Sawar, Abraham van den Broek and Nicolaas Puijk, left for Banten and never returned. They were replaced by Jacques Obelaer as chief merchant (*opperkoopman*) or factor, Abraham Willemz de Rijk as his deputy, and one Hector Roos who is described as a specialist in diamonds (*diamantkenner*).[62]

News of the Twelve Years Truce, which arrived at the Johor court in late November or early December 1609, confronted the Raja with yet another fait accompli. Admiral Verhoeff and other leading VOC servants in Asia had insisted that the May 1606 Treaty had been transformed into a standing blueprint for future co-operation in both war and commerce. Indeed, if this was the case, did the ratification of the Twelve Years Truce not represent an open and manifest infringement of Article 10 that, as has already been seen, clearly states: 'Neither party shall enter into peace with the King of Spain without the consent of the other'? Raja Bongsu had never been consulted on the forging of the truce. What were the Dutch really up to? Could they even be trusted? What about Admiral Verhoeff's request to construct a fortification on 'Johorean soil?'

Raja Bongsu's Fall

Materials of primarily Dutch origin account for the substantial challenges faced by Raja Bongsu and his faction immediately preceding, but especially after news of the Twelve Years Truce arrived at the Johor royal court. The Portuguese of Melaka cleverly exploited the growing gaps between arriving and departing VOC vessels in Johor waters to launch a two-pronged offensive on the royal court aimed at breaking the respect and authority wielded by Raja Bongsu's pro-Dutch faction. One aspect of the Portuguese strategy was to impose a naval blockade in the lower reaches of the Johor River, as a result of which the densely populated upstream settlements along the river, including

61 De Jonge, *Opkomst*, vol. 3, 82, 307 et seq.

62 Netscher, *De Nederlanders*, 17, 26, 27. Batu Sawar had extensive trading links with both Sambas and Sukadana on the great island of Borneo, both of which were significant diamond-exporting regions. See also Van Opstall, *De reis*, vol. 2, 255, note 2.

Batu Sawar, experienced a severe reduction in commercial activity. It is important to bear in mind that the riverine blockade of 1609 (imposed by the Portuguese after the departure of Admiral Verhoeff's two guard vessels from the Johor River estuary on 10 May 1609)[63] dealt a crippling blow to the economy of the upstream towns. This was no mean feat, for several surviving reports touching on the commercial activity in and around the Johor River region claim that there were many in Batu Sawar who lived only on trade,[64] chiefly in pepper but also in diamonds (chiefly procured from around Sambas and Sukadana), sappan wood, cottons and textiles generally. According to contemporary eyewitnesses the river was frequented by ships from as far away as Arabia, Persia, Gujurat, the Ryukyus and China. This sharply contrasts with the situation described for Melaka at roughly the same time, where – due to the lack of trading activity – local *casados* fell back on farming to eke out a living.[65]

It is little surprise that the latest Portuguese blockade of the Johor River acted as the proverbial final straw for many of the courtiers and *orang kaya* (notables, merchants) at Batu Sawar and other upstream towns. Their dissatisfaction, combined with the prospect of Johor having to possibly wage the war against Portuguese Melaka on its own, precipitated the sudden and for the Dutch clearly unexpected fall or marginalisation of Raja Bongsu at the Johor court.[66] Admittedly, it is difficult to reconstruct precisely what role the Portuguese of Melaka played in engineering Raja Bongsu's fall, but a role they certainly had. Lavish gifts and extravagant promises were dished out to those

63 Van Opstall, *De reis*, vol. 2, 252. The original plan had been that the vessels hold guard until 1 July 1609, see Netscher, *De Nederlanders*, 17.

64 See Borschberg, 'Jacques de Coutre', 90, quoting from the *Vida de Jacques de Coutre:* 'The court of the king is in the city of Batu Sawar, and was constructed after the destruction of Old Johor [that is Johor Lama]. We now call this city New Johor. It is a port city hosting many ships of different nations.... There is a beautiful river [that is the Johor River] and a port with many large and small ships. This land [of Johor] maintains a vast network of trade and produces a surplus of food'. See also Madrid, National Library of Spain, ms. 2780, *Vida de Jaques de Coutre*, appendices, fol. 273r: 'In the aforementioned city of Johor [that is "New Johor" or Batu Sawar] there are many people who make a living only from merchandise and [from] sailing from one land to another'. (My translations).

65 P.A. Tiele etc., 'De Europeërs in den Maleischen Archipel', part 6, *Bijdragen van het Koninklijk Instituut voor Land-, Taal-, en Volkenkunde*, 30 (1882) 229, note 2.

66 The situation was apparently already desperate at the time of Admiral Verhoeff's visit to the Batu Sawar court in January 1609. See especially the 'Oost-Indische Voyagie' in Commelin, *Begin ende Voortgang*, vol. 3, 208, stating how 'the [Johor] Kings are currently in a state of great despair and poverty', that they had come to this precisely on account of their alliance with the Dutch, and that they were in genuine danger as they do 'not know how to resist the enemy' without 'money, ammunition of war, and ships'.

who opposed the pro-Dutch raja, such as notably the Raja Siak, the *laksamana* (and/or the Raja Laut), the *shahbandar* of Singapura (the Sri Negara di Raja), almost certainly the *bendahara* Tun Sri Lamang together with an unspecified number of *orang kaya*; in other words, to those men identified earlier as leading members of the Lusophile or pro-Portuguese faction. No doubt, the Portuguese worked on key players at the court, exploited existing rifts and differences among the four royal brothers and their respective supporters. Most important of all, the Portuguese held out the tangible material benefits that would derive from normalising relations with Melaka and the *Estado da Índia* in general.

Reports of European provenance touching on the Johor royal court indicate that Raja Bongsu and King Alauddin's leadership were never uncontested. Rumors had been circulating as early as 1607 – that is in the year immediately following the unsuccessful joint attack on Melaka – that factions at the court were pushing for a peace with the Portuguese. Admiral Matelieff even attests to having seen draft peace clauses with his very own eyes.[67] It is uncertain, however, whether these draft clauses were ever formally accepted. With the ratification of the Twelve Years Truce in Europe, and subsequently its implementation in Asia by April 1610, the Dutch and Portuguese would attempt to make the Johor court their new battle-ground. This was a new war, fought not with artillery, weapons, or the latest military tactics, but with gifts, bribes, promises and also some hard-nosed diplomatic manoeuvres. It was a very different kind of warfare that, with the benefit of hindsight, the Dutch quickly lost. Instrumental to Portuguese success was the dispatch of a senior, experienced negotiator to Johor known from Portuguese sources as João Lopes de Morero which in certain other documents is also spelled Lopes d'Amoreira or 'Lopes de Morere Tonbongon'.[68] This Portuguese envoy is described in various documents as a citizen of Melaka, the Portuguese colony's *temenggong* of foreigners, as well as an old friend of Raja Ali Jalla, the late father of King Alauddin, Raja Bongsu, Raja Siak and Raja Laut.[69] Lopes de Morero arrived in Batu Sawar in October 1610 to forge a peace treaty with Johor. Raja Bongsu's power base at the court was now in tatters, his downfall at the court almost complete.

The approximate date is noteworthy. The Twelve Years Truce had come into effect in the Asian theatre only six months before. The Dutch factor in Batu

67 See Rietbergen, *De eerste*, vol. 2, 207. The 'Historische Verhael', 131, also alludes to a peace agreement that followed attacks on Batu Sawar in 1607.

68 See also Netscher, *De Nederlanders*, 27–28; Rouffaer, 'Was Malaka', 451. The term 'Tombongon' is evidently a corruption of the Malay title *temenggong*.

69 R.A. Bulhão Pato and A. da Silva Rego (eds.), *Documentos Remettidos da Índia ou Livros das Monções* (Lisbon, 1880–1982), esp. vol. 4, 315; Rouffaer, 'Was Malaka', 451–452, note 3.

Sawar watched as the Raja Siak and his Lusophile faction engineered Raja Bongsu's fall with Portuguese assistance.

According to the testimony of the VOC factor in Batu Sawar, Jacques Obelaer, the Portuguese envoy named João Lopes de Morero arrived at the court to finalise a peace deal with Johor on 16 October 1610. Less than one week later, on 22 October, the Treaty was also endorsed by the governor of Melaka, Dom Francisco Henriques, in the presence of Archbishop Dom Frei Cristóvão de Sá e Lisboa and two unnamed Johorean envoys.[70] According to the historian Manuel Teixeira, Johor's ruler Alauddin Riayat Shah himself ventured to the Portuguese colony of Melaka in order to attend the signing ceremony, but Raja Bongsu was, in any case, conspicuously absent.

At a formal level, the bureaucracy of the *Estado da Índia* ensured further delays in the full ratification of the Luso-Johor peace. According to the period testimony of Dutch Admiral Steven van der Hagen, the Portuguese Viceroy in Goa, Rui Lourenço de Távora, objected to the wording of specific clauses, and delayed the full ratification and implementation of the Treaty until the objectionable passages had been either altered or deleted.[71] It is uncertain whether this was ever accomplished, especially since no copy of the 1610 Luso-Johor Treaty appears to survive, a problem that António Saldanha has also noted.[72]

How the peace deal of October 1610 was eventually handled in the notorious red tape of the *Estado da Índia's* Goa-based administration is admittedly of little concern to the main thrust and argument of this exposé. Far more important to the present focus were the events that immediately began to unfold. According to a letter by Obelaer dated 25 November 1610, Raja Bongsu paid a visit late at night at the premises of the Dutch factory in Batu Sawar.[73] This letter probably yields the strongest testimony yet that the Raja had been marginalised and virtually forced to give his nod to the peace with Portuguese Melaka.[74] Not surprisingly, Raja Siak and his supporters are named as the instigators. But Raja Bongsu's problems ran deeper than the political manoeuvres at the Johor court. He evidently caved in to a deal for another reason

70 De Jonge, *Opkomst*, vol.3, 304, letter by Obelaer of 25 November 1610.

71 Tiele and Heeres, *Bouwstoffen*, vol. 1, 129, letter by Admiral Steven van der Hagen to the Heren XVII, 10 March 1616.

72 A. Vasconcelos de Saldanha, *Iustum Imperium, dos tratados como fundamento do império dos portugueses no Oriente* (Lisbon, 1997), 371, note 10.

73 De Jonge, *Opkomst*, vol. 3, 306.

74 De Jonge, *Opkomst*, vol. 3, 305, quotes Raja Bongsu as having claimed that he was driven by 'poverty', that is 'necessity', into signing the agreement with the Portuguese. This could be an indirect reference to the crippling blockade imposed on the Johor River and the upstream towns in 1609. See also Netscher, *De Nederlanders*, 27–28.

mentioned in Obelaer's written communication: there was a real danger of an imminent popular uprising in Johor, but it is not exactly clear what the people were rising up against. There was certainly a lot of pent-up frustration with the dire economic state brought on the upstream towns by the latest riverine blockade. It appears that many at the time identified Raja Bongsu's anti-Portuguese, pro-Dutch stance as the principal source of Johor's economic plight.

Johor had been successfully tugged into the greater sphere of Portuguese mercantile, political and hegemonic interests. The battleground was not the Johor River, but the royal court itself. With his authority broken at the court, Raja Bongsu must have been deeply 'saddened' to see the rapid changes taking place after October 1610.[75] The inhabitants of Batu Sawar who had been starved of supplies by the periodic riverine blockades – and especially the blockade of 1609 – were almost overnight strutting around in the latest Luso-Indian fashion. Once the deal with Melaka had been sealed – with or without the Portuguese viceroy's objections – the merchants of Melaka quickly descended on the riverine towns to sell their wares, mainly cloth pieces, finished clothing, and also dried or preserved food. To the average man on the street the abundant wares and food provisions in the riverine towns of Johor amounted to those tangible benefits the pro-Portuguese faction had so deeply desired from the forging of peace with Melaka. These material benefits defused the heightened threat of a popular uprising. The fall of Raja Bongsu and his pro-Dutch faction at the court was now complete.

Acehnese Intervention (1613)

No account of this important period in the history of the Johor Kingdom would be complete without making two additional observations about the Luso-Johor peace of October 1610 and its medium-term aftermath.

First, it is important to step back and assess the nature of Luso-Johor and Johor-Dutch relations from a longer-term perspective. Prior to the arrival of the Dutch in Johorean waters in the final weeks of 1602 or the beginning of 1603, relations with the Portuguese were very fluid, an oscillating on-again

75 David Bassett does not see Raja Bongsu as having been abandoned by the Dutch, but argues that he felt inadequately supported. His comment makes little sense against the backdrop of the Twelve Years Truce and its provisions. See D.K. Bassett, 'European Influence in the Malay Peninsula, 1511–1786', *Journal of the Malayan Branch of the Royal Asiatic Society*, 33.3 (1960) 16, '...the sultan of Johore felt himself to be so inadequately supported by the Dutch Company that he made peace with the Portuguese in October 1610'.

off-again situation that was not exactly uncommon in the Southeast Asian world of politics. Luso-Johor relations remained in a state of flux, and this despite the severe political, economic and demographic shocks suffered as a result of the Acehnese invasions of 1613 and 1615, as well as despite the subsequent reversal of fortunes for Raja Siak and his Lusophile faction in the wake of the 1613 Acehnese invasion.

The second concerns the political comeback of Raja Bongsu. By the close of 1610, his position among the high-ranking courtiers had been severely weakened. The unexpected turn in Raja Bongsu's fortunes took place against the backdrop of the Acehnese invasion in 1613, in the course of which the upstream towns, including Batu Sawar and also Singapura, were burnt to the ground. The royal residence was garrisoned by Acehnese troops and members of the court were brought to Aceh.[76] There are mixed reports about the fate of King Alauddin. Some claim he had been brought to Aceh as well, but a far more credible story had him flee to the Riau island of Bintan where he passed away around 1615.[77] Meanwhile, Raja Bongsu, who had been brought to Aceh in June 1613 with other leading members of the Johor court, was married off to an Acehnese princess and returned to Johor in September or October 1613 where he ruled as Abdullah Hammayat Shah until his death around 1623.[78]

Once returned to Johor as the new monarch the former Raja Bongsu sought almost immediately to mend fences with the VOC. A lot had changed with regards to the Twelve Years Truce, and by that point in time it was pretty much a dead letter in the Asian theatre. But important changes had also taken place in the regional balance of power. Melaka – and the *Estado da Índia* at large – were from the perspective of the new Johor ruler no longer the principal threat. The power to watch was now Aceh which had expanded rapidly and aggressively on the great island of Sumatra as well as on the Malay Peninsula during the late 16th and at the beginning of the 17th centuries. King Abdullah tested the willingness of the VOC to revive their alliance with Johor in the wake of the major setback brought on by the pro-Portuguese faction and the subsequent devastation caused by Aceh. The Johor ruler simply restarted the conversation with the Dutch where they had effectively ended at their last meeting with Admiral Verhoeff in 1609.[79] The Dutch company dispatched Jan Gommerszoon Cocq and Adriaen van der Dusschen to treat with King Abdullah

76 See also D. Lombard, *Le Sultanat d'Atjéh*, 92, and Rouffaer, 'Was Malaka', 449, esp. note 1.

77 Gibson-Hill, 'The Alleged', 128.

78 Gibson-Hill, 'The Alleged', 134.

79 Tiele and Heeres, *Bouwstoffen*, vol. 1, 68, letter by Jan Pieterszoon Coen to the Heren XVII, 10 November 1614.

and also select a site for the proposed fortification. Jan Gommersz passed away shortly after arriving at Batu Sawar, leaving Adriaen van der Dusschen to conduct the negotiations for the VOC on his own. After inspecting several sites along the banks of the Johor River and also along the northern coast of Bintan, he settled for the northeastern tip of Karimun Besar (Great Carimon).[80] It was in many ways an ideal strategic location from where it would be possible to monitor shipping between Java, Makassar, the Maluku and Banda Islands, and to Timor, as well as to and from all ports east of the Malay Peninsula through the Singapore Straits.

As late as January 1611, the VOC administration was seriously toying with the idea of establishing a permanent Asian base in or around Johor. In the light of unfolding events, however, especially the fall of the pro-Dutch faction in Batu Sawar, the proposed scheme of transferring the VOC administration to Johor was quickly abandoned. Johor's political instability had been exacerbated by news of the Twelve Years Truce, the on-again off-again relations with Portuguese Melaka, and the Acehnese invasion of 1613. These developments ensured that the construction of the Dutch fortress on Johor soil would never materialise.

Ms. Raffles 18 and the Revision of the Sejarah Melayu (Malay Annals) in 1612

It was during this interlude between the fall or marginalisation of Raja Bongsu's pro-Dutch faction (end of 1610 or latest by early 1611) and the Acehnese invasion in May 1613 – a period in other words of just over two years – that the text of the *Sejarah Melayu* recorded in Ms. Raffles 18 was supposedly commissioned and/or completed.[81] It is not the objective of the present chapter to delve into the detailed historical background to, or the literary qualities of, the *Sejarah Melayu*. What this chapter can contribute, however, is to provide a synopsis of the developments at the Johor court and the region of the Straits and the

80 Tiele and Heeres, *Bouwstoffen*, vol. 1, 70–79.

81 Brown, *Sějarah Mělayu*, xxv–xxvi; R. Winstedt., 'The Date, Author and Identity of the Original Draft of the Malay Annals', in *Sejarah Melayu. The Malay Annals. Raffles ms. 18* (new Romanised edition, compiled by B.K. Cheah, Kuala Lumpur, 1998), 47–56 and esp. 47–48. Rouffaer suggests that the *Sejarah Melayu* was most probably commissioned on the occasion of a *majilis* (*kroonraad* in Dutch), held every 6 years on the Prophet Mohammad's birthday, that is on 13 May 1612. This would place the commissioning of the work, rather than its completion, in 1612. See Rouffaer, 'Was Malaka', 446, 450.

Peninsula at large against which the genesis and revision of this important work of Malay literature and history can be placed. In keeping with this agenda, I wish to highlight a number of connections that can be drawn from the commissioning and revision of the *Sejarah Melayu* in or around 1612, and the wider political and diplomatic developments discussed in this chapter.

Text-critical analysis conducted during the past century on the *Sejarah Melayu*, such as notably by Brown, Shellabaer and Winstedt, have added considerably to our present-day understanding of the work, its structure and evolution from a Malay kinglist into a more comprehensive story or narrative.[82] Crucial for the revision of an earlier core into the text of Ms. Raffles 18 in or around 1612 was a 'hikayat Melayu yang dibawa orang dari Goa' or translated liberally a 'Malay hikayat [story, or liberally, history] brought [by someone] from Goa'.[83] Two observations are worth making in the present context. The first concerns the name 'Goa'. In the early to mid-20th century, a number of prominent authors on Malay history and literature, such as notably Rouffaer and Gibson-Hill, took the name Goa as a reference to the capital of Portuguese India. By contrast, Winstedt contended that the name 'Goa' does not in fact refer to the seat of the Portuguese viceroy in India, but to another town (Gowa) situated in Bugis-controlled region of Sulawesi (Celebes). In a similar vein, Linehan saw 'Goa' as a corruption of 'Guo', but treated this as a reference to a town in Pahang. Although the interpretations of Winstedt and Linehan amount to little more than guesswork, their positions are readily and often uncritically embraced among authors of Malay language and history today. The name 'Goa' may very well refer to the capital of Portuguese India. With a view cast on the broader developments staked out in this essay, two reasons stand out for revisiting this older, now clearly unfashionable interpretation: one, there can be no doubt that the Portuguese were in possession of certain Malay texts or in the case of Tomé Pires, Affonso d'Albuquerque, João de Barros, Diogo do Couto,

82 See also Hj.M. Khalid-Taib, *Sastera Sejarah in the Malay World: A Structural and Contextual Study of Folkloristic Elements in a Transitional Genre* (Unpublished Ph.D. Thesis, Indiana University, 1981), 126, 'It has now been generally agreed among the Malay Studies scholars that the *Sejarah Melayu's* prototype was a kinglist. This kinglist was a very sketchy compilation which emphasised the genealogical relationships of the Malacca royal dynasty'.

83 Brown, *Sĕjarah Mĕlayu*, xxiv; C.-A. Gibson-Hill, 'The History Brought from Goa', *Journal of the Malayan Branch of the Royal Asiatic Society*, 29.1 (1956) 185–188. Rouffaer, 'Was Malaka', 467. In some surviving manuscripts of the *Sejarah Melayu*, the name of the person who brought the 'history from Goa' is indicated as one 'orang kaya Sogoh'. See R.O. Winstedt, 'The Preface of the Malay Annals', in *Sejarah Melayu*, 57–73.

and Manoel Godinho de Erédia, of certain recorded oral traditions.[84] The Portuguese chroniclers, especially Barros and Do Couto, incorporated passages from these Malay narratives into their important *Décadas da Ásia* which were published successively after 1552. Two, as has been evidenced by this essay, Johor and Portugal were at peace in 1612. When negotiating for the Luso-Johor peace agreement of October 1610, Portuguese Melaka was sure to select and dispatch a senior, experienced hand who not only had a sound command of the Malay language, but is also described in period sources as an old friend of the late Raja Ali Jalla. Is it not very well conceivable that, among the gifts passed to the courtiers, João Lopes de Morero presented a copy of a Malay manuscript? Would this not have been a means not only of deepening formal and personal ties, but also of impressing on the Portuguese envoy's Malay hosts: 'We know all about you[r past] and understand you?'[85] Could the date of this presentation – October 1610 – also have been of any significance? Was it a coincidence that the presentation of the text would have taken place near the 100th anniversary of the fall of the Melaka Sultanate to the Portuguese?

The second observation concerns the text brought from 'Goa' and used for the revision of the *Sejarah Melayu*. If we accept that the 'hikayat from Goa'

84 The most authoritative text of Pires is the critical Portuguese language edition published in 1978. See *A Suma Oriental de Tomé Pires e o Livro de Francisco Rodrigues* (ed. A. Cortesão, Coimbra, 1978) and separately the text of the Lisbon manuscript in R.M. Loureiro, *O Manuscrito de Lisboa da 'Suma Oriental' de Tomé Pires (Contribuição para uma Edição Crítica)* (Macao, 1996). See also T. Pires, *Suma Oriental* (ed. and transl. A. Cortesão, London, 1944, 2 vols.) and G.B. Ramusio, *Delle navigationi et viaggi in molti luoghi corretta, et ampliata nelle quale si contengono da descrittione dell'Africa, & del paese del Prete Ianni, con varij viaggi,...*(Venice, 1554); M. Godinho de Erédia, *Malaca L'Inde Méridionale e le Cathay: Manuscrit original autographe de Godinho de Eredia appartenant à la Bibliothèque Royale de Bruxelles* (ed. and transl. M. Léon Janssen, Brussels, 1882); A.L. Caminha, *Ordenações da Índia do Senhor Rei D. Manoel*, etc. (Lisbon, 1807) [This source contains the original Portuguese language edition of Erédia's *Informação da Aurea Chersoneso, ou Peninsula, e das Ilhas Auríferas, Carbunculas e Aromaticas*]; B. de Albuquerque, *The Commentaries of the Great A. Dalboquerque, Second Viceroy of India* (transl. W. de Gray Birch, London, 1875–95, 4 vols.); J. de Barros and D. do Couto, *Da Ásia, Dos feitos que os Portuguezes fizeram no conquista, e descubrimento das terras e mares do oriente* (Lisbon, 1778, 23 vols.).

85 C.-A. Gibson-Hill, 'The History Brought from Goa', *Journal of the Malayan Branch of the Royal Asiatic Society*, 29.1 (1956) 185, especially note 4, 'according to Rouffaer, the mission of 1611/12 which returned the Annals was headed by an envoy named de Amoreira. MacGregor is searching for Portuguese sources for further details of the presents carried by the mission to Johore'. The reference to Rouffaer is almost certainly his article 'Was Malaka', 469.

does not refer to a manuscript brought from Gowa on Sulawesi, or Guo in Pahang, but to a manuscript given by the Portuguese to the court as an official gift in October 1610, then the question invariably arising is this: What manuscript might that have been, and do any copies survive today? As a means of fuelling a fresh debate on this matter, it is worth repeating the deliberations of Rouffaer on this very issue.[86] After identifying four Malay manuscripts that were all modelled on Persian (or Moghul) originals and were likely used during the revision of the *Sejarah Melayu*,[87] Rouffaer narrows down the list of possibilities and singles out the *Hikayat Koris* as the likely text from 'Goa'. Citing from the introduction (page viii) to Wilkinson's Malay-English Dictionary of 1903, Rouffaer underscores:[88]

> The *Hikayat Koris*, which is exceptional in that it contains many local references, clearly belongs to the period of the Portuguese rule in Melaka.... It was probably written in the Peninsula as it contains descriptions of the Semang and Pangan aborigines,...and it shows a friendly spirit to Europeans, rare thing in those days. The Dutch are not mentioned.... The *Hikayat Indera Mengindera* approaches the *Hikayat Koris* so closely in point of style as to suggest the same authorship or at least the same school of authorship.

If Rouffaer's deliberations can be deemed correct, then the *Sejarah Melayu* was revised on the basis not of a single major manuscript, but by using three different *Hikayats* (which are also mentioned in the *Sejarah Melayu*) that were based on a Persian or Moghul model. These included the *Hikayat Koris* which had brought by the Portuguese from 'Goa'; and an unnamed family *Hikayat* plotting the 'family tradition' of Si-Guntang, Palembang, Singapura and Melaka.[89]

If commentators disagree over the text from 'Goa' as well as the range and number of sources underlying the revised text, there is a clear consensus that the revisions were undertaken by the Bendahara Paduka Raja (Tun Sri Lanang), and that the project was evidently the brain child of Raja Bongsu. Given the immediate historical backdrop of the Raja's shifting fortunes among Johor's

86 Rouffaer, 'Was Malaka', 464 ff.

87 The three texts identified by Rouffaer are the *Hikayat Iskandar, Hikayat Sajidina Hamzah, Hikayat Huhammad Hanifijah,* and the *Taju as-Salatin*. See Rouffaer, 'Was Malaka', 464, 465, 467.

88 Rouffaer, 'Was Malaka', 468.

89 Ibid., 468–470.

high-ranking courtiers, as well as his vision of a New Melaka, the motives for revising the *Sejarah Melayu* in or around 1612–15 become clearer. The project can be placed within the more immediate context of the deepening divisions among Raja Bongsu's siblings and their respective followers; the Raja's 'fall' or 'marginalisation' in the wake of the Luso-Johor peace deal, as well as the Acehnese attack on Johor in 1613.[90] The work also serves as a reflection of Raja Bongsu's vision to reclaim the Melaka legacy for himself, which he had already expressed well before the events that brought him down after October 1610.

Conclusions

What was the role and significance of the Twelve Years Truce in the Asian theatre? To answer this question we can look at the impact of the Truce from two different vantage points, namely the bigger picture in Asia, as well as specifically with reference to and within the context of Johor.

As an agreement to silencing the arms between the VOC (as the Dutch Republic's proxy in Asia) and the Iberian crowns of Spain and Portugal, the truce was a failure. There was no willingness among the politicians, diplomats and VOC directors in Europe to make it work. Plundering the Iberian enemy helped the bottom line of the VOC in the first years of its corporate lifespan. On the ground – that is in the VOC factories and outposts across Asia – the truce was greeted with a mixture of excitement, confusion and consternation. When news of the memorial of 11 April 1608, arrived in Asia in February 1609, the VOC agents on the ground scrambled to grab and consolidate their position. They did this by signing treaties with Asian rulers and also by stepping up attacks on Iberian targets across Southeast Asia. As a trigger for devising and executing new forward strategies in Asia, the memorial of April 1608 proved to be of greater significance to the servants of the VOC on the ground in Asia than the actual Treaty of Antwerp (April 1609). It was not the (attempted) silencing of arms that rendered the 1608 memorial so important, but rather the proposed opening of all markets across Asia to the Dutch where the Iberian powers exerted no direct or indirect control. This provision would have marked a clear break from earlier Spanish and Portuguese policies aimed at creating an exclusive trading preserve for the Iberian powers by forcefully impeding, obstructing and excluding their European competitors. By contrast – and this is an important point to bear in mind – Asian princes and traders had until

90 Aceh finally brought Johor's ally Aru into complete submission by 1612. See also note 20.

then not been singled out as a principal target of Iberian policies of obstruction or exclusion. This, however, was to change over the next few years.

The Twelve Years Truce left its most lasting mark on the VOC's treaty partners across Asia, but specifically among allied rulers in what this chapter has identified as front-line polities. The Kingdom of Johor stands out as a fairly well-documented case. In this study attention has been focused on how news of the truce immediately impacted developments on the ground at Johor's court. The Portuguese were quick to exploit existing divisions at the court to bring this strategically located and commercially important polity out of the Dutch and into their sphere of influence. The Portuguese in Melaka allied with friendly factions in Johor to hammer out a peace agreement and engineer the downfall of Raja Bongsu and his pro-Dutch supporters. The pro-Portuguese faction subsequently held sway until the Acehnese invasion of Johor in May and June 1613. Importantly also, the present chapter yields the immediate political and historical context for the revision of the *Sejarah Melayu* in or around 1612. But important questions continue to linger: How does this new context change our interpretation of the authorial intentions behind that Malay text? To what extent, if at all, does the *Sejarah Melayu* mirror politics, factions and divisions prevailing at the royal court in the period 1603–13 at large? The debate continues.

CHAPTER 6

The Tactical Military Revolution and Dutch Army Operations during the Era of the Twelve Years Truce (1592–1618)

Olaf van Nimwegen

Introduction

In the summer of 1610, the States General of the Dutch Republic ordered an army of 136 infantry companies and 36 cavalry companies,[1] amounting to some 10,000 to 11,000 effective fighting men,[2] to the Holy Roman Empire to besiege the town of Jülich occupied by Imperial-Habsburg troops a few months after the death (March 1609) of the last Duke of Jülich, John William. From the start Maurice, Count of Nassau and Commander-in-Chief of the Dutch army[3] since 1590, made use of this opportunity to display to the world Dutch military might. Besides being accompanied by a powerful siege train of fifteen guns, Maurice moved ostentatiously along the River Rhine toward the Spanish held fortress of Rheinberg. Near Xanten, the Dutch force was drawn up in battle-array, and, fitting to the close proximity of *castra Vetera*, the ancient Roman army camp, Maurice aligned the infantry battalions and cavalry squadrons in three successive lines following the chessboard pattern of the Roman legions. Perhaps even more impressive to contemporaries was the novel way in which the foot-soldiers were organised. Traditionally, they fought in bodies composed

1 Simon Stevin, *Castrametatio, dat is legermeting* (Rotterdam, 1617), 16–19, facsimile edn. in W.H. Schukking (ed.) *The principal works of Simon Stevin*, vol. 4, 'The art of war' (Amsterdam, 1964). The 'Ordre de bataille' for the 1610 campaign mentioned by F.J.G. ten Raa and F. de Bas, *Het Staatsche leger, 1568–1795* (Breda, 1911–21), vol. 3, 14–15, tallies well-nigh with Stevin's list.

2 On paper this army numbered more than 15,000 men, but due to fighting, illness, desertion and fraud the real or effective strength of Dutch companies was always a third to a quarter less than prescribed. See Olaf van Nimwegen, *'Deser landen crijchsvolck'. Het Staatse leger en de militaire revoluties (1588–1688)* (Amsterdam, 2006), 52–54. An English translation by Andrew May of this study is forthcoming.

3 Throughout this paper the army of the States General of the Republic of the United Netherlands will be called the Dutch army, notwithstanding it was composed of many 'nations': Dutch, German, Walloon, French, English, Scots, Swiss. All European armies of the Early Modern Age were recruited on an international military labour market. The Spanish army consisted of Spaniards, Italians, Walloons, Burgundians, Germans, Irish, and English.

 | DOI 10.1163/9789004274921_008

of a core of pikemen with on either side a 'sleeve' of soldiers with firearms. In 1610, the Dutch no longer followed this practice. They had separated the pike from the shot. In this way the soldiers with firearms could form a continuous firing-line resulting in volley fire dominating the battlefield rather than the push of pike.[4]

The main purpose of Maurice's demonstration of Dutch military power was to impress upon the Spanish General Ambrogio Spinola (1569–1630) that, notwithstanding the conclusion of the Twelve Years Truce in 1609, the army of the States General was ready to continue the fight. In fact, Maurice hoped that Spinola would take up the challenge, because he believed that a long suspension of hostilities would only benefit Spain. In 1605 and 1606, Spinola had made territorial gains in the eastern provinces of Gelderland and Overijssel, providing him with a basis for continuing his assault on the Republic. In view of this, Maurice was of the opinion that a truce would lull the Dutch regents into a false feeling of security, lessening their resolve to maintain a strong army. However, the Archdukes in Brussels had no intention of endangering the truce. For the time being Albert (1559–1621) and his wife Isabella (1566–1633), joint sovereigns of the Spanish Netherlands, considered the Jülich-crisis an Imperial affair; the ships with the Dutch siege artillery and ammunition sailed past Rheinberg without meeting any difficulty from the Spanish governor. In 1614, the Archdukes changed their stance, but they instructed Spinola not to engage Maurice. Since suffering defeat at the Battle of Nieuwpoort (1600), Brussels would not permit its generals to fight another pitched battle with the Dutch. In the 1570s and 1580s, the Spaniards had confidently faced the Dutch rebels wherever they encountered them, and with good reason: of the nine battles waged in these years, the Spaniards had won eight (see Appendix I).[5] Nieuwpoort was the turning-point. The discipline, training and tactical skill of the Dutch troops became the benchmark for Europe's armies. To understand this remarkable reversal it is necessary to study the theoretical framework of the Dutch military innovations and their subsequent practical implementation. Rome's military legacy had inspired military thinkers for centuries, but the credit for turning the military teachings of the Ancient Greeks and Romans into tools relevant for early modern warfare is traditionally, and deservedly so,

4 Royal Archives The Hague (KHA) Archief van Frederik Hendrik A14-IX-2, 'Première forme d'ordre de battaille dressée l'an 1610 en marchant depuis Vorstenborch [Fürstenberg]'; National Library The Hague (KB) special collections (BC) Ms. Simon Stevin 128-A-19, 'Tweede slachoirden alsoo se daernae verstelt wiert in 't marcheren van Voorstenberch naer de stadt Gulik op den 22en augustus in 't jaer 1610'.

5 The only battle the rebels won was Heiligerlee in 1568.

given to the three Nassau cousins William Louis, the already-mentioned Maurice and Count John (VII) of Nassau-Siegen.[6] William Louis (1560–1620), Stadholder of Friesland, Groningen and Drenthe – the three north-eastern provinces of the Dutch Republic – was second-in-command of the Dutch army. His younger brother John VII (1561–1623) was an astute student of ancient military training and tactics and its adaptation to armies and warfare in his own time. The tactical revolution of the Nassau's was all but completed in 1609 and 1610. However, the States General in The Hague wished no more than the central government in Brussels to decide the Jülich Succession War by forcing a decisive battle. The political and military reasons for this decision will be addressed in the second part of this chapter.

The Dutch Army and the Tactical Military Revolution (1592–1618)

In the 1580s, the Dutch Revolt was at its nadir. In 1579 Alexander Farnese, the Duke of Parma and the newly appointed Governor General of the Netherlands, had started a counter-offensive that seemed unstoppable. He rounded off the recapture of the southern provinces with the siege of Antwerp in 1585. In the northern Netherlands, Spanish troops had in the meantime lodged themselves in the strongholds of Groningen, Delfzijl, Oldenzaal, Steenwijk, Coevorden, Zutphen and Nijmegen, and to cap it all on 10 July 1584 William of Orange, the Dutch rebel leader, was assassinated. In 1586, the areas under full rebel control were reduced to a mere four provinces: Holland, Zeeland, Utrecht and Friesland. The undisciplined and underpaid Dutch troops were on the verge of mutiny. But even if they were willing to fight, they were no match for the army of Philip II. Discipline and training made the difference between triumph and defeat on the battlefield. Spain's crack infantry regiments – the *tercios* and the German Landsknechts – were deemed by contemporaries to be all but unbeatable. Dutch troops lacked the *esprit de corps* of their adversaries. But that was not all. They also lacked the proper weapons for fighting in the open field. To be able to face attacking infantry or cavalry without cover a sufficient number of pikes was needed. The pikemen – soldiers armed with an ash pole fitted with an iron point with a total length of eighteen feet (c. 5½ metres) – formed a living palisade behind which the musketeers and calivermen could find

6 Olaf van Nimwegen, 'The army of the Dutch Republic and the military revolutions', in Louis Ph. Sloos (ed.), *Warfare and the Age of Printing. Catalogue of early printed books from before 1801 in Dutch military collections with analytical bibliographic descriptions of 10,000 works* (Leyden/Boston, 2008), vol. 1, 84–109 at 85–86.

refuge when threatened by a cavalry charge or infantry assault. Muskets and calivers, smoothbore firearms with a calibre of 20 mm and 17.4 mm respectively and an effective range of approximately 75 paces of two-and-a-half feet (c. 55 metres), required an average loading time of one minute between shots. In damp or rainy weather, they were sensitive to misfires because they were fitted with a matchlock firing mechanism. On pulling the trigger a cock holding a smouldering slow-match was forced down into a pan filled with fine priming powder. The lightly armoured musketeers and calivermen had no hope of survival in hand to hand combat with swordsmen, halberdiers or horsemen. Bayonets that could be fitted onto the muzzle of the musket without impeding loading and firing would not be invented until the end of the 17th century.[7] In German regiments, approximately half of the soldiers were therefore armed with polearms and swords,[8] and in Spanish units this could be as high as seventy percent.[9] In contrast, the Dutch rebel infantry of the 1570s and early 1580s numbered just twenty to twenty-five percent pikemen,[10] halberdiers and swordsmen; approximately 70 percent of each company being armed with calivers (see Appendix II). Consequently the Dutch troops were far inferior in fighting strength to the Spaniards. The rebellious provinces were spared further defeats by Parma only because Philip II ordered his victorious general to shift his attention to England and France. In 1588, Parma had to keep his main army in readiness at the Flemish seaports in order to set sail for England as soon as the 'Invincible Armada' arrived from Spain, and after this plan had failed, Philip II ordered him in 1590 to intervene in France to prevent the Huguenot Henri de Bourbon (Henry IV) from acquiring the French throne which had become vacant on 1 August 1589 when King Henry III was murdered.[11]

7 Van Nimwegen, *Deser landen crijchsvolck*, 86–87 and 336.

8 Eugen von Frauenholz, *Das Heerwesen in der Zeit des freien Söldnertums*, vol. 2, 'Das Heerwesen des Reiches in der Landsknechtszeit' (Munich, 1937), 298–299, appendix XXVI 'Der deutschen knecht articuln' (1570).

9 Geoffrey Parker, *The Army of Flanders and the Spanish Road 1567–1659. The logistics of Spanish victory and defeat in the Low Countries' Wars* (2nd edn., Cambridge, 1990), 276.

10 The Dutch General Philips Count of Hohenlohe-Langenburg (1550–1606) complained in July 1582 that it was difficult to find pikemen in the Netherlands 'because those of these lands much rather set out to carry a caliver than [put on] a pikeman's armour'. Gelders Archief, Archief Huizen Waardenburg en Neerijnen (AHWN) 743, Letter to Bernhard of Merode, lord of Rummen, Lieutenant-Stadholder of Friesland, Hemert 17 July 1582.

11 Geoffrey Parker, *The Dutch Revolt* (2nd edn., London, 1990), 219 and 225–227.

Spain's French imbroglio prompted William Louis to urge the States General to mount a limited counter-offensive.[12] According to ancient wisdom those 'who want to gain honour with soldiers, must pay well and punish immediately'.[13] The first condition was met by the introduction of the 'repartitiestelsel' in 1588. This system allotted a portion of the payment of the Dutch troops to each of the member provinces organised in the Union of Utrecht (1579) according to their financial wherewithal.[14] Well paid soldiers were not however synonymous with skilled ones. William Louis and his cousin Maurice agreed with the notion dating from Classical Antiquity that wars were not won by the largest army but by the one whose discipline and training was superior. In the 1590s, Maurice and William Louis started a series of reforms that resulted in a tactical military revolution. Their new, more scientific approach to the art of war marked by study of Greek and Roman military treatises, theoretical discussions on the practical use of ancient tactics for contemporary warfare, subsequent experiments with a diversity of tactical formations using 'tin soldiers', and eventually in exercises with actual soldiers, established the basis for the systematic exercising and drilling of troops. This was a prerequisite for challenging the Spanish army in the open field. The ambitions of Maurice and William Louis did not end here. It was not just that they wanted to make Dutch soldiers the equals of their adversaries; they aimed at surpassing the enemy in fighting-power. They hoped to achieve this through optimising the use of firearms on the battlefield.

The Theoretical Framework of the Tactical Revolution

Central to the tactical military revolution was the development of sustainable volley fire, i.e. the simultaneous firing of shots by whole ranks of soldiers. Because of the low rate of fire, and the limited effective range of each shot, musketeers and calivermen would only be able to participate in battles on an equal footing with the pikemen if they could defeat an enemy at a distance. This required that they attacked their adversary with a hail of shots and that

---

12 Everhart van Reyd, *Oorspronck ende voortganck van de Nederlantsche oorloghen* (2nd edn., Arnhem, 1633), 284; E.H. Waterbolk, 'Van grafrede naar biografie' in Ubbo Emmius, *Willem Lodewijk, graaf van Nassau (1560–1620). Stadhouder van Friesland, Groningen en Drenthe* (1621) translated from the original Latin text by P. Schoonbeeg (Hilversum, 1994), 9–27 at 23.

13 KB, BC, 1702 C 60, *Der bussen meesterije*, (Amsterdam, 1588), 28.

14 Van Nimwegen, *Deser landen crijchsvolck*, 70–71.

each subsequent volley followed after no more than a short interval. Otherwise the opponents had the opportunity to regroup or throw themselves at the firing unit. Optimising the use of firearms had baffled military thinkers for the past hundred years. The Frenchman Fourquevaux (1508–1574) dismissed them as useless in open battle, because most soldiers were more interested in making noise (*faire bruit*) than in firing accurately.[15] This complaint was shared by the Dutch military author Adriaen Duyck (†1628) who in 1588 lamented that Dutch soldiers preferred firearms to pikes, since only a few cavalry would be needed to compel these marksmen 'to throw themselves as ducklings (*eendekuyckens*) into a moat'.[16]

William Louis was not deterred by the contempt in which his contemporaries held firearms. He acknowledged the technical imperfections of these weapons, but instead of resigning to the idea that soldiers with firearms could only play a subordinate role in combat, he devoted himself to finding a tactical solution that would overcome this problem. However, two preconditions had to be fulfilled to make the introduction of regular volley fire possible. First, the soldiers had to be armed, drilled and exercised in the same way, so that they could be deployed in identical tactical formations. Second, the troops had to be disciplined to perfection so that they could perform their complicated tactical manoeuvres under combat conditions and would face their enemies with perfect calm. William Louis's efforts were fully endorsed by Maurice. Both subscribed to the notions propounded by the philologist Justus Lipsius (1547–1606) on what made a good army.

Lipsius or Joost Lips was born near Leuven (Louvain), in the province of Brabant. Already in 1574, he established a scholarly reputation with the publication of a reliable edition of the works of the 1st-century Roman historian Tacit. In 1578, Lipsius accepted a professorship at the University of Leyden. In 1583–84, Maurice was one of his students. In these years, Parma's counteroffensive reached its high watermark. The impact of these military setbacks on Lipsius's state of mind is clearly visible in his book *De Constantia* published in 1584. In this philosophical treatise, Lipsius outlined his neo-stoic ideas which he had derived from the study of Roman stoicism (1st century). Stoics emphasised duty and constancy under adversity, two qualities that were also of great significance for soldiers. After all the greatest danger that could happen to an

15 KB, BC, 427 C 41, Raymond de Beccarie de Pavie, seigneur de Fourquevaux, *Instructions sur le faict de la guerre* or *La discipline militaire* (Paris, 1548), 11v. This publication is also available on the internet: gallica.bnf.fr.

16 KB, BC, 1702 C 60, Adriaen Duyck, *Instructie van de crijchs-oorts stellinghe* (Leiden, 1588), 101.

army on the battlefield was to be seized by panic. In 1586, Lipsius started working on a political and military manual based on his philosophical ideas. The *Politicorum sive civilis doctrinae libri sex*[17] published in 1589 was an immediate bestseller.[18] A Dutch translation appeared just one year later.[19] Book V on 'military providence' dealt directly with practical military matters. In this part of his work, Lipsius argued that the infantry was the most important part of an army as all writers from Classical Antiquity agreed.[20] Foot-soldiers could be used for occupying terrain and for the attack and defence of towns. Moreover the upkeep of infantry was much less expensive than that of cavalry. Lipsius warned his readers, however, that a large armed force would be worthless if the troops were not 'pious', i.e. disciplined and dutiful, besides being proficient in the use of their weapons. Nature provides only a few 'pious' men, Lipsius remarked, but good training provides us with many. Following the example of the Greeks and Romans, Lipsius was therefore an ardent advocate of exercising and drilling the troops on a daily basis, of mock combats, and of improving the stamina of the soldiers through manual labour, such as the digging of a ditch, throwing up of entrenchments and the carrying of weights.[21] In 1591, Lipsius left Leyden for the University of Leuven. There he wrote *De militia Romana* (1595), a commentary on Book 5 of Polybius's *Historiae* which deals with the organisation of the Roman army during the second Punic War (218–201 BC) between Rome and Carthage.

William Louis shared Lipsius's veneration for devotion to duty and discipline as it matched well with his Calvinist upbringing. Together the maintenance of strict discipline and moral education would have to transform the unruly mercenaries employed by the Dutch Republic into disciplined and loyal

---

17 Gerhard Oestreich, 'Justus Lipsius als Theoretiker des neuzeitlichen Machtsstaates', *Historische Zeitschrift*, 181 (1956) 31–78 at 58–59 and 'Der Römische Stoizismus und die oranische Heeresreform', Ibid., 176 (1953) 17–43 at 22 and 25–28; Jan Waszink, Introduction to his annotated English translation of Lipsius's *Politica. Six books of politics or political instruction* (Assen, 2004), 1–221 at 28–29.

18 Between 1589 and 1618 no less than 25 reprints of the Latin edition of the *Politica* were published, besides translations into Dutch and French. See Gerhard Oestreich, *Antiker Geist und moderner Staat bei Justus Lipsius (1547–1606). Der Neustoizismus als politische Bewegung* (doctoral thesis 1954, posthumous ed. Nicolette Mout, Göttingen, 1989), 191.

19 *Politica van Iustus Lipsius, dat is van de regeeringhe van landen ende steden in ses boecken begrepen* (transl. into Dutch Marten Everart, Franeker, 1590). Library Utrecht University, BC, 122 H 52.

20 Lipsius based his views predominantly on the writings of the Romans Tacitus, Vegetius and Frontinus and the Greeks Polybius en Xenophon.

21 *Politica van Iustus Lipsius*, 189–190 and 208.

professional soldiers.[22] That said, William Louis did not indiscriminately adopt the Greek and Roman military teachings. Although there were important similarities between 16th-century combat and Classical warfare – the armies were predominantly infantry based and the taking of towns was pivotal – there was also a fundamental difference: the Greeks and Romans did not have firearms and cannon. A critical approach of the classical military treatises was therefore necessary. William Louis was inspired above-all by the book on tactics by the Greek Aelian (late 1st century-early 2nd century) and the military manual compiled by Leo VI, called the philosopher, Emperor of the Byzantine Empire from 886 to 912. Both Aelian and Leo VI discussed matters of tactics and strategy that were relevant to 16th-century warfare, and no less important their ideas were readily accessible through 'modern' editions in Latin, French and Italian.[23] An inventory of Maurice's library shows that he owned four editions of these two works.[24]

In his *Tactica*, Aelian described the tactics of the Greek-Macedonian-Hellenistic tradition.[25] It was not an original work because Aelian mainly voiced the opinions of earlier authors and in particular those of Asclepiodotus the philosopher (1st century BC).[26] In Ancient Greece, military affairs were part of the study of philosophy and this explains the logical and systematic way with which the Greeks dealt with the matter of tactics. They had worked out the distribution of troops into units down to the lowest level of command, thereby ensuring that the command structure was crystal clear.

22 Oestreich, *Geist und Gestalt*, 328, idem, 'Der Römische Stoizismus', 37 and idem, 'Justus Lipsius', 59 and 61.

23 Werner Hahlweg, *Die Heeresreform der Oranier und die Antike. Studien zur Geschichte des Kriegswesens der Niederlande, Deutschlands, Frankreichs, Englands, Italiens, Spaniens und der Schweiz vom Jahre 1589 bis zum Dreißigjährigen Kriege* (Berlin, 1941), 47.

24 A.A. Wiekart, 'De bibliotheek van prins Maurits', in J.P. Puype and A.A. Wiekart (eds.), *Van Maurits naar Munster. Tactiek en triomf van het Staatse leger. Catalogue of objects in the exhibition of the same name at the Army Museum in Delft, and a reconstruction of the library of Maurice of Nassau* (1998), 17–52 at 31 and 43.

25 I used the following three editions of Aelian's *Tactica*: *The tacticks of Aelian* (transl. into English and annotation Captain John Bingham, London, 1616; facsimile edn, Amsterdam/New York, 1968), *Aelianus' Theorie der Taktik*, transl. into German and annotation H. Köchly and W. Rüstow, in *Griechische Kriegsschriftsteller*, vol. 2, 'Die Taktiker', 1st section (1855, facsimile edn., Osnabrück, 1969), 199–471, and Henry Augustus Viscount Dillon, *The tactics of Aelian, comprising the military system of the Grecians* (London, 1814).

26 Asclepiodotus, *Tactics* (1st century BC) translated and annotated by C.H. and W.A. Oldfather, in *Aeneas Tacticus, Asclepiodotus, Onasander* (London/Cambridge, Mass., reprint 1948), 227–340 at 236–237 (introduction); Hahlweg, *Heeresreform*, 41–42, 49, 51, 119, 122 and 125.

All movements the troops had to make together (e.g. facing about, turning to the left or right, the closing and opening of ranks and files) had their specific word of command. Aelian warned his readers that these had to be short and unambiguous to avoid confusion. 'For example, if I say "Face", some of those who hear this command may face to the right and others to the left, and this will produce no small confusion. As the word "face" is a general one I should not say "Face – right," when I want to turn to the right or the left, but "Right – face." Therefore I must prefix the special to the general [direction], so that all will do the same together'.[27] The Greek words of command were very appropriate for 16th-century warfare. William Louis and Maurice faced the same problems as ancient generals when moving large bodies of men on the battlefield. Besides Aelian's teachings on the words of command William Louis was fascinated by the Greek's treatment of the 'choreain' or Cretan countermarch.[28]

The greatest threat to a Greek and Macedonian phalanx (a pike unit with a depth of eight and sixteen ranks respectively) was an attack from the rear, because the most skilled soldiers were positioned in the front ranks. It was therefore of vital interest to be able to about-turn and then to march as quickly as possible to the rear, so that the best troops would again be facing the enemy. This was a complex manoeuvre that could easily throw the unit into disorder. To prevent this from happening the Greeks and Macedonians had developed the countermarch. It existed in three variants of which the Cretan or 'choreian' was according to William Louis the most suitable for warfare in his day because of the possibilities it offered for use with firearms. The 'choreian' countermarch derived its name from the movements that were performed by the chorus during Greek religious festivals and plays. The dancers moved rhythmically, organised in ranks and files and when they had reached the limits of the stage 'they retired one through the ranks of the other, exceeding not the bounds of the place', explains Captain John Bingham in his 1616 translation of Aelian's *Tactics*.[29]

27 Aelian, *Tactics*, (Bingham) 149–150 (ch. 52) (Köchly and Rüstow) 459–463 (ch. 40.1–4) and (Dillon) 158 (ch. LI); Asclepiodotus, *Tactics*, 331, 333 (ch. 12.11). I based the translation on Köchly and Dillon.

28 Hahlweg, *Heeresreform*, 77.

29 Aelian, *Tactics*, (Köchly and Rüstow) 393 and 399 (ch. 27.4 and 28.3); notes by John Bingham, 129 (quote) Köchly and Rüstow, 'Introduction', 1–101 at 8–10; Asclepiodotus, *Tactics*, 305, 307 (ch. 10.15); Xenophon, *Cyropaedia* (transl. Walter Miller, reprint, London, 2000–1) vol. 1, 303 and 305 (book 3. 3.70); KB, BC, Ms. Simon Stevin 128A-9I, notes on the countermarch, fo. 45.

Leo VI's military manual impressed William Louis with its clear treatment of all facets of warfare, and in particular those of drill and weapons training.[30] Leo VI was of the opinion that soldiers had to exercise on a daily basis, because idleness led to moral corruption. Before taking up their places within the unit, recruits first had to be instructed individually in the use of their weapons. Next they had to be taught the meaning of the words of command, so that they would perform their movements together. In imitation of the Greek General Xenophon (c. 430–354 BC), Leo VI advocated the staging of sham battles arming the soldiers with blunt pikes and ordering them to throw clods at each other. These exercises were especially important in peacetime to maintain fighting ability but also in wartime during the winter when armies lay dormant in numerous garrisons. Mock fights mentally prepared the troops for real battle so that they would not panic when they came face to face with the enemy.[31]

Maurice also studied ancient tactics and warfare but rather those of the Romans than of the Greeks. Partly this preference for the Roman army can be attributed to the influence of Lipsius but even more so to 'the more mathematical bias of Maurice, nourished by the ingenuity of Simon Stevin'.[32] Stevin (1548–1620), mathematician, fortifications engineer, and expert in logistics, was an important advisor to the commander-in-chief on military matters. Maurice was attracted by the matter-of-fact way with which the Romans approached warfare and their skill in fortifying army camps and besieging towns. Maurice was impressed by the lessons taught in the *Historiae* written by Polyb. In Book 6, he described in detail the Roman military system in the war with the Carthaginian General Hannibal (247–183 BC), and in Book 18 he thoroughly analysed the tactical shortcomings of the massive Macedonian phalanx when confronted by the flexible Roman legion. The Romans subdivided their legions in ten small units of 420 men each. These cohorts (battalions) consisted of three maniples, each with a depth of ten ranks. The maniples were aligned three lines deep in a chequer-wise pattern. The main advantage of this

30 I used the annotated German translation by J.W. von Bourscheid, *Kaisers Leo des Philosophen Strategie und Taktik. Aus dem in der kais. königl. Bibliothek befindlichen Orginal* (Vienna, 1777–81). KB, BC, 535 J 46. This book can also be found on the internet (google books) but unfortunately not all pages are properly scanned.

31 Leo VI, *Strategy and tactics*, vol. 2, 7th Institute, 283 and 287–295; Xenophon, *Cyropaedia*, vol. 1, 185, 187 and 189 (book 2.3.17–20).

32 E.H.Waterbolk, 'Willem Lodewijk als opvoeder' in *Omtrekkende bewegingen. Opstellen aangeboden aan de schrijver bij zijn tachtigste verjaardag* (Hilversum, 1995), 160–178 at 170 (quote) and 'Met Willem Lodewijk aan tafel 17-3-1560 – 13-7-1620' in *Verspreide opstellen aangeboden aan de schijver bij zijn aftreden als hoogleraar aan de Rijksuniversiteit te Groningen* (Amsterdam, 1981), 296–315 at 303–304, 310 and 315.

deployment was that the troops in the front line could be relieved or reinforced by the units disposed further to the rear without this leading to disorder. Polyb pointed out that the attack of the phalanx could only come to fruition on a battlefield that was level and open. The Romans on the other hand could fight anywhere because they could easily adjust their battle order to fit the terrain.[33] Maurice saw clearly the relevance of the analysis offered by Polyb for the tactical problems faced by the Dutch in their fight against the Spanish army.

The Tactical Military Revolution: From Theory to Practice (1592–1618)

The moment at which Maurice and William Louis started to implement their tactical reforms can be dated to July 1592. At first, they focused on drilling and exercising, and on improving the distribution of weaponry in each company. Training and disciplining soldiers to perfection together with increasing the numbers of pikemen and musketeers per unit was a precondition for all further reforms. The additional pikes were needed to enable the Dutch army to face the enemy in the open field and the replacement of calivers by muskets would increase firepower. Musket balls weighing 41 grams could penetrate any body armour something which the much lighter caliver shot of just 20.5 grams could not. As mentioned earlier in the 1570s and early 1580s, Dutch infantry companies were predominately armed with calivers. Maurice and William Louis doubled the number of pikemen in each company, tripled those of the musketeers and reduced the calivermen by almost half as is clearly shown by the composition of William Louis's Frisian regiment. This regiment served as a model for the rest of the Dutch army.

The new standards of military proficiency to which the Nassau cousins aspired were high indeed. In the summer of 1592, they used every opportunity to drill the infantry serving in the field in 'turning, wheeling, retreating and advancing the battalions without breaking formation'.[34] This entry in the

33 Polyb, *Historiae*, 6.19.42, 18.28-32 (transl.W.R. Paton, London/New York, 1923–26), vol. 3, 311–367 and vol. 5, 145–159; Stevin, *Castrametatio*, 47; Werner Hahlweg (ed.), *Die Heeresreform der Oranier. Das Kriegsbuch des Grafen Johann von Nassau-Siegen* (Wiesbaden, 1973), 32–33. See also Marcus Junkelmann, *Die Legionen des Augustus. Der römische Soldat im arcäologischen Experiment* (9th edn.; Mainz, 2003), 213 and 241–245.

34 *Journaal van Anthonis Duyck, advokaat-fiscaal bij den Raad van State (1591–1597, 1600–1602)* (transcription and annotation Lodewijk Mulder (The Hague/Arnhem, 1862–66), vol. 2, 104.

TABLE 1 *Composition of the Frisian regiment for the 1587, 1592, 1594, 1595 and 1601 campaigns (rank and file)*

Date	Pike	Musket	Caliver	Halberd	Broadsword	Total (100%)
23 Sep. 1587	305 (28%)	143 (13%)	479 (44%)	90 (8%)	63 (6%)	1080 men
1592	971 (42%)	384 (16%)	887 (38%)	91 (4%)	–	2333 men
1594	694 (40%)	288 (17%)	684 (40%)	56 (3%)	–	1722 men
23 July 1595	980 (41%)	425 (18%)	920 (39%)	45 (2%)	5 (0.2%)	2375 men
15 Aug. 1595	859 (40%)	385 (18%)	864 (40%)	54 (2.5%)	4 (0.2%)	2166 men
15 July 1601	1146 (40%)	700 (25%)	980 (35%)	–	–	2826 men

SOURCES: ROYAL ARCHIVES THE HAGUE (KHA), A24-IV-H10, BATTLE ARRAY OF 1594; TRESOAR (PROVINCIAL ARCHIVES OF FRIESLAND), FRIES STADHOUDERLIJK ARCHIEF (FSA) 5, BATTLE ARRAYS OF 1592, OF 23 JULY AND 15 AUGUST 1595, AND OF 15 JULY 1601; FSA 700, SPECIFICATION OF THE TROOPS ORDERED FOR THIS CAMPAIGN, 23 SEPTEMBER 1587.

journal of Anthonis Duyck (c. 1560–1629), who as advocate-fiscal was an eyewitness to the campaigns of the Dutch army from 1591 to 1602, forms an important indication that Maurice and William Louis wanted to train the Dutch troops according to the Roman tactical system. The aforementioned battalions had a strength of 800 to 900 men each, reduced a few years later to between 500 and 600 men. These units combined tactical flexibility with staying-power. They were strong enough to fight independently yet without compromising manoeuvrability which had been the major drawback of the Macedonian phalanx and of the Swiss and German *Gewalthaufen*. For battle Maurice and William Louis distributed the battalions in three lines following the Roman chequer-wise pattern. Next to defence in depth, the division of the army in many small units had the added advantage of minimising the effect of local setbacks during battle. The defeat and flight of one or two units was no longer tantamount to losing the fight, which had been a root-cause for the string of defeats suffered by the Dutch rebels in the 1570s and 1580s.

Nothing is known about the drilling and exercising of the Dutch army in 1593 but the following year would be crucial for the development of the new infantry tactic of volley fire. In Oktober 1594, Maurice and William Louis met in Arnhem in preparation to besieging the Spanish held town of Groenlo. This operation had to be postponed but their meeting was nonetheless of great significance. One day while travelling together in a coach William Louis and Maurice discussed in detail Hannibal's famous victory at Cannae (216 BC). In this battle the Carthaginian general with 40,000 men enveloped and then utterly destroyed a Roman force of no less than 70,000 men. Maurice had his doubts whether the Romans had deployed their troops in the way William Louis assumed. The Frisian Stadholder decided to use the coming winter and spring to explore the matter further hoping that it would yield insights that could be used to improve the tactical performance of the Dutch troops.[35] On 8 December 1594, he sent Maurice a long letter in which he gave a detailed preliminary account of his findings.[36] The importance of this famous letter can hardly be overstated and therefore merits that we study it in detail.

The occasion for writing this letter was the sending of a Latin translation of Leo VI's book on warfare to Maurice.[37] William Louis was confident that many of the lessons taught in this manual were appropriate 'for our modern age'. Of course, this required a careful translation into Dutch of the relevant tactical concepts and words of command that Leo VI had adopted from Aelian. William Louis included these in his letter. He informed his cousin that he had not indiscriminately copied Aelian and Leo VI but had only selected those parts of which he had first tested the suitability with his own regiment at the drill ground in Leeuwarden. What mattered above-all, William Louis contended, was that the troops learnt to open and close their ranks and files without fault and that they could turn and face about on battalion level without falling into disorder. Following the example of the Greeks and the Romans William Louis demanded of his soldiers absolute silence during drill and exercise so that they could not misunderstand what they were ordered to do. He underscored Aelian's prescription that all words of command had to be short and unambiguous: 'If a say "Turn about – right," the soldier on hearing the word turn will just as easily turn to the left before he has understood or expected to hear the word "right turn." But if I say first the word "Right about – turn," the soldier knows and understands that he has to do something to the right and awaits the order'.

After finishing his exposition on Aelian, William Louis did not end his letter with a closing remark but continued with a detailed discussion of a method he had devised to make it possible to fire continuous volleys in the open field.

---

35 Werner Hahlweg, 'Wilhelm Ludwig von Nassau und das Cannae-Problem', *Nassauische Annalen*, 71 (1960) 237–242 at 240–241, Letter of William Louis to Maurice, Leeuwarden 9 April OS/19 April NS 1595; Geoffrey Parker, 'The limits to revolutions in military affairs: Maurice of Nassau, the battle of Nieuwpoort (1600) and the legacy', *The journal of military history*, 71 (2007) 331–372 at 337.

36 William Louis's letter is printed in full in Hahlweg, *Kriegsbuch des Grafen Johann von Nassau-Siegen*, 606–610. See also Parker, 'The limits in revolutions in military affairs', 338–339.

37 This was probably the 1554 translation by the Englishman Sir John Cheke (1514–1557). A new edition of this work was published in Basel in 1595. See Wiekart, *Van Maurits naar Munster*, 43.

> I have found *ex evolutionibus* [that is, from Aelian's discussions of drill] a method suitable not only for training the musketeers and calivermen to fire, but maintain that this method can [also] very easily be used in battle order (namely that they are not skirmishing or [use the cover of] hedges…) and that everyone can fire carefully and well, in the following manner: namely that as soon as the first rank has fired simultaneously it steps back *per evolutionem et versum* [i.e. makes an about-turn and returns to the rear of the block]; the second [rank] steps forward or stands still and shoots simultaneously, then marches back; the third and the following do the same. Thus before the last rank has fired the first has reloaded.

William Louis explained what he had in mind using a diagram. He subdivided the soldiers with firearms into blocks numbering nine men across by five ranks deep. After the musketeers or calivermen had fired together by rank they were to make an about-turn to the right and march to the rear between the files; an adaptation of the 'choreian' countermarch. It is highly unlikely that this firing method was used in such a form in practice. When loading a musket or caliver a soldier needed already at least three feet of space to manoeuvre on either side. During the loading process he had to swing his firearm around and move it from his right side to his left while simultaneously making sure that his smouldering match did not ignite another soldier's gunpowder. Moreover, William Louis's proposal required a 'street' measuring three feet across to be kept free between each file, so that soldiers who had fired could return to the rear of the column, so the files stood a total of six feet apart. As a consequence a unit of 314 pike, 36 halberd, 144 musket and 306 caliver (the composition of one of the Frisian battalions in 1594), with a depth of nine ranks, had a front of no less than 405 feet (c. 127 metres): 300 feet for the musketeers and calivermen (50 men x 6 feet) and 105 feet for the pikemen (35 men x 3 feet). The halberdiers were positioned in the rear of the calivermen. In the field, such an open and wide formation presented an easy target for the cavalry, who could exploit the spaces to penetrate the unit speedily. Based on a hitherto unknown sketch of the Frisian regiment's battle array dating from 1594 preserved in the Dutch Royal Archives,[38] and two letters that William Louis wrote to Maurice in December 1594 and April 1595,[39] it is plausible that the Frisian Stadholder tried

38 KHA, A24-IV-H10. This sketch is discussed in detail in Van Nimwegen, *Deser landen crijchsvolck*, 95–96.

39 That of 8 December 1594 in which William Louis explains the countermarch and that of 9 April 1595 in which he discusses the battle of Cannae. See note 35.

out his tactical ideas at the drill ground in the winter of 1594 and the spring of 1595, which made him realise that a modified formation was preferable. William Louis himself had doubts about the practicality of the new firing method, witness the warning to Maurice in his letter of December 1594: 'If your Excellency wants to joke about it, let that be in private and amongst friends'. Furthermore, William Louis did not want this manner of shooting to be adopted by the colonels of the other regiments before he was wholly certain of his case.

In the summer of 1595, William Louis had his regiment demonstrate the revised firing method in the presence of Maurice and the Dutch army's senior officers.[40] The major change involved the way musketeers and calivermen moved to rear of the unit after firing a salvo. They no longer made an about-turn individually but made a right turn as a rank before marching in file to the rear of the unit. To that end the blocks of musketeers and calivermen were separated from each other by a street of six feet, 'so that once it has fired the front rank can march through it to the rear of his troop to get ready again & can there properly prepare itself for firing by the time it has once again become the front rank', to quote Simon Stevin.[41] William Louis's original solution for achieving a continuous hail of gunfire was in principle preserved, but the front of each battalion could be reduced considerably, because the soldiers now marched to the rear via the streets between the blocks rather than between the individual files. By simultaneously reducing the number of soldiers in each block of musket and caliver from nine to five or six men per rank it was, moreover, possible to increase the rate of fire. This meant the troops who had fired could clear the front of the battalion more rapidly, so the following rank could loose its salvo sooner. It is very likely that William Louis had come to this solution after a careful re-examining of the text of Leo VI. To counter a threat from the rear the Greeks instead of using the countermarch sometimes resorted to a manoeuvre called the 'metabole', that is a complete reversal of front. In order to achieve this, half the men in the front rank made a turn to the right and the other half to the left; next they moved to the flanks of the unit and then quickly retired one after the other to the rear, where they again aligned facing the enemy. All the other ranks did the same until the entire unit had changed its front.[42]

40 Tresoar, FSA 5, Battle formations of 13 July and 5 August 1595. See also Duyck, vol. 1, 636–637 and 664.

41 KB, BC, Ms. Simon Stevin 128-A-18, 'Formen van slachorden (soowel ten deel als in 't geheel) van 't leger'. A French version of the same text is to be found in KHA, A14-IX-2, 'Ordres de batailles'.

42 Leo VI, *Strategy and tactics*, 7th Institute, vol. 2, 326–327. Leo VI's description of the metabole is much more clear than that of Aelian.

This variation on the countermarch was known as the conversion and was approved of by Maurice and the senior army officers. In October 1595, training the soldiers in the new firing method started. Maurice had the battalions 'advance towards each other as if they were going to shoot in order to practise this same thing'. He and William Louis took care that after the field army had retired to its garrisons, the soldiers continued their firing-practice during the winter months in order that at the start of the 1596 campaign all companies would be able to fire volleys in the same manner. The infantry captains were provided with an extra supply of gunpowder and the Council of State in The Hague, charged with the responsibility of military affairs, had four supervisors tour the garrisons to be kept informed of the progress made by the troops.[43] Captains found negligent were reprimanded. When it came to the attention of William Louis that the Frisian companies hardly ever practised firing, and that their captains sold the gunpowder, he immediately took steps to remedy this abuse. He ordered the captains to start exercising forthwith and have the soldiers fire continuously 'so with files as ranks and every fourteen days [they had to fire] at a target as well'.[44]

Troops who were trained to handle their weapons in the same way could, self-evidently, more readily fight side by side. Maurice and William Louis devoted attention to this as well, although they felt no need to set down the method followed in writing, seeing as they did not have to work with companies made up exclusively of fresh recruits and could therefore focus on standardising the exercise of troops who were for the most part experienced. The renowned drill manual first published in 1607, *Wapenhandelinghe van roers, musquetten ende spiessen*,[45] was not authored by Maurice and William Louis but by John VII of Nassau-Siegen, who had served in the Low Countries in 1592 and 1593. Later on he led the Swedish troops against the Poles in Livonia (1601–1602). Armed with this practical experience, he subsequently endeavoured to establish a 'Militia Force' (*Landesverteidigung*) for the County of Nassau. Being too poor to raise a sizeable professional army, the county's core defence had to be provided by the inhabitants themselves. In order to instil the rudiments of the art of war

43 National Archives (NA) The Hague, Archief van de Staten-General (SG) 4889, Council of State to the SG, The Hague 23 July 1598; Duyck, vol. 1, 683–684 (quote), 689, footnote 1 (Resolutions of the Council of State 18 and 20 November 1595).

44 Tresoar, FSA 1, William Louis to 'the garrisons in Friesland', Leeuwarden 29 December 1595 OS/8 Januari 1596 NS.

45 This work was published in facsimile with an introduction by J.B. Kist, *The Exercise of Armes: A Commentary* (Lochem, 1971). Soon after its initial publication the manual was translated into all major European languages and was even published in polyglot editions.

into these inexperienced soldiers, John VII produced a drill manual in which he described every manoeuvre with musket, caliver and pike, and illustrated them with drawings, which were subsequently artistically engraved by Jacob de Gheyn. He based this drill on practices he had observed in the Dutch army. John VII also turned his mind to the way in which soldiers should be led as a group in battle, but his ideas about this were elaborated only in notes for personal use.[46]

In the Spanish, French and German armies the recruits were taught by veteran soldiers. Under Maurice and William Louis the Dutch company commanders were still entrusted with the instruction of young, inexperienced soldiers, but they no longer allowed captains to do this according to their personal insights. Moreover, the corporals had to 'instruct with gentle words, not with beating, swearing and scolding'.[47] They were above all not to 'suffer the old soldiers to mock or jeer the younger if they do not do their postures as they ought, seeing that every man in every science and profession must have a time of learning before he can be perfect'.[48] The notion that Dutch officers had to drill their troops with the *Wapenhandelinghe* in hand is a stubborn misconception. This drill manual was intended solely for individual instruction of 'young or untrained soldiers'.[49] It was not intended for groups of soldiers who had already undergone basic training, though this was often the case even seventy years after its publication. In 1679, Captain Louis Paen complained that the drill manuals were:

> (…) misused by many officers, who practise it with a great troop standing in ranks and files, for a soldier should understand the correct use of the musket before he is ranged in ranks and files. Therefore, when a troop stands in ranks and files no other command should be used after the musketeers have readied themselves than *present* and then *give fire*, so that the soldiers might give due consideration to the necessary skill.[50]

---

46 Hahlweg, *Heeresreform*, 3–5, 21 and 41; Kist, *Exercise of Armes*, 4–5 and 13–15.

47 Johan and Christoffel le Hon, *Ordres van batailjen gepractiseert in de legers der Vereenighde Nederlanden onder het beleydt van sijn excellentie Mauritius en sijn hoogheydt Frederick Hendrick* (Amsterdam, 1672), 33v.

48 Henry Hexham, *Principii ofte de eerste gronden van de oorloghskonste gelijck se in dese Vereenichde Nederlanden ghepractiseert wort onder het gouvernement van sijn hoogheyt mijnheer den prince van Orangien* (The Hague, 1642), 2–3.

49 Johan Boxel, *Vertoogh van de krijghsoeffeninge soo in 't particulier van musquet en spies, als in 't generael van een corpus of gros der compagniën te voet van de guardes* (The Hague, 1670), titlepage of the first of the three parts.

50 Louis Paen, *Den korten weg tot de Nederlandsche militaire exercitie. Inhoudende eenige consideratien tot het manuael, soo van musquet, picq als andere noodige evolutiën, &c.* (Leeuwarden, 1679), Introduction.

In 1600, William Louis's and Maurice's tactical innovations were put to the most severe test imaginable: a pitched battle without the option of retreat. On 2 July 1600, approximately 11,000 Dutch and an equal number of Spanish troops faced each other on the beach and dunes near the Flemish seaport of Nieuwpoort. Battle was joined at around half past three in the afternoon. For a long time the battle wavered, but then the Dutch troops started to bend before the Spanish attack. The Spaniards interpreted this as proof that victory was imminent and pushed on, but their attacking drive proved to be a drawback. In contrast to the battles of the 1570s and 1580s, the Dutch infantry did not turn heels, but maintained its battle order and poured volley after volley into the enemy. When the Spanish infantry had moved so far forward that its flanks were left unprotected, Maurice saw his chance to decide the battle. He had kept a few companies of horse in reserve and now these fresh troopers went on the offensive. The Dutch cavalrymen hit the Spaniards in the flank and scattered them. The Spanish army's retreat began at around 7 PM. Both parties had sustained heavy losses. The Dutch army suffered 1000 fatalities and 700 wounded, but on the Spanish side there were 3000 or so fatalities and a further 600 Spaniards were taken prisoner.[51]

The Completion of the Tactical Revolution (1609–1618)

After the discarding of the caliver by the Dutch army in 1609, a model battalion consisted of 250 pikemen and 240 musketeers divided into five blocks of pike, each five men across and ten men deep, and six blocks of musket, each four men across and ten men deep. Such a unit had a front of only 183 feet (c. 57 metres): 49 x 3 feet + 6 streets of 6 feet. After each salvo the line that had fired split itself 'into two parts, one half [marching] to the rear via the right-hand side and the other half via the left; this moves them out of the way of the other musketeers sooner'.[52] But Maurice and William Louis were not yet satisfied with this formation. It may have provided a satisfactory solution to making continuous volleys of musket fire possible, but in close combat it was less suitable, 'seeing that in the clash of the battle orders the musketeers must pull back'. Musketeers were no match for armoured pikemen or halberdiers in close combat, but this was not the sole disadvantage of this formation. During the Battle of Nieuwpoort, it became evident that the pikemen were unable to

51 Duyck, vol. 2, 671–679; Parker, 'Limits to revolutions in military affairs', 351–353.

52 KHA, A23-VII-Db-O, 'De woorden van commandement waerdoor de capiteynen hunne soldaten gebieden ende exerceren', Leeuwarden 1630.

provide adequate cover for the musketeers and calivermen when they were subjected to a cavalry charge, 'insofar as the pikemen must serve as the breastwork of the musketeers and that with their being in two parts, to the right as well as to the left side [of the pikes], ... if they were charged by cavalry they [could] not retreat behind a group of pikes without confusion'.[53]

At first, Maurice and William Louis did not venture to radically alter the tried and tested infantry formation, because 'the slightest alteration overwhelms the common soldier',[54] but when the war with Spain was suspended for twelve years in 1609, they seized the small-scale Jülich War of Succession as an opportunity to improve the tactical formation. 'And when one subsequently devoted further consideration to the matter, ... [one] found that it was better to remove all the musketeers away from the flanks of the pikemen & to arrange them behind their pikes, ... & that thereby the whole battle order gained greater security, being serried closer together', Simon Stevin noted.[55] When they had to fire, all the musketeers advanced and formed a closed line in front of the pikemen. As mentioned earlier this new tactical formation was employed for the first time in 1610. Soon thereafter, it became standard practice to combine three battalions into a brigade. This made it possible to fire salvoes with 72 musketeers at once (three times 24 musketeers per battalion). In the rules and regulations of 1618, the essence of the new tactic was formulated as follows: 'Exercise of musketeers. The two front ranks make ready, present, give fire (and so on until all the ranks have discharged)'.[56] It was also possible to have two front ranks fire simultaneously, a coordinated salvo by 144 men. 'If one wants to have the two front ranks fire simultaneously', Stevin noted, 'one should have the musketeers in the front rank either crouch or kneel and have the second rank shoot over their heads in order to inflict greater damage on the enemy in the same amount of time'.[57] Geoffrey Parker draws the conclusion that William Louis's original proposal from December 1594 had some two decades later been transformed 'into a production line of death'.[58] Volley fire was to dominate land-based warfare until the mid-19th century.

And yet the increased firepower of the infantry did not foreshorten wars. On the contrary they became even more protracted. Writing in the early 18th

53 Le Hon, *Ordres van batailjen*, fol. 6v.

54 NA, Collectie Van der Hoop 124, Memorandum by Lieutenant-General Daniël de Savornin (1669–1739).

55 KB, BC, Ms. Simon Stevin 128-A-18, 'Formen van slachorden', fols. 5v and 6 (quote).

56 NA, Archief van de Stadhouderlijke Secretarie 1449, 'Ordre', The Hague, 5 December 1618.

57 KB, BC, Ms. Simon Stevin 128-A-9I, fol. 45 and verso.

58 Parker, 'Limits to revolutions in military affairs', 353.

century, the French quartermaster-general and theorist, De Puységur, retrospectively formulated the view that:

> the greatest change in the Ancient battle orders has occurred since the employment of firearms. For since then it has not been possible for the men to bear defensive arms, to protect themselves from strikes, as they did previously. The long range and power of firearms have obliged the armies to maintain an even greater distance from one another.[59]

In other words, the introduction of firearms and the development of orderly volley fire in particular had fundamentally altered tactics, but the likelihood of achieving a decisive victory was at the same time reduced. Owing to the fact that joining battle at a distance had become prevalent, from then on hand-to-hand fighting rarely arose in the open field. Infantry armed with pikes, halberds and swords had an offensive capability and could carry the battle by knocking out the enemy in the hand-to-hand struggle. The introduction of the matchlock musket in the mid-16th century had reinforced the defensive, because battle could then be joined at a distance.[60]

The Jülich War of Succession (1610–1616)

The Jülich War of Succession offers an intriguing example of the ways in which the Dutch and the Spaniards sought to avoid the premature ending of the Twelve Years Truce, while at the same time availing themselves of this conflict to display their military power. The distribution of Duke John William's inheritance was a matter of both German and European concern. Besides Jülich he had ruled over the duchies of Cleves and Berg, the counties of Mark and Ravensberg, and the Ravenstein seigniory, an enclave in States-Brabant (modern day North-Brabant). The partitioning of this sizeable inheritance was closely entwined with confessional politics. The late duke had been a Catholic but those who had the strongest claim to the succession – John Sigismund (1572–1619), Elector of Brandenburg and husband to a niece of John William, and Wolfgang William (1581–1653), Count of Neuburg, a nephew of the deceased – were Lutheran. The Emperor, the Catholic German princes, and

59 Jacques François de Chastenet, marquis De Puysegur, *Art de la guerre, par principes et par règles* (2nd edn., Paris, 1749), vol. 1, 105.

60 Bert S. Hall, *Weapons and Warfare in Renaissance Europe. Gunpowder, technology, and tactics* (Baltimore/London, 1997), 170 and 175.

also the King of Spain, had in the past already made clear that they would not permit the legacy to fall into the hands of Protestants. In response Brandenburg and the Palatinate, an electorate ruled by a Calvinist prince, had in 1605 concluded an alliance with the States General of the Dutch Republic, who had pledged themselves to secure the duchies of Jülich and Cleves for John Sigismund. The Dutch had agreed to this because of the strategic position of these territories, located on both banks of the River Rhine and bordering the Northern and the Southern Netherlands. King Henry IV of France (1589–1610) also readied himself to intervene. However, whereas the Dutch wanted a limited war that would end in a partition treaty satisfying both sides, the French King seemed intend on igniting a general European war. Henry IV's murder in May 1610 abated this threat. The heir to the French throne, Louis XIII (1610–1643), was a mere nine years old and Nicolas de Neufville (1542–1617), Marquis de Villeroy, Minister for Foreign Affairs and the *de facto* leader of the French government, was of the opinion that, without a powerful king, France could not allow herself to become involved in a war against the Habsburgs. Maria de Medici (1575–1642), the Queen Regent, did indeed send troops to the Holy Roman Empire, but the French operational objective was limited to dislodging the Imperialists from Jülich in association with the Republic. This was precisely what Johan van Oldenbarnevelt, the dominant political leader of the Dutch Republic, wanted.[61]

As mentioned earlier, the Dutch army marched on Jülich in July 1610. On reaching the vicinity of the disputed town the Dutch troops set up camp in the Roman manner fortifying it with entrenchments and surrounding it with a ditch. Simon Stevin, quartermaster general of the Dutch army, supervised the construction of the defences and assigned each regiment a location for building huts. All troops belonging to the same regiment hutted together so that in case of alarm the army could easily be arrayed in battle order.[62] The siege of Jülich went well. By the middle of August all the outworks were in Dutch hands. The French troops joined the Dutch army on 17 August and two weeks later the Imperialists surrendered Jülich. Maurice granted the garrison a free withdrawal. About 1650 men, plus 150 sick and wounded, marched out on 2 September; Maurice estimated that during the siege the defenders had suffered 150 fatalities.[63] A garrison paid by both John Sigismund and Wolfgang

61 A.Th. van Deursen, *Maurits van Nassau 1567–1625. De winnaar die faalde* (Amsterdam, 2000), 235–237; Geoffrey Parker (ed.) *The Thirty Years' War* (2nd edn., London/New York, 1997), 21–24; J. den Tex, *Oldenbarnevelt* (Haarlem/Groningen, 1960–72), vol. 3, 104.

62 Simon Stevin, *Castrametatio*, 34–35.

63 NA, SG 4922, Maurice to the SG, before Jülich, 1 and 3 September 1610.

William, the two 'possessing' princes, was billeted in the town of Jülich, but the castle's garrison was Dutch and Frederik Pithan, a Dutch army major, was appointed as governor of Jülich. Pithan was to defend Jülich 'for the common profit and service' of the two princes and, not least, of the Republic.[64] Maurice broke up his encampments in mid-September, marking the end of the 1610 campaign.

New problems arose around the Jülich legacy three years later. Elector John Sigismund converted to Calvinism, while Count Wolfgang William married a sister of Maximilian, Duke of Bavaria (1591–1651), head of the Catholic League of German princes established in 1609. In May 1614, Wolfgang William drove the Brandenburg troops out of Düsseldorf, whereupon he demonstratively attended Mass there, prompting Pithan to relieve the Neuburg troops of their duties in Jülich and send them away. By April 1614, the two Archdukes had pronounced that should The Hague side with Brandenburg, then Wolfgang William could depend on Spanish military support. Unlike four years earlier, Albert and Isabella did not remain above the fray this time. In 1614, Brussels dared to pursue a policy of confrontation, since now no French intervention was to be expected. The Queen-Regent and Villeroy were keen to establish closer relations with Spain, to be better able to tackle internal difficulties. Spinola was instructed to raise an army.[65] The Spanish preparations for war gave Maurice serious cause for concern. In the middle of June, he warned William Louis that the Spaniards already had 9800 men ready for field service and that they would soon be joined by a further 13,200 men.[66] A month later, there could have been no shadow of a doubt that Spinola would set out on campaign in early August 1614, seeing as the Spanish troops had hired 1200 wagons for the conveyance of their baggage, victuals and munitions. Maurice reinforced the garrison of Jülich (seven companies strong) with an additional 2000 men and dispatched sufficient food supplies and munitions for a protracted siege. He hereby hoped to gain sufficient time to assemble a relief army. The prospects did not, however, bode well for this, because no fewer than 228 of the Dutch army's 352 infantry companies were needed for garrison duties. 'You yourself can judge that 124 companies (which are at the moment so feeble) is a small number to be deployed on campaign', Maurice lamented to William Louis.[67] Maurice told his cousin that the majority of infantry

64 Ten Raa, *Het Staatsche leger*, vol. 3, 17.

65 Den Tex, *Oldenbarnevelt*, vol. 3, 104 and 116.

66 KHA, A22-IX-A1-414, Maurice to William Louis, The Hague, 15 June 1614, with 'Estat de l'armée des Archiduqz juing 1614' as an appendix.

67 KHA, A22-IX-A1-417, Maurice to William Louis, The Hague, 15 July 1614 (quote) and KHA, A22-IX-A1-418, The Hague, 17 July 1614, with 'Besettinge van[de] garnisoenen' as an appendix.

companies numbered just seventy men, so 'we [shall be] entering the campaign with a meagre army and therefore consider it urgently necessary to gather together as many companies as is feasible'. William Louis would in any case have to march with the majority of the Frisian companies, each of them being 100 strong.[68] By drawing additional troops from towns that were not under serious threat Maurice expected to be able to raise an army composed of 136 infantry companies and 40 cavalry companies.[69]

In the latter half of August 1614, Spinola gathered about 15,000 men near Maastricht and used them to occupy Aachen and thereafter Wesel (5 September), two towns with garrisons from Brandenburg.[70] He left Jülich undisturbed. Maurice then marched on Rees with an estimated 18,000 men. Spinola subsequently established a position near Xanten, whereupon he opened negotiations with Maurice about a neutrality pact. He explained that the two Archdukes were prepared to withdraw from Wesel and the other places occupied by Spanish troops in Jülich, 'so when my lords the States General want to promise ... [that they] shall not come back with their army hereafter ... into the lands of the possessing princes to occupy any places there', Maurice wrote to William Louis. 'We already consider these to be trifles and that they are seeking nothing else but to delay us', he continued, with regard to reinforcing the defences of Emmerich, Rees and Jülich.[71] The parties ultimately agreed a provisional partition of the Jülich estate. In the Treaty of Xanten of 12 November 1614, Jülich and Berg were allocated to Count Wolfgang William, while Cleves, Mark, Ravensberg and Ravenstein were assigned to Elector John Sigismund. The accord was not implemented immediately, the mutual distrust between the parties being too great, nevertheless confrontations between Spanish and Dutch troops failed to materialise. During the winter of 1614 to 1615 a total of about seventy Dutch infantry companies were quartered in Jülich, Cleves and Mark.[72]

Looking ahead, Maurice considered this buffer essential, for when the Twelve Years Truce expired it would be advantageous to ensuring the security

68 KHA, A22-IX-A1-419, Ditto to ditto, The Hague, 24 July 1614.

69 NA, SG 4929, 'Liste van de comp[ag]ni[e]ën die men dit jaer 1614 te velde soude connen gebruycken', 19 July 1614.

70 KHA, A22-IX-A1-423, Maurice to William Louis, The Hague, 13 August 1614, with an overview of the strength of the Spanish field army as an appendix. See also Parker, *The Thirty Years' War*, 32.

71 KHA, A22-IX-A1-439, Maurice to William Louis, The Hague, 19 March 1615.

72 KHA, A22-IX-A1-434, Ditto to ditto, The Hague, 3 January 1615, with a 'Liste van de besettinghe van de garnisoenen in den lande van Gulich, Cleve en[de] van der Marck' as an appendix.

of the Betuwe, a strategically important region between the Rivers Waal and Lower-Rhine, and the towns along the River IJssel. The Dutch troops would then be in a position to sever the lines of communication between the Spaniards and their bases in the eastern parts of the provinces of Gelderland and Overijssel. Spinola wanted to retain Wesel, situated in the Duchy of Cleves, for similar reasons. Direct hostilities between Spain and the Republic did not materialise in 1615 either. Nevertheless, in April 1616, Spinola tightened his control of the disputed territories by occupying Soest,[73] a town in the easternmost part of the County of Mark. The capture of Soest did not pose any immediate threat to the Republic, but for Maurice Spinola's action represented additional proof of Madrid's hostile intentions. Maurice believed it would be better for the States General to turn the 'cold war' as soon as possible in a real one, but Van Oldenbarnevelt did not share this viewpoint. The Truce was not even ruptured when in 1618 the Thirty Years War broke out, and King Philip III sent an army to support his Austrian relatives. In 1621, the Dutch army was once again brought to its wartime strength. Over the summer the Dutch field army established positions between Emmerich and Rees. By establishing this forward position, Maurice could protect the Betuwe and the towns along the River IJssel, but he could not prevent the Spaniards surrounding Jülich on 5 September 1621. After a blockade of five months the food supplies were exhausted and Governor Pithan was forced to capitulate. Jülich was evacuated on 2 February 1622.[74]

Conclusion

Long-drawn exchanges of musket fire were bloody affairs as the Battle of Nieuwpoort had clearly demonstrated. Losses resulting from combat had to be repaired by the captains themselves, because until the second half of the 17th century, Europe's rulers and political bodies were of the opinion that caring for the mercenaries that fought their wars was not their responsibility. They considered the upkeep and recruiting of troops a private matter only of concern to the company commanders. That this bred fraud, hampered army growth, and put severe limitations on the offensive capabilities of armies, was accepted as inevitable by the Spanish government in Brussels as well as the States General in The Hague. Maurice and William Louis shared this opinion but at the same time were averse from risking their soldiers' lives. The high level of training and

73 KHA, A22-IX-A1-423, Ditto to ditto, The Hague, 5 and 13 April 1616.

74 Ten Raa, *Het Staatsche leger*, vol. 3, 73–74, 78, 84 and 91.

discipline required for the implementation of the tactical innovations had increased the value of veteran troops too an even higher level. Maurice and William Louis were resolved not to be forced into fighting a second Nieuwpoort, where defeat would have resulted in the destruction of the Dutch field army. They would only join battle again if the designs of the enemy could not be thwarted in any other way, and then only when they were assured of a clear-cut numerical superiority, when the enemy positions were not overly strong, and when the withdrawal of the Dutch army was secure. However, the changes that such an opportunity would present itself were slim. According to William Louis, 'the enemy ... has learnt so much from [the Battle of] Nieuwpoort ... that he will only face us in such an advantageous [position] where he can receive us [i.e. fight] gloriously'.[75] The southern as well as the northern parts of the Netherlands were ideally suited to a defensive war: rivers, streams, woodland and marshes offered countless opportunities to establish strong positions.[76] As a result of this military impasse the Dutch and the Spaniards were careful not to engage one another in open battle from 1600 onwards. Sieges and skilful marches characterised the second part of the Eighty Years War. After Nieuwpoort, Maurice never again fought a battle. Frederick Henry, commander-in-chief of the Dutch army from 1625 to 1646, followed this example to a fault, notwithstanding contemporary military authors vigorously advocated the seeking of battle. Henri II, Duke of Rohan (1579–1638), argued that only victory in the field 'leads to quick conquests. But nowadays one wages war more as a fox than as a lion'.[77] A similar complaint was made by Captain John Bingham who wrote in his introduction to *The art of embattailing an army* (1629), a sequel to his translation of Aelian's *Tactics*:

> And whereas many hold opinion that it sorteth not with the use of our times, they must give me leave to be of another mind. Indeed our actions in warre are onely now a dayes and sieges oppugnations of cities. Battailes wee heare not of, save onely of a few in France and that of Newport in the Low-Countries. But this manner will not last alwayes, nor is there any conquest to be made without battailes.[78]

---

75 A.J. Veenendaal sr., *Johan van Oldenbarnevelt. Bescheiden betreffende zijn staatkundig beleid en zijn familie* (The Hague, 1962), vol. 2, no. 6, Letter of William Louis, 29 March 1602.

76 Jamel Ostwald, 'The "Decisive" Battle of Ramillies, 1706: Prerequisites for decisiveness in Early Modern Warfare', *The Journal of Military History*, 64 (2000) 649–677 at 660.

77 Henri duc De Rohan, *Le parfaict capitaine. Autrement, l'abrégé des guerres de Gaule des commentaires de César* (Paris, 1636, facsimile edn., Osnabrück, 1972), 257.

78 John Bingham, *The art of embattailing an army* (Londen, 1629, facsimile edn. Amsterdam/New York, 1968), 'The epistle dedicatory'.

The major pitched battles during the Thirty Years' War – Breitenfeld (1631), Lützen (1632) and Nördlingen (1634) – as well as the Battle of Rocroi (1643) seemed to proof Bingham right. However, none of these victories achieved a decisive outcome: the struggle in the Holy Roman Empire continued through to 1648 and the Franco-Spanish War did not end until 1659.

APPENDIX I *Battles 1568–1581.*

Year	Battle	Forces of the Dutch rebels		Forces of the King of Spain		Losses		Result
		Infantry	Cavalry	Infantry	Cavalry	Rebels	Royal troops	
24 April 1568	Dalem (modern Rheindalen, east of Roermond)	5000 to 6000		1100	300	1500 to 2000	100 to 200	A
23 May 1568	Heiligerlee (Groningen)	3000	300	3000	300	50 to 70	1500	B
21 July 1568	Jemmingen (East-Friesland)	8000	500 to 600	17,000	1000	7000 to 8000	Negligible	C
13 December 1572	1st Manpad (Holland)	4000	200	5500	60	600 to 800	Negligible	A
8 July 1573	2nd Manpad	c. 4000		–*		700	Negligible	A
14 April 1574	Mook (Limburg, near Nijmegen)	5500 to 6000	1700	4000	765	3000	190	A
31 January. 1578	Gembloux (Namur)	20,000 to 22,000		20,000	2500	6000	Negligible	A
16 June 1580	Hardenberg (Overijssel)	1800	1200 to 1400	3000	500 to 600	?	?	A
30 September 1581	Noordhorn (Groningen)	4000	500	5000 to 6000	500	1600 to 2000	500 to 600	A

APPENDIX I *Battles 1568–1581.* (cont.)

Legend:
A Royal victory
B Rebel victory
C Rebel army annihilated

* Two Spanish tercio's and an unknown number of other Royal troops took part in the second battle of the Manpad.

Note: all figures are estimates. Losses are for the most part killed, both sides hardly taking any prisoners.

Sources:

Dalem: Gelders Archief, Arnhem, Archief Huizen Waardenburg en Neerijnen 718, Bernhard de Merode, 'Discours … sur le rencontre avenu à Dalem', Cologne 9 May 1568; Felix Rachfahl, *Wilhelm von Oranien und der niederländische Aufstand* (The Hague, 1924), vol. 3, 302–304.
Heiligerlee: L.L. Doedens, '"The day the nation was born". The Battle of Heiligerlee, 1568', in Marco van der Hoeven (ed.), *Exercise of arms. Warfare in the Netherlands* (1568–1648) (Leyden/New York/Cologne, 1997), 57–67, 63–64; Rachfall, *Wilhelm von Oranien*, vol. 3, 325, 331; J.W. Wijn, *Het krijgswezen in den tijd van prins Maurits* (Utrecht, 1934), 487–489.
Jemmingen: Rachfall, *Wilhelm von Oranien*, vol. 3, 426; Wijn, *Krijgswezen*, 489–491.
Manpad: J.W. Wijn, *Het beleg van Haarlem* (Amsterdam, 1942), 38–40, 189–191.
Mook: Wijn, *Krijgswezen*, 493–497.
Gembloux: W.J.F. Nuyens, *Geschiedenis van den Opstand in de Nederlanden van de Gentsche bevrediging tot aan den dood van Willem van Oranje* (Amsterdam, 1867), vol. 3.1, 198; Wijn, *Krijgswezen*, 497–498.
Hardenberg: Koninklijk Huisarchief, The Hague, A11-XII-6, Instructions of William of Orange to General Hohenlohe, Antwerp 16 June 1580; Wijn, *Krijgswezen*, 498–500.
Noordhorn: Zeeuws Archief, Middelburg, States of Zeeland 887, Jacob Valcke, Leeuwarden 14 September 1581; Wijn, *Krijgswezen*, 500–503.

APPENDIX II *Weaponry (rank and file) of eleven Dutch and nine English infantry companies, mustered in Holland from 1573 to 1578*

Dutch companies

Date of muster	Captain	Pike	Halberd	Broad sword	Rondache[a]	Feder[b]	Musket	Caliber[c]	Caliver	Total (100%)
20 Nov. 1573	Reinier van Zittart	9 (7%)	9 (7%)	3 (2%)	–	3 (2%)	-	–	106 (82%)	130
3 Dec. 1573	Jacques Hennebaert	8 (5%)	4 (3%)	4 (3%)	–	–	10 (7%)	–	124 (82%)	150
20 Dec. 1573	Claes Gijsbrechts alias Aecker	25 (17%)	4 (3%)	6 (4%)	–	–	–	–	115 (76%)	150
14 Jan. 1574	Hans van Cremnitz	16 (12%)	1 (0.7%)	7 (5%)	–	–	–	–	111 (82%)	135
17 Aug. 1574	Daniël van Eck	13 (11%)	9 (8%)	3 (3%)	–	–	2 (2%)	–	90 (77%)	117
22 Feb. 1575	Dito	14 (11%)	9 (7%)	3 (2%)	–	–	6 (4%)	–	101 (76%)	133
14 Dec. 1575	Hans Bouwinga	23 (16%)	1 (0.7%)	4 (3%)	–	–	4 (3%)	–	114 (78%)	146
Sept. 1575	Diedrik van Renesse	22 (21%)	1 (1%)	5 (5%)	–	–	6 (6%)	–	73 (68%)	107
Dec. 1575	Dito	23 (21%)	1 (1%)	3 (3%)	–	–	7 (6%)	–	76 (69%)	110
16 April 1576	Dito	20 (19%)	3 (3%)	6 (6%)	–	–	9 (8%)	–	68 (64%)	106
21 Dec. 1575	Johan van Ham	23 (22%)	–	2 (2%)	–	–	1 (1%)	4 (4%)	75 (71%)	105
6 Sept. 1576	Willem van Wijngaerden	24 (17%)	1 (0.7%)	5 (4%)	–	–	7 (5%)	3 (2%)	98 (71%)	138

APPENDIX II *Weaponry (rank and file) of eleven Dutch and nine English infantry companies, mustered in Holland from 1573 to 1578.* (cont.)

Dutch companies

Date of muster	Captain	Pike	Halberd	Broad sword	Rondache[a]	Feder[b]	Musket	Caliber[c]	Caliver	Total (100%)
30 July 1577	Dito	17 (15%)	–	3 (3%)	3 (3%)	–	12 (10%)	5 (4%)	76 (65%)	116
13 Aug. 1577	Jacques Cristal	4 (4%)	–	2 (2%)	3 (3%)	–	8 (8%)	33 (34%)	47 (48%)	97
1576, '77 or '78	Evert Wolters	20 (16%)	4 (3%)	5 (4%)	–	1 (1%)	–	–	95 (76%)	125

English companies

Date	Captain	Pike	Halberd	Broad sword	Rondache	Bow	Musket	Caliber	Caliver	Total (100%)
27 April 1573	Lt.-col. Rowland York[d] (two companies)	–	24 (9%)	–	3 (1%)	–	–	–	237 (90%)	264
6 June 1573	Edward Chester (two companies)	38 (10%)	15 (4%)[e]		5 (1%)				340 (85%)	398
10 June 1573	Gillis Gainsford, lieutenant of captain Wore	15 (19%)	–	–	–	–	–	–	64 (81%)	79
1 July 1573	Wore	24 (24%)[f]	–	–	2 (2%)	3 (3%)	–	–	70 (71%)	99
10 June 1573	Mauris	12 (12%)	12 (12%)	–	–	–	–	–	75 (76%)	99

APPENDIX II *Weaponry (rank and file) of eleven Dutch and nine English infantry companies, mustered in Holland from 1573 to 1578.* (cont.)

Dutch companies

Date of muster	Captain	Pike	Halberd	Broad sword	Rondache[a]	Feder[b]	Musket	Caliber[c]	Caliver	Total (100%)
23 June 1573	Lieutenant Grene	–	12 (8%)	–	–	–	12 (8%)	117 (83%)[g]	–	141
7 July 1573	G. Gascoigne	–	20 (15%)[h]	–	–	10 (8%)	–	–	101 (77%)	131

Notes:

a A rondache is a small round shield carried by a soldier armed with a short sword.

b A 'feder' is a short, sturdy pike.

c A 'caliber' was a firearm that fired a ball that was heavier than that of a caliver, but lighter than that of a musket. Apparently it did not meet the approval of the soldiers, because the caliber was discarded at the end of the sixteenth century.

d In August 1573 it was decreed that both companies should muster 18 rondachiers, 20 pikemen and halberdiers and 112 calivermen each. NA, Handschriften Derde Afdeling 478 (Datebase correspondence of William of Orange: http://www.inghist.nl/Onderzoek/Projecten/WVO/letter/11597). York was lieutenant-colonel of Morgan's regiment.

e This number consisted of halberdiers and soldiers with short pikes.

f They were armed with long and short pikes.

g The 12 musketeers were gentlemen. The 117 'common shot' were armed with muskets and calibers.

h Their armament consisted of halberds and other short polearms.

Source: NA, Collectie Ortel 5, 6, 10, 12, 15, 16, 18, 19, 29, 34, 39, 45, Muster-rolls.

CHAPTER 7

'Une oppression insupportable au peuple'

The Impact of Contributions on Armistice, Peace and Truce Negotiations

Tim Piceu[1]

Introduction

It is common knowledge that during the truce negotiations, dozens of pamphlets informed the Dutch citizens about the advantages of war or peace and attempted to convince them one way or the other. The *Boeren-litanie ofte Klachte der Kempensche Landt-lieden, over de ellenden van deze lanck-duerighe Nederlandtsche Oorloghe* (*Farmers' Litany or Complaint by the Villagers of the Campine Region about the Miseries Caused by This Continuing War in the Netherlands*) is such a pamphlet and it is a striking text. Striking because, unlike most other pamphlets, it did not focus on religion, colonial trade or independence, but gave voice to the Dutch rural population and its interests. Striking furthermore, because it is the only pamphlet listed by Knuttel that is fully dedicated to the countrymen's desire for a long and stable peace.

The *Boeren-litanie* carefully enumerates the reasons why for the inhabitants of the Campine region, peace was to be preferred over the scourges of war. According to the pamphlet, never before, villagers had to endure the atrocities and uncertainties of war for such a long period of time. Looting was widespread and was eagerly engaged in by so-called *cheesehunters* (*kaes-jaegers*), freebooters, mutineers and others. Buying off these pillagers by paying contributions on a regular basis was not a lasting solution, because 'this peace doesn't last long, and [therefore] can't set us free'. For these reasons, villagers in both the Northern and the Southern Low Countries longed for a 'general peace, solid and sincere'.[2] The afore-mentioned living conditions in rural areas did not only prevail in the Campine region, but along the entire frontline which divided the Low Countries. Indeed, the farmers of the Campine region

---

1 I'm very grateful to Hans Cools, Bernardo García García and Werner Thomas for their useful suggestions. José Javier Ruiz Ibáñez deserves my special gratitude for letting me read two valuable articles in press, as well as Marjan De Smet for her revision of this text.

2 Johannes Van Vloten, *Nederlandsche Geschiedzangen, naar tijdsorde gerangschikt en toegelicht* (Amsterdam, 1864) vol. 2, 395–396.

 | DOI 10.1163/9789004274921_009

can easily be interchanged with villagers in Northern Flanders, Northern Brabant, Guelders, Overijssel or Drenthe. Inhabitants of these regions all experienced similar living conditions, *viz.* conditions of insecurity and endemic violence as a result of raiding enemies or mutineers, violent skirmishes, looting, ambushes, abductions, the levying of contributions, etc.[3]

The contributions mentioned in the *Boeren-litanie* were a periodical payment by villages vulnerable to enemy looting in exchange for a *sauvegarde*, a document promising exemption from being looted. Concerned about the fate of the inhabitants, houses and movables of a village, communities as a whole might decide to pay contributions, but it was not uncommon for relatively well-off individuals to pay contributions to protect their private possessions. Violence and the use of force were the key elements in the system of contributions. The villagers would only remain eager to pay contributions as long as they feared retaliation of enemy marauders; as soon as they believed themselves to be safe from the enemy's military might, these regular payments would instantly cease. As a consequence, contributions were an unreliable source of income for the warring parties: as long as the local balance of military power was in favour of the exactors, income would rise and the contribution paying area tended to enlarge; income collapsed as soon as villages estimated they could successfully stand up against the enemy garrisons and marauders.[4]

The payments mentioned here should not be confused with two similar, related types of levies. Indeed, regular taxes, imposed by a sovereign with the consent of the local states, were also called 'contributions'.[5] Wartime

3 On unofficial war, see Frank Tallet, *War and Society in Early Modern Europe, 1495–1715* (War in Context 5; London, 1995) 148–151; Jonathan R. Hale, *War and Society in Renaissance Europe, 1450–1620* (Fontana History of European War and Society 4; Bath, 1985) 179–209. See Geoffrey Parker, *The Army of Flanders and the Spanish Road, 1567–1659. Logistics of Spanish Victory and Defeat in the Low Countries' War* (Cambridge, 1972) 12–18, on the position of unofficial warfare in the Low Countries' War.

4 L. Van der Ent, '"Oostersche Contributiën". Contributie aan de vijand in Drenthe, 1621–1633' in W. Fritschy, J.K.T. Postma and J. Roelevink (eds.) *Doel en Middel. Aspecten van Financieel Overheidsbeleid in de Nederlanden van de Zestiende Eeuw tot Heden* (NEHA-Series III, 22; Amsterdam, 1995) 35–57, esp. 37.

5 Wantje Fritschy, *Gewestelijke financiën ten tijde van de Republiek der Verenigde Nederlanden, Deel I: Overijssel (1604–1795)* (Rijks Geschiedkundige Publicatiën. Kleine Serie 66; The Hague, 1996) 185–186. In France, Spanish exactions were frequently labelled as 'tailles'. José Javier Ruiz Ibáñez, 'La guerre, les princes et les paysans. Les pratiques de neutralité et de sauvegarde dans les Pays-Bas et au Nord du royaume de France au XVIe et au début du XVIIe siècle' in *Neutralités, sauvegardes, accommodements: Microhistoire des arrangements face à la guerre et à l'occupation à l'Époque moderne et contemporaine* (Bern, forthcoming).

contributions should also be carefully distinguished from the proceeds of *brandschatting*. The latter practice entails 'a payment in money or kind extorted by an enemy under the threat of force'. The sum demanded amounted to the value of the property that under the laws of war could be looted and burned. In exchange for the payment, the receiver promised to leave the house, farm, monastery or even a whole village or town unscathed.[6] The boundary between wartime contributions and *brandschatting* is very vague indeed, and contemporary sources from the Low Countries often use these expressions indiscriminately. This notwithstanding, abundant evidence testifies to the fact that *brandschatting* was a once-only payment extracted by raiding soldiers from villages that could not be forced to pay contributions on a regular basis (often because they were too far away from the nearest enemy stronghold); it might also be a once-only fine for having resisted the payment of contributions to be paid on joining the community of villages already paying the enemy contributions.[7]

In this Chapter, I will examine the impact of contributions on the lengthy negotiations for an armistice, for peace and for a truce. The role played by these levies has been overlooked by accounts concentrating on the bargaining leading up to the Antwerp Treaty.[8] This is hardly surprising, since contributions and looting belonged to the unofficial war (*guerre guerroyante, kleine Krieg*), an aspect of early modern conflicts which has received little attention in comparison with the development of strategy and major military operations. The main reason for this neglect is that historians have long thought that contributions were introduced during the Thirty Years War by Tilly and Spinola. According to Moritz Ritter, Wallenstein would have perfected the rudimentary system of contributions introduced by his colleagues.[9] This view was adjusted by Geoffrey Parker, who found evidence of the Spanish Army of

6 Fritz Redlich, 'Contributions in the Thirty Years' War', *The Economic History Review*, 12 (1959) 247.

7 Tim Piceu, *Over vrybuters en quaetdoenders. Terreur op het Vlaamse platteland (eind 16de eeuw)* (Louvain, 2008), 16–17.

8 Paul C. Allen, *Philip III and the Pax Hispanica, 1598–1621. The Failure of Grand Strategy* (New Haven, 2000); W.J.M. Van Eysinga, *De wording van het Twaalfjarig Bestand van 9 April 1609* (Verhandelingen van de Koninklijke Nederlandse Akademie van Wetenschappen. N.S. 66.3; Amsterdam, 1959).

9 Moritz Ritter, 'Das Kontributionssystem Wallensteins', *Historische Zeitschrift*, 55 (1903) 247. Ritter's opinion was shared by Fritz Redlich, who argued that 'The *Kontribution* is distinctly from seventeenth century origin', Redlich, '*Contributions*', 253 and more recently by Etienne Rooms, 'Oorlogscontributies' in Paul Janssens (ed.), *België in de Zeventiende Eeuw* (Ghent, 2006) vol. 1, 86–87.

Flanders establishing 'a regular, permanent and rational contributions system' in Holland during the 1570s,[10] but detailed studies have only recently unravelled the mechanisms of the Dutch and Spanish levies during the 1570s, 1580s, 1590s and the 17th century.[11]

After some introductory remarks on the evolution of the contributions system during the Dutch Revolt, I will argue that the 1607 armistice and the Truce of Antwerp contain several innovative legal solutions introducing practices that would become standard in 17th-century warfare.

Pillaging and Contributions before the Armistice

The recapture of the Southern Low Countries by Alexander Farnese created a frontline stretching from Flanders to Friesland. In the period before the truce, looting and violence by soldiers, mutineers and the so-called *vrybuters* (freebooters) flared up in the frontier regions. The freebooters – often civilians who had fled their homes and whom poverty forced to plunder for a living – were based in Dutch or Spanish frontier towns, from which they raided the vulnerable countryside under the enemy's control, pillaging houses, abducting travellers, stealing cattle, attacking convoys and murdering opponents. In doing so, they caused widespread panic. Defensive measures devised by Brussels, The Hague or local administrations, such as the construction of redoubts, the recruitment of a special armed corps to oppose these freebooters and the

10 Parker, *The Army of Flanders*, 142.

11 Adriaan M.J. De Kraker, 'Een Staatse strategie in een "uitgestorven" land: organisatie en ten uitvoerlegging van de brandschat in Vlaanderen, 1585 tot 1604', *Bijdragen en Mededelingen betreffende de Geschiedenis van de Nederlanden*, 121 (2006) 3–34; Piceu, *Over vrybuters en quaetdoenders*; N.J. Tops, 'De Heffing der Spaanse Contributiën tot 1635 in het Oosten der Republiek of de "landbederfelijke" rol van Grol, Oldenzaal en Lingen', *Bijdragen en Mededelingen Gelre*, 78 (1978) 34–64; Van der Ent, *'Oostersche Contributiën'*; Olaf van Nimwegen, *'Deser landen crijchsvolck'. Het Staatse leger en de militaire revoluties 1588–1688* (Amsterdam, 2006), esp. 127–30; Erik Swart, *Krijgsvolk. Militaire Professionalisering en het ontstaan van het Staatse leger, 1568–1590* (Amsterdamse Gouden Eeuw Reeks 1; Amsterdam, 2006), esp. 147–55; Griet Vermeesch, *Oorlog, steden en staatsvorming. De grenssteden Gorinchem en Doesburg tijdens de geboorte-eeuw van de Republiek (1572–1680)* (Amsterdamse Gouden Eeuw Reeks 2; Amsterdam, 2006), esp. 139–47; Leo Adriaenssen, *Staatsvormend Geweld. Overleven aan de Frontlinies in de meierij van Den Bosch, 1572–1629* (Tilburg, 2007); Ruiz Ibáñez, 'La guerre, les princes et les paysans'; idem, 'Vivir en el campo de Marte. Población e identitad en la frontera entre Francia y los Países Bajos' in *Las sociedades fronterizas del Mediterráneo al Atlántico (ss. XVI–XVIII)* (Madrid, forthcoming).

announcement of significant rewards on their heads, failed to stop the freebooters.[12]

An important consequence of the actions of the freebooters was that the economic recovery of the countryside was slowed down. Whereas agriculture in Holland quickly recovered and trade flourished once the war had left the county,[13] the small-scale hostilities by freebooters made the war linger on in the frontier regions. The warlike conditions of life and the continuing uncertainty prevented the villagers, fled for Farnese's conquering army, to return to their farms and houses. Available material for the County of Flanders abundantly shows at the more exposed a region was to raids, the harder the economic crisis hit the region and the longer economic recovery failed to materialize. The *Brugse Vrije* (the 'Freedom of Bruges'), the large rural district surrounding the town of Bruges, for instance, extending from the river Yser to the Scheldt estuary, was hit hard by Farnese's ruthless way of waging war. All available economic indicators show that agriculture and local economy came to a standstill in 1584, when the Spanish army operated in the area. Grain prices and prices of consumer goods skyrocketed; agricultural production and the consumption of meat, beer and wine plummeted. Although the extreme hardship of the years 1584, 1585 and 1587 did not continue in the following years, the crisis dragged on. The persistency of economic distress is well-illustrated by the fiscal records. In the fiscal year 1597–1598, for instance, fourteen years after the Spanish *reconquista* of the region, the total tax income in the *Brugse Vrije* still barely amounted to 4, 6% of the tax income of 1575–1576. When discussing the causes of the dramatic economic performance of the County, the States of Flanders pointed towards the Dutch stronghold of Ostend as the 'root of all evil'. Although Ostend did certainly not monopolise the violence in Flanders's countryside, the Flemish States were right to blame the enemy raids and contributions as the chief cause of their problems.[14]

---

12 Piceu, *Over vrybuters*, 65–96; José Javier Ruiz Ibáñez, 'Corsarios de la Tierra. La Guerra Irregular en el Norte de Francia a Fines del Siglo XVI' in Juan Luis Castellano Castellano and Miguel Luis López-Guadalupe Muñoz (eds.) *Homenaje a Antonio Domínguez Ortiz* (Granada, 2008), vol. 2, 711–713; Jean-Pierre Andrault, 'Une capitale de province sous les armes au temps de la Ligue: la guerre de course menée par Poitiers entre 1589 et 1593' in André Corvisier and Jean Jacquart (eds.) *Les malheurs de la guerre. I. De la guerre à l'ancienne à la guerre réglée* (Paris, 1996), 39–63.

13 Jan De Vries and Ad Van der Woude, *Nederland 1500–1815. De eerste ronde van moderne economische groei* (Amsterdam, 1995), 242–243.

14 Klaas Maddens, 'Het uitzicht van het Brugse Vrije op het einde van de XVIe eeuw', *Handelingen van het Genootschap voor Geschiedenis*, 97 (1960) 31–73. On the economic consequences of the Revolt: Geoffrey Parker, 'War and Economic Change: The Economic

From the 1590s onwards, pillaging in enemy territory by freebooters and soldiers was slowly replaced by the levy of contributions. Villagers in frontier regions were eager to pay the enemy garrison a contribution on a regular basis since, in exchange for these regular payments, the villages received a safeguard. The payment of contributions thus promised the oppressed villagers the security they so desperately needed for economic recovery. For the Spanish and the Dutch governments, the system meant a new source of income.[15]

Both the Spanish and Dutch administrations created mechanisms to enforce the extortion of money in enemy territory. To secure this source of income, the Council of State of the United Provinces appointed in frontier towns such as Ostend (up until 1604), Sluys (from 1604 on) and Bergen-op-Zoom three officials. The collector of the contributions had to fix the amount of contributions that every village, situated in the vicinity of the Dutch exclave, had to pay. He summoned the villagers with incendiary letters to come and pay their contributions and ordered an 'execution', a violent, punitive raid on the village by the garrison of the Dutch exclave, if the villagers refused to pay or ran up unacceptable arrears. A meticulous account was to be kept of all the revenues from contributions, which was inspected by the auditor of the contributions. This auditor also checked the accounts of the third official, the collector of the confiscations, charged with the task of collecting the charges imposed on ecclesiastical domains in enemy territory.[16] The Archdukes inherited a similar system which had been developed during the late 1580s and early 1590s by the Spanish administration in Brussels. Accountants stationed in Den Bosch, Lingen and Groenlo every month received and entered into the books the contributions from Drenthe, Guelders and Overijssel. Just like their Dutch counterparts, they tried to enlarge the area under their control and ordered execution in case of arrears. The Roermond audit office checked the accounts. It goes without saying that the conquest by Spinola of Oldenzaal, Lingen and Groenlo vastly enlarged the territory in which the Archdukes could effectively collect contributions.[17]

Costs of the Dutch Revolt' in Geoffrey Parker (ed.) *Spain and the Netherlands, 1559–1609. Ten Studies* (Glasgow, 1979), 178–185; E. Scholliers, 'De eerste schade van de scheiding. De sociaal-economische conjunctuur 1558–1609' in J. Craeybeckx, F. Daelemans and F.G. Scheelings (eds.) *'1585: On Separate Paths ...' Proceedings of the colloquium on 'The separation of the Low Countries' held on 22–23 November 1985 in Brussels* (Colloquia Europalia 6; Louvain, 1988), 35–51.

15 Parker, *The Army of Flanders*, 12–18; Piceu, *Over vrybuters*, 98–141.

16 Piceu, *Over vrybuters*, 141–161; De Kraker, Een staatse strategie, 16–28.

17 Tops, 'De Heffing der Spaanse Contributiën', 35–38; Van der Ent, 'Oostersche Contributiën', 45–49. A similar organisation was found in Northern France, where the audit office of

The Spanish and Dutch efforts to collect contributions in the frontier regions suffered from some deficiencies. The collectors as well as the governors of the frontier towns managed to embezzle quite large sums of money by making the villagers pay more than was stated in the accounts. The publication by the States General of a placard forbidding the levy of contributions by private persons was to no avail, as is shown by its frequent republications. Moreover, soldiers and freebooters openly ignored the issued safeguards and pillaged villages that had diligently paid their contributions. In a letter to the States General, Michiel Everwijn, the collector of the contributions in Ostend, demonstrated how the freebooters boasted that they were 'the masters of the forests of Flanders' and illustrated how their actions eroded the authority of the States General as guarantor of the *sauvegardes*. Their wild actions caused great mischief and irritation with the collectors and the villagers alike, the latter resenting the fact that the contributions had not provided them with the security they craved so much.[18] The greatest challenge for the system of contributions, however, was political resistance. In The Hague as well as in Brussels, many resented the fact that their subjects had to pay the enemy contributions. While the cash-strapped government in Brussels deplored the continuous sapping of its subjects' finances, the States of Zeeland feared that the contributions and the peace and quiet they promised would lure the emigrated Flemish and Brabant merchants and craftsmen back to their homes and herald the economic recovery of the Southern Low Countries. This in turn would enable the Spanish army to launch an attack on the Zeeland isles. The result of these fears was that both sides occasionally forbade their subjects to pay contributions to the enemy.[19]

In spite all these tribulations and political considerations, both sides imposed contributions on large parts of enemy territory throughout the 1590s and 1600s and monthly channelled considerable sums of money to their chests. From August to December 1597, for instance, the Dutch collector of the contributions in Ostend received more than 140,000 guilders in contributions from West-Flanders.[20] The generally well-informed papal nuncio, Guido Bentivoglio, estimated that the Dutch annually extracted 900,000 guilders from the archducal territories. It is hard to properly assess the value of Bentivoglio's estimate,

Lille watched over the Spanish receivers of the contributions. Ruiz Ibáñez, 'La guerre, les princes et les paysans'.

18 Piceu, *Over vrybuters*, 167–180.

19 Piceu, *Over vrybuters*, 180–183.

20 Michiel Everwijn to the States General, 31 December 1597, The Hague, National Archive, *States General*, 4888.

since we have no information regarding the total amount of Dutch contributions at our disposal, but even after a considerable adjustment of the nuncio's figures to allow for some exaggeration or misinformation on his side, the contributions system still appears to have been highly profitable.[21] So when the warring parties agreed to initiate negotiations, the stakes were high. Never before had the levying of contributions been so well-organised. Nevertheless, because of the injection of American silver and the staggering amounts of taxes paid by Castile and Holland, contributions did not yet become the principal way of financing the war effort, a role they would acquire during the Thirty Years War and the wars of Louis XIV.[22] Still, the size of the levies meant multiple questions relating to the contributions would have to be answered during the coming negotiations: should the collecting of contributions continue or cease when peace was signed and, if continued, should there be specific areas in which the levying of contributions would still be tolerated? In the Southern Netherlands, the different provinces had already clearly voiced their ardent desire for a complete end to violence on different occasions, such as the meeting of the Southern States General in 1600 and the Joyous Entries of the Archdukes.[23] The war-torn eastern provinces of the Republic were as eager to

21 Guido Bentivoglio, *Histoire des Guerres de Flandre par le Cardinal Guido Bentivoglio, traduite de l'Italien par M. Loiseau, l'aîné, Chanoine de l'église d'Orléans* (Paris, 1770), vol. 4, 526–527. The nuncio's estimate seems greatly exaggerated, as the annual average of Dutch levies in the period 1637–1642 amounted to 400,947 guilders. Marjolein C. 't Hart, *The Making of a Bourgeois State: War, Politics and Finance During the Dutch Revolt* (Manchester, 1993), 99.

22 On the role of contributions and taxes in the financing of the Dutch Revolt: 't Hart, *Making of a Bourgeois State*, 94–100; Jan Glete, *War and the State in Early Modern Europe. Spain, the Dutch Republic and Sweden as Fiscal-Military States, 1500–1660* (Warfare and History 8; London/New York, 2002), 100–110. On the key role played by contributions in the financing of other conflicts, see Ronald G. Asch, 'Kriegsfinanzierung, Staatsbildung und ständische Ordnung in Westeuropa im 17. und 18. Jahrhundert', *Historische Zeitschrift*, 268 (1999) 651–655; John A. Lynn, 'How War Fed War: The Tax of Violence and Contributions during the *Grand Siècle*', *Journal of Modern History*, 65 (1993) 303–309; H. Landberg et al. (eds.) *Det kontinentala krigets ekonomi. Studier i krigsfinansiering under svensk stormaktstid* (Acta Universitatis Upsaliensis. Studia Historia Upsaliensa 36; Uppsala, 1971); Ronald Fagerlund, 'Kontribution, försträckning och kaduck. Svensk krigsfinansiering i Östersjöprovinserna 1655–1661', *Historisk Tidskrift för Finland*, 66 (1981) 321–337.

23 Louis P. Gachard, *Actes des Etats Généraux de 1600* (Brussels, 1849), *passim*; Ioannes Bochius, *Historica narratio profectionis et inavgvrationis serenissimorvm belgii principvm Alberti et Isabellae, Avstriae archidvcvm. Et eorum optatissimi in Belgium Aduentus, Rerumque gestarum et memorabilium, Gratulationum, Apparatuum, et Spectaculorum in*

put an end to violence as their southern counterparts. Linked to the matter of contributions was the problem of the possession of frontier towns such as Sluys, Bergen-op-Zoom, Breda, Grave, Rheinberg, Groenlo, Oldenzaal and Lingen. Apart from the strategic importance of these towns, most of the places mentioned functioned as a seat of the collectors. If the Archdukes and the States General were to reach an agreement on an exchange of towns under their authority, this would seriously hamper the levying of contributions deep in Flanders, Brabant, Guelders, Overijssel and Drenthe in case of a renewal of the conflict. Finally, as the military commander, Maurice of Nassau had been assigned a portion of the spoils and booty of war. Although peace would provide him with a higher income from his domains in Zeeland and Brabant, Maurice was nevertheless expected to react reluctantly to efforts to ban contributions and *brandschattingen.*[24]

Finding solutions for these three related issues presented itself as a difficult task. Mutual distrust hampered the negotiations. Furthermore, no ready-made answers could be found in the writings of Pierino Belli, Francisco de Vitoria, Baltasar de Ayala or Alberico Gentili.[25] And 16th-century treaty practice alike provided virtually no clues for the negotiators. Most of the Franco-Habsburg treaties of the 16th century used standard phrases to put an end to all hostile actions, liberate all prisoners of war and return to a stable peace, while truces forbade the troops to cross the border.[26] This does not mean that no contributions were levied during the Valois-Habsburg wars, but these levies did not yet function as a coherent, state-run system. Contributions in the wars before and during the first phases of the Dutch Revolt – petty amounts of money extorted

---

ipsorum Susceptione et Inavguratione hactenus editorum accurate description. Avctore Ioanne Bochio S.P.Q.A à secretis (Antwerp, 1602), e.g. 345–347.

24 Kees Zandvliet, 'Het Hof van een dienaar met vorstelijke allure', in Kees Zandvliet et al. (eds.) *Maurits. Prins van Oranje* (Zwolle, 2000), 40–41.

25 Neither the law of booty nor the concept of *occupatio* were thoroughly treated in 16th-century international law: Heinhard Steiger, '"Occupatio bellica" in der Literatur des Völkerrechts der Christenheit (Spätmittelalter bis 18. Jahrhundert)' in Markus Meumann and Jörg Rogge (eds.) *Die besetzte res publica. Zum Verhältnis von ziviler Obrigheit und militärischer Herrschaft in besetzten Gebieten vom Spätmittelalter bis zum 18. Jahrhundert* (Herrschaft und soziale Systeme in der frühen Neuzeit 3; Munster, 2006), 232–233, n. 165.

26 Randall Lesaffer, *Europa. Een zoektocht naar vrede? 1453–1763 en 1945–1997* (Louvain, 1999), 235–238. Treaties (and preliminary armistices) of Noyon, Madrid, Cambrai, Crépy, Cateau-Cambrésis, Vervins and the Truces of Breda, Bomy and Cabanes in Jean Dumont, *Corps universel diplomatique du droit des gens* (Amsterdam, 1726–1731), vol. 4.1, 224–228, 399–410 and 433–434; vol. 4.2, 7–15, 153–154; 159 and 279–287 and vol. 5.1, 34–46 and 561–565.

in a small area by local commanders for their private use – [27] had not the far-reaching financial consequences of the 17th-century conflicts and were therefore no political problem that had to be solved by means of a treaty. The corpus of treaties and political texts produced during the Dutch Revolt also did not provide the negotiators with much inspiration. Only Article 7 of the Perpetual Edict promised to do justice to those soldiers that had committed 'oppressions, contributions & compositions'.[28] The stream of *édits* issued during the French wars of religion likewise offered them scant support.[29] By 1607, however, the well-organised, profitable and state-run contributions had transformed into a problem that could no longer be ignored. Complicating the issue even more was the fact that the Archdukes, and to a lesser extent also the Republic, perceived their levies as expressions and confirmations of their sovereign rights over the frontline countryside.[30]

Contributions and the Armistice

The first step towards ending the war in the Low Countries was a suspension of arms. The first, hesitating contacts leading to negotiations were undertaken by Walrave van Wittenhorst, a country squire with family connections to Cornelis van Aerssen, registrar of the States General, and Jan Gevaert, registrar of the small town of Turnhout and, according to nuncio Guido Bentivoglio, a man well-known in the Dutch ruling classes 'because of his frequent journeys into Holland to pay the contributions of that part of Brabant Turnhout belongs to'.[31] When the suspicious States General of the United Provinces in April 1607 accepted the archducal confirmation of their independence, both parties agreed on an eight-month armistice beginning on the 4th of May. All sieges of and surprise attacks on enemy strongholds, invasions into enemy territory and

27 On the roots of the contributions system, see Fritz Redlich, *De praeda militari. Looting and Booty, 1500–1815* (Vierteljahrschrift für Sozial- und Wirtschaftsgeschichte. Beihefte 39; Wiesbaden, 1956); 45–48. Concerning the development of contributions, Vermeesch, *Oorlog, steden en staatsvorming,* 141, distinguishes different phases in the development of the contributions: from *brandschatting* over local contributions to the largescale contributions of the Revolt.

28 Article 7 of the Perpetual Edict in Dumont, *Corps universel diplomatique,* vol. 5.1, 287.

29 The *Edit de Poitiers* (15 September 1577) forbade local commanders to levy contributions after the conclusion of the edict. Dumont, *Corps universel diplomatique,* vol. 5.1, 306–308.

30 Van der Ent, 'Oostersche Contributien', 38–39.

31 Bentivoglio, *Histoire des Guerres de Flandre ...*, vol. 4, 439.

the construction of new fortresses would cease from that date onwards.[32] While it was clear that all major military operations on land were to be abandoned for the rest of the year, the fate of minor actions such as the occasional execution of villages refusing to pay contributions still hung in the balance. Everything depended on the interpretation of the clause forbidding 'invasions of all provinces'. For the collectors of contributions, the situation was confusing indeed. In Flanders, for instance, 21 villages in the valley of the river Mandel, a small tributary of the river Lys, had revolted just before the cessation of arms, rejecting the payment of contributions. They counted on the military units and redoubts at their disposal to press home their arguments. The Dutch collector in Sluys feared that, now an armistice had been signed, the Archdukes could 'obstruct and prevent the villagers to pay contributions', because executions were no longer allowed.[33] A clarification of the armistice text was certainly needed.

Therefore, Jan Neyen, the archducal envoy who had brokered the armistice, was sent once more to the States General. The possible return of Neyen raised suspicion in the Republic, especially among Maurice and the representatives of Zeeland who would have preferred to refuse a passport to the archducal envoy. The other provinces, however, overruled the objections of Zeeland and admitted Neyen to the meeting of the States General so that he might present his proposals for an amplification of the armistice.[34] On 7 May 1607, Neyen requested from the States a cessation of all hostilities at sea and a clarification of how the word 'invasions' was to be interpreted. The Dutch Council of State deliberated several times over the issue. A draft of the extended armistice 'concerning the word invasion, the armistice on land ... and the limits of the mentioned armistice', met with the opposition of the representatives of Zeeland, who were unwilling to engage in new negotiations with the enemy, and of Maurice, who was concerned about the precise wording of the document, so as not to relinquish any sovereignty claims. Their objections, however, were to no avail. The recently arrived French envoys analysed the situation well when stating that 'since he [Maurice] learned that other provinces had accepted [the

32 Emanuel Van Meteren, *Historie van de Oorlogen en Geschiedenissen der Nederlanden, en derzelver Nabuuren, Beginnende met den jaare 1315, en eindigende met den jaare 1611. ... Negende deel* (Gorinchem, 1760), 229.

33 F. Van Belle and F. Roussel to the States General, 5 May 1607, The Hague, National Archives, *States General*, 4915.

34 H.P.H. Rijperman, *Resolutiën der Staten-Generaal van 1576 tot 1609. Veertiende Deel, 1607–1609* (Rijks Geschiedkundige Publicatiën, Grote Serie 131; The Hague, 1970) 52 (5 May 1607).

draft of the extended armistice], despite some noticeable considerations made by His Excellency, he would yield, giving good prospects that also those of Zeeland would let them instruct on this issue'. Indeed, Oldenbarnevelt and the other provinces got their way. On 2 July 1607, both parties exchanged the extended armistice text.[35]

Although the learned historiographer of the States General, Dominicus Baudius, was of the opinion that 'it is not proper for a first-rate historiographer, nor interesting for later generations to describe such matters in detail', the text the States came up with is well worth a closer look.[36] The States and the Archdukes agreed on the creation of clearly demarcated zones where enemy contributions – and if necessary also executions – were to be tolerated. In Brabant, the Dutch collectors of the contributions would be allowed to collect money in all villages north of the rivers Dijle and Demer, but they had to respect the neutrality of the Prince-Bishopric of Liège. In Flanders, the collector of Sluys commanded the area north of the rivers Scheldt, Lys and Mandel. Villages situated on the left bank of the Yser or south of the line Roeselare-Diksmuide were exempt from paying contributions. Archducal accountants, for their part, could rightfully exact payments from the Brabant villages controlled by the Dutch. In the east of the Republic, the fiefdom of Wedde, Drenthe, the villages north of the river Vecht and west of the river IJssel enjoyed freedom from contributions, as did the lands between the rivers Maas en Waal. It is striking that the Overkwartier of Guelders was not mentioned in the text. Most likely, the States General did not want to compromise their claims regarding that region. One was not allowed to change the rate of taxation during the armistice. The situation of the inhabitants of the embattled periphery of the Low Countries in the Holy Roman Empire did not improve as a result of the armistice, since people and property 'outside the aforementioned exempted limits ... [are] subjected to the law and rigors of war'.[37] The Dutch historiographer Emanuel Van Meteren narrates how garrisons at the outskirts of the Low Countries continued to harass each other 'as they were allowed to do by the treaty'. This was illustrated by the violent death of Count Adolf van

35 C.M. Van der Kemp, *Maurits van Nassau, Prins van Oranje, in zyn leven, waardigheden en verdiensten voorgesteld* (Rotterdam, 1843), vol. 1, 118–121; Rijperman, *Resolutiën der Staten-Generaal ... 1607–1609*, 53–61 (26 and 28 May and 1 June 1607).

36 Dominicus Baudius, *Van't Bestant des nederlantschen oorlogs Drie Boecken: beschreven door Dominicvm Bavdivm, Doctoor in de Rechten ende voornaemste Professeur der Historiën in de hooghe Schole van Leyden. Vertaelt door P. Iacobi Austro-Sylvium* (Amsterdam, 1616), 13.

37 Middelburg, Zeeland Archive, *States of Zeeland*, 22, 162–164.

Nassau-Siegen. Attracted by the spoils Adolf's horsemen had captured in the area, soldiers of the Spanish garrison of Rheinberg ambushed the Count's troops. Adolf died in combat, but his men eventually succeeded in defeating the Rheinberg garrison and recapturing their booty (Figure 7.1).[38]

No faith was pinned on a small-scale armistice such as had been reached during the negotiations leading up to the Vervins Treaty. Henry IV, who had wanted to keep up military pressure on Philip II and could not afford to leave his allies in the lurch, only agreed to a limited armistice restricted to a four-mile radius around Vervins.[39] It seems almost surreal that two governments that had in the previous decades spent much of their energy trying to eliminate enemy contributions, now publicly permitted enemy levies in their territory, but with this agreement, Brussels and The Hague created clarity for the coming period, for their rural subjects and for themselves. By clearly marking the borders of the contribution paying areas and by freezing the contribution rates, the warring parties attempted to keep tensions from running high. Indeed, in the years before 1607, quarrels about contribution rates had often caused conflicts to flare up in the frontier regions. If one party raised the contributions the enemy villages had to pay, the other party retaliated by doing the same, thus creating a spiral of ever higher demands. If no side backed down or tempered its financial claims, both sides ended up with their villages being executed for not having paid the unrealistic contribution duties. Thanks to the transparent extended armistice, it was unlikely that the issue of contributions would ever again cause such chain reaction of mounting demands and disrupt the lengthy negotiations that lay ahead.

Within the territory of the Low Countries, the Archdukes and the States ordered their commanders and (military) personnel to obey these new clauses. However, violations were manifold. Van Meteren noted that 'both parties organised some raids, under different pretences'. The garrison of Bergen-op-Zoom, for instance, apparently found it hard to abandon its habit of attacking travellers in the neighbourhood of Antwerp, while soldiers of the Spanish force in Rheinberg captured all the Dutch merchants who were travelling to the Frankfurt fair without a passport. Rittmaster Du Boys, an experienced officer who 'trusted the armistice too lightly', was shot by raiders when he returned to his garrison and the governor of Grave entered Den Bosch as a prisoner. The mutineers in Diest, for their part, also did not bother to

38 Van Meteren, *Historie… Tiende Deel*, 94–96.

39 *Memoires de Bellievre, et de Silleri. Contenant Un Journal concernant la Negociation de la Paix Traitée à Vervins l'an 1598. entre Henri IV. Roi de France, & de Navarre, Philippes II. Roi d'Espagne, & Charles Emanuel Duc de Savoye. Premiere Partie* (The Hague, 1696), 15–16.

FIGURE 7.1 *Contribution zones in the Low Countries, 1607–1609*

observe the armistice.[40] For the year 1607, the resolutions of the States General mention violations of the agreement by either side on 16, 18, 21 and 28 July, 18 September and 1, 2 5, 15, 16, 19, 27 and 31 October 1607.[41] However, in the end, the additional clauses to the armistice succeeded in addressing the contributions as a root of conflict. During the peace congress both parties reacted calmly to violations of the armistice and promised swift rectification.[42]

Contributions during the Peace Negotiations

With the problem of contributions temporarily settled, the negotiators could tackle more fundamental issues during the Congress of The Hague. The instructions of the Archdukes for their delegation did not mention the levying of contributions – peace would make an end to those – but did address the related problem of the *limites*, the demarcation of the frontier, and consequently also the exchange of possessions. Both parties had to agree on marking their borders in order to establish where archducal or Dutch territory started and – consequently – where sovereign rights could be exercised. Brussels knew that it would be a major gain 'if we could have frontiers so that nature separates us from each other, for instance in Flanders by the sea and in Brabant and Guelders by the Rhine and Waal'. In exchange for the formidable Dutch strongholds in Flanders and Brabant, the Archdukes were willing to give up the fortresses on the Rhine and the towns of Lingen, Oldenzaal and Groenlo. Albert realised that this was an unequal exchange, so in case of resistance, the Brussels delegation was authorised to renounce the claims on Geertruidenberg and Heusden, two places which had always been part of Holland, and argue that 'the many things we let [the Dutch] deserves that they do something for us…' If necessary, it was even conceivable that Rheinberg would be returned to the Elector of Cologne. Finally, to obtain that 'Flanders would be fully ours, the case that matters most', the envoys could promise that Grave or other places

40 Van Meteren, *Historie… Negende Deel*, 255–256.

41 H.P.H. Rijperman, *Resolutiën van de Staten-Generaal … 1607–1609*, 33–34, 38, 40–41, 61, 66 and 179. See also F.J.G. Ten Raa and F. De Bas, *Het Staatsche Leger 1568–1795* (Krijgsgeschiedkundige Geschriften 15; Breda, 1911–1921), vol. 2, 95.

42 A.J. Veenendaal, *Johan van Oldenbarnevelt. Bescheiden betreffende zijn Staatkundig Beleid en zijn Familie* (Rijks Geschiedkundige Publicatiën, Grote Serie 108; The Hague, 1962), vol. 2, 182–184.

would not be garrisoned.[43] This insistence on Flanders is hardly surprising. If the archducal negotiators succeeded in making their Dutch counterparts give up the Republic's foothold in Flanders, Brussels would regain control over the southern bank of the Scheldt estuary and the isle of Cadzand, thereby depriving the Republic of an excellent base for a seaborne invasion of Flanders. Gaining control of Flanders had also another benefit: it would once more reunite the province that provided Brussels with the highest tax incomes.[44]

Although surrendering control over the above-mentioned fortresses in Flanders and Brabant would drastically alter the strategic balance in the Low Countries, many in the Republic – according to the French ambassador Pierre Jeannin even 'les plus sages' – were willing to consider the Archdukes' proposition. Accepting would allow the needy States to discharge more than 6000 men garrison troops.[45] Others, however, strongly opposed it on the grounds that in this way, the Spanish King would deprive them of possessions 'he could impossibly take in six years', while offering in exchange only minor towns that had been conquered in sixteen days.[46] The French King Henry IV shared this opinion. In a letter to Jeannin and Russy of 27 February 1608, he declared that he considered the issue of sovereignty over disputed territory of paramount importance, more significant even than religion or the trade on the Indies. Unlike colonial trade, which the King considered to be a domain where only the personal wealth of some merchants was at stake, the possession of the strategic strongholds in Brabant and Flanders influenced the unity and security of the entire Republic. Henry clearly feared a Spanish strategy of peace,[47] *viz.* that Madrid would succeed in weakening its opponent's military position by means of peace talks and would afterwards resume war from a dominant military and financial position. 'If they [the Dutch] relinquish these towns in Brabant and Flanders', Henry stated, 'they should not count on their independence that had been granted them previously [as a Dutch precondition to initiate talks]'. The French King forbade Jeannin to make any overture regarding this issue, thereby ignoring Richardot's requests in this direction.[48]

---

43 Copy of the Instruction given by the Archdukes to their envoys, Brussels, 6 January 1608. J.A.C. Buchon (ed.), *Négociations Diplomatiques et Politiques du Président Jeannin (1598–1620)*(Paris, 1875), 18–20.

44 Bentivoglio, *Histoire des Guerres de Flandre ... Quatrième Partie,* 426–427.

45 Jeannin to Villeroy, 29 March 1608. Buchon, *Négociations,* 317.

46 Jeannin and Russy to Henry IV, 16 February 1608. Buchon, *Négociations,* 276–277.

47 On the foreign fears that Spain would exploit peace talks to achieve what its army couldn't, see Allen, *Philip III and the Pax Hispanica,* viii–x.

48 Henry IV to Jeannin and Russy, 27 February 1608. Buchon, *Négociations,* 285–286.

Instead, Jeannin, who was well aware of the strategic importance of the cities involved and had been informed that the States would walk out of the talks if the Archdukes insisted on an exchange, urged Richardot to keep this issue for another conference, to be held after peace had been concluded. The French ambassador also realised that the fact that the peace-weary Maurice of Nassau now *de facto* possessed the family domains of Breda and Grave and claimed the overlordship of Lingen, was an additional reason to postpone the whole discussion.[49] Backed by Jeannin, Oldenbarnevelt stood firm in rejecting the poisoned gift of Brussels. Father Neyen and Richardot, who understood that the States were not willing to give in on any of the major points listed up in their instruction, regretted this and loudly voiced their grieves: 'that, if they [the Dutch] also wanted to keep the cities of Brabant and Flanders, they [Neyen and Richardot] did not perceive how this negotiation could in any way benefit the King and the Archdukes'.[50] Notwithstanding the efforts of the archducal delegation, they failed to obtain control of the towns in Flanders and Brabant.

This did not mean that the problem of the boundaries was abandoned also. The warring parties still had to agree on a strict and clear delineation of their possessions in the Low Countries. The Dutch envoys pushed for an agreement stating that their side controlled the Brabant villages subjected to Breda and Grave and those situated in the Marquisate of Bergen-op-Zoom; this seemed reasonable to them, considering the fact that they held the *chef-ville* of these specific regions. Brussels strongly opposed this suggestion, since the Archdukes feared that relinquishing sovereignty over the villages in Northern Brabant would not only reduce their territory, but would also imply giving the Republic *carte blanche* to introduce reformed religion there. Richardot argued that his masters were the sovereigns of Brabant and thus by right possessed the whole Duchy, except for the walled towns occupied by the Dutch. Oldenbarnevelt countered with the Dutch argument that the sovereignty claims of the Dutch Republic, which could be traced back to the Union of Utrecht, predated those of the Archdukes, which were barely a decade old. Of course, the archducal delegation staunchly opposed these arguments and offered suggestions for a compromise.[51]

In the search for a compromise concerning the sovereignty over the countryside, the topic of contributions popped up again. On 6 June 1608, the envoys representing the Archdukes suggested that control over the countryside

49 Jeannin and Russy to Henry IV, 16 February 1608. Buchon, *Négociations*, 276–277.

50 Veenendaal, *Johan van Oldenbarnevelt. Bescheiden*, vol. 2, 205.

51 Jeannin and Russy to Henry IV, 6 April 1608. Buchon, *Négociations*, 323–324.

of Brabant, Flanders and the Overkwartier of Guelders was to be relinquished to them, while the countryside on the other side of the Rhine was to be controlled by the States. With this overture, Richardot gave up all claims to sovereignty over the countryside of the Overkwartier and Lingen in order to obtain it for Flanders and Brabant. The States rejected the proposal because they considered it an unbalanced deal. In the ensuing debate the archducal delegation claimed that the States could not act as sovereigns over the Brabant countryside as they had never levied taxes there, an argument the Dutch immediately rejected by saying that they had levied contributions there for years, thus carefully exploiting the two meanings of the word and presenting their levies of contributions as a sovereign right.[52] This argument certainly did not help to bridge the gap between the bickering parties and as a result neither the problem of the contributions, nor that of the *limites* had been resolved by the time both sides agreed that the negotiations had reached a deadlock, abandoning all hope of a lasting peace and settling for a prolonged truce, brokered by the foreign ambassadors Pierre Jeannin and Ralph Winwood.

Contributions and the Truce Negotiations

At the beginning of 1609, Richardot once more put the issue of the contributions on the negotiation table. A truce, after all, would not automatically end all hostilities.[53] The drafts of the articles of a truce, drawn up earlier by Jeannin and Winwood, had proposed the unhindered levying of contributions in the armistice zones during the truce years. Richardot had agreed on this point: the draft of the articles of a future truce he had written himself had gone even further and stated that the situation in the countryside was to be left as it had been before the armistice.[54] In other words, violence and extortion could return to large parts of the Low Countries. Brussels knew that accepting the enemy's levies would cause great displeasure among its rural subjects. Moreover, contributions would serve to prolong tensions between North and South and it was not totally inconceivable that these might, in the long run, spark off a renewal of the conflict. Finally, the Dutch collectors managed to extract larger amounts of money from the enemy's countryside than their archducal counterparts. If we are to believe a Danish envoy, the Dutch monthly

52 Veenendaal, *Johan van Oldenbarnevelt. Bescheiden*, vol. 2, 217–219.

53 Lesaffer, *Europa: een zoektocht naar vrede?*, 238–239.

54 Jeannin to Oldenbarnvelt, 12 February 1609. Buchon, *Négociations*, 598.

collected 34,000 guilders in Brabant and Flanders, a sum which the Archdukes found hard to match.[55]

For all the reasons mentioned above, Richardot urged Jeannin to have the States accept the fact that all contributions would cease after a truce had been signed. He argued that contributions could only be collected by use of force. Jeannin realised that the Archdukes would never give in on this subject and tried to convince Oldenbarnvelt of the reasonableness of this demand concerning, as Jeannin called it, 'a minor issue'. If the States were to accept Richardot's proposition, however, this would also affect the financial position of Maurice. Indeed, the Stadholder received a part of the contributions and Jeannin pressed Oldenbarnvelt to find ways to compensate him for this loss of revenues.[56] Henry IV agreed with his ambassador's course of action because continuing the contributions 'would be an unbearable oppression of the people'.[57]

The States, for their part, did not yield easily. In order to reconcile North and South, the ambassadors drew up a compromise whereby contributions could still be levied in distinct zones for some years. Brussels flatly refused the ambassadors' proposals.[58] On 18 March, the ambassadors explained to the States General that the only problem left to be solved was that of the contributions. Eventually, the Dutch agreed to abolish contributions.[59] This decision freed large parts of the Republic of a constant strain – which Oldenbarnvelt considered a major achievement of the Twelve Years Truce[60] – but also created two new problems: Maurice's loss of income had to be compensated for and Brussels and The Hague had to agree on a frontier, marking precisely where enemy territory started.

The first of these problems was quickly resolved. The Stadholders and Frederik-Hendrik accepted a large financial settlement. Under impulse of Jeannin, the States General indemnified Maurice by more than doubling the

55 Danish envoy quoted in Ten Raa and De Bas, *Het Staatsche Leger,* vol. 2, 405. Another, apparently exaggerated estimate in Bentivoglio, *Histoire des Guerres de Flandre ... Tome Quatrième* (Paris, 1770), 526–527.

56 Jeannin and Russy to Henry IV, 23 February 1609. Buchon, *Négociations,* 602.

57 Henry IV to Jeannin and Russy, 29 February 1609 [sic]. Buchon, *Négociations,* 610.

58 Baudius, *Van't Bestant des nederlantschen oorlogs,* 215–216.

59 Jeannin to Oldenbarnvelt, 10 March 1609; Speech of Jeannin to the States General, 18 March 1609; Jeannin and Russy to Henry IV, 21 March 1609. Buchon, *Négociations,* 624, 630–634 and 635–637.

60 M.L. Van Deventer, *Gedenkstukken van Johan van Oldenbarneveldt en zijn tijd, verzameld en met inleiding en aanteekeningen uitgegeven. Derde deel. 1604–1609* (The Hague, 1865), 311–312.

wages for his political functions and increased the remuneration for his military functions with 61,000 guilders. Besides this handsome salary increase, the Archdukes promised 100,000 guilders in recompense for lost revenues from the Nassau domains in the Southern Netherlands. For Maurice, the 1609 Truce meant the end of his financial problems.[61] The ambassadors faced a more difficult problem. They had drafted a proposal according to which all villages belonging to the Marquisate of Bergen-op-Zoom or coming under the authority of Breda and Grave would be part of the Republic. Jeannin realised that a similar proposal had met with fierce resistance from the Archdukes only months ago, but he was nevertheless confident that they would accept it now. After all, Brussels had to choose between unbridled contributions or an agreement on the frontiers and it opted for the latter.[62] To mollify the opposition, the ambassadors agreed on adding a certificate to the Truce Treaty stating that neither the States General nor Maurice would influence the religious situation in the Brabant countryside.[63]

The result was that Article 2 of the Truce put an end to 'tous actes d'hostilité, de quelque façon qu'ilz soyent, ... tant par mer, ... que par terre ... et pour tous leurs subjects et habitans...' The next Article stated that both parties would be left in the possession of the cities they had controlled before the signing of the Truce 'en quoy on entend comprendre les bourgs, villages, hameaulx et plat pays, qui en dependent'.[64]

Additional Treaties

The conclusion of the Truce and the subsequent pause in hostilities caused great rejoicing throughout the Netherlands. Caution, however, remained. The succession crisis in Cleves-Jülich made the future of the Antwerp Treaty look bleak. Moreover, numerous bones of contention had not been discussed thoroughly during the negotiations. Brussels and The Hague had postponed several issues – such as the opening of the river Scheldt, the religious situation in the countryside in Twente and Overijssel, confiscated goods and the sovereignty of

61 A. Th. Van Deursen, *Maurits van Nassau. De winnaar die faalde* (Amsterdam, 2002), 217; Zandvliet, 'Het hof van een dienaar met vorstelijke allure', 41.

62 Jeannin and Russy to Henry IV, 21 March 1609; Jeannin to Villeroy, 25 March and 3 April 1609, Buchon, *Négociations,* 635 and 638, 644.

63 Certificate published in Buchon, *Négociations,* 659–660.

64 Victor Brants, *Recueil des Ordonnances des Pays-Bays. Règne d'Albert et Isabelle, 1597–1621* (Brussels, 1909–1912), vol. 1, 403.

contested territories outside Brabant – to conferences which were to be held once a truce was concluded. A first cycle of reunions produced a first additional treaty, concluded in The Hague on 7 January 1610, in which predominantly the issues of the confiscated goods and property were tackled. Contributions and the related issue of sovereignty were dealt with during the negotiations leading up to a second explanatory treaty on 24 June 1610.

The Truce only pertained to the sovereignty and religious situation in the Duchy of Brabant. The overlordship over the villages in Twente (the so-called 'Twente quaestie') still needed to be established. Furthermore, the frontiers in Flanders were challenged by the city of Bruges which claimed the possession of Sluys, the harbour city it had bought in 1566. As a result of the hiatuses in the 1609 Treaty, Brussels' agents tried to gain control over the disputed villages in Twente and Flanders, possession of which would enable the Archdukes to levy taxes and influence the religious situation there. In Flanders, for instance, a man nicknamed *Duyveljager* (devilhunter) received a commission from the magistrate of the *Brugse Vrije* to levy taxes in the area controlled by the Dutch.[65] A flood of similar incidents startled the States. The Republic did not fail to voice its concern to its allies[66] and complained loudly to Brussels. On 12 April 1610, the States General showed their teeth in a letter to the Archdukes. 'If the Archdukes have exercised jurisdiction and sovereignty somewhere in Twente', the *Hoog Mogenden* commented, 'then there are ten times as much villages in Brabant and Flanders and other areas, now claimed by the Archdukes by virtue of the Treaty [of Antwerp], where the States have done the same'.[67] After months of hard bargaining the same compromise that had broken the deadlock in Brabant was used to resolve the matter of Twente. In the second additional treaty, the Archdukes gave up their claims to Twente 'on the explicit condition nonetheless, that concerning the matter of religion all will remain in the same condition as it was on the day of the conclusion of the aforementioned Treaty [of Antwerp]'. The town of Oldenzaal was to remain under archducal control.[68] Negotiations concerning the frontiers of Flanders quickly floundered. With reference to the Truce, Bruges demanded the restitution of

65 Rijperman, *Resolutiën der Staten-Generaal ... 1607–1609*, 882–883 (15 June 1609).

66 Van Meteren, *Historie ... Tiende Deel*, 336–338, lists thirteen archducal infractions or unreasonable demands.

67 A. Th. Van Deursen, *Resolutiën der Staten-Generaal. Nieuwe Reeks 1610–1670. Eerste Deel, 1610–1612* (Rijks Geschiedkundige Publicatiën, Grote Serie 135; The Hague, 1971), 85–86 (12 April 1610).

68 'op expresse conditie niet te min dat roerende het stuck ende exercite van de Religie, alle saecken aldaer sullen blyven in den selven staet soo die geweest zijn ten dagen van het besluyt des voorsz bestants'. Dumont, *Corps universel diplomatique*, vol. 5.2, 142.

Sluys, while the government of the *Brugse Vrije* claimed sovereignty over the part of the Flemish countryside conquered by Maurice in 1604. In the Republic, nobody ever seriously considered giving up the bridgehead protecting the island of Walcheren against a direct invasion. While maintaining the status quo during the truce, Bruges, the *Brugse Vrije* and Zeeland entered upon a century-long juridical quarrel in which the respective arguments fell on deaf ears.[69]

Also matters relating to the contributions had not yet been settled completely. The Dutch collectors of the contributions wrestled with the question of what they were to do with villages that had accumulated high arrears in the years before the truce. Referring to the treaty, villages in Brabant and Flanders now stubbornly refused to pay. The States General were determined to collect these arrears and ordered their collectors to execute the villages in Brabant in order to raise at least half of the arrears. Brussels, however, urged the States to be patient and pursued a compromise for the whole issue.[70] In the end, the negotiators of the second additional treaty overcame these problems. On 23 June 1610, the States promised to behave reasonably with regard to the contributions. The next day, the second explanatory treaty stated that 'concerning the arrears from the contributions in Brabant, the villages will immediately furnish a third part, and concerning the rest the Lords States General will treat with them [the villages] with reason'.[71]

Arrears could amount to thousands of guilders. In spite of several remittances, some villages in Peel, in the area near Grave, had run into arrears of more than 117,000 guilders. They desperately needed some leniency from the States. And yet we find that, years later, some of those villages were still struggling to meet the arrears. In May 1612, the Dutch Council of State lamented that several Brabant villages blamed bad harvests for their inability to fulfil their financial obligations towards the Republic. Moreover, villages situated in the vicinity of towns flatly refused to hand over the money to settle their arrears. Even as late as July 1614, Weert, a village near Roermond, suffered execution at

69 Bruges, Rijksarchief, *Fonds Brugse Vrije – Ongeordende Procesbundels*, 22,541; Middelburg, Zeeland Archive, *Vrije van Sluis*, 451.

70 Van Deursen, *Resolutiën der Staten-Generaal ... 1610–1612*, 84–86, 102, 121, 120, 145 (10 and 28 April, 17 and 23 May 1610).

71 'Aengaende de restanten van de Contributien in Brabant, dat mits by de selve promptelijck furnerende een derdendeel, sal by den voorsz Heeren Staten Generael noopende de reste met hun gehandelt worden in alle redelijckheyt'. Dumont, *Corps universel diplomatique*, vol. 5.2, 142–143. On 9 June 1610, villages in Flanders obtained confirmation of the States General that there would be no new Dutch levies, but that arrears had to be paid. Van Deursen, *Resolutiën der Staten-Generaal ... 1610–1612*, 145 (9 June 1610).

the hands of the Dutch; this event gave rise to discussions in The Hague as to whether this action was a violation of the second additional treaty. Thereafter, resolutions of the States General no longer mention similar actions, suggesting that five years after the Truce was concluded contributions no longer caused troubles in the Low Countries.[72]

An Innovative Treaty

Ordinary people in the Low Countries experienced an important consequence of the articles of the 1609 Truce regarding contributions, when war resumed in 1621. Contributions and *brandschatting* were as widespread in the second phase of the war as they had been before the truce, but unlike had been the case in the 1590s, both parties now refrained from attempting to thwart the enemy levies. Such attempts during the first phase of the conflict had robbed the inhabitants of the frontier regions of virtually all protection: they had to endure the wrath of the central government if they paid contributions to the enemy, but if they did not, they had to face the enemy.[73] The text of the armistice and the long drawn-out negotiations during 1607–1611 turned out to be a veritable watershed, since now, for the first time, enemy levies in large parts of one's own territory became openly acceptable. Indeed, both Brussels and The Hague now accepted contributions as an integral part of the practices of war. The warring parties appreciated their advantages and no longer forced their subjects to resist the levies that could not be prevented. Agreements were drawn up regarding the amounts villages had to pay and the delineation of the areas where contributions had to be paid. For a decade, both Brussels and The Hague managed to respect each other's levies, thus rendering the war in the Low Countries more humane. The most remarkable example of this trend was to be found in the fact that along certain parts of the frontier one and the same person collected and administrated both the Spanish and the Dutch contributions.[74] Hugo Grotius also commented on this evolution, when he mentioned contributions as a contemporary example of moderation in war. In his *De iure belli ac pacis libri tres*, he described the positive effects of the levies: '[If the

72 Van Deursen, *Resolutiën der Staten-Generaal … 1610–1612*, 390, 413, 633 and 734 (30 May, 28 June 1611, 2 May, 18 September 1612); Van Deursen, *Resolutien der Staten-Generaal. Nieuwe reeks 1610–1670. Tweede Deel, 1613–1616* (Rijks Geschiedkundige Publicatiën, Grote Serie 151; The Hague, 1984) 291 (29 July 1614).

73 Van Deursen, *Maurits van Nassau*, 90–92.

74 Tops, 'De heffing der Spaanse contributiën', 36.

enemy has means of subsistence from other sources], it is best to leave agriculture undisturbed even along the common frontier. This we see in recent times was the arrangement for a considerable period in the war of the Netherlands against the Empire, with payment of contributions to either party'. Other scholars and lawyers followed suit.[75]

Nevertheless, war remained a grim business.[76] The practice of carving up the Low Countries into contribution zones was abandoned and both parties did their utmost to extend the area paying contributions to them as much as possible. Furthermore, there is ample evidence from the 1620s that both parties abducted clerics to enforce their financial demands. When from 1629 onwards, the fortunes of war started to favour the Dutch, Brussels reverted to the old practice of forbidding the Brabant villages to pay contributions to the Dutch. After the capture of Rheinberg (1633), villages north of the great rivers were no longer allowed to pay the Spanish collectors. In 1635, the beginning of the involvement of France in the conflict finally put an end to a decade and a half of more 'humane' warfare.[77] The atrocities committed by the French soldiers (e.g. pillaging the small town of Tienen in 1635) had not been witnessed in the Low Countries in recent years, giving the war along the French border a particularly brutal character. But in the long run, the French did grasp the benefits of contributions to finance their war efforts. Under Louis XIV, contributions became one of the main ways of financing French military efforts. In order to prevent an escalation of the demands and to secure a reliable income, French and Spanish officials held three rounds of talks between 1676 and 1678

75 Hugo Grotius, (1625, text of 1646 and translation, Classics of International Law; Oxford, 1925, 2 vols.). On the legal restrictions on pillaging and the development of contributions in the 18th century, see Redlich, *De praeda militari,* 58–77.

76 Martin Rink, 'Die noch ungezähmte Bellona – Der kleine Krieg und die Landbevölkerung in der frühen Neuzeit' in Stefan Kroll and Kersten Krüger (eds.) *Militär und ländliche Gesellschaft in der frühen Neuzeit* (Herrschaft und soziale Systeme in der frühen Neuzeit 1; Munster, 2000) 172–179 and 187–189, rightly observes that the ever stricter regulations on plundering and contributions did not immediately bring about the desired effects.

77 Van Nimwegen, *Deser landen crijchsvolck,* 128–129; Vermeesch, *Oorlog, steden en staatsvorming,* 146; A. Impe, 'Nota betreffende de dorpen 'subject aen de contributie' en de toestand in 't Noorden van de kasselrij in 1621 en volgende jaren', *Handelingen van de Geschied- en Oudheidkundige Kring Kortrijk,* 9 (1930) 60–68; A. Bauwens, 'Gijzelingen van protestantse en rooms-katholieke geestelijken in het grensgebied tussen Staats-Vlaanderen westelijk deel en de Spaanse Nederlanden tijdens de zeventiende eeuw', in A. Wiggers et al. (eds.) *Rond de Kerk in Zeeland. Derde verzameling bijdragen van de Vereniging voor Nederlandse Kerkgeschiedenis* (Delft, 1991), 159–176.

in Deinze, near Ghent, which culminated in a set of rules to be applied to the contributions system of the Spanish Netherlands. With regard to one specific aspect, the conferences in Deinze were clearly influenced by the 1607 armistice clauses. Great emphasis was put on the importance of natural borders, such as rivers, to separate the area free from contributions from *la terre de contribution*. As the negotiators had done in 1607, the French and Spanish officials agreed on creating clear contribution zones in order to stop the vicious circle of ever increasing contribution demands. To enhance the clarity of their agreements – a novelty in comparison with the 1607 armistice – the delegations at Deinze approved that the prefatory bargaining on the amount of contributions to be paid was to be conducted by administrators of rural districts, instead of those of individual villages. Although the Deinze conferences did not produce a treaty, nor prohibit the French to levy huge contributions during the *Guerre des Réunions*, the practices agreed upon proved to be of a lasting quality.[78]

Not only the 1607 armistice, but also the Truce and the additional treaties inspired later treaty makers with regard to their position towards contributions. As contributions became the most important and a generally accepted way of financing an army during the Thirty Years War, articles relating to contributions could no longer be absent from treaties. The years after the 1609 Truce saw the breakthrough of contributions in treaties. Without doubt, the central role such contributions played in financing the wars in Germany was the main cause of the proliferation of articles relating to contributions.[79] But the influence of the Antwerp Truce articles cannot be brushed aside, as is witnessed by the wording of the articles of later treaties. Most notably, in 1648 Spain had to swallow the humiliating Article 3 that assigned the Bailiwick of Den Bosch and the districts of Breda and Bergen-op-Zoom to the Republic. The principle that villages followed the *chef-ville* was implemented once more. The fact that the Archdukes had given up their sovereignty, although temporarily, over Twente and the villages near Bergen-op-Zoom and Breda in 1609 now had a very bitter side-effect. Moreover, Article 64 of the Treaty of Munster of 30 January 1648 stipulated that 'le payement des arrierages de contributions qui lors dela conclusion du traicté resteront à payer pour les personnes & biens de part & d'autre sera regleé & determine par ceux qui de part & d'autre ont la

78 Hubert Van Houtte, *Les occupations étrangères en Belgique sous l'ancien régime* (Ghent, 1938), vol. 1, 213–229; Lynn, 'How War Fed War', 300–301.

79 After 1618, numerous treaties deal with contributions, as is illustrated by Dumont, *Corps universel diplomatique*, vol. 6.1, e.g. 21, 33, 35, 43, 52–53, 58, 85, 120–121, 156, 167, 229, 244, 286 and 303.

surintendance des Contributions'.[80] As in 1610, both parties accepted that the payment of arrears continued after the conclusion of the peace. Agreeing that arrears had to be paid after the conclusion of a peace eventually became standard practice during the second half of the 17th century. Similar clauses are found in the Treaties of Aachen (1668) and Nijmegen (1678/1679) and in the Truce of Regensburg (1684). France accepted Spain's demand to depart from the principle in the Treaty of Riswick (1697), but in 1713 the obligatory payment of arrears returned in the Peace Treaty of Utrecht as Article 28. Different interpretations and subsequent violations of these clauses caused French and Spanish officials to draw up extensive *traités*, which carefully dictated the exact point in time when the contributions and the payment of the arrears were to stop.[81]

Conclusion

The Dutch Revolt transformed the Low Countries into Europe's *School of War*, the main battleground where the art of war could be learned and practiced. This is most famously illustrated by the tactical innovations by Maurice of Nassau, but the school of war also provided other lessons. By the 1590s, both sides had perfected the levying of contributions in enemy territory and, in spite of stiff resistance and corruption, managed to uninterruptedly drain considerable sums of money from the enemy's countryside. The high degree of organisation, the duration and the size of these levies constituted new elements in late 16th-century warfare. The innovative character of the Treaty of Antwerp stems from the fact it was a truce which ended a prolonged period of conflict in a civil war. Without real peace and a clearly delineated border between the Northern and the Southern Netherlands, Article 2, which put an end to all hostilities, would remain a hollow phrase. So the possibility of a truce caused the negotiators to consider what was to become of the contributions during such a prolonged cessation of arms, and effectively forced them to agree on explicit legal and geographical limits for such contributions. In doing so, they laid the groundwork for future treaties with regard to the attitude towards contributions and set a standard for the practice of levying in the Low Countries and Western Europe. The Twelve Years Truce was a defining moment in the

80 Dumont, *Corps universel diplomatique*, vol. 6.1, 430–434.

81 Van Houtte, *Les occupations étrangères en Belgique*, vol. 1, 168–176, 475–497.

development of the contributions system, because it set the legal standards for the century to come.

During the lengthy negotiations, Brussels had caved in on many issues, but its hard bargaining on contributions yielded some valuable results. The Archdukes no longer had to tolerate Dutch financial claims and military raids on their territory and put an end to violence for a period of twelve years. For the country-folk of the war-torn frontier regions the truce meant security and peace. For those living in the Campine region and others living near the front-line, the end of the imposition of new levies was one of the most important aspects of the truce as it guaranteed them the 'general peace, solid and sincere' they so longed for.

PART 3

Truce and Law

CHAPTER 8

The United Provinces

'Free' or 'Free and Sovereign'?

Beatrix C.M. Jacobs

Introduction[1]

In the very first article of the Twelve Years Truce of 1609, the Archdukes Albert and Isabelle declare, both in their own names and in the name of the King (Philip III, 1598–1621), that they are pleased to conclude a treaty with the States General of the United Provinces *qualitate qua*, and that they consider these provinces free lands, provinces and states, to which they do hold no claims:

> Firstly, the Archdukes declare, both in their own names and in the name of the King, that they are content to treat with the Lords States General of the United Provinces in that capacity, holding them to be free Countries, Provinces and States, to which they do not pretend, and to arrange with them in these names and capacities, as they now do herewith, a Truce on the conditions described and declared hereafter.[2]

In the Treaty of Munster of 30 January 1648 it is the King himself (Philip IV, 1621–1665) who declares and recognises in Article 1 that the States General of

1 This text is a revision of my conference paper of April 2009. I cordially thank Professor Simon Groenveld of Leyden University for sending me the text of his lecture at the Institut für Europäische Geschichte in Mainz on 7 May 2009. This lecture has been published as 'Der Zwölfjährige Waffenstillstand in den Niederlanden von 1609. Ein halber Frieden zwischen *libertates* und religiones', *Jahrbuch für Europäische Geschichte*, 11 (2010), 161–187. I am also grateful to Professor Simon Groenveld and to Professor Randall Lesaffer, Dr Raymond Kubben and Mr Dick Broeren of Tilburg Law School for their substantive and editorial comments on my text.

2 My translation. A recent Dutch edition of the Truce can be found in Simon Groenveld, *Unie – Bestand – Vrede. Drie fundamentele wetten van de Republiek der Verenigde Nederlanden* (Hilversum, 2009), 115–127: 'Inden eersten die voorsz Heeren Eertztoghen verklaren, soo in haren namen, als inden naem van den voorsz Heere Coninck, dat syluyden te vreden zijn te tracteren mette voorsz Heeren Staten Generael van de Vereenichde Provincien, in qualiteyt, ende als de selve houdende voor vrije Landen, Provincien, ende Staten, op de welcke syluyden niet en pretenderen, en*de* te maecken met haer inde voorsz namen ende qualiteyten, gelijck sy doen by desen jegenwoordige, een Bestandt, opte conditiën hier nae beschreven ende verclaert'.

 | DOI 10.1163/9789004274921_010

the United Provinces and the provinces themselves with all the associated territories, cities and dependent lands are 'free and sovereign states, provinces and lands', to which neither he nor his issue holds or will hold any claims.

> Firstly, the asforesaid Lord King declares and recognises that the aforesaid Lords States General of the United Netherland and the respective provinces thereof, with all their associated districts, cities and dependent lands, are free and sovereign states, provinces, and lands, upon which, together with their associated district, cities and lands aforesaid he, the Lord King, does not now make any claim, and he himself and his successors descendants will in the future never make any claim; and therefore is satisfied to negotiate with these Lords States, as he does by these presents, a perpetual peace, on the conditions hereinafter described and confirmed.[3]

While the Truce of 1609 only used the term 'free' to refer to the lands, provinces and states of the Republic, the 1648 Treaty added 'sovereign'. Furthermore, and remarkably enough, the 1648 document asserts that the States General and the provinces are recognised as free and sovereign entities. The problem I would like to address here is whether these differences in terminology have any special meaning or whether the contracting parties meant the same in both cases.

In literature, it is sometimes simply assumed that the 1609 Truce recognised sovereignty. What complicates matters here is that in the literature different concepts of sovereignty are used. For example, in their introduction to the inventory of the archives of the Dutch emissaries and consuls up to 1813, Pennings and Thomassen conclude that the Republic's allies France and England considered the Truce of 1609 to entail recognition of the sovereignty of the States General. Their conclusion rests on the fact that France and England had already established ambassador-level diplomatic relations with

3 Translation in Wayne te Brake, *Shaping History. Ordinary people in European Politics, 1500–1700* (Berkeley/Los Angeles/London, 1998), 109. Groenveld, *Unie – Bestand – Vrede*, 160: 'Inden eersten verclaert den voors Heer Coninck ende erkent, dat de voors Heeren Staten Generael vande Vereenichde Nederlanden, en de respective Provincien vandeselve, met alle haer geassocieerde Landschappen, steden en aenhorige Landen, sijn vrije ende Souveraine Staten, Provincien en Landen, opde welcke, noch op haer geassocieerde Landschappen, Steden en Landen voors hij heer Coninck niet en pretendeert, noch nu, ofte namaels, voor hem selven, syne successeurs en nacomelingen immermeer ijets sal pretenderen; Ende dienvolgens te vreden te sijn met deselve heeren Staten te tracteren, gelijck hij doet by dese jegenwoordige, een eeuwige Vrede, opde conditien hier naer beschreven en verclaert'.

the Republic in 1609 and that before 1648 the Ottomans, Hamburg and Lübeck, Venice and Denmark had followed suit. The authors then say that with the 1648 Peace Treaty of Munster the Republic was also recognised as a sovereign state by other powers. What Pennings and Thomassen may have failed to notice is that they are referring to the sovereignty of two different entities, i.e., the States General and the Republic, and that they suggest that the Republic's allies and other states and sovereigns recognise the Republic as a sovereign state.[4]

An example of the equation of free and sovereign can be found in Richard Tuck's *The Rights of War and Peace*, in which he describes Grotius' idea of state sovereignty. Grotius (1583–1645) saw the provinces as sovereign states, Tuck argues, and the Union was an alliance to which no participating country had ceded any part of its sovereignty. Grotius also wrote that the United Provinces handled the conduct of war on behalf of the provinces, but left the *summa potestas* with the States of the provinces. In other words, the Republic of the United Provinces was a union of free nations and rulers. According to Tuck, in this context 'free' undoubtedly meant 'sovereign', and this refers to the Truce of 1609, so he states.[5] However, given that the text of the Truce does not explicitly mention either 'sovereignty' or 'sovereign' in relation to the Republic, can such an argument make a plausible case for the recognition of the Republic's sovereignty during the Twelve Years Truce?

To answer this question, I will present an analysis of the meaning given to the phrase 'free and sovereign'. For this purpose, I will examine the truce negotiations as well as the theoretical development of the concept of sovereignty in the 16th and 17th centuries.[6] The arguments the States General themselves

---

4 J.C.M. Pennings and Theo H.P.M. Thomassen (eds.), *Archieven van Nederlandse gezanten en consuls tot 1813. Deel 1. Overgedragen archieven van gezanten en consuls in de Christelijke wereld* (The Hague, 1994), 20–25. They refer to O. Schutte (ed.), *Repertorium der Nederlandse vertegenwoordigers residerende in het buitenland, 1584–1810* (Rijks Geschiedkundige Publicatiën; The Hague, 1976). See www.historici.nl/retroboeken/schutte.

5 Richard Tuck, *The Rights of War and Peace. Political Thought and Political Order from Grotius to Kant* (Oxford, 1999), 83–84. I do not consider the discussion whether the States General possessed sovereignty or not. In the United Provinces many people shared Grotius' view of the provinces possessing sovereignty and of the provincial States therefore lawfully exercising it. In the trial against Oldenbarnevelt this issue proved an important one. On this trial, see H. Gerlach, *Het proces tegen Oldenbarnevelt en de 'maximen in den staet'* (Haarlem, 1965).

6 On the later negotiations in the years before the Treaty of 1648, see Laura Manzano Baena, 'Negotiating Sovereignty. The Peace Treaty of Münster, 1648', *History of Political Thought*, 28 (2007), 617–641; J.J. Poelhekke, *De Vrede van Munster* (The Hague, 1948); Jonathan Israel, *The Dutch Republic and the Hispanic World* (Oxford, 1982), 347–374.

used in another case will also help to clarify the concept of sovereignty as it was then understood and applied.

The Negotiations

Both the United Provinces and Spain were faced with serious financial problems, which in part explain their willingness to enter into negotiations at the beginning of the 17th century. As Spain also eyed the conquests of the Dutch East India Company with great suspicion, there was sense in Philip III's apparently sudden move in 1606 to recognise the rebellious provinces as a free state, provided they withdrew from the overseas territories in Asia, Africa and America. Informally at first, but soon in a more formal setting, prolonged negotiations were conducted, in which the Archdukes Albert and Isabella, the Spanish commander Ambrogio Spínola and the Grand Pensionary (*raadpensionaris*) of Holland, Johan van Oldenbarnevelt played crucial roles.[7]

In April 1607, an armistice was signed, but it contained little in the way of concessions the United Provinces would be required to make. Of course, this stirred up feelings of ill will on the Spanish side, and these feelings intensified when in that same month the Spanish lost the Battle of Gibraltar.[8] However, as a consequence of resistance within the provinces, Oldenbarnevelt's oral promises could not be honoured. Even full peace and recognition as a free state could not persuade the provinces to sacrifice the East India Company and to allow free practice of the Roman Catholic faith.

In the course of 1607, the provincial representatives to the States General used both the term 'sovereignty' and the term 'freedom' in their deliberations.[9] Count William Louis of Nassau (1560–1620), to give an example, put forward that the provinces should agree that they would not make any concession on 'sovereignty and religion'. The Council of State advised the States General that

7 On the negotiations, see Simon Groenveld, *Het Twaalfjarig Bestand, 1609–1621. De jongelingsjaren van de Republiek der Verenigde Nederlanden* (The Hague, 2009), 33–66; Groenveld, *Unie – Bestand – Vrede*, 94–106; Israel, *The Dutch Republic and the Hispanic World*, 1–28; W.J.M. van Eysinga, *De wording van het Twaalfjarig Bestand van 9 April 1609* (Verhandelingen der Koninklijke Nederlandse Akademie van Wetenschappen, afdeling Letterkunde, NS. 66.3; Amsterdam, 1959), 67–155.

8 In this naval battle of 25 April 1607 a Dutch fleet attacked and destroyed an anchored Spanish fleet.

9 On the discussions, see H.H.P. Rijperman (ed.), *Resolutiën der Staten Generaal van 1576 tot 1609, veertiende deel, 1607–1609* (Rijks Geschiedkundige Publicatiën, Grote Serie, 131; The Hague, 1970), 42–109. See: www.historici.nl/retroboeken/statengeneraal/#14OR%3A0.

they should press the emissaries of the Archdukes for more details concerning their position on 'the free state and religion'. The representatives from Utrecht used the term 'free state' in conjunction with the concept of 'authority'. Representatives from Holland used the phrase 'freedom of the land', whereas the representatives from Friesland, Overijssel and Groningen used the term 'sovereignty'. The representatives from Zealand did not address sovereignty and religion as separate, if related, issues, but considered religion to be an integral element of sovereignty. Responding to the views expressed by the Zealand representatives, Utrecht, Friesland, Overijssel, and Groningen and Ommelanden referred to 'free state of the land'. In their final common position, the States General used the term 'sovereignty'. It would appear then that the terms 'free state', 'freedom' or 'liberty' and 'sovereignty' did not represent fundamentally different concepts for the representatives of the provinces, although it is also possible that they, or some of them, disguised the differences deliberately, as the negotiators, mediating emissaries and envoys were to do in the further negotiations. One thing is clear, however. In all cases external sovereignty was the implied antecedent: an entity's independence or exclusive competence to exercise authority on its own territory.

In the meantime, prospects of a peace or truce looked increasingly bleak. When negotiations were resumed in 1608, Oldenbarnevelt could only make limited promises in the face of growing resistance within the provinces. It was only fear of the costs of warfare and reluctance to raise taxes to cover these costs that made the opposing regents choose his side.

In the negotiations of 1608 too, 'free state' and 'sovereignty' were used interchangeably. Now internal sovereignty also entered the fray, raising such questions as who was competent to exercise authority and how did internal and external sovereignty connect. For instance, it was suggested that the King of Spain and the Archdukes should 'abandon' the provinces – i.e., renounce their sovereignty by relinquishing their authority to exercise power in these provinces – and that the Lords States General should be regarded as their 'good friends and neighbours'. Yet, Their Highnesses the Archdukes did not want to relinquish their provincial titles and coats of arms. The Spanish negotiators argued that their counterparts representing the States General should not unduly complicate matters: by all means, call the new entity a kingdom, a duchy, a free and sovereign republic or however one sees fit, but why kick up such a fuss about titles and coats of arms?[10]

---

10 Rijperman, *Resolutiën der Staten Generaal van 1576 tot 1609, veertiende deel, 1607–1609*, 358. See also the comment on this point from J.J. Poelhekke in his review of Rijperman,

The English emissaries recommended that the King and the Archdukes renounce the United Provinces in Article 1 and repeat their recognition of the 'free state' in Article 2.[11]

In the end, the only realistic result of the negotiations was a truce, given that the Dutch did not want to give up on the East India Company and the matter of religion remained unresolved. Moreover, this truce could only be achieved because in the end Spain yielded. But this is not to say that the truce was hailed as a resounding success throughout the United Provinces. Although in the text of the truce the United Provinces were called 'free lands, provinces and states', the city fathers of Amsterdam noted correctly that such a recognition carried but little weight in what was after all a temporary arrangement.

In the States General debates it had been urged that the negotiations should not focus on temporary but on permanent recognition. The princes Maurice and William Louis of Nassau finally submitted to the provinces that wanted to accept a truce, provided that the emissaries of the Kings of France and England declared that the Spanish rulers had abandoned their sovereignty over the provinces in sufficient manner. Not only would the Spanish renunciation have to last beyond the truce, the English and French Kings would also have to pledge to help maintain the provinces' freedom both during and after the truce. The only province that persisted in its opposition was Zealand, precisely because it considered the guarantees of sovereignty and religion to be insufficient.

Jonathan Israel states with regard to this aspect of the treaty that the United Provinces were recognised 'as if' they were a sovereign state.[12] However, Groenveld has shown that this is just one possible interpretation, as the United Provinces negotiators had objected to the French phrase 'comme avec états libres' being translated into 'als met vrije landen, provincies en staten' ('as with free lands, provinces and states'), i.e., as if they were a free state. And so the Dutch version of the truce stated that the Archdukes were content to negotiate with the States General of the United Provinces *qualitate qua* and regarded them 'as' free lands, provinces and states. The ambiguous wording rendered the text acceptable to both parties.[13] The resulting margin of interpretation

---

Resolutiën der Staten Generaal van 1576 tot 1609, veertiende deel, 1607–1609 in *Bijdragen en Mededelingen betreffende de Geschiedenis der Nederlanden,* 86 (1971), 407–411.

11 Rijperman, *Resolutiën der Staten Generaal van 1576 tot 1609, veertiende deel, 1607–1609,* 332–474 and 637–675.

12 Jonathan Israel, *The Dutch Republic: Its Rise, Greatness and Fall, 1477–1806* (Oxford, 1995), 399–405.

13 Groenveld, *Het Twaalfjarig Bestand,* 59–60. On the negotiations and the deliberate ambiguous phrasing, see also John Lothrop Motley, *History of the United Netherlands,* vol. 4,

had already been remarked on by the envoys of the German princes in February 1608, when they had been asked to examine the mandates of the King of Spain and of the Archdukes to see if they could find anything which was relevant. The envoys had stated that the express purpose of these mandates should be to transfer the sovereignty over the land to the States. They also believed that negotiating '*with* a free state' was different from negotiating '*as if* with a free state'.[14]

In spite of this controversy, by calling the Truce Spain had taken a significant, if temporary, step towards recognition of the Republic. The United Provinces interpreted the formula 'as holding them for free lands, provinces and states' as a *de facto* recognition. Spain did not, but accepted the United Provinces as a treaty partner. In response to the 1609 Truce various European and other powers established ambassador-level diplomatic relations with the United Provinces, which effectively constituted an implicit recognition.

In the 19th century, John Lothrop Motley phrased it in even more strongly:

> Mankind were amazed at this result – an event hitherto unknown in history. When before had a sovereign acknowledged the independence of his rebellious subjects, and signed a treaty with them as with equals?

And:

> The King's Government might seek solace in syntax. They might triumph in Cardinal Bentivoglio's subtleties, and persuade themselves that to treat with the republic as a free nation was not to hold it for a free nation then and for ever. But the whole world knew that the republic really was

1600–1609 (London, 1860–1867) It is remarkable that the 1611 edition of Emanuel van Meteren's, *Belgische of Nederlandsche Oorlogen ende Geschiedenissen, beginnende van tJaer 1598 tot 1611, mede vervatende enighe haerder gebueren handelinghe*, fol. 321v.–323v., contains the Dutch text version 'ende als dezelve houden voor' (and regarding them as), whereas in Van Meteren's, *Historie van de oorlogen en geschiedenissen der Nederlanderen en der zelver Naburen: beginnende met den Jare 1315, en eindigende met den Jare 1611* (Gorinchem, 1748–1763), vol. 10, 101–113, the text reads 'als met, en die houdende voor' (as with, and regarding them as), in other words, a translation of the French version.

14 This period witnessed the start of the development of the international law principle that the possibility of concluding a treaty with a de facto regime does not equal or imply recognition of the regime. J.A. Frowein, *Das de facto-Regime im Völkerrecht. Eine Untersuchung zur Rechtsstellung 'nichtanerkannter Staaten' und ähnlicher Gebilde* (Cologne and Berlin, 1968), 2–3, 96–97.

> free, and that it had treated, face to face, with its former sovereign, exactly as the Kings of France or Great Britain, or the Grand Turk, might treat with him. The new commonwealth had taken its place among the nations of the earth. Other princes and potentates made not the slightest difficulty in recognising it for an independent power and entering into treaties and alliances with it as with any other realm.[15]

But was this true? Did the phrase 'free lands, provinces and states' point to a *de jure* recognition by Spain? As the representatives from Zealand insisted, the phrase is ambiguous. The Antwerp Treaty was concluded with the States General and the provinces were considered to be free lands, but only for the purpose and the duration of the truce.

That the Spanish *de facto* recognition did not amount to a *de jure* recognition became apparent in the following years, when Francisco Gómez de Sandoval y Rojas, the Duke of Lerma (c. 1552–1625) made a confidential offer to Oldenbarnevelt of perpetual peace and of recognition of the United Provinces as a 'free state' in exchange for the provinces' renunciation of their possessions in the Eastern and Western Indies and for allowing public practice of the Roman Catholic faith. The secret negotiations led to nothing.[16] Only the European peace negotiations that were opened in the 1640's would signal a change.

It was these negotiations, which were officially launched in 1644, that the Republic, through France as its intermediary, was invited to join. Groenveld notes that the Republic demanded recognition of the sovereignty of the United Provinces and that it wanted to be ranked after the Emperor, the Kings of France, Spain and Portugal, England, Denmark and Sweden and after the Republic of Venice, but before the smaller princes and sovereigns. As Philip IV had already agreed to the Dutch negotiators having the status of ambassador in 1640, recognition of sovereignty no longer proved to be an obstacle to the negotiations.[17]

Even so, the point was raised. When the negotiations were opened and the French were allowed to inspect the Spanish mandates, they advised the negotiators from the Republic to object to the fact that only Don Gaspar de Bracamonte y Guzmán, 3rd Count of Peñaranda (c. 1595–1676) had authorisation from the Spanish King Philip IV and that Joseph Bergaigne (1588–1647)

---

15 Motley, *History of the United Netherlands*, vol. 4, 378.

16 Israel, *The Dutch Republic*, 405–410.

17 Simon Groenveld, *T'is ghenoegh, oorloghsmannen. De Vrede van Munster: de afsluiting van de Tachtigjarige Oorlog* (The Hague, 1997), 62–67.

and Antoine Brun (1599–1654), whom he was entitled to appoint as his deputies, did not. Poelhekke quotes the French advisers: 'Traicter par substituts avec Messieurs les Etats n'est pas correspondre à la reconnaissance de la Souveraineté et au Tiltre d'Excellence donné à leur Ambassadeurs'. And he adds as a comment: 'as if the sovereignty had already been recognised!'[18]

In reaction to the draft provisions the Dutch negotiators had submitted, their Spanish counterparts declared that the first article was acceptable to His Royal Majesty as a mere declaration, without modification or restriction, concerning the freedom and sovereignty of the Lords States General of the United Provinces and their respective provinces, as far as a truce could acknowledge, in general and indefinite terms. It was added that, because His Majesty on this fundamental point, which carried such great weight, offered such a dignified and complete satisfaction to the Lords States General, they hoped that they would reward His Majesty with regard to other points of less consideration.

The Dutch negotiators also presented the demand that the declaration of freedom and sovereignty of the Lords States General in Article 1 of the truce not be limited to the present. Events obviated the need to address this particular issue: the parties decided not to renew the truce, but to conclude a peace treaty.

The Theory behind the Terminology

In his *De Antiquitate Reipublicae Batavicae*, printed in 1610 and published in the same year as *Tractaet van de Oudheydt vande Batavische, nu Hollandsche Republique*, Grotius expresses the view that the province of Holland had always been a free country without any relationship of dependence vis-à-vis any foreign power and that in this country the States had traditionally possessed sovereignty, but that this sovereignty was limited by the quasi-monarchical authority of the Stadholder.[19] In other words, Grotius eloquently describes both the external and the internal sovereignty of the province. The question of what internal sovereignty meant in the Republic had to be answered from a double perspective: Provincial States versus States General and Provincial States (particularly the States of Holland) versus the Stadholder.[20]

18 Poelhekke, *De Vrede van Munster*, 230–231 (My translation).

19 Gees van der Plaat, *Eendracht als opdracht. Lieuwe van Aitzema's bijdrage aan het politieke debat in de zeventiende-eeuwse Republiek* (Hilversum, 2003), 13–14. Grotius later distanced himself from this theory of the Batavian myth which many authors had endorsed.

20 Van der Plaat, *Eendracht als opdracht*, 178–180; J.V. Rijpperda Wierdsma, *Politie en Justitie. Een studie over Hollandschen staatsbouw tijdens de Republiek* (Zwolle, 1937), 1–9.

Grotius also writes about the negotiations and their results. When the Archdukes and King Philip III showed themselves willing to discuss the freedom of the States, negotiations had been started, with emissaries of the Kings of France, England, Denmark and of other sovereigns acting as mediators. Because peace ultimately proved unattainable, in 1609 a twelve years truce was concluded. Article 1 contained a declaration from the Archdukes, both in their own name and in the name of Philip III, who had instructed them on the declaration, in which they indicated that they concluded the truce with the States General as with the States of free lands and peoples and that they regarded them as such and that the Archdukes would not infringe on their rights. Philip ratified the treaty by reiterating this statement.[21] In other words, Grotius too is somewhat ambiguous.

The question, of course is, to what degree the terms used (free, sovereign, independent) mesh with the development of theories on sovereignty in the 16th and 17th centuries? Any attempt to answer this question must begin with an analysis of this development.

From the mid-13th century onwards, the terms 'sovereign' and 'sovereignty' were used for a lord and his supremacy or supreme power, i.e., his authority to make decisions independently from other lords. Decisions that could not be legally affected were regarded as sovereign decisions. From the 14th until the 16th centuries, the concept became increasingly limited to the decisions of the King (in France and England), parliament or certain other institutions that were also called 'sovereign', such as the 'sovereign' Council of Brabant in the Netherlands.[22] In the 16th century, royal power was no longer referred to as sovereignty, but as absolute power.

The use of the concept of sovereignty in the medieval period calls for caution. Sovereignty was but a component of royal powers and was therefore not

21 '[...] et cum pacem difficultates magnae morarentur, ad ultimum, anno MDCIX factae in duodecim annos induciae; praeposita testatione ab Archiducibus tum suo, tum Philippi, a quo id mandati acceperant, nomine, qua se pacisci eas inducias cum Ordinibus Federatis, ut cum liberarum nationum ac civitatum Ordinibus, profitebantur, talesque eos a se haberi, et nihil a se in ipsos iuris obtendi. Philippus pacta rata habuit, repetita eadem professione'. Hugo de Groot, *Liber de Antiquitate Reipublicae Batavicae* (translated into Dutch and introduced by the Collegium Classicum c.n. E.D.E.P.O.L., Arnhem, 1995), caput 7, 80–81. This modern edition is based on the first edition of 1610, but with notes on the variations in the later editions of 1617, 1630 and 1633. On Grotius' position, see e.g. Arthur Eyffinger, *Oorlog, Vrede of Bestand? 1609 door de ogen van Hugo de Groot* (The Hague, 2009), 15 and 29.

22 This Council was the highest court in the Duchy of Brabant. It recognised no higher court, not even (or particularly not) the Great Coucil of Malines for the Burgundian Netherlands.

the same as *seigneurie* or supreme royal power or *summum imperium*. In the Middle Ages, and beyond, sovereignty shifted its meaning.[23]

In the 16th century, Jean Bodin (1530–1596) in his *Six Livres de la République* and earlier in his *Methodus ad Facilem Historiarum Cognitionem*, redefined the concept of sovereignty as the absolute and eternal power of a state.[24] Not only did Bodin regard sovereignty as absolute, but more importantly, sovereignty implied that within a state it was the sovereign who possessed all political power, and this power was based on the sovereign's right to legislate. In Bodin's view sovereignty was no longer a list of competences; with some exceptions all power within the state accrued to the sovereign. At its core was the indivisible power to legislate, and not, as had been assumed before, the power to adjudicate.

According to Kossmann, such a view did not fit the ideology of the Dutch Revolt. Those involved in the rebellion adhered to the traditional view that as a judge the sovereign had to uphold existing privileges. Because in the rebels' perception the ruling monarch, Philip II, had failed to do so, the inescapable conclusion was, so Kossmann writes, that he had dissociated himself from the constitution and consequently from his sovereignty. For that reason the States were no longer under an obligation to recognise him as their sovereign. Yet it took several years before it was pronounced that the sovereignty of the 'land' rested with the Provincial States. Apart from that, the States actually did know – as opposed to what they had originally put to Francis, the Duke of Anjou (1555–1584), when they negotiated with him about assuming the position of Philip II – the terms 'sovereign' and 'sovereignty'. They were also aware of Bodin's views. By the time of the Antwerp Truce the work of Johannes Althusius (1557–1638) expresses the view that indivisible and inalienable sovereignty rested not with the prince but with the people, that is to say, the estates and their assembly and its members representing them, and that this sovereignty only implies the control of power.[25]

23 Helmut Quaritsch, *Souveränität. Entstehung und Entwicklung des Begriffs in Frankreich und Deutschland vom 13. Jh. bis 1806* (Schriften zur Verfassungsgeschichte 38; Berlin, 1986), *passim*.

24 C.G. Roelofsen, 'De periode 1450–1713', in A.C.G.M. Eyffinger (ed.), *Compendium volkenrechtsgeschiedenis* (2nd edn., Deventer, 1991), 43–131 at 46; Bodin, *Methodus ad Facilem Historiarum Cognitionem*, multiple editions between 1566 and 1650. *Method for the Easy Comprehension of History* (transl. Beatrice Reynolds, New York, 1969/e-book Ann Arbor, 2008).

25 E.H. Kossmann, 'Volkssoevereiniteit aan het begin van het Nederlandse Ancien régime', in E.H. Kosmann, *Politieke theorie en geschiedenis. Verspreide opstellen en voordrachten* (Amsterdam, 1987), 59–92, esp. 61–78; E.H. Kossmann, 'Bodin, Althusius en Parker, of:

Various authors, such as Quaritsch, note that the ideas of Bodin and of other French writers, such as Theodorus Beza (1519–1605) and Philippe du Plessis-Mornay (1549–1623), did influence the Dutch Revolt, and that this also applies to terms of fairly recent date they all used, such as 'sovereignty', next to more ancient terminology, such as *summum imperium*, *summa potestas* or *majestas imperii*.

Further Use of the Concept of Sovereignty in the 17th Century

Quaritsch also remarks that in the year 1609 the word 'sovereignty' could be found in a German text for the first time. The text concerns a message in the *Aviso*,[26] one of the first newspapers in Europe, about the conclusion of the Truce. In the very first *Aviso* of the end of January of that year it was reported with the news of 2 January (O.S.) that the States General accepted that the King of Spain completely relinquished his sovereignty of the provinces, and in the 3 March (O.S.) issue of that same year the cession by the King of the sovereignty of the provinces was mentioned. In reports concerning other countries, however, the term 'sovereignty' was not yet used. In those cases the correspondents still used 'power', 'supreme power' and 'supreme lord'. Quaritsch leaves aside whether this difference in terminology can be attributed to the correspondent in the Netherlands or to the specific situation in the Netherlands where the concept of sovereignty had already been used in the 16th century.[27] In the light of the discussion on the meaning of the phrase 'regarding them

over de moderniteit van de Nederlandse opstand', in E.H. Kosmann, *Politieke theorie en geschiedenis*, 93–110.

26 With the *Relation*, the *Aviso* is among the oldest newspapers in Europe. They both date from 1609. The first issue of the *Aviso* is dated 15 January 1609, but was actually printed a few days later. The dating follows the Julian calendar (Old Style, O.S.). The Gregorian (or New Style) date would have been 10 or 11 days later, 27 or 28 January. The newspaper was published weekly from 1609 until 1632. Information by courtesy of Dr Martin Welke, Pressehistoriker, Stiftung Deutsches Zeitingsmuseum. For the news in the *Aviso* and the *Relation*, see also Thomas Schröder, *Die ersten Zeitungen. Textgestaltungen und Nachrichtenauswahl* (Tübingen, 1995), 26–29. For the news on the Treaty of 1609, see M. Dlugaiczyk, *Der Waffenstilstand (1609–1621) als Medienereignis. Politische Bildpropaganda in den Niederlanden* (Munster, 2005), 253–256. Dlugaiczyk claims that the Truce merely signalled *de facto* sovereignty for the Northern Netherlands or the Republic and that only the Peace Treaty of 1648 granted *de jure sovereignty*. She also asserts that *de facto* sovereignty of the States General rested on the Truce, 273.

27 Quaritsch, *Souveränität*, 81–82.

[the provinces] as free countries, provinces and states'. it is remarkable that the term 'sovereignty' was used in the German press. It effectively distributed the Dutch interpretation of the text.

In the negotiations leading up to the Westphalian Peace Treaties of 1648 the term 'sovereignty' was used more regularly, for example in the phrase 'in omnibus aliis suis souverenitatis juribus vel supremitatis'.[28] It is, however, questionable, whether the negotiators had really reflected upon the term. Sovereignty was frequently described as *jus territorii et superioritatis*, but not so in the Spanish-Dutch Treaty. Article 1 refers to 'free and sovereign' states, provinces and lands. Article 3 then adds the phrase 'stay with the aforesaid Lords States in all and the same rights and parts of sovereignty and superiority'.[29] This dovetails with the demands of the States of Zealand, which did not wish to accept a declaration that was any less strong. They also desired that the full sovereignty and superiority of the Bailiwick of 's-Hertogenbosch and other conquered lands must not be impaired in any way. The States of Zealand repeated this demand a few months later, now referring to full and absolute sovereignty. In this matter they received support from several other provinces.[30] This is another instance of the concepts of external and internal sovereignty being used alongside one another.

The States General and their Notion of Sovereignty in the Gemert Dispute

On other matters too, the States General ran into sovereignty issues, for example in their conflict with the Teutonic Order over the Seigniory of Gemert.[31]

28 Quaritsch, *Souveränität*, 82. See also Klaus Malettke, 'La perception de la "superiorité territoriale" et de la "souveraineté" des princes d'Empire en France au XVIIe siècle', in Jean-Francois Kervégan and Heinz Mohnhaupt (eds.), *Wechselseitige Beeinflussungen und Rezeptionen von Recht und Philosophie in Deutschland und Frankreich. Influences et réceptions mutuelles du droit et de la philosophie en France et en Allemagne* (*Ius commune*, Sonderhefte 144; Frankfurt, 2001), 69–90.

29 My translation. Groenveld, *Unie – Bestand – Vrede*, 161.

30 Quaritsch, *Souveränität*, 84–85; Poelhekke, *De Vrede van Munster*, 395 and 401. See also Manzano Baena, 'Negotiating Sovereignty: The Peace Treaty of Münster, 1648', 617–641.

31 This case is described in B.C.M. Jacobs, 'Om het behoud van de soevereiniteit van Gemert. De Duitse Orde contra de Staten Generaal, 1648–1662', in E.C. Coppens, J. Hallebeek, D. Heirbaut, Th. Van der Meer and C.H. van Rhee (eds.), *Fabrica Iuris. Opstellen over de 'werkplaats van het recht' aangeboden aan Sjoerd Faber* (Nijmegen, 2009), 75–90.

In the 17th century, Gemert was a sovereign seigniory, which by then had long belonged to the *Ordo Domus Sanctae Mariae Theutinicorum Hierosolymitanorum* (the Teutonic Order for short). When Frederick Henry, Prince of Orange and Stadholder of the Republic, conquered the city of 's-Hertogenbosch in 1629, the States General attempted to exert their authority in Gemert under the pretext that the Seigniory of Gemert belonged to the Bailiwick of 's-Hertogenbosch and for that reason now fell under the authority of the States General as the successors of the Duke of Brabant. The claim that the Bailiwick had automatically come under the control of the States General upon the conquest of the city of 's-Hertogenbosch was heavily debated and it took considerable time before the Spanish conceded it. In Gemert itself, the claim of the States General also met with fierce resistance, and for a number of years there was a stalemate. In 1648, the year of the Peace, the States General unexpectedly had a new oppportunity to assert their alleged authority over Gemert. The then commander of the Teutonic Order in Gemert, Caspar Ulrich of Hoensbroek (Commander 1635–1655), who had always defended the sovereignty and neutrality of the seigniory, came into conflict with his superior, the governor of the *landcommanderij* Alden Biesen and made an appeal to the States General, asking them to reinstate him as commander. The States General supported him in the interest of preserving Gemert's sovereignty ('conservatie van de souverainiteijt'). The Teutonic Order countered, claiming that it was Hoensbroek's appeal that threatened the freedom and neutrality of the Seigniory of Gemert.

Both external and internal sovereignty came to bear on the debate. On the one hand, the parties invoked the 'sovereignty and neutrality' or the 'freedom and neutrality' of the seigniory. On the other hand, the States General argued (as did several other parties) that as Gemert had originally fallen under the 'sovereignty' of the Duke of Brabant, it had since the Munster Peace Treaty come under the dominion of the States General as successors to the Duke in the conquered northern part of the Duchy. Eventually, Philip IV embroiled himself in the debate, contending that Gemert had remained a 'free seigniory' of the German Empire and that as he had succeeded the Duke of Brabant he was entitled to the supreme tutelage of Gemert.

Learned lawyers advising the Teutonic Order discussed the concepts of freedom and sovereignty with reflections on *imperium, libertas, jurisdictio, superioritas* and *suprema potestas*. They averred that the concept of neutrality did not imply that Gemert and the Teutonic Order had purposely or consciously occupied a position of non-involvement and dissociation during an armed conflict between third parties, but rather that a more elevated freedom (*sublimor libertas*) existed, which entailed complete immunity from any submission to the Duke of Brabant. As before in, for instance, Article 3 of the Munster

Peace Treaty and the demands of the Zealand negotiators before the treaty was concluded, most records in this case use the terms *souveraineté* and *superioritas*. In some cases, however, 'sovereignty' was used alongside 'independence'.

Although this conflict was put before arbiters from the Chambre Mi-Partie,[32] after intense diplomatic discussions it was finally resolved in 1662 by the conclusion of a treaty. Under its terms, the States General renounced their 'superiority and sovereignty' over the seigniory to the Teutonic Order, in exchange for which the Order undertook to accept the reformed religion in Gemert and not to establish Roman Catholic monasteries there. In addition, the Order committed itself to paying 40.000 guilders to the States General.

Conclusion

In this Chapter, I have argued that the parties negotiating and drafting the Twelve Years Truce often used the concepts 'free' and 'sovereign' interchangeably and that they merged the external and internal dimensions of sovereignty. To some extent they did this on purpose. The resulting apparent equivalency and sense of vagueness made it easier to reach an agreement on the first article of the Truce and to accommodate a wider margin of interpretation. It made the Truce sufficiently acceptable to the signatories. The Peace Treaty of 1648 simply puts the words 'free' and 'sovereign' side by side as attributive adjectives. Yet, even this seemingly straightforward pair of modifiers is not void of indeterminateness. While the text does read that the States General are free and sovereign lands, it is likely that this statement was not meant to be taken at face value, but was only understood (albeit tacitly) to refer to the recognition of the States General as a negotiating party in its own right, in addition to (but separate from) the recognition of the independence of the United Provinces. In any event, the States General themselves began to use the term 'sovereignty' regarding other territories, and they did so both at the time of the peace negotiations and in subsequent years. In this way, they contributed to the integration of the external and internal concepts of sovereignty into political parlance and reality.

32 The Chambre Mi-Partie was a court of justice and arbitration for conflicts between Spain and the Republic of the United Provinces, created in Article 21 of the 1648 Munster Peace Treaty. As the conflict was not between signatories to the treaty the court itself could not be seized, but members of the court were asked to decide the case as independent arbiters. See C. Streefkerk, 'Cedant arma togae: De sententiën van de Cambre Mi-Parti, 1654–1657', *Bronnen van het Oud-Vaderlands Recht, Verslagen en Mededelingen,* NS 6.5 (1987), 103–116.

CHAPTER 9

How 'Sovereign' were the Southern Netherlands under the Archdukes?

Georges Martyn

The Many Meanings of 'Sovereign'

The 'autonomy', 'sovereignty', 'independence', etc. of the (Southern) Netherlands under the rule of Albert and Isabella has been debated by many scholars since many years.[1] It pretty much depends on the perspective one takes to decide whether the glass is 'half empty' or 'half full'. It also pretty much depends on the sense one attributes to words such as 'sovereignty', 'autonomy', 'independence' and similar ones.[2] In this Chapter, I shall defend the thesis that the Archdukes, in fact and legally, really can be considered sovereign rulers of the (Southern) Netherlands.[3]

According to Webster's dictionary of the English language[4] 'sovereign' means today:

1 E.g. Charles H. Carter, 'Belgian "autonomy" under the Archdukes, 1598–1621', *Journal of Modern History*, 36 (1964) 245–259; Hugo De Schepper, 'De overheidsstructuren in de Koninklijke Nederlanden 1580–1700', in *Algemene Geschiedenis der Nederlanden* (Haarlem, 1975), vol. 5, 388–405, 390, is rather sceptical, especially because of the presence of Spanish ministers in Brussels, *infra*; Ernest Gossaert, *La domination espagnole dans les Pays-Bas à la fin du règne de Philippe II* (Brussels, 1906), 208–213, holds the same. More moderate, and even in favour of a high degree of independence, are the studies of: Victor Brants, *L'autonomie internationale de la Belgique sous les Archiducs Albert et Isabelle* (Mâcon, 1901); Joseph Lefèvre, 'La souveraineté d'Albert et Isabelle', *Revue générale Belge*, 89 (1953) 967–983; Werner Thomas, 'Andromeda unbound. The reign of Albert & Isabella in the Southern Netherlands, 1598–1621', in Luc Duerloo and Werner Thomas (eds.), *Albert & Isabella (1598–1621)* (Brussels, 1998), 1–14; L. Willaert, 'Négociations politico-religieuses entre L'Angleterre et les Pays-Bas catholiques', *Revue d'Histoire Ecclésiastique*, 8 (1907) 99, cites Richardot : 'Le transport des Pays-Bas n'est qu'une chose simulée'.

2 Thomas, 'Andromeda', 2, talks of 'dependent independence'.

3 It is just one possible thesis, of course. One could also defend, completely the other way around, that the Archdukes had not an own military power, nor any autonomy in international matters, two essential characteristics to define a 'sovereign' state. This is why, further on, I shall stress the 'internal' sovereignty of Albert and Isabella.

4 Naples (Florida) 1997, 522.

 | DOI 10.1163/9789004274921_011

– exercising or possessing supreme jurisdiction or power;
– free, independent, autonomous as in a sovereign state;
– supremely excellent, great, or exalted;
– extremely potent or effective, e.g. a sovereign remedy;
– total, unmitigated, e.g. sovereign hate;
– of chief importance, supremacy, etc., e.g. sovereign claims.

Obviously, only the first and second meaning should be considered here. In this contribution, special attention will be given to particular aspects of the 'supreme jurisdiction or power' of the Archdukes and to the question whether the Low Countries under their rule can be seen as 'free, independent or autonomous'. These are the two classical meanings of 'sovereign' in public (international) law.[5]

The etymological basis of the word 'sovereignty' is to be sought in the (vulgar) Latin word 'superanus', evolving via the French 'souverain' to the Dutch 'soeverein' and the English 'sovereign', which words start appearing in these languages in the 13th century. When Philippe de Beaumanoir, for instance, in 1283 wrote his commentary on the customs of the French region of Beauvaisis, he stated about the king:

> Li rois est souverains par dessus tous, et a de son droit la générale garde de tout son royaume; par quoi il peut faire tous establissements comme il li plest pour le commun pourfit, et ce qu'il establit doit estre tenu.[6]

In this expression – 'the king is sovereign above all' – lies one of the seeds of the modern sense of sovereignty in public (national and) international law.

5 S. Benn, 'Sovereignty', in P. Edwards (ed.), *The Encyclopedia of Philosophy* (New York, 1967), vol. 7, 501–505. The concept of sovereignty has been studied by many scholars and the interpretations of the word are uncountable, Jens Bartelson, *A Genealogy of Sovereignty* (Cambridge, 1995); Ryan Goodman and Jinks Derek, 'Toward an institutional theory of sovereignty', *Stanford Law Review*, 55 (2003) 1749–1788; Kenneth Pennington, *The Prince and the Law 1200–1600. Sovereignty and Rights in the Western Legal Tradition* (Berkeley, 1993); Daniel Philpott, *Revolutions in Sovereignty. How ideas shaped modern international relations* (Princeton, 2001); Helmut Quaritsch, *Souveränität. Entstehung und Entwicklung des Begriffs in Frankreich und Deutschland vom 13. Jh. bis 1806* (Berlin, 1986); Helen Stacey, 'Relational sovereignty', *Stanford Law Review*, 55 (2003) 2029–2059; Luc Wintgens, 'Alles is relatief... ook relativiteit', *Rechtskundig Weekblad*, 64 (2000–2001) 1289–1304.

6 Philippe de Beaumanoir, *Coutumes de Clermont-en-Beauvaisis*, ed. Amédée Salmon (Paris, 1899), § 1043. Susan Reynolds, *Fiefs and vassals. The medieval evidence reinterpreted* (Oxford 1994), 36, refers to the 13th-century meaning of 'superior dominus' (French 'sovereign seignour') in the sense of 'the lord with jurisdiction over the fiefholder's lord'.

But the scope of different uses of the term 'sovereign' is much larger. In a very broad sense, in every relation between two persons or institutions, one can be qualified as 'superior', i.e. 'higher', than the other. Moreover, even without any comparison to others, one individual subject can be called 'sovereign',[7] i.e. independent or autonomous. In the Middle Ages, the County of Flanders knew 'sovereign truths', some kind of general assemblies of the free men of a resort, where debated matters of law were settled.[8] In this case, 'sovereign' has nothing to do with the sense as we understand the word today.

The Use of the Word 'Sovereign' around 1600

We shall have a look at some of the many notions of sovereignty,[9] especially at the times of Albert and Isabella.[10] In feudal law, the 'sovereign' is the overlord. The Archdukes are certainly 'sovereign' in this feudal sense. They reign the

7 Mark Van Hoecke and Luc Wintgens, 'Het individu als soeverein rechtssubject – De natuurfilosofie van Frank van Dun', *Rechtskundig Weekblad*, 51 (1987–88) 689–697; see also Hendrik Kaptein, 'Geciviliseerde soevereiniteit? Kleine kaleidoscopie van civielrechtelijke onmacht en autonomie', in Hendrik Kaptein, H. Prakken and B. Verheij (eds.), *Legal Evidence and Proof: Statistics, stories, logic* (Farnham, 2009) 1–14.

8 G. Van Acker, 'Placita Generalia en soevereine waarheden in Vlaanderen', *Handelingen van de Maatschappij voor Oudheidkunde en Geschiedenis te Gent*, 3 (1948) 142–164.

9 Hubert Van Houtte, 'Conquête et transfert de souveraineté sous l'ancien régime', *Belgisch Tijdschrift voor Filologie en Geschiedenis*, 9 (1930) 1244–1248; Guus Van Nifterik, *Vorst tussen volk en wet. Over volkssoevereiniteit en rechtsstatelijkheid in het werk van Fernando Vázquez de Menchaca (1512–1569)* (Gouda, 1999); M. Wilks, *The problem of sovereignty in the later Middle Ages* (Cambridge, 1963).

10 Albert and Isabella are not the only rulers in the Southern Netherlands calling themselves 'sovereign'. Also several landlords consider themselves to be 'sovereign' within their territory, holding all powers sovereign princes have: legislation, low, middle and high justice, grace, etc. This is for instance the case with Jean Richardot, as president of the Privy Council being the first civil officer of the 'nation', but as lord of the small village of Lembeek claiming 'laditte terre est neutrale, et n'est comprinse dans aulcune des dixsept provinces, ne se relevant que de Dieu et du Soleil [...] toutte justice, haulte, moienne, et basse, avecq droict de confiscation, de faire grace [...] item peult ledict Seigneur asseoir et imposer toutes amendes pour le maintènement de la police à observer audict Lembecque, et ce à cause de sa souveraineté', Brussels, Algemeen Rijksarchief/Archives Générales du Royaume, fund d'Ursel, n° L1220; more complete transcription in Georges Martyn, *Geschiedenis van de politiek en van het publiekrecht* (Bruges, 2008), 106–107.

Duchy of Brabant as dukes, the County of Flanders as counts, etc.[11] in their personal names, not as representatives of another duke or the count. Within every duchy and county, many vassals resort under the Archdukes as their overlord. Albert and Isabella sit on top of the feudal pyramid. Looking from the bottom to the top, Albert and Isabella are the sovereigns of all (or at least most) lower feudal lords. Moreover, while their ancestors, the Dukes of Burgundy in the 15th century had been, at least theoretically,[12] still vassals of a higher sovereign, i.e. the German emperor (Brabant, Hainaut, etc.) or the French king (Flanders, Tournai, Artesia), these highest feudal bonds had been cut by Charles V, in relation to the Holy Roman Empire, in the Augsburg Transaction (1548), and, in relation to France, in the Madrid Peace (1526). According to the first treaty between the Emperor and the *Reichstag*, the Habsburg Netherlands did no longer belong to the resort of the *Reichskammergericht* and legislation of the Empire was not applicable in the Netherlands. By consequence, even if, *de iure*, the feudal bond was thereby not broken, the emperor no longer exercised any real feudal power in practice.[13] According to the second treaty, confirmed by the 1529 Cambrai Peace Treaty of the Ladies, the feudal bonds between France on the one hand and the County of Flanders, Franche-Comté, Tournai and Artesia on the other were broken; from that moment on, appeal to the *Parlement de Paris* was no longer possible.[14]

11 There is no general title for all of the (Southern) Netherlands together. The attempts to acquire a common royal crown were never realised. Also during the reign of Albert and Isabella, a request was sent to the pope, Piet Lenders, 'Onstaan en ontwikkeling van de moderne staat in de Nederlanden', in Herman Coppens and Karin Van Honacker (eds.), *Symposium over de centrale overheidsinstellingen van de Habsburgse Nederlanden, Brussel, 3 December 1994. Tien bijdragen over de staat, de regering en de ambtenaren van de 16de tot 18de eeuw* (Brussels, 1995), 1–42 at 28; Paul Bonenfant, 'Les projest d'érection des Pays-Bas en royaume du XVe au XVIIIe siècle. Aperçu de l'évolution de ce concept politique', *Revue de l'Université de Bruxelles*, 41 (1935–36) 151–169.

12 Philippe Godding, *La législation ducale en Brabant sous le règne de Philippe le Bon (1430–1467)* (Académie royale de Belgique. Mémoires de la Classe des Lettres. Collection in-8°, 3e série, vol. 42; Brussels 2006), 29.

13 For a different appraisal, see Chapter 2.

14 Article 10 of the Madrid Treaty stated that 'demeurera le dit seigneur Empereur pour luy, ses hoirs, successeurs et ayant cause quite, exempt et absous à perpétuité et à tousjours de tout et quelconque droit de resort, de souveraineté que le dit seigneur roy ou ses successeurs de la couronne de Franse pourront pretender et quereller sur les comtéz de Flandres et d'Artois', Jean Dumont (ed.), *Corps universel diplomatique du droit des gens* (Amsterdam 1731), vol. 4, 399, see Serge Dauchy, 'Keizer Karel, een soevereine vorst?', in Hugo Soly and René Vermeir (eds.), *Beleid en bestuur in de oude Nederlanden. Liber amicorum prof. dr. M. Baelde* (Ghent, 1993), 65–72.

By the Late Middle Ages and Early Modern Times, the term 'sovereignty' is used to qualify the highest power, also outside the feudal context, as the citation of Beaumanoir already showed and as will be developed further. By the end of Early Modern Times, more and more enlightened scholars held that the people itself had the highest power. This popular sovereignty is the basis of modern democracy. On the other hand, even in democracies, some levels of power or some institutions are qualified 'higher' than others. Within a constitutional democracy, the sovereign power can be in the hands of a president, a king, a parliament, a supreme court, the basis of this highest and all lower powers still being popular sovereignty. This leads us to making a distinction between the idea of sovereign power as a factual and legally established highest institution of power on the one hand, and, on the other, the idea of sovereign power as the legitimating source of power: the people, God, the king, etc.

It is my opinion that Albert and Isabella can be seen, both as the legitimated highest institution of power in the (Southern) Netherlands on the one hand, and as the legitimating source of power on the other hand. They really held and used most of the factual power, even if they cannot be said to be completely and exclusively sovereign, or, *a fortiori*, absolute. Historians normally underscore the lack of complete sovereignty, especially regarding military and international matters.[15] In this sense, one can say that the Archdukes are mostly considered 'internally' sovereign, but not 'externally' sovereign. Internal sovereignty means that there are no competing powers within the territory of a government, while external sovereignty refers to the fact that outside, or better higher powers are to be recognised. In the Middle Ages, emperor and pope were legally considered higher powers above internal sovereigns, but also today the member states of international organisations for instance can be said to be limited in their external sovereignty.

The competence of the Archdukes in the field of military and international (commercial and state) affairs was certainly limited by Spain. So indeed, Albert and Isabella could not be considered to be completely externally sovereign. Nevertheless, they did have quite a few elements of external sovereignty. I shall come back to this point further. Moreover, exactly the same can be said on their internal sovereignty. Although undoubtedly respected as sovereign princes, the Archdukes are in fact obliged to take the advices and wishes of internal competing powers into account, e.g. the provincial states in fiscal matters, and, in legislative and judicial matters, the provincial councils, exclusively

15 Hugo De Schepper, 'The Decision-making Process in the Government of the Catholic Netherlands under the Archdukes, 1596–1621', in Geoffrey Parker (ed.), *Spain and the Netherlands, 1559–1659. Ten studies* (Glasgow, 1979), 164–176 at 166–173.

composed of natural Dutch councillors, and the collateral councils, almost exclusively composed of 'nationals'. If 'sovereignty' as 'exercising or possessing supreme jurisdiction or power' in Webster's first sense should mean fully 'free, independent and autonomous' in Webster's second sense, then the Archdukes cannot be considered to be – even internally – sovereign. But then, the question arises whether ever one prince has really been sovereign. Even the French absolute kings had to respect some *lois fondamentales* and the influence of estates and councillors. But if we define internal sovereignty as the right to unconditioned respect for the dignity of the prince by all subjects and internal institutions,[16] then, for sure, the Archdukes are to be considered internally sovereign.[17]

This internal sovereignty was displayed in all legislative, administrative and judicial acts. Statutes (*édits, placards, ordonnances, décrets...*)[18] were promulgated by the Archdukes in their personal names, using as '*intitulatio*' their feudal titles as Dukes of Brabant, Counts of Flanders, etc., titles they were justified to wear *'par la grâce de Dieu',* a diplomatic formula commonly used by sovereign princes.[19] In the legislative procedure, there was no intervention by the Spanish King. Both legislation on request, as well as legislation *motu proprio*, were the products of the Brussels collateral councils, mostly based on the advices of a variety of lower institutions. In judicial matters, there was no appeal or any other ordinary or extraordinary recourse to a higher – read 'Spanish' – instance. Within the Southern Netherlands, the Brussels Privy Council and the Great Council of Malines – except for the Duchy of Brabant – were the supreme administrative and judicial institutions and they rendered judgments in the name of the Archdukes. Based on the Joyous Entry, the

---

16 Or in other words: the legally based acceptance that the prince has the final word in all decisions.

17 According to Franciscus Zypaeus, *Judex, magistratus, senator, libris IV exhibitus* (Antwerp, 1673), 326, Albert, before swearing his oath to the Estates, asked Dutch and foreign advisors to investigate whether in the Dutch customs and constitutions nothing was against his dignity. For Zypaeus, publishing in 1635 one of the first general books on the legal system of the Southern Netherlands, the prince had '*soveranum imperium*'. He was not to use it in an absolute way, but for the common good.

18 Jean Bodin, *Les six livres de la République* (Paris 1578), 131: 'La première marque de souveraineté, est donner la loy aux sugets...ce que ne puit faire celuy qui est subiects aux lois ou à ceux qui ont commandement sur lui; c'est pourquoy que la loi dit que le Prince est absolus de la puissance des lois'. Merio Scattola, 'Diritto medioevale e scienza politica moderna nella dottrina della sovranità di Jean Bodin', *Ius Commune. Zeitschrift für Europäische Rechtsgeschichte*, 26 (1999) 165–209.

19 Arthur Giry, *Manuel de diplomatique* (Paris, 1925), 319.

Council of Brabant claimed the privilege of being 'sovereign',[20] which meant that no appeal could be made against its judgments.[21] However, here again, the sentences were rendered in the name of Albert and Isabella as Dukes of Brabant.

The Terminology of the Act of Cession

When most authors hold the thesis that there are reasons to consider the Archdukes to be not or at least less 'externally' sovereign, this is commonly based on the special conditions[22] of the Act of Cession of the Netherlands (1598),[23] and more particularly on the articles on Spanish garrisons[24] in the Netherlands and the prohibition of commerce with the Spanish colonies.

In general, however, we can conclude that Philip II really transferred 'sovereign' power to the Archdukes by his act of 6 May 1598, as approved by the Estates General.[25] As he did this under the condition of starting a new dynasty

20 Arthur Gaillard, *Le Conseil de Brabant* (3 vols., Brussels, 1898–1902); Eddy Put, 'Raad van Brabant (ca. 1430–1795)', in Raymond Van Uytven, Claude Bruneel, Chris Coppens and Beatrys Augustyn (eds.), *De gewestelijke en lokale overheidsinstellingen in Brabant en Mechelen tot 1795* (Brussels, 2000), 147–171 at 157–159.

21 Compare with the claim of the Council of Flanders to be 'sovereign' in criminal matters, as described by the Flemish proctor-general Jean-Baptiste van Steenberghen in his *Esclaircissement du droit de souveraineté...*, mentioned in Jos Monballyu, 'De raad van Vlaanderen, een soevereine justitieraad in strafzaken?', in *Handelingen van het tweede Hof van Holland Symposium gehouden op 14 November 1997 in de Trêveszaal te Den Haag* (The Hague, 1998), 77–90. The French Council of Flanders, established at the end of the 17th century by Louis XIV, is also 'sovereign', Jacques Lorgnier, 'La justice du Roi Soleil dans las anciens Pays-Bas. Organisation de la justice dans le ressort du Conseil souverain de Tournai', in Olav Moorman-van Kappen (ed.), *Les juridictions supérieures. Actes des Journées internationales tenues à Leeuwarden du 20 au 23 mai 1993* (Rechtshistorische Reeks van het Gerard Noodt Instituut 32; Nijmegen, 1994), 19–32.

22 Both the public and the so-called 'secret' ones. These were only secret in the sense that they were not published by letters patent, not in the sense that the people should not know about them.

23 Victor Brants (ed.), *Recueil des ordonnances des Pays-Bas. Règne d'Albert et Isabelle. 1597–1621* (Brussels, 1909), vol. 1, 7–11.

24 The presence of these garrisons in Ghent, Antwerp, Cambrai... in 1598 was a matter of fact. Keeping them there was a necessity, given the military situation. They were paid for by Spain.

25 Robert Wellens, 'Les Etats Généraux de Bruxelles en 1598 et la cession des Pays-Bas aux Archiducs Albert et Isabelle', *Cahiers Bruxellois*, 23 (1978) 23–34. According to

and Albert and Isabella finally died without offspring, things returned to the original status. If, however, a child would have been born, it would have inherited the (Southern) Netherlands and, very probably, a sovereign state would have emerged and might have continued to exist. However, this is counterfactual history.

The wording of the Act of Cession is clear. King Philip II makes a marriage donation: 'à l'advancement dudict marriage, faire à nostredicte fille donation d'iceulx noz pays et avecq tout ce qu'en dépend'. It is a patrimony that he is transferring ('céder et transporter').[26] As the legitimate owner, he disposes of a part of his possessions, and he gives it completely. As he is spending part of his heritage, his son and future inheritor and successor intervenes and confirms the act explicitly.[27] Philip II wants to give the Dutch people a proper and 'natural' prince: 'de se trouver régy et gouverné à la veue et par la présence de son prince et seigneur naturel'. So, if Philip has sovereign power of his own, he is now transferring it to his daughter and son-in-law: 'donnons, cédons, délaissons, transférons et renonçons et accordons en dot, en fief et arrière fief et par quelconcque meilleure voie, manière et forme que de droict faire se puist et doibve valoir'. The description of the content of these sovereign powers sounds like a catalogue of sovereignty taken from Jean Bodin's *Six livres de la République*:[28]

> tous noz pays d'embas et chacune province d'iceulx, ensemble le pays et conté de Bourgoigne y comprins celluy de Charolois, et les duchez,

contemporary authors such as Zypaeus and Tuldenus, the Netherlands had a mixed constitution, based on a contract between the sovereign and the States as representatives of the people, Victor Brants, '1598.-Quelques notes sur les théories politiques et les Etats généraux aux Pays-Bas sous le règne des archiducs Albert et Isabelle', *Bulletin de l'Académie Royale des Sciences, des Lettres et des Beaux-Arts de Belgique*, 68 (1898) 92–112.

26 Many articles of the Act of Cession tend to keep the patrimony in the family (prohibition to transfer to third parties (Art. 5), obligation to marry sons and daughters to Spanish princes or, at least, to take the Spanish King's advice at this point (Arts. 6–7), but they do not stand for a retention of part of the patrimonial rights. In this same sense should be interpreted the oath of loyalty to the Spanish King in 1616, when the Estates explicitly accept that, given the childless situation of the archducal marriage, the Netherlands will return under the sovereignty of Spain at some point.

27 See the Act of 4 May 1598, Brants, *Recueil*, vol. 1, 11–12. It is confirmed by a declaration of Philip III during his reign (Valladolid, 1 February 1601), Joseph Lefèvre, 'La souveraineté', 969.

28 And to the list of competences Zypaeus enumerates as *iura maiestatis*, Zypaeus, *Judex, magistratus*, 305–323.

> principaultez, marquisats, contez, baronies, seigneuries, villes, châteaux et fortz qui sont en nosdicts pays d'embas et de Bourgoigne, ensemble touttes régales (the royal competences!), fiefs, hommages, droicts, libertez, franchises, droictz de patronnaiges, rentes et revenus, domeine, aydes, confiscations et fourfaictures avecq tous et quelzconcques droictz et actions que pourrons et pourrions prétendre à cause d'iceulx pays d'embas et conté de Bourgoigne, ensemble touttes prééminences, prérogatives, privilèges, exemptions, gardiennetez, advoueries, jurisdictions, haulteurs, ressorts et autres superioritez quelzconcques comme et en quelle sorte elles soyent, et à quelque cause et occasion elles nous puissent compéter et appertenir, soit de patrimoine ou aultrement à quelque titre et comme que ce soit.

Isabella receives the competence to do 'tout ce qu'une vraye princesse et dame naturelle et propriétaire desdictz pays, de droict coustume et aultrement peult et doibt faire' (Art. 13). Although 'sovereignty' is not explicitly handed over, the word '*souverain*' is mentioned once, when the King describes that Isabella will take his place with regard to the subjects:

> sermens de fidélité, foy et hommaige, promesse et obligations qu'ilz avoient à nous, comme à leur seigneur et prince souverain, veuillant, ordonnant et enjoignant bien expressément à iceulx qu'en ayent à jurer et recepvoir ladicte infante, nostre fille, pour leur vraye princesse et dame, et à luy facent et présentent les deuz sermens de fidélité, foi, homage (…)

From these wordings, we can conclude that in the eyes of Philip II, Albert and Isabella became the real and legal sovereigns of the Netherlands, a new and independent state, apart from Spain. And this is still the case in 1609, when he gives procurement for the conclusion of the Twelve Years Truce, referring explicitly to the Archdukes as the 'principes y senores soberanos proprietarios dellos'.[29] In Article 1 of the Twelve Years Truce, the Archdukes handle 'tans en leurs noms que dudit Sieur Roi'.[30]

If in 1598 the purpose to transfer (almost) complete sovereignty was very clear, a fact confirmed by the, eventually unsuccessful, quest for a new royal crown, to my opinion, things only started to weaken when it became clear that

29 Brants, *Recueil*, 407.

30 See R. Lesaffer, *Europa: een zoektocht naar vrede? 1453–1763 en 1945–1997* (Leuven, 1999), 378.

the main condition, a new dynasty, was no longer a possibility. It is in this light, for instance, that Philip III, in 1616, asked the provincial States to swear an oath of allegiance to his person.

Elements of Sovereignty between 1598 and 1621

That not only according to the words of the Spanish ruler, but also in fact, the Archdukes acted as sovereigns, is illustrated in various ways.

The *Consejo de Flandes*, having emerged implicitly through the ages but being explicitly established in Madrid in 1588, to discuss and give advice on all Dutch problems ('Flandes' stands here as *pars pro toto* for all of the Netherlands), did not function during the reign of Albert and Isabella.[31] Officially, the Spanish King did not have an advisory board on the Low Countries matters. Why should he? The Netherlands were another State, no longer his.

In Brussels, there was a Spanish ambassador residing just like there were many other foreign ambassadors.[32] Furthermore, Albert and Isabella made use of their right to send out their own ambassadors to Rome, Paris or London (not to Madrid!). These are two prerogatives only sovereign princes enjoy.[33] Moreover, in many senses, Brussels could be considered to be at the heart of the Spanish diplomacy. Indeed, having diplomats of their own did not mean there was no cooperation between Madrid and Brussels in international affairs. Philip III and his sister and brother-in-law were certainly no rivals, but worked together to defend the Spanish hegemony in Europe. Let us not forget that between 1539 and 1691, Madrid repeatedly considered creating an independent kingdom in the Netherlands, or ceding them to England, France or Bavaria.[34]

31 Francisco Tomas y Valiente and José Luis Bermejo Cabrero, 'Het geografisch en institutioneel kader van Spanje', in Jean-Marie Duvosquel and Ignace Vandevivere (eds.), *Luister van Spanje en de Belgische steden, 1500–1700* (Brussels, 1985), 41.

32 'Parmi les prérogatives reconnues aux archiducs, comme princes souverains, se trouve celle de recevoir des agents diplomatiques et d'en accréditer', Joseph Lefèvre, 'Les ambassadeurs d'Espagne à Bruxelles sous le règne de L'Archiduc Albert (1598–1621)', *Belgisch Tijdschrift voor Filologie en Geschiedenis*, 2 (1923) 61–80.

33 Lefèvre, 'La souveraineté', 980.

34 The Spanish *Consejo de Estado* debated on the cession of sovereignty of the Netherlands to France in 1544 and 1602, to England in 1554 and 1623, and to Bavaria in 1684 and 1691. More than twenty projects are conserved in the Spanish archives, Rafael Valladares, 'Decid adiós a Flandes. La monarquia hispánica y el problema de los Países Bajos', in Luc Duerloo and Werner Thomas (eds.), *Albert & Isabella (1598–1621)* (Brussels, 1998), 47–54 at 48.

'L'alliance du roi d'Espagne avec les princes des Pays-Bas est l'union des plus puissants potentats d'Europe avec des souverains qui régissent un petit état. Elle n'a pourtant jamais entrainé la soumission des seconds au premier', Lefèvre wrote.[35] Especially the 1604 London Peace Treaty with England can be considered a personal achievement of Albert. Also in the evolution towards the acceptance of the Twelve Years Truce, the Archduke's personal pacifist role was of paramount importance. Especially the provisional truce of 13 March 1607 was Albert's achievement. However, if Albert was allowed to play his role, he could not act with complete autonomy or without keeping in close touch with Madrid. If, formally, he acted as a sovereign, substantially spoken his (external) sovereignty was limited. Two out of the four Spanish ambassadors who succeeded each other in Brussels between 1598 and 1621, Balthazar de Zuniga y Fonseca being the first one and the Marquis of Bedmar the last, can certainly not be considered to be 'ordinary' ambassadors. For that, their influence on the Archdukes was too strong. It makes Joseph Lefèvre conclude that 'la Belgique n'est durant ces vingt ans, ni un état indépendent, ni une province de la monarchie espagnole. L'archiduc n'est, pour le roi d'Espagne, ni un souverain étranger, ni un simple gouverneur'.[36] However, in diplomatic correspondence between Brussels and other powers, we see that the same formulas were used as in that used among sovereigns. Moreover, in official meetings, the representatives of the Archdukes took place immediately behind the royal ones, but in front of the republics. These formal elements illustrate that the Archducal Netherlands were 'recognised' as a sovereign State, if we are allowed to use this modern term to describe the early modern situation, without risk of 'Hineininterpretierung'.

The Spanish influence was especially weighing through the so-called 'Spanish Ministry' in Brussels.[37] All through the 16th and 17th centuries, different Spanish noblemen (originally all military officers) and prelates have been playing an intermediary role between the Spanish king and his general governor in the Netherlands. They did not disappear from the Brussels court scene between 1598 and 1621. The already mentioned Spanish ambassador was just one of them. Others were the head of the Spanish army and the Secretary of State and War.[38] Together with the presence of Spanish garrisons in the

---

35 Lefèvre, 'La souveraineté', 973–977.

36 Lefèvre, 'Les ambassadeurs', 80.

37 Joseph Lefèvre, 'Le Ministère espagnol de l'Archiduc Albert, 1598–1621', *Bulletin de l'Academie royale d'archéologie de Belgique*, 1 (1924) 202–224.

38 The *veedor general*, the *contador general*, the *pagador general* and the surintendant for the military justice are other members of this so-called 'Spanish Ministry'.

Netherlands, the presence of these Spanish men was certainly a *de facto* limitation of the external sovereignty of the (Southern) Low Countries. Most important was the role of the Genovese military leader Ambrogio Spinola, confident of Philip III. Joseph Lefèvre did not hesitate to call him a viceroy. On the other hand, we should not forget that he was presented to Philip III by Albert himself and that he was an Italian, not a Spaniard.[39] Another important go-between was the Secretary of State and War, the link between the administrations in Madrid and Brussels. From the first days of Albert's reign until the day he died in 1618, this office was held by Juan de Mancicidor. He was a royal minister, not an archducal one. Thirdly, Albert's confessor, the Dominican friar Iñigo de Brizuela, was another important brake on Albert's sovereign aspirations. It is known, for instance, that Brizuela played an important role in pressing Albert to accept the oath of allegiance wanted by Philip III. Lefèvre concludes: 'Alors que les conseillers belges, qui exercèrent une réelle influence sur la marche des affaires, se bornent en somme à trois: Richardot, Verreycken et Pecquius, il n'y a pas moins de neuf fonctionnaires espagnols de rang supérieur'.[40] Nevertheless, it should be underlined that all Spanish civil servants were explicitly confirmed as servants of Albert and Isabella, and, when a place became vacant, selection and nomination were done in Brussels, without any intervention of the Madrid court. The legislative and judicial activities of the Archdukes, as expressions of their internal sovereignty, have been mentioned before. Special attention should be drawn to the fact that between 1598 and 1621 several important ordinances were promulgated and, especially after the Edictum Perpetuum of 1611, a serious amount of customs were homologated, more than ever before or after.[41] Albert and Isabella were also very generous in granting pardons,[42] another expression of a sovereign royal power.

---

39 'Albert respected and accepted the military advice of the best soldier of Europe, while Spinola deferred willingly to the sovereignty of the archduke (…) whose actions conformed with Albert's policy, not Madrid's', Carter, 'Belgian autonomy', 252–253.

40 Lefèvre, 'Ministère Espagnol', 224.

41 Georges Martyn, *Het Eeuwig Edict van 12 juli 1611. Zijn genese en zijn rol in de verschriftelijking van het privaatrecht* (Brussels, 2000), 44–50.

42 Hugo De Schepper and Jean-Marie Cauchies, *Justice, grâce et législation. Genèse de l'état et moyens juridiques dans les Pays-Bas, 1200–1600* (Cahiers du centre de recherches en histoire du droit et des institutions 2; Brussels, 1994), 79; Dutch version: 'Justicie, gracie en wetgeving. Juridische instrumenten van de landsheerlijke macht in de Nederlanden, 1200–1600', in Hugo Soly and René Vermeir (eds.), *Beleid en bestuur in de oude Nederlanden. Liber amicorum prof. dr. M. Baelde* (Gent, 1993), 127–181; see also Hugo De Schepper, 'Justitie door gratie krachtens vorstelijke wetgeving in de Nederlanden (1400–1621)', in Erik-Jan Broers and Beatrix Jacobs (eds.), *Interactie tussen wetgever en rechter voor de Trias*

Also in everyday court life, in granting popular feasts and cultural and religious events, Albert and Isabella demonstrated that they were sovereign rulers. Their portraits figure on finely chiselled coins and a multitude of paintings, carvings, drawings, prints.[43] Also, the Joyous Entries in many different towns can all be seen as important moments of display of their sovereign aspirations.[44] And for the people it was the moment to express their thankful wish that, after all these years, finally decisions would again be taken in the Netherlands and not in Madrid. During the Antwerp Joyous Entry of 1599, for instance, paintings and allegorical representations symbolised the transfer of sovereignty from Philip II to his daughter.[45]

Although the list of 'sovereignty proofs' could still be lengthened, this enumeration suffices to allow for the conclusion that the Archdukes certainly were formally sovereign, at least internally.

Conclusion

When, in contemporary law, judges or policy makers are called 'sovereign', this does not mean at all that they are not bound by any legal rule or principle.[46] In public international law, misunderstandings about 'sovereignty' have been the cause of many wars. Understood as an undisputed respect for the dignity of the prince by subjects and institutions, Albert and Isabella can rightly be portrayed as true sovereigns, legitimated and legitimising sources of law and order.

Politica (The Hague, 2003), 109–130, and Hugo De Schepper and Marjan Vrolijk, 'La grâce princière et la composition coutumière aux Pays-Bas bourguignons, 1384–1633', in Jacqueline Hoareau-Dodinau and Pascal Texier (eds.), *Anthropologies juridiques. Mélanges Pierre Braun* (Limoges, 1998), 735–760.

43 E.g. Cordula Schumann, 'Court, city and countryside: Jan Breughel's Peasant Weddings as images of social unity under archducal sovereignty', in Luc Duerloo and Werner Thomas (eds.), *Albert & Isabella (1598–1621)* (Brussels, 1998), 151–160.

44 Margit Thofner, 'The ideal of sovereignty in the Joyous Entries of the Archduke Albert and Infanta Isabella', in Luc Duerloo and Werner Thomas (eds.), *Albert & Isabella (1598–1621)* (Brussels, 1998), 55–66. Especially Isabella was defined as 'Domina & Princeps proprietaria'.

45 Jan Van Den Broeck, 'Het beeld van de vorst bij de Blijde Inkomst van Albrecht en Isabella in Antwerpen', *Bijdragen tot de Geschiedenis*, 71 (1988) 123–139 at 128; Edmond Geudens, 'Blijde inkomst der aartshertogen Albertus en Isabella te Antwerpen in 1599', *Bijdragen tot de Geschiedenis*, 10 (1911) 120–140.

46 Etienne Cerexhe, 'Subsidiarité, proportionnalité, souveraineté, concepts antinomiques?', in Georges de Leval et al. (eds.), *Liber amicorum Paul Martens. L'humanisme dans la résolution des conflits. Utopie ou réalité?* (Brussels 2007), 201–211.

This does not exclude that other persons and institutions had competing powers. Susan Reynolds wrote: 'The containment of conflict between layers and types of authority seems to be a problem of all governmental systems, even where elaborated theories of sovereignty purport to eliminate it'.[47] Although the theories were not really elaborated around 1600 in the Netherlands, there seems to have been a common knowledge and acceptance of the state of affairs, embracing respect for Albert and Isabella's sovereignty.

---

47 Susan Reynolds, *Kingdoms and communities in Western Europe, 900–1300* (Oxford, 1997), 222. Certainly in the Middle Ages, according to the author, there was 'no idea that sovereignty should be single and precisely located: government consisted of layers of authority, and loyalties were attracted to each layer accordingly', Ibid., 331.

CHAPTER 10

The Early Doctrine of International Law as a Bridge from Antiquity to Modernity and Diplomatic Inviolability in 16th- and 17th-Century European Practice

Carlo Focarelli

Introduction

At the risk of oversimplifying a complex question, it can be assumed that among several possible approaches to the history of international law, two stand out: *a*) international law as an essentially European law that emerged at the beginning of the Early Modern Age, more or less around the times the Twelve Years Truce was made;[1] and *b*) international law as a law deeply rooted in Antiquity, going back even to the 3rd millennium BC.[2] Broadly speaking, while the former approach emphasises discontinuity and Euro-centrism and tends mostly to be adopted by international lawyers, the latter emphasises continuity and universalism and is generally taken by historians.[3]

1 The classical formulation of this approach is famously found in Lassa F. Oppenheim, *International Law* (London: Longman Green, 1948, 7th edn. by Hersch Lauterpacht), vol. 1, 68: 'International law as a law between sovereign and equal states based on the common consent of those States is a product of modern Christian civilisation, and may be said to be about four hundred years old.' For a restatement see Josef L. Kunz, 'Pluralism of Legal and Value Systems and International Law', *American Journal of International Law*, 49 (1955) 370–376; Jan H.W. Verzijl, *International Law in Historical Perspective* (Leyden, 1968), vol. 1, 403–404.

2 Cf., e.g., Brougham H. Leech, 'Ancient International Law', *Contemporary Review*, 43 (1883) 260–274 and 890–904; Coleman Phillipson, *The International Law and Custom of Ancient Greece and Rome* (2 vols., London, 1911); Sergej A. Korff, *Introduction à l'histoire du droit international public*, *Recueil des Cours de l'Académie de Droit International*, 1 (1923) 5–23; Isidoro J. Ruiz Moreno, *El derecho internacional publico antes de la era cristiana* (Buenos Aires, 1946); Wolfgang Preiser, 'Zum Völkerrecht der vorklassischen Antike', *Archiv des Völkerrechts*, 4 (1954) 257–289; Idem, 'Die Epochen der antiken Völkerrechtsgeschichte', *Juristenzeitung*, 11 (1956) 737–744; Stephan Verosta, 'International Law in Europe and Western Asia between 100 and 650 AD', *Recueil des Cours de l'Académie de Droit International*, 113 (1964) 491–613.

3 A purportedly non-Eurocentric approach may not necessarily imply that international law existed in or before 'classic' Antiquity (Greece, Rome and other civilisations of the

 | DOI 10.1163/9789004274921_012

Adherents to the latter approach have held that current international law is 'nothing else but the last transformation of the European law of nations, which has an uninterrupted tradition since the days of the ancient Greek city-states,'[4] if not 'pre-classic' international law in the Ancient Near East.[5] This is not necessarily to deny that international law is *somehow* 'European' in its origins, but with the qualification that the European origin of international law is rooted in the ancient world covering the Mediterranean and Mesopotamia. Such

---

Mediterranean basin after the demise of the Roman Empire). Ago emphasised that international law originated in the 9th century AD including rules applicable to relations between the Roman Sacred Empire, the East Roman Empire and the Islamic Caliphate of Baghdad: see Roberto Ago, 'Pluralism and the Origins of the International Community', *Italian Yearbook of International Law*, 3 (1977) 3–30; for a later analysis of *earlier* international law insisting on disproving the traditional belief that international law is of exclusively Christian, European descent, see Roberto Ago, 'The First International Communities in the Mediterranean World', *British Yearbook of International Law*, 53 (1982) 213–232. In favour of the Christian origins of international law see, e.g., Giorgio Balladore Pallieri, *Diritto internazionale pubblico* (Milan, 1962), 3–7. For a discussion on this point see Heinhard Steiger, 'From the International Law of Christianity to the International Law of the World Citizen – Reflections on the Formation of the Epochs of the History of International Law', *Journal of the History of International Law*, 3 (2001) 180–193. Paradisi made the point that the origins of international law are to be traced to the dissolution of the Roman Empire: see Bruno Paradisi, *Civitas Maxima. Studi di storia del diritto internazionale* (2 vols., Florence, 1974). A somewhat compromising position is taken by other scholars, such as Josef L. Kunz – reviewing Georg Stadtmüller's *Geschichte des Völkerrechts* (Hannover, 1951) in *American Journal of International Law*, 46 (1952) 374 – who argues that the history of 'our' international law 'goes back to the European Middle Ages.' For an analysis of Euro-centrism in international law see Wilhelm G. Grewe, 'Vom europäischen zum universellen Völkerrecht. Zur Frage der Revision des "europazentrischen"Bildes des Völkerrechtsgeschichte', *Zeitschrift für ausländisches öffentliches Recht und Völkerrecht*, 42 (1982) 450–478; Yasuaki Onuma, 'Eurocentrism in the History of International Law', in idem (ed.), *A Normative Approach to War. Peace, War, and Justice in Hugo Grotius* (Oxford, 1993), 371–386. For the well-known view that Euro-centrism emerged only in the 19th century see Charles H. Alexandrowicz, 'Treaty and Diplomatic Relations between European and South Asian Powers in the Seventeenth and Eighteenth Centuries', *Recueil des Cours de l'Académie de Droit International*, 100 (1960) 207–321; Idem, 'The Afro-Asian World and the Law of Nations (Historical Aspects)', Ibid., 123 (1968), 117–214; Idem, *An Introduction to the History of the Law of Nations in the East Indies (16th, 17th and 18th Centuries)* (Oxford, 1967).

4 Karl-Heinz Ziegler, 'Grotius Topical, or the Import of Antiquity into the International Law of Europe', *Grotiana*, N.S. 12–13 (1991–1992) 78–87.

5 Wolfgang Preiser, 'Über die Ursprünge des modernen Völkerrechts, in Internationalrechtliche und staatsrechtliche Abhandlungen', in *Festschrift für Walter Schätzel zu seinem 70. Geburtstag* (Düsseldorf, 1960), 373–387.

concepts as 'treaties' made by mutual oaths, 'brotherhood' between sovereigns, 'sovereignty' itself (as traceable to the sovereignty of God), 'just war,' 'natural law,' 'arbitration,' 'diplomatic inviolability,' and so forth, are regarded as clearly found in pre-classic and classic Antiquity. Moreover, earlier modern European writers systematically used examples drawn from biblical, historical and other ancient (as well as medieval) sources as 'leading cases' as we would call them today, for constructing a legal world order.

It is also a fact, however, that a 'science' of international law emerged precisely in Europe at the beginning of the Early Modern Age, just around 1609 AD, and that the world at that time was quite different from the one prevailing in Antiquity. This led the so-called 'founding fathers' of modern international law to 're-imagine' the world in order to identify a law that could work in that new world, a world that was marked by the discovery of America, the Protestant Reformation and the ensuing need for legal rules that could govern religious wars (and wars for dominance) in Europe as well as wars aimed at the control of overseas colonies.[6] Some historians have argued that the purported 'ancient international law' is far from constituting a true 'system' of law and is hardly conceivable as either 'international' or 'law' proper.[7] Most ancient sources are actually open to different, even opposing interpretations. It seems that ancient inter-societal rules are too dependent on questionable (if not simply legendary) sources and events, and even when the latter's authenticity is proven, serious doubts remain as to their legal characterisation. Historians may be satisfied that certain peoples made a treaty in Antiquity, but lawyers may still wonder whether such 'treaties' were treaties in a 'technical' sense – assuming that the very term 'technical' is meaningful in this context –, whether and in what sense they were 'legally' binding, and, last but not least, whether they were actually observed.

Both approaches appear to capture some truth, but neither is fully convincing. My argument is that international law is indeed rooted in Antiquity, but this is reasonably true to the extent that Antiquity was taken as a given by early modern European writers. I would suggest that the question whether an ancient international law objectively existed does not need to be answered in order to show that international law is rooted in Antiquity, although this does not imply that the question should necessarily be answered in the negative.

---

6 The need for 're-imagining' a world order after the discovery of the New World has been emphasised by Douglas M. Johnston, *The Historical Foundations of World Order: The Tower and the Arena* (Leyden, 2008); for a detailed discussion of this book see my review in the *Journal of the History of International Law*, 11 (2009) 187–201.

7 This point will be discussed *infra*, para. 2.

Early modern European writers unquestionably used past historical examples, opinions and concepts and drew from them a legal discourse on international law, thereby operating as a bridge between Antiquity and Modernity. This may be proved even in case the existence of a 'true' international law in Antiquity should be dismissed.

The approach suggested here could be developed in virtually all areas of international law, a task that is clearly beyond the scope of this paper. I shall confine myself to taking ambassadors' inviolability and remedies against their abuse in criminal matters as an illustration. I would also like to show that while ancient 'examples' were central in the 16th- and 17th-century doctrinal debate on ambassadors' inviolability, in actual state practice ancient principles and purported legal rules were 'adjusted' to the newly emerging states system by carefully considering political expediency. As a matter of fact, a set of rules on ambassadors' inviolability – along with other rules on ambassadors' privileges – emerged as a result of a common interest of European states to control each other and no doubt permanent diplomacy offered a valuable instrument to this end.

After briefly resuming the debate around the existence of international law in Antiquity, I shall review a few well-known writers who worked in the 16th and 17th centuries and elaborated on the question of the inviolability of ambassadors, especially pointing to their ancient sources and to the way they drew legal rules from them. I shall then turn to the 16th- and 17th-century practice in Europe and see to what extent doctrines were confirmed, disconfirmed or expanded.

The Question of the Existence of an International Law in Antiquity

It is still a common belief that international law as we know it was born in Europe at the beginning of the Early Modern Age.[8] This view has been defended in the past, notably in the 19th century, by relying on a variety of purported

8 The more general view has been particularly developed by the so-called English School of International Relations whereby international society originated in Europe at the beginning of the Modern Age and eventually expanded globally, although states systems are found also in Antiquity and in regions of the world other than Europe. See Hedley Bull, 'The Importance of Grotius in the Study of International Relations', in Hedley Bull, Benedict Kinsbury and Adam Roberts (eds.), *Hugo Grotius and International Relations* (Oxford, 1992), 80 (the 'society of Christian or European states [became] global or all-inclusive') and, notably, Hedley Bull and Adam Watson (eds.), *The Expansion of International Society* (Oxford, 1985). From this

features of ancient law signalling its 'primitiveness.' Advocates of such a view insisted that an international law could not develop in Antiquity – unless treaties were made, it is sometimes pointed out – for a variety of reasons: because of a state of 'permanent hostility' and normal war relations between ancient peoples;[9] because of lack of a universally shared values, especially concerning justice and humanity,[10] or of any advanced civilisation;[11] because of lack of common interests given the (geographical, racial, religious and cultural) isolation then prevailing between different peoples;[12] because of lack of legal (as opposed to religious) sanctions;[13] because of lack of the notion of

perspective the global 'expansion' of the originally European States system took place by 'admission' in the circle of 'civilised nations,' namely, of States that fulfilled a 'standard of civilisation' determined and proclaimed by the European great powers and reflecting their own organisational structures and values. See Georg Schwarzenberger, 'The Standard of Civilisation in International Law', *Current Legal Problems*, 8 (1955) 212–234; Dietrich Schindler, 'Völkerrecht und Zivilisation', *Annuaire Suisse de droit international*, 13 (1956) 79–96; Gerrit W. Gong, *The Standard of 'Civilisation' in International Society* (Oxford, 1984); Brett Bowden, 'The Colonial Origins of International Law. European Expansion and the Classical Standard of Civilization', *Journal of the History of International Law*, 7 (2005) 1–23. This approach, albeit remaining dominant, has attracted various criticisms, e.g., as methodologically Eurocentric, see Yasuaki Onuma, discussed *infra*, note 23, or as essentially State-centric, see Paul Keal, *European Conquest and the Rights of Indigenous Peoples, The Moral Backwardness of International Society* (Cambridge, 2003), 3–6 and 25–37.

9 Cf., e.g., François Laurent, *Histoire du droit des gens et des relations internationales. Etudes sur l'histoire de l'humanité* (Bruxelles, 1861), vol. 1, 19–20 and 46–48; Michael I. Rostovtseff, 'International Relations in the Ancient World', in Edmund A. Walsh (ed.), *The History and Nature of International Relations* (New York, 1922), 35–36 and 43.

10 Cf., e.g., James Kent, *Commentaries on American Law* (12th edn. by O.W. Holmes, Boston, 1873), vol. 1, 5; Henry Sumner Maine, *Ancient Law. Its Connection With the Early History of Society, and Its Relation to Modern Ideas* (London, 1861), 25; Lord Arundell of Wardour, *Tradition Principally with Reference to the Mythology of the Law of Nations* (London, 1872), 379.

11 Cf. G. Fusinato, *Deo feziali e del diritto feziale. Contributo alla storia del diritto pubblico esterno di Roma* (Rome, 1884), 11 ff.; Idem, 'Le droit international de la république romaine. Les étrangers, les récupérateurs, les fétiaux', *revue de droit international et de législation comparée*, 17 (1886) 278–312.

12 Cf. M.K. Nawaz, 'The Law of Nations in Ancient India', *The Indian Year Book of International Affairs*, 6 (1957) 173, arguing that, alongside 'a remarkable body of inter-State rules' in the ancient Indian state practice, there existed in the past a number of international societies that 'lived in isolation from each other, separated by geographical factors and racial considerations.'

13 Cf. C. Vergé, *Introduction*, in Georg F. de Martens, *Précis du droit des gens moderne de l'Europe* (Paris, 1864), viii; August W. Heffter, *Das Europäische Völkerrecht der Gegenwart*

sovereignty;[14] because of the formalistic character of ancient law;[15] because of a religious (as opposed to legal) character of existing rules;[16] because existing rules at the time were too few and hardly coherent.[17] Since the end of the 19th century, these arguments have been more and more opposed by other writers, among whom Giovanni Baviera – a regrettably little known (abroad) Italian Roman law scholar writing in the second half of the 19th century – stands out.[18]

In fact, few doubt today that some inter-societal or inter-group rules have existed since Antiquity in all parts of the world. Few also would deny that there were in Antiquity independent political entities powerful enough to co-exist as equals and to form a 'system' that might be called 'international.'[19] What is denied by detractors is that these rules constituted an international law proper, they being neither 'international' nor 'legal' in any comprehensible or acceptable sense. Even rules on diplomatic intercourse, which no doubt are attested to everywhere since the most remote times,[20] are thought to be at best the

---

auf den bisherigen Grundlagen (Berlin, 1881), 12; Amos S. Hershey, 'The History of International Relations during Antiquity and the Middle Ages', *American Journal of International Law*, 5 (1911) 901.

14 Cf. Vergé, *Introduction*, in Martens, *Précis*, viii; James L. Brierly, *The Basis of Obligation in International Law and Other Papers* (Oxford, 1958), 20.

15 Cf. Maine, *Ancient Law*, 25; Paul Vinogradoff, *Outlines of Historical Jurisprudence* (London, 1920), 364.

16 Cf. Guy Kestemont, *Diplomatique et droit international en Asie occidentale (1600–1200 av. J.C.)* (Louvain-La-Neuve, 1974), 201–204.

17 A. Maury, *Histoire des religions de la Grèce antique* (Paris, 1859), 401–402.

18 Giovanni Baviera, *Il diritto internazionale dei Romani* (Modena, 1898). For other critical writings moving in the same direction, despite some different nuances, see Phillipson, *International Law and Custom*, vol. 2, 167; and the review made by Moreno, *El derecho internacional publico*, 19–91.

19 See David J. Bederman, *International Law in Antiquity* (Cambridge, 2001), 16–21.

20 See, e.g., Phillipson, *International Law and Custom*, vol. 1, 302–346; Ragnar Numelin, *The Beginnings of Diplomacy; A Sociological Study of Intertribal and International Relations* (London, 1950); J.M. Munn-Rankin, 'Diplomacy in Western Asia in the Early Second Millennium BC', *Iraq* 18 (1956) 68–110; Ludo Rocher, 'The "Ambassador" in Ancient India', *Indian Yearbook of International Affairs*, 7 (1958) 344–360; Louise-Marie Wéry, 'Le meurtre de hérauts de Darius en 491 et l'inviolabilité du héraut', *L'antiquité classique*, 34 (1966) 468–486; Idem, 'Le fonctionnement de la diplomatie à l'époque homérique', *Revue international des droits de l'antiquité*, 14 (1967) 169–205; Derek J. Mosley, *Envoys and Diplomacy in Ancient Greece* (Wiesbaden, 1973); Franck E. Adcock and Derek J. Mosley, *Diplomacy in Ancient Greece* (London, 1975); Donald Lateiner, 'Heralds and Corpses in Thucydides', *Classical World*, 71 (1977) 97–106; Peter Karavites, 'Diplomatic Envoys in the Homeric

result of mere reciprocity, a sort of mutual expectation that was not backed by legal rules. Ancient sources on 'international law' are often mythological and extremely difficult to be evaluated in legal terms. In sum, to say that there existed an 'international law' in Antiquity appears a rather hazardous proposition unless a number of qualifications are made. On the other hand, advocates of ancient international law have objected that its existence is evidenced by archaeological finds, historical literature, and so forth.[21] Other scholars have taken a somewhat mid-way path.[22]

The problem with all these positions is that they are centred on whether international law *as such* existed in the past, thus preliminarily assuming a certain notion of international law, inevitably reflecting its current notion or at least what is regarded as its 'core' meaning. Evidently, international law exactly 'as we know it' cannot be found in the past. Moreover, international law is made up of various rules whose history may not coincide with that of international law as a whole: a specific rule, such as the one concerning diplomatic inviolability, may well be traceable to Antiquity but this does not imply that international law as such, i.e. as a coherent body of rules, can equally be said to have existed in ancient times. In addition, not infrequently an ideological bias and a promotional goal for present times is easily detectable in positions advocating the existence of an international law in Antiquity aiming at showing, e.g., how current international law is biased for Western values and arguing in favour of the Third World.[23] This understandable stance is a reaction to the

World', *Revue international des droits de l'antiquité*, 34 (1987) 41–100; T.R.S. Broughton, 'Mistreatment of Foreign Legates and the Fetial Priests: Three Roman Cases', *Phoenix*, 41 (1987) 50–62; Margaret M. Mitchell, 'New Testament Envoys in the Context of Greco-Roman Diplomatic and Epistolary Conventions: The Example of Timothy and Titus', *Journal of Biblical Literature*, 111 (1992) 641–662; Bederman, *International Law in Antiquity*, 106–120.

21 Cf. Dominique Gaurier, *Histoire du droit international. Auteurs, doctrines et développement de l'Antiquité à l'aube de la période contemporaine* (Rennes, 2005), 25–36, and *Journal of the History of International Law*, 9 (2007) 291–298 for my critical review.

22 Cf. Johnston, *Historical Foundations of World Order*, 145, arguing that it is 'more accurate' to see the system of international law, as we know it, as a gradual accumulation of elements – ideas, norms, practices, institutions 'and especially values' – that were shared 'in some degree' among pre-modern peoples, elements which might be regarded as 'preconditions' or 'early glimmerings' of 'what would evolve into 'world community law.' For an enquiry into 'a broader vision of intellectual origins' of international law see Bederman, *International Law in Antiquity*, 1 and 267–280, concluding that 'there was a common *idea* held in antiquity that international relations were to be based on the rule of law.'

23 See, e.g., Chan Nay Chow, *La doctrine du droit international chez Confucius* (Paris, 1940); Hiralal Chatterjee, *International Law and Inter-State Relations in Ancient India* (Calcutta,

opposite claim underlying the traditional Eurocentric thesis, which has manifestly been advanced to emphasise European (or Western) centrality, and moral superiority, relative to other civilisations.

That modern European practice and doctrine provides the fundamental material of international law as we know it is hardly questionable. This does not imply, however, that Eurocentrism is inherently part of international law, much less that international law should be understood in Eurocentric terms. Nor would the proof that international law existed in Antiquity in regions of the world other than the Mediterranean (such as in India or in China) mean that modern Europe did not contribute, or contributed less, to the development of international law. It is a fact that the basic ideological assumptions and the content of many rules of international law derive from European legal history and doctrine, including the very concept of 'law' that has been transplanted into the domain of international law.[24] This picture is, however, largely built upon rules that were believed to exist in Antiquity. In this respect it is not decisive to ascertain whether such rules were 'legal' and 'international', a problem largely open to speculation. What matters is that they have been *regarded* as such by later writers and by sovereigns. For example, it is unclear whether the Romans usually made declarations of war and, if so, whether this practice was considered as imposed by what we would call today 'law' rather than by considerations of morality or religion or other; equally unclear is whether such rules were 'international' or 'domestic,' assuming that this very distinction was known and relevant at the time. In other words, to say that the Romans actually made declarations of war and that this practice was followed by a sense of legal obligation, two questions that are far from easy to answer, is not enough if it is apparent that such declarations of war were simply made in

---

1958); H.S. Bhatia (ed.), *International Law and Practice in Ancient India* (New Dehli, 1977). A different position has been adopted by Onuma, whereby international law has actually been imposed by Europe to all other peoples, but should be seen today from an inter- or trans-civilizational (as opposed to a Eurocentric) perspective: Yasuaki Onuma, 'When was the Law of the International Society Born?', *Journal of the History of International Law*, 2 (2000) 1–66; cf. also *Journal of the History of International Law*, 6 (2004) 1–41, and some comments on Onuma' study by R.P. Anand, A. Anghie, J. Fisch, E. Jouannet, Li Zhaojie and N. Onuf. For a recent comprehensive articulation of the trans-civilizational theory, see Idem, *A Transcivilizational Perspective on International Law: Questioning Prevalent Cognitive Frameworks in the Emerging Multi-polar and Multi-civilizational World of the Twenty-first Century* (Leyden, 2010).

24 See Adda B. Bozeman, *The Future of Law in a Multicultural World* (Princeton, 1971), xi–xvii and 35–49.

compliance with Roman law and irrespective of any relationship with the legal expectations of the other belligerent. War may be the subject of both domestic and international law and a domestic legal rule, i.e. a rule that was not understood to apply to the relations between two sovereigns, cannot be equated with international law, even though it governs war and would later be governed (also) by international law. If all these questions are highly problematic, what is certain is that the 'founding fathers' of international law did assume the declarations of war made by the Romans – according to the sources – as imposed by *jus gentium*, and this latter was understood as a law different from Roman law or from the law of any specific political communities.[25] To this effect, it is also undisputable that ancient international law as related by historians and other sources profoundly affected international law as we know it and its knowledge is vital to any treatment of the history of international law.[26]

It follows that so-called ancient international law, even assuming that it was neither 'international' nor 'law' proper, at the very least is to be considered part of the history of international law to the extent that it provided examples and arguments – hence historical continuity – for a theoretical construction of international law and its individual norms, as well as for offering models of behavior that began to be followed in state practice at the beginning of modern times.[27]

---

25 See, for example, Alberico Gentili, *De jure belli libri tres* (1598, text of 1612 and translation, Classics of International Law; Oxford/London, 1933, 2 vols.) 1.1 and 2.3.

26 It is worth noting that the approach taken here is different from asking whether modern scholars like Hugo Grotius (1583–1645) were 'influenced' by ancient law and culture. This latter question generally presupposes that some ancient law did exist and proved influential in later times. I do not assume, however, that there was anything like international law in Antiquity, even although I do not either deny that some international law existed. My argument is that even assuming that 'ancient international law' is fanciful, still this fancy did provide the basis for imagining an 'international world order' and an 'international law' at the beginning of early modern European history.

27 An analysis somehow based on a similar approach – albeit limited to Roman law and to Grotius – has been recently conducted by Benjamin Straumann, *Hugo Grotius und die Antike. Römisches Recht und römische Ethik im frühneuzeitlichen Naturrecht* (Baden, 2008), reviewed by Randall Lesaffer, 'On Roman Ethics, Rhetoric and Law', *Journal of the History of International Law*, 10 (2008) 343–347. See also Arthur Nussbaum, 'The Significance of Roman Law in the History of International Law', *University of Pennsylvania Law Review*, 100 (1951–1952) 678–687; Ziegler, 'Grotius Topical', 78–87; and Randall Lesaffer, 'Argument from Roman Law in Current International Law: Occupation and Acquisitive Prescription', *European Journal of International Law*, 16 (2005) 25–58.

The 16th and 17th Century Doctrine of International Law on Diplomatic Inviolability

At the turn of the 17th century, a large number of new issues emerged in Europe concerning diplomacy: multilateral treaty-making, permanent embassies and so-called ambassadors' extra-territoriality, inviolability of ambassadors' residence, rank or precedence of ambassadors (hence of their sovereigns), exemption from subpoena as a witness, exemption from taxation and customs duties, renunciation and duration of immunities, ambassadors' privileges in third-party States, immunity of the ambassador's entourage from local jurisdiction, right of chapel, immunity of ambassadors' dispatches, and so on. One of the most sensitive and controversial question was certainly the one concerned with the treatment of ambassadors, or more precisely the question of their 'inviolability' or 'sacredness' and of possible remedies against abuse of their functions.[28]

The principle of territorial States and of the supremacy of local law (as distinct from personal law) was hardening. The right to send and receive ambassadors increasingly came to be viewed as a litmus test of sovereignty: gradually, immunities were not recognised by sovereigns to persons who did not represent entities regarded as 'equally' sovereigns, including rebels aspiring to become independent States, and this contributed to the emergence of a states system in Europe.[29] An impressive number of dissertations and doctrinal contributions were produced in the 16th and 17th centuries on the subject of diplomatic privileges.[30]

---

28 See Ernest Nys, 'Les commencements de la diplomatie et le droit d'ambassade, jusqu'à Grotius', *Revue de droit international et de législation comparée* (1883–1884) 577–586; Edward R. Adair, *The Extraterritoriality of Ambassadors in the Sixteenth and Seventeenth Centuries* (London/New York/Toronto, 1929); Charles H. Carter, 'The Ambassadors of Early Modern Europe: Patterns of Diplomatic Representation in the Early Seventeenth Century', in Charles H. Carter (ed.), *From the Renaissance to the Counter-Reformation* (New York, 1965), 269–295; M.S. Anderson, *The Rise of Modern Diplomacy, 1450–1919* (Harlow, 1993); Linda S. Frey and Marsha L. Frey, *The History of Diplomatic Immunity* (Columbus, 1999), 119–260; John Watkins, 'Toward a New Diplomatic History of Medieval and Early Modern Europe', *Journal of Medieval and Early Modern Studies*, 38 (2008) 1–13.

29 The topic was discussed at length in the first ever history of international law written by Robert Ward, *An Inquiry into the Foundation and History of the Law of Nations in Europe, from the Time of the Greeks and Romans, to the Age of Grotius* (London, 1795), vol. 2, 359–465; and by Geoffrey Butler and Simon Maccoby, *The Development of International Law* (London/New York, 1928, reprint 2003), 11 and 28–32; see also Frey and Frey, *History of Diplomatic Immunity*, 125–128.

30 For a collection of extracts from numerous 16th and 17th-century treatises on ambassadors see Vladimir E. Hrabar, *De Legatis et Legationibus Tractatus Varii* (Dorpat, 1905),

Ancient law, especially Roman law as related by Livy, Cicero, and others, was taken as a reference point. In this context the word used was *legatus*, which meant both an envoy from a foreign people outside the Roman Empire and a representative of a municipality or a province within the Empire. Ancient sources reported episodes that attested to (or could be understood as implying rules on) both respect for inviolability of ambassadors (its breach giving rise to a cause of war) and justified reactions against their abuses (this also capable of involving a war). In the Middle Ages, the classical sacredness of ambassadors was reinforced by the sanctity (sanctioned by canon law) surrounding the papal legate or *nuncio*, who represented the best-known type of ambassador at the time.[31] Roman law, canon law, emerging territorial, medieval personal law, all contributed to the acceptance of ambassadors' inviolability in the 16th century.

The classical source of ambassadors' inviolability, cited by all early modern writers, is the text attributed to Pomponius and found in D. 50.7.17 ('Si quis legatum hostium pulsasset, contra ius gentium id commissum esse

---

covering treatises published before 1625; Idem, *De Legatorum Jure Tractatuum Catalogus Completus ab Anno usque ad annum 1700* (Dorpat, 1918), dealing with treatises published from 1625 to 1700. See also B. Behrens, 'Treatises on the Ambassador Written in the Fifteenth and Early Sixteenth Centuries', *English Historical Review*, 60 (1936) 619–620.

31 The 13th-century *legatus* ordinarily refers to a papal legate and only rarely to a secular diplomat, while at the time secular diplomats were either *nuncii* (in use for centuries) or *procuratores* (appeared only in the 12th or 13th century, who supplemented, but not supplanted, *nuncii*). A *nuncius* was basically a messenger used to send and obtain information; a procurator, as defined by Ulpian in D. 3.3.1: 'is one who administers another's affairs by the mandate of the principal.' See R. Maulde, 'Les instructions diplomatiques au Moyen Age', *Revue d'histoire diplomatique*, 6 (1892) 602–632; George P. Cuttino, *English Diplomatic Administration, 1259–1339* (London, 1940), 84–85; Donald E. Queller, 'Thirteenth-Century Diplomatic Envoys: Nuncii and Procuratores', *Speculum*, 35 (1960) 196–213; George P. Cuttino, *English Medieval Diplomacy* (Bloomington, 1985); Igor de Rachewiltz, *Papal Envoys to the Great Khans* (Stanford, Calif., 1971). The origins of the modern office of ambassador, according to the prevailing view, date back to the 13th-century Italy: cf. François L. Ganshof, 'Le Moyen Age', in Pierre Renouvin (ed.), *Histoire des relations internationals* (Paris, 1953), vol. 1, 268; Garrett Mattingly, *Renaissance Diplomacy* (Boston, 1955; repr. New York, 1988), 24–25 and 47–60. Before the 13th century, the term *ambaxador* was in use but with no technical meaning, denoting any person sent by any other who was a public authority and had provided the ambassador with adequate credentials or letters of credence. Eventually, the term took to indicating someone representing the person of his principal – similarly to the medieval *nuncius* – while the procurator was someone merely acting in his principal's name.

existimatur, quia sancti habetur legati').[32] All writers accepted ambassadors' inviolability. A brief account of the most representative ones (Belli, Ayala, Gentili and Grotius) and of certain passages from their works is helpful for our purposes.

Pietrino Belli

Pietrino Belli (1505–1575), an Italian scholar, wrote his major work *De re militari et bello tractatus* (*A Treatise on Military Matters and Warfare*) in 1563.[33] He devoted Paragraphs 10 and 11 of Chapter 9 in Book 2 to diplomacy. Two propositions found in his book are of relevance.

First, Belli stated that envoys of the enemy ('legati hostium') are immune, and this was more likely because of a practice based on *jus gentium* than because of a tacit agreement between commanders.[34] He pointed out that this inviolability was scrupulously observed in early times, quoting as a proof the above-mentioned Pomponius' passage in the Digest,[35] along with the passage in the *Decretum Gratiani* defining *jus gentium* found in the Digest,[36] as well as the passage of Livy where the story of Tarquin is described to show that the Romans adhered to *jus gentium* even though Tarquin's ambassadors were enemies and were plotting secretly to restore him to the throne.[37]

Second, Belli noted that he did not believe that in his days envoys were immune 'if they attempted such a thing' (as that of Tarquin's ambassadors) because 'they ought not to overstep the bounds of their commission.' Also this

32 'When anyone strikes the envoy of our enemy, he is considered to be guilty of an act against the Law of Nations, because envoys are considered sacred,' translation by Samuel P. Scott, *The Civil Law* (Cincinnati, 1932), available at http://www.constitution.org/sps/sps.htm. All translations of the *Digest* provided hereinafter are from this work. Citations from the writers discussed in this section actually refer to D. 50.7.18.

33 Pietrino Belli, *De re militari et bello tractatus* (1563, text and translation, Classics of International Law; Oxford, 1936, 2 vols.).

34 Belli cites D. 2.14.5: 'There are three kinds of conventions, some of which relate to public matters, and some to private affairs. Those which are private are either based upon legislative enactments or upon the Law of Nations.'

35 D. 50.7.17.

36 D. 1.1.9: 'All nations who are ruled by law and customs make use partly of their own law, and partly of that which is common to all men. For whatever law any people has established for itself is peculiar to that State, and is called the Civil Law, as being the particular law of that State. But whatever natural reason has established among all men is equally observed by all mankind, and is called the Law of Nations, because it is the law which all nations employ.'

37 *Ab urbe condita* 2.4.7.

proposition was based on Roman sources[38] and illustrated by the Senones' punishment of Rome when Roman ambassadors abused their functions and violated *jus gentium* as related by Livy.[39] He also recalled the killing of Tatius by the Laurentines for having allowed their envoys to be flogged 'contrary to *jus gentium*,' again drawing from Livy.[40]

Belli thus held, first, that inviolability of the enemy's envoys is grounded in *jus gentium*. Second, he used Roman stories as a 'precedent' ('quo exemplo') to assert a rule that he thought should be applied in his days. Third, *jus gentium* was assumed to prohibit *both* ill-treatment of envoys and abuses committed by envoys. Fourth, abuse was regarded as a conduct outside the diplomatic functions, thus justifying the denial of inviolability. This last proposition is particularly important since it is also found, as will be seen, in 15th- and 16-century State practice.[41]

Balthazar Ayala

Turning to Balthazar Ayala (1548–1584), a Spanish writer from the Spanish Netherlands whose masterpiece *De jure et officiis bellicis et disciplina militari libri tres* (*Three Books on the Law of War and on the Duties Connected with War and on Military Discipline*) was published in 1582.[42] Chapter 9 of Book 1, devoted to diplomacy and entitled *De iure legatorum*, deserves some consideration.

Ayala began making an impressively clear statement: 'Ambassadors were safe and inviolable among all peoples. This was provided by *jus gentium*' ('Legati apud omnes gentes semper tuti, & inviolabiles fuerunt, quod iure gentium inductum est'), citing D. 50.7.17.[43] Interestingly, he rooted inviolability in *jus gentium* and referred it to 'all peoples.' He had no doubts about the universality of the rule on ambassadors' inviolability as found in the Roman *jus gentium*.

Second, Ayala recalled that those who assaulted or ill-treated an ambassador were ordinarily surrendered to the enemy, citing again D 50.7.17, and

38 C. 4.35.21.

39 *Ab urbe condita* 5.35.4 ff.

40 *Ab urbe condita* 1.14.1 ff.

41 Among theorists, Belli was not alone in holding that ambassadors who abused their position could no longer enjoy privileges. See, e.g., Conradus Brunus, *De legationibus* (Moguntiae, 1548); Niccolò Machiavelli, *Discorsi sopra la prima deca di Tito Livio*, in Mario Martelli (ed.), *Tutte le Opere* (Florence,1971), vol. 2, 243–245.

42 Balthazar Ayala, *De jure et officiis bellicis et disciplina militari libri III* (1582, text and translation, Classics of International Law; Washington DC, 1912, 2 vols.).

43 Ayala, *De jure et officiis bellicis* 1.9.

adding that if they were not surrendered or if the state was involved in the violation, custom would have justified a declaration of war.[44]

Third, like Belli, Ayala stressed that ambassadors were not allowed to do anything outside the scope of their embassage, citing a passage attributed to Paulus from the Digest.[45]

Alberico Gentili

Also worth mentioning is Alberico Gentili (1552–1608), an Italian scholar who has been traditionally credited with being the most important of Grotius' precursors. In his work *De jure legationis*, published in 1585,[46] he significantly stated, in Chapter 19 of Book 1, that embassies are found 'among all nations,' thus reiterating what his predecessors had stated. This proposition is supported by Roman, Greek and biblical sources that attested, in Gentili's view, to the reception of ambassadors by the Hebrews, the Carthaginians, the Gauls and Alexander the Great. He stressed that embassies arose after the separation of the nations, a clearly biblical motive. Citing again D. 50.7.17, he stated that the right of embassy is 'sacred among all peoples' as well as 'of universal application, and admitted and recognised even by barbarous peoples.'[47]

We do not need to go into Book 2 of the *De jure legationibus*, which is specifically devoted to the treatment of ambassadors, except for emphasising that it was Gentili's belief that 'the rights of embassy ought not to be disturbed on account of religious differences, since 'this intercharge is the universal practice now, just as it was the regular practice in the olden time' (Chapter 11) and that an ambassador suspected of conspiring against the local sovereign should be ordered to depart rather than to be put to death (Chapter 18).[48]

Hugo Grotius

A similar approach is also found in Grotius, whose masterpiece *De jure belli ac pacis libri tres* was published in 1625.[49] Grotius devoted Chapter 18 of Book 2 to diplomacy. Again, we do not need to examine in detail Grotius' treatment of the subject. It is sufficient to note that he also cited, among plenty of other

---

44 Ibid.

45 D. 50.7.9.2.

46 Alberico Gentili, *De legationibus libri tres* (1585, text from 1594 and translation, Classics of International Law; New York, 1924, 2 vols.)

47 Ibid.

48 Ibid. See also below, note 63.

49 Hugo Grotius, *De jure belli ac pacis libri tres* (1625, text of 1646 and translation, Classics of International Law; Oxford, 1925, 2 vols.).

ancient sources, D. 50.7.17 to underscore that mention of the inviolability of ambassadors is found 'everywhere.'[50] He also held that diplomatic immunities are rooted in *jus gentium*, understood as 'volitional law' ('ex voluntate gentium modum accipit'), i.e. grounded in the will of nations.[51] To his mind, once admitted in a state, ambassadors were 'extra-territorial' and not subjected to local law; they could however be detained and interrogated, but ultimately had to be allowed to return home.[52]

Summary

Ancient 'examples' were regarded by early-modern international law scholars as 'precedents' to be used to defend a rule on diplomatic inviolability and forfeiture of privileges in case of abuse. This rule was grounded in the Roman *jus gentium* and believed to be of universal application. It prohibited offenses against ambassadors, including envoys of the enemy, and allowed some remedy to abuses of diplomatic functions. Abuses entailed forfeiture of privileges insofar as the ambassador was deemed to have acted beyond his functions, thus becoming a private individual.

Some methodological points are also worth being made. First, no one apparently questioned the historical truth of the facts narrated in ancient sources. Historical truth and moral/legal truth were felt to be intertwined. Second, sources that were known at the time were considered, especially biblical, Greek, Roman and medieval. 'All peoples,' for example, meant all the peoples recounted in the sources available, including some that were at the time actually unknown except for a few hints found in existing sources, such as certain peoples mentioned in the Bible. *Jus gentium* was regarded as a law common to 'all peoples,' but this hardly referred to all 'real' peoples, as we would say today. Third, these episodes and rules are hardly conceivable of as an 'international law' proper. There remains the fact, however, that those episodes were seriously considered and discussed at the time and early international law scholars drew from them the rules that eventually became the international law that we know. Fourthly, a general – albeit not necessarily consistent – practice developed in Europe on the basis of these doctrines. Finally, plenty of archaeological and historical material is available today testifying that even 'classical' practice taken into account by early-modern international law scholars was

50 Grotius, *De jure belli ac pacis* 2.18.

51 Ibid., 2.18.1.

52 Ibid., 2.18.1.

inspired by a more ancient practice, especially from the Ancient Near East.[53] This suggests that, somehow, today's international law reflects an 'image' of world order that can be traced back to the 3rd millennium BC, regardless of the classical question whether one can properly speak of an 'international law' in Antiquity.

Diplomatic Inviolability in Criminal Matters and Remedies to Abuse of Diplomatic Functions in the 16th and 17th Century European Practice

Turning to the 16th- and 17th-century state practice, a few preliminary words need to be said. The general trend in works concerning the history of international law is to analyse, more or less accurately, doctrinal works. Attention has been rarely drawn on empirical verification in order to check whether and to what extent doctrinal theories reflected actual practice.[54]

As hinted earlier, Roman and canon law were important in the scholarly construction of rules on diplomatic inviolability, but also concrete facts were of relevance. In particular, the establishment of permanent embassies in the 15th century, first in Italy and later throughout Europe, involved a virtually uncontrolled growth of diplomatic personnel and immunities, and a number of unprecedented problems to the then emerging sovereigns.[55] Personal law continued to apply to ambassadors while territorial law (along with territorial

53 See, e.g., Jonathan Rosner Ziskind, *Aspects of International Law in the Ancient Near East* (Columbia University, Ph.D., 1967).

54 This task was indeed embarked upon by Adair in 1929 in his book on the extraterritoriality of ambassadors in the 16th and 17th centuries: cf. Adair, *Extraterritoriality of Ambassadors*, 4. See also, more generally, Georg Schwarzenberger, 'Historical Models of International Law: Towards a Comparative History of International Law', in William E. Butler (ed.), *International Law in Comparative Perspective* (Alphen aan den Rijn, 1980), 228–229.

55 See Otto Krauske, 'Die Entwickelung der ständigen Diplomatie. vom fünfzehnten Jahrhundert bis zu den Beschlüssen von 1815 und 1818', *Mittheilungen des Instituts für österreichische Geschichtsforschung*, 10 (1889) 501–552; Adolf Schaube, *Zur Entstehungsgeschichte der ständigen Gesandtschaften* (Leipzig, 1885); Garrett Mattingly, 'The First Resident Embassies: Medieval Italian Origins of Modern Diplomacy', *Speculum*, 12 (October 1937) 423–439; Angelo P. Sereni, *The Italian Conception of International Law* (New York, 1943), 9 and 15; Fritz Ernst, 'Über Gesandtschaftswesen und Diplomatie an der Wende vom Mittelalter zur Neuzeit', *Archiv für Kulturgeschichte*, 33 (1950) 64–95; Luis Weckmann, 'Les origines des missions diplomatiques permanentes', *Revue générale de droit international public*, 56 (1952) 161–188; Frey and Frey, *History of Diplomatic Immunity*, 121–125.

states) was coming to prevail. The Protestant Reformation might imply that a Catholic ambassador could not be subjected to local law in a Protestant state; he should also be protected from the mob. There was apparently an interest of all States to send their ambassadors to other States (especially to gather intelligence information) and have them protected, but this implied that they had to do the same within their territory with regard to ambassadors from other States.

That said, I shall now briefly review a number of cases from the 16th and 17th centuries dealing with diplomatic inviolability in criminal matters and, in particular, the reaction of sovereigns to abuse of diplomatic functions.

In 1525, Charles V's (1516–1558) ambassador to England (Louis de Praet, 1488–1555) was discovered to have sent home reports that Henry VIII (1509–1547) was untrustworthy, even advising that a separate peace be made with France against England. These dispatches were seized by Thomas Wolsey (c. 1470–1530), then Lord Chancellor, and de Praet was summoned before him and some members of the King's Council, ordered to keep to his house and to forbear any further correspondence with Charles V. He was eventually allowed to leave the country. Wolsey argued that de Praet had overstepped the bounds of his office and consequently was no longer an ambassador, so he could be punished at the king's will.[56]

---

56 Cf. *Letters and Papers, Foreign and Domestic, Henry VIII*, available at http://www.british-history.ac.uk/catalogue.aspx?type=3&gid=126, vol. 4, § 1083 (Wolsey to Sampson, the English agent with Charles V, 13 February 1525) and §§ 1247 and 1248 (Margaret de Savoy, the then governor for Charles V of the Netherlands for whom De Praet was also acting, to Wolsey and to Henry VIII, 6–7 April 1525); Ibid., § 1237 (Sampson to Wolsey, 1 April 1525); *Harleian Manuscripts* (in the British Museum), No. 304, pp. 40–41; *Calendar of State Papers, Spain*, available at http://www.british-history.ac.uk/catalogue.aspx?type=3&gid=136, vol. 3.1, § 20 (de Praet to Charles V, 25 February 1525), §§ 31–32 (letters of Henry VIII and Wolsey to Charles V, 8 March 1525), § 38 (de Praet to Charles V, 10 March 1525), as well as § 28 (memorandum, entitled 'Justification des Anglais', bearing no date, but presumably sent on 7 March 1525 to Spain and the Low Countries soon after the occurrence and de Praet's despatch), § 47 (de Praet to Charles V, 25 March 1525), §§ 50–51 (Charles V to Henry VIII and Wolsey, 26 March 1525), § 52 (Charles V to de Praet, 26 March 1525), § 55 (Charles V to de Praet, 27 March 1525), § 61 (the Commissioners to Margaret of Austria, 30 March 1525), § 63 (de Praet to the Archduchess Margaret, 31 March 1525), § 100 (Charles V to de Praet, 29 May 1525), § 103 (Instructions to the Imperial Ambassadors in England); Edward Hall, *Henry VIII* (London, 1904), 27–28, 38; Adair, *Extraterritoriality*, 42–43; Mattingly, *Renaissance Diplomacy*, 161 and 238–239; A.F. Pollard, *Wolsey, Church and State in Sixteenth-Century England* (New York, 1966), 158; Frey and Frey, *History of Diplomatic Immunity*, 143–144.

In 1526, the Spanish ambassador to England (Iñigo de Mendoza, 1476–1535, Archbishop of Burgos) was seized and imprisoned as a reprisal against an alleged (but untrue) imprisonment by Charles V of the English and French ambassadors. To ensure Mendoza's safe return, Charles retained the English ambassador as hostage. Only in 1529 the two ambassadors were exchanged at the frontier between France and Spain near Perpignan.[57]

In 1533, an unofficial French envoy, by birth a Milanese (Giovonalberto Maraviglia) was arrested and decapitated by the Duke of Milan, Francesco Sforza (1450–1466), for plotting against the State. Francis I of France (1515–1547) protested, even towards the pope and other kings, arguing that the execution of his agent was contrary to *jus gentium* and to custom, but Francesco Sforza replied that Maraviglia was not an ambassador, since he had been never formally received him as such at court and was thus simply a criminal, subject of the Duke of Milan, guilty of both sedition and conspiracy, who deserved punishment. This occurrence seems *a contrario* to confirm that if Maraviglia had been a formal ambassador, then he would have enjoyed a better treatment.[58]

In 1557, the Spanish ambassador in Rome (Garcilasso de la Vega) was imprisoned by Pope Paul IV (1555–1559) with the charge of urging the Duke of Alba to wage war against him.[59] When Spain protested, the pope replied that the

57 Cf. *Letters and Papers, Foreign and Domestic, Henry VIII*, available at http://www.british-history.ac.uk/catalogue.aspx?type=3&gid=126, vol. 4, § 2626 (Sir Robert Wingfield to Wolsey, 14 November 1526); *Calendar of State Papers, Spain*, available at http://www.british-history.ac.uk/catalogue.aspx?type=3&gid=136, vol. 3.1, § 410 (Instructions of Mendoza, 2 May 1526), § 469 (Mendoza to the Emperor, 26 June 1526), § 619 (Mendoza to the Emperor, 21 November 1526), §§ 632 and 645 (the Emperor to Mendoza, 13 December and 28 December 1526); ibid., vol. 3.2, § 8 (Mendoza to the Emperor, 19 January 1527); *Calendar of State Papers, Venice*, available at http://www.british-history.ac.uk/catalogue.aspx?type=3&gid=140, vol. 3, §§ 1381 and 1422 (reports of Gasparo Spinelli, 11 August 1526, and Andrea Navagero, 7 October 1526; Frey and Frey, *History of Diplomatic Immunity*, 134.

58 Cf. *Calendar of State Papers, Spain*, available at http://www.british-history.ac.uk/catalogue.aspx?type=3&gid=136, vol. 4.2, § 1107 (Eustace Chapuys to the Emperor, 30 July 1533) and § 1109 (Cifuentes to the Emperor, 5 August 1533); §§ 1147, 1148 and 1164 (Cifuentes to the Emperor, 6 and 9 November 1533, and Chapuys to the Emperor, 23 December 1533); ibid., vol. 5.1, § 35 (Cifuentes' dispatch, 2 April 1534); ibid., vol. 5.2, § 52 (Francis I to the Pope, 11 May 1536); Jocelyne Russell, *Peacemaking in the Renaissance* (London, 1986), 230; Martin Du Bellay and Guillaume Du Bellay, *Mémoires de Martin et Guillaume Du Bellay* (Société de l'Histoire de France, Paris, 1908–1919, 4 vols.), vol. 2, 206–226; V.-L. Bourrilly, 'Les diplomates de François Ier: Maraviglia à Milan (1532–1533)', *Bulletin italien* (1906) 133–146; Adair, *Extraterritoriality of Ambassadors*, 44; Frey and Frey, *History of Diplomatic Immunity*, 131–133.

59 Cf. Paolo Sarpi, *Istoria del concilio tridentino* (Bari, 1935), vol. 2, 218–219 (original Latin edition of 1658); Karl von Martens, *Causes célèbres du droit des gens* (Paris, 1827), vol. 2,

ambassador, by getting involved in plots and seditions, had acted beyond the limits of his instructions and was thus punishable like any private individual.[60]

In 1569, the Spanish ambassador in England (Don Guerau de Spes, 1524–1572) was put under guard in his own home for 'acting against the alliance of the two kingdoms.' Against the ambassador's protests, the Queen replied that he had acted beyond his instructions and was thus like any other resident alien, presumably under the influence of Belli. He was then ordered to leave England within three days.[61]

In 1571, the ambassador of Mary, Queen of Scots (1542–1567/1587) at the court of Queen Elisabeth of England (1558–1603), John Leslie (1527–1596, Bishop of Ross) was accused of plotting against the Queen and handed over to the care of the Bishop of Ely. Five of the most distinguished civil lawyers were consulted (Daniel Lewis, Valentine Dale, William Drury, William Aubrey and Henry Jones), who concurred that he had forfeited his privileges. The ambassador was summoned before the Privy Council. In the end, however, he was released and ordered to leave the country (1573).[62]

489–490; Adair, *Extraterritoriality of Ambassadors*, 45; Frey and Frey, *History of Diplomatic Immunity*, 119.

60 'If Vega has kept within the limits of his instructions and the function of his embassy, he would have suffered no injury. But when he became a participant in plots, seditions, and machinations secretly contrived against the prince to whom he had been sent, he was guilty of misdemeanour as a private individual and as such merited punishment,' quoted in Cornelius van Bynkershoek, *De foro legatorum liber singularis. A Monograph on the Jurisdiction over Ambassadors in Both Civil and Criminal Cases* (Oxford, 1946), 97.

61 Cf. *Calendar of State Papers, Spain*, available at http://www.british-history.ac.uk/catalogue.aspx?type=3&gid=136, 1568–1579, § 70 (de Spes to the King of Spain, 8 January 1569), § 71 (de Spes to the duke of Alba, 10 January 1569), § 78 (de Spes to the King of Spain, 14 February 1569), § 82 (de Spes to the duke of Alba, 28 February 1569), § 84 (statement made by the English ambassador to France as to de Spes' treatment, 28 February 1569), § 85 (Philip to de Spes, 28 February 1569), § 88 (de Spes to the King of Spain, 12 March 1569), § 110 (de Spes to the King of Spain, 22 June 1569), § 115 (de Spes to the King of Spain, 5 July 1569), § 295 (de Spes to the duke of Alba), § 296 (de Spes to the King of Spain, 24 December 1571), § 301 (de Spes' relation of his embassy), § 309 (de Spes to the King of Spain, 25 February 1572); Adair, *Extraterritoriality of Ambassadors*, 46–47; Frey and Frey, *History of Diplomatic Immunity*, 166.

62 Cf. T.B. Howell and T.J. Howell, comps. *Cobbett's Complete Collection of State Trials and Proceedings for High Treason and Other Crimes and Misdemeanors from the Earliest Period to the Present Time* (London 1809–1828, 34 vols.), vol. 5, 499–500; William Camden, *History of the Most Renowned and Victorious Princess Elisabeth, Late Queen of England* (1688,

In 1584, the Spanish ambassador to England (Bernardino de Mendoza, c. 1540–1604) was summoned before the Privy Council for plotting against the Queen. Alberico Gentili and Jean Hotman (1552–1636) were consulted. The ambassador was given 15 days to leave the country.[63]

In 1587, the French ambassador to England (De l'Aubespine) was summoned for plotting to murder Queen Elisabeth and planning an invasion of England. He pleaded innocent and was later received by the Queen who admitted his innocence.[64]

In 1614, the envoy of the Duke of Savoy (Colonel Alard) to Dauphiné committed a cold-blooded murder. The Parliament ordered his arrest, but the Marshal Lesdiguières (1543–1626) demanded and obtained his release on grounds that the imprisonment of an envoy was contrary to *jus gentium*. This was approved by the King of France.[65]

In 1618, the Spanish Ambassador at Venice (Alfonso de la Cueva, c. 1574–1655) was charged with having conspired against the Republic. The Senate demanded his recall and even defended him from the Venetian mob.[66]

In 1618, the French representative in England (Le Clerc) was summoned before the Privy Council for high treason and plotting against King James, but

---

Chicago, 1970, ed. by Wallace T. MacCaffrey), 164–165 and 198; Adair, *Extraterritoriality of Ambassadors*, 48–49; Frey and Frey, *History of Diplomatic Immunity*, 174–176.

63 Cf. *Calendar of State Papers, Spain*, available at http://www.british-history.ac.uk/catalogue.aspx?type=3&gid=136; *Cottonian Manuscripts* (in the British Museum), Vesp. c. vii, fols. 390–392; William Camden, *History*, cit., p. 296; Alberico Gentili, *De legationibus*, 79; Jean Hotman, *De la Charge et Dignité de l'Ambassadeur* (1604), fo. 66; Mattingly, *Renaissance Diplomacy*, 175–176 and 240; De Lamar Jensen, *Diplomacy and Dogmatism: Bernardino de Mendoza and the French Catholic League* (Cambridge, Mass., 1964); Frey and Frey, *History of Diplomatic Immunity*, 159–160 and 167–174.

64 Cf. *Calendar of State Papers, Venice*, available at http://www.british-history.ac.uk/catalogue.aspx?type=3&gid=140, vol. 8, § 468 (Dolfin to Doge, 13 February 1587); *State Papers, Domestic*, Add. Eliz. (Public Record Office), XXX, 3 (12 January 1587); A. Teulet (ed.). *Papiers d'Etat, pièces et documents inédits ou peu connus relatifs à l'histoire de l'Écosse au 16e siècle* (Paris, 1852–1860), vol. 2, 865–867, 898, 903–906, 909–912 and 914–917; Camden, *History*, 377–379; Adair, *Extraterritoriality of Ambassadors*, 50.

65 Cf. Abraham de Wicquefort, *Mémoires touchant les ambassadeurs et les ministres publics* (The Hague, 1677), 54–56; A. Degert, 'Louis XI et ses ambassadeurs', *Revue historique*, 154 (1927) 4; Adair, *The Extraterritoriality of Ambassadors*, 56–57.

66 Cf. *Calendar of State Papers, Venice*, available at http://www.british-history.ac.uk/catalogue.aspx?type=3&gid=140, vol. 15, §§ 565–566 (17 and 19 October 1618); Giovan Battista Nani, *Historia della Republica veneta* (Bologna, 1680) t. 1, liv. III; Adair, *Extraterritoriality of Ambassadors*, 57; Frey and Frey, *History of Diplomatic Immunity*, 195–196.

he was not arrested, just restrained to his house and ordered not to come back to England. He was recalled by the King of France, who refused to see the English agent in Paris, who in turn was also recalled. Nothing further happened.[67]

In 1620, the agent of Brandenburg, resident and Dutch subject in The Hague (Christopher Sticke) was charged with coining false money, a crime of *laesa majestatis*. He was tried and found guilty and beheaded.[68]

In 1624, the Spanish ambassador in London (the Marquis of Inojosa) was accused of having publicly denounced an attempt to dethrone James. He was allowed to return to Spain.[69]

In 1641, the agent of the Duke of Lorraine, resident in England (Anthony Fortescue) was the victim of a seizure of his papers by English authorities, but was soon restored by the House of Commons.[70]

In 1644, the Duke of Lorraine's envoy was again the victim of another seizure. He was ordered to leave the Parliament quarters, but did not obey and in 1647 was still protesting. He was finally ordered to leave the country within 10 days.[71]

67 Cf. *Calendar of State Papers, Venice*, available at http://www.british-history.ac.uk/catalogue.aspx?type=3&gid=140, vol. 15, §§ 548, 555, 563 and 570 (Contarini to the Doge, 28 September, 5 October, 12 October, 26 October 1618); *State Papers, Domestic*, Charles I (Public Record Office), CCCX, 102; Samuel R. Gardiner, *History of England from the Accession of James I. to the Outbreak of the Civil War: 1603–1642* (London, 1863), vol. 3, 143–144; Adair, *Extraterritoriality of Ambassadors*, 51.

68 Cf. *Calendar of State Papers, Venice*, available at http://www.british-history.ac.uk/catalogue.aspx?type=3&gid=140, vol. 16, §§ 375 and 492 (Venetian Secretary to the Doge, 2 June and 12 August 1620); Adair, *Extraterritoriality of Ambassadors*, 57; Frey and Frey, *History of Diplomatic Immunity*, 239.

69 Cf. *Calendar of State Papers, Venice*, available at http://www.british-history.ac.uk/catalogue.aspx?type=3&gid=140, vol. 18, §§ 399, 410, 450, 463 and 477 (Valaresso to the Doge, 24 May, 31 May, 21 June, 28 June and 5 July 1624); *State Papers, Domestic, James I*, available at http://www.british-history.ac.uk/catalogue.aspx?gid=59, vol. 164, § 10 (Locke to Carleton, 3 May 1624) and § 12 (D. Carleton to Carleton, 3 May 1624); *Harleian Manuscripts* (in the British Museum), 304, fols. 40–41 (27 April 1624); *Additional Manuscripts* (in the British Museum), 12496, fo. 411; Howell Howell, comps. *Cobbett's Complete Collection*, vol. 5, 495–499; Gardiner, *History of England*, vol. 5, 226, 228, 268; Adair, *Extraterritoriality of Ambassadors*, 24–26 and 51–52; Frey and Frey, *History of Diplomatic Immunity*, 189–190.

70 Adair, *Extraterritoriality of Ambassadors*, 52–53.

71 Cf. *Calendar of State Papers, Venice*, available at http://www.british-history.ac.uk/catalogue.aspx?type=3&gid=140, vol. 27, §§ 118 and 251 (10 June 1644 and 27 July 1645); Adair, *Extraterritoriality of Ambassadors*, 53.

In 1654, the French agent in England (the Baron de Baas) was accused of plotting against the Protector, but only ordered to leave the country.[72]

Once established that practice generally militates against the denial of inviolability, even when an abuse was believed to have been committed, the question arises whether this practice – which was associated at the time with *jus gentium* and *jus gentium* was commonly understood as a law common to all peoples – reflects some legal rules. It is not enough to gather cases and information for legal purposes. To answer this extremely difficult question, the only possible way is to check whether those concerned considered that they were acting because of legal reasons. It may be that they also (or only) acted in pursuing of their interests, but their awareness that their conduct was in any case in accordance with law is of autonomous importance. Restraint was certainly inspired by political expediency and presumably *jus gentium* and natural law, in addition to Roman law (which was generally relied on to support the punishment of abuses), were mentioned in certain cases to provide some form of legal justification to what appeared as strategically necessary. In fact, ambassadors were granted personal *legal* privileges that other people did not enjoy, despite the development of the State into a territorial legal entity. To this effect, practice was ahead of doctrine.[73]

To sum up, state practice was particularly – even surprisingly – in favour of lenient reactions against abuses. Abusers were generally ordered to leave the country; on occasion, their recall was demanded. Punishment was only reserved to local subjects and in very few instances. Governments clearly endeavoured to avoid raising disputes with other governments on these matters. They even defended foreign ambassadors from the rage of the local mob.

Conclusion

While writers tended to repeat Roman law maxims and often to copy from one another, sovereigns tried to both assert their power and ensure their survival,

72 Cf. *Calendar of State Papers, Venice*, available at http://www.british-history.ac.uk/catalogue.aspx?type=3&gid=140, vol. 29, § 284 (Paulucci to Sagredo, 2 July 1654); John Thurloe, *A Collection of State Papers of John Thurloe, Esq.; Secretary, First to the Council of State, and Afterwards to the Two Protectors, Oliver and Richard Cromwell* (London,1842, ed. Thomas Birch), available at http://www.british-history.ac.uk/catalogue.aspx?type=2&gid=101, vol. 2, p. 309 ff.; Cardinal Mazarin, *Lettres du Cardinal Mazarin pendant son ministère* (Paris, 1872–1906, ed. P. Chéruel), vol. 6.1, 157–158, 201–202, 220–221; Adair, *Extraterritoriality of Ambassadors*, 54–55; Frey and Frey, *History of Diplomatic Immunity*, 226.

73 Adair, *Extraterritoriality of Ambassadors*, 65.

feeling that ambassadors had to be exchanged and protected at any price, even against popular will. The advantages of sending ambassadors outweighed the disadvantages of receiving them. Protection of foreign ambassadors had to be secured in order to obtain protection of one's own ambassadors. The grant of immunities was the result of the stress on political realism. This web of *mutual interests* gradually gave rise to *rules* that developed from courtesy to custom. Embassies proved indispensable within the emerging states system to learn others' hostile intentions and to maintain alliances for survival, although mutual distrust was pervasive. It was thus practice that pressed writers to turn to actual cases and to adjust ancient episodes related by Livy, the Bible, and so on, to current necessities, thus paving the way for what will eventually be called a positivist approach to international law.

CHAPTER 11

From Antwerp to Munster (1609/1648)

Truce and Peace under the Law of Nations

Randall Lesaffer, Erik-Jan Broers and Johanna Waelkens

Introduction

On 27 August 1609, Pierre Jeannin (1540–1622), the French representative at The Hague, appeared together with the diplomatic representatives from England and the German princes before the States General of the United Provinces. In the weeks before, the negotiations for a peace treaty between the United Provinces and the Archdukes Albert (1559–1621) and Isabella (1566–1633) had broken down on the Spanish refusal to withdraw or mitigate their demands regarding freedom of worship for Catholics in the Northern Netherlands and the exclusion of the Dutch from the Indies.[1] Jeannin had now come to the States General, after having well prepared the ground on different sides, to revive the negotiations by suggesting that the warring parties try to reach a long-term truce rather than a peace treaty. In his speech, Jeannin laid out the main conditions under which the truce would be made: the United Provinces would be recognised as 'Estats libres', implying, at least to those who wanted to hear this, full say over internal religious matters as well as the right of free trade in the Indies, Spain and the Southern Netherlands.[2] The idea to try and achieve a long-term truce rather than a peace treaty was not new and had been suggested before. The Armistice of 24 April 1607 which had been made to

1 For a survey regarding the negotiation process, see Paul C. Allen, *Philip III and the Pax Hispanica, 1598–1621. The Failure of Grand Strategy* (New Haven/London, 2000), 172–233; Miguel Antonio Echevarría Bacigalupe, *La diplomacia secreta en Flandes, 1598–1643* (Bilbao, 1984); Simon Groenveld, *Het Twaalfjarig Bestand 1609–1621. De jongelingenjaren van de Republiek der Verenigde Nederlanden* (The Hague, 2009), 33–59; W.J.M. van Eysinga, *De wording van het Twaalfjarig Bestand van 9 april 1609* (Verhandelingen der Koninklijke Nederlandse Akademie van Wetenschappen, Afdeling Letterkunde, N.S. 66.3; Amsterdam, 1959); Jesús María Usunáriz, *España y sus tratados internacionales: 1516–1700* (Pamplona, 2006), 233–272; Martine Van Ittersum, *Profit and Principle: Hugo Grotius, Natural Rights Theories and the Rise of Dutch Power in the East Indies (1595–1615)* (Leyden/Boston, 2006), 189–358.

2 J.A.C. Buchon (ed.), *Négotiations diplomatiques et politiques du Président Pierre Jeannin (1598–1620)* (Paris, 1875), 405–406; H.H.P. Rijperman (ed.), *Resolutiën der Staten-Generaal 1607–1609* (Rijks Geschiedkundige Publicatiën, Grote Serie 131; The Hague, 1970), vol. 14, 443–444.

 | DOI 10.1163/9789004274921_013

allow negotiations between the belligerents for an encompassing settlement had already referred to the possibilities of both permanent peace as well as a truce of twelve, fifteen or twenty years.[3] Later on, at the actual peace negotiations in The Hague in March 1608, Johan van Oldenbarneveldt (1547–1619), Grand Pensionary of Holland, had suggested to lift the matter of the Dutch trade in the Indies from the peace treaty and suffice with a temporary solution – a nine years truce – on this point, or even to continue hostilities in the Indies.[4] The Spanish government in Madrid, which shouldered the larger part of the war effort, had been in favour of a long-term but temporary agreement, all along, hoping to benefit from a break to restore the strength and finances of the Spanish Monarchy and to resume the war afterwards with more success. Halfway through July 1608, two weeks before the Spanish had to agree to concede on religion and trade for the Dutch not to break off negotiations, the Spanish King Philip IV had already indicated his willingness to accept a truce in a letter to Archduke Albert.[5]

The Spanish, the French and the other mediators, as well as some on the Dutch side now all favoured a long-term truce because they believed that it would bring many of the benefits of a peace, while it allowed reserving some major issues for future settlement, either through peaceable or forcible means. In the words of Jeannin, the truce would allow the Dutch to enjoy 'en effet par les moyens d'icelle de toutes commoditez & avantages que la paix vous eust donnés'.[6] It would take a lot of pressure from the French, including King Henri IV (1589–1610) himself, on Stadholder Maurice van Nassau (1585–1625) before he gave up his resistance against a truce and the States General agreed on the idea (14 November 1608).[7] In the ensuing negotiations about the truce, Jeannin played a pivotal role as chief mediator. In September 1608, Brussels had suggested to expand the existing armistice which had been in place since 24 April 1607 with another seven months.[8] This was a minimal solution as it demanded no further negotiations, but would also imply a general *status quo*, meaning

3 Armistice of 24 April 1607 and ratification by Philip III in Jean Dumont, *Corps universel diplomatique du droit des gens* (Amsterdam/The Hague, 1726–1731), vol. 5.2, 83–84.

4 M.L. Van Deventer, *Gedenkstukken van Johan van Oldenbarnevelt en zijn tijd* (The Hague, 1865), vol. 3, 188.

5 Allen, *Philip III*, 218; Van Esinga, *Wording van het Twaalfjarig Bestand*, 129; Letter of Philip III to Albert of 15 July 1608, Henri Lonchay and Joseph Cuvelier (eds.), *Correspondance de la Cour d'Espagne sur les affaires des Pays-Bas au XVIIe siècle* (Brussels, 1923), vol. 1, 284–286, nr. 661.

6 Buchon, *Négociations du Président Jeannin*, 405.

7 Van Eysinga, *Wording van het Twaalfjarig Bestand*, 127–134.

8 On 9 September 1608, Van Eysinga, *Wording van het Twaalfjarig Bestand*, 129.

that the belligerents would retain all their possessions, rights as well as claims as they had them at the time of the end of the hostilities in 1607. The 1607 Armistice held very few stipulations. It entailed an agreement to end hostilities – originally only on land, but later extended to sea warfare in Europe – and implicitly affirmed the *status quo*. Its main purpose was to freeze all military action in order for negotiations on a definitive peace or a truce to take place. Its main legal implication was that in the armistice the Archdukes conceded that they would negotiate with the United Provinces as 'free states' on which they held no pretences.[9]

But once the negotiations really took off, the parties rejected this minimal solution and produced a far more encompassing treaty. In the end, the Treaty of Antwerp of 9 April 1609 became an elaborate treaty which contained many detailed stipulations similar to those in peace treaties. Moreover, the Antwerp Treaty was later supplemented by two additional and interpretative treaties, which detailed its clauses even more and made it further resemble a proper peace.[10]

Contrary to what Jeannin and others had hoped, the Antwerp Truce was not prolonged and did not evolve into a definite peace. After its expiration in 1621, the war between the Spanish Monarchy and the Dutch Republic was resumed. However, when in 1646, negotiations between the Spanish and the Dutch for a new settlement began in earnest at Munster, the Antwerp Treaty text resurfaced. In their initial phase, the Munster negotiations did not aim at a final peace settlement, but at a new truce. When the Dutch plenipotentiaries arrived at Munster at the beginning of 1646, their brief was to conclude a new truce for at least twelve years and to do this on the basis of the 1609 text.[11] On 17 May 1646, the Dutch diplomats tabled a draft truce of 71 Articles.[12] These articles, of which 60 were accepted by the Spanish with only minor amendments, had for the larger part been taken from the 1609 Antwerp Truce and the two additional treaties of 1610. The negotiations on the truce and the major points of contention went so well in 1646 that in September of that year the States of Holland proposed converting the negotiations into proper peace

9 Dumont, *Corps universel*, vol. 5.2, 83–84, see also Papel nº 5 'Cessación de armas para ocho meses', Brussels and The Hague, 24 April, 1607, Biblioteca Nacional de España, Manuscript 11.187, fols. 8r–v and Papel nº 6 'Cessación de las armas por la mar', The Hague, 1 June 1607, BNE, MS 11.187, fols. 9r–10r.

10 Treaties of 7 January and 24 June 1610, in Dumont, *Corps universel*, vol. 5.2, 119–120 and 142–143 and in Cornelis Cau, Simon van Leeuwen et alii, *Groot Placcaet-boeck* (The Hague, 1658–1797), vol. 1, 71–80 and vol. 2, 581–586.

11 Instruction of the States General of 28 October 1645 in Lieuwe van Aitzema, *Verhael van de Nederlandsche Vreede Handeling* (The Hague, 1650), vol. 1, 570–607, esp. Arts. 4–6.

12 Aitzema, *Vreede Handeling*, vol. 2, 54–78.

negotiations. The motion of Holland was carried in the States General and the Spanish were ready to accept this. The draft truce was speedily rewritten into a peace treaty, mainly through the addition of some articles, bringing the total up to 79. By 27 December, the parties had reached an agreement on the text, which afterwards only underwent slight changes before the peace was finally signed on 30 January 1648. By and large, the 1609 Antwerp Truce was kept intact throughout the Munster negotiations as the basis for the 1648 peace instrument.[13]

Since at least the 13th century, jurists had been aware of the distinction between short-term armistices and long-term truces and had discussed the nature of the latter. Did a truce pertain to the domain of war or did it constitute a kind of temporary peace? But few if any of the medieval or early-modern writers prior to 1609 had delved all too deeply into the matter and doctrine had failed to provide a clear definition of what a 'truce' was or a clear description of what it entailed. Due to its negotiation history and particularly due to its relation to the 1648 Munster Peace Treaty, the Antwerp Truce of 1609 may shed an interesting light of what constituted a truce at the beginning of the 17th century and what its relation to a proper peace treaty was.

This chapter falls into three parts. In the next section, a brief survey of what medieval and early-modern jurists up to Hugo Grotius (1583–1645) had to say on the subject of truce will be offered. In the following section, the implications of the distinction between truce and peace at Antwerp and Munster will be examined, through the comparative study of three texts: the Antwerp Truce of 1609, the Dutch draft truce of May 1646 and the final Munster Peace Treaty of 1648. In the concluding section, a brief comparison with other early modern long-term truces will be added.

Indutiae, Treuga, Pax in Late-Medieval and Early-Modern Doctrine

Truce and its relation to peace were already subject to debate among the civilians and canonists of the Late Middle Ages (12th–15th centuries). Both the

13 Aitzema, *Vreede Handeling*, vol. 2; Jonathan Israel, *The Dutch Republic and the Hispanic World 1606–1661* (Oxford, 1982), 347–374; Randall Lesaffer and Erik-Jan Broers, 'Private Property in the Dutch-Spanish Peace Treaty of Münster (30 January 1648)', in Michael Jucker, Martin Kintzinger and Rainer Christoph Schwinges (eds.), *Rechtsformen internationaler Politik. Theorie, Norm und Praxis vom 12. Bis 18. Jahrhundert* (Zeitschrift für Historische Forschung, Beihefte 45; Berlin, 2011), 174–175; J.J. Poelhekke, *De Vrede van Munster* (The Hague, 1948).

authoritative sources of Roman and canon law contained references to the matter, allowing the medieval jurists to comment and expand upon. Digest 49.15.19.1 held a definition of *indutiae* by the classical jurist Paul:

> Indutiae sunt, cum in breve et in praesens tempus convenit, ne invicem se lacessant: quo tempore non est postliminium.[14]

The term *indutiae* was not absent from the canonist text tradition, as Saint Isidorus of Seville (c. 560–636) had included it in his definition of *jus gentium*,[15] but it had been superseded by the term 'treuga'. The *Liber Extra* (1234) of Pope Gregory IX (1227–1241) contained a title 'De treuga et pace'. This title cited two decretals by Pope Alexander III (1159–1181) of 1179, which actually dealt with the peace and truce of God – the immunity of some categories of persons from violence and the prohibition to fight at certain times –,[16] but later on, canonists would use this title as a *sedes materiae* to elaborate on peacemaking and truces in general.[17] In all, the comments and expositions of medieval civilians and canonists on the subject of armistice, truce and peace and their interrelation remained brief and sketchy. The *Tractatus Universi Juris*, a huge collection from the late 16th century of mainly 15th- and 16th-century treatises written by canonists contained two treatises entitled 'De treuga et pace', but these added little to existing discussions and opinions.[18] For more systematic expositions on truces, one had to await the great treatises on the laws of war of the later 16th century, such as those of Pierino Belli (1502–1575),[19] Balthasar Ayala (1548–1584)[20] and Alberico Gentili (1552–1608).[21] In his *De jure belli ac pacis* of

14 There is an armistice if one agrees that, for a short time entering immediately, one will not attack one another. During that time, there is no *postliminium*.

15 *Etymologiae* 5.6 Quid sit ius gentium.

16 X. 1.34.

17 Some canonists made a distinction between conventional and canonical truces; the former term referring to negotiated truce and the latter to the peace and truce of God. See Hostiensis, *Summa aurea, De treuga et pace* 5.

18 In book 11 of the collection, entitled 'De judiciis criminalibus', treatises by Octavianus Volpellius and Nicolaus Moronus, actually dealing with conflicts and violence between persons in general. *Tractatus Universi Juris* (apud Franciscum Zilettum, Venetiis, 1583–1586, 18 vols.).

19 Pierino Belli, *De re militari et bello tractatus* (1563, original text and translation, Classics of International Law; Oxford, 1936, 2 vols).

20 Balthasar Ayala, *De jure et officiis bellicis et disciplina militaris libri tres* (1582, original text and translation, Classics of International Law; Washington DC, 1912, 2 vols.)

21 Alberico Gentili, *De jure belli libri tres* (1598, text of 1612 and translation, Classics of International Law; Oxford/London, 1933, 2 vols.).

1625, Hugo Grotius (1583–1645) treated the subject of truces somewhat extensively.[22]

Already some of the medieval civilians acknowledged that a distinction could be made between short-term and long-term suspensions of hostilities. The distinction reflected reality, as both in ancient and medieval practice instances of both kinds of agreements were to be found. A sharp dividing line in terms of duration cannot be indicated, but one has to think in terms of days to months, possibly one or a couple of years for short-term agreements and in terms of many years, decades or even a century for long-term agreements. But there is more to divide these two types of suspension of hostilities than their duration. Whereas truces – as we will henceforward call long-term agreements – normally apply to all hostile actions between two belligerents and are generally entered into by the sovereign, armistices – as we will henceforth call short-term agreements – can be made by battlefield commanders as well as sovereigns and often are limited to certain theatres of war.[23]

In the *Glossa Paciscuntur* at D. 2.14.15, Accursius († 1263) defined *treuga* as a long-term agreement and *inducie* as a short-term agreement.[24] This distinction and use of terminology were adopted by several civilians and canonists during the Late Middle Ages.[25] From the Roman historical sources, which became important sources for the study of the laws of war under the influence of humanism, the jurists of the 16th century and later knew that the Romans had at times entered into long-term agreements of suspension of hostilities, lasting years, decades or even a century.[26] But as Pierino Belli indicated, they had used the term *indutiae* for these treaties, just as the term *treuga* was used by the canonists without much distinction as well.[27]

The problem of the distinction between a short armistice and a long-term truce was vexing to many of the later authors, precisely because it raised the question of what the relation of a long-term truce of many years to peace was. That question became all the more relevant, as in the second half of the 15th and first half of the 16th century the terminological distinction between truce

22 Hugo Grotius, *De jure belli ac pacis libri tres* (1625, text of 1646 and translation, Classics of International Law; Oxford, 1925, 2 vols.).

23 See for Roman practice, Karl-Heinz Ziegler, 'Kriegsverträge im antiken römischen Recht', *Zeitschrift der Savigny-Stiftung für Rechtsgeschichte, romanistische Abteilung*, 102 (1985) 40–90.

24 '(…) Ut treugas sunt in longum tempus. Item inducias sunt in breve (…)'.

25 E.g. Angelus de Ubaldis (1328–1407), *Consilia et responsa* (Antonius de Carcano et Zaninus Ripa, Pavia, 1478), Treuga et indutie.

26 Ziegler, 'Kriegsverträge'.

27 Belli, *De re militari* 5.1.1.

and peace was sometimes abandoned in treaty practice and during the same period, peace treaties were sometimes limited to the lifespan of one or both of the signing princes, with or without some additional years. While this held together with the private, *intuitu personae* character of peace treaties which were rather to be considered contracts between persons than public treaties between bodies politic, it did help confound the questions about the character and implications of truces.[28] By 1550, these limitations had disappeared; long-term truces for a certain number of years, however, continued to exist.[29]

There were four major problems relating to the character of a truce that were debated in late-medieval and Renaissance literature. The first problem pertained to the question of who held authority to make a long-term truce. This matter was particularly of interest to the writers of the 16th and 17th centuries. These were writing at a time when princes and central governments tried to increase their control over foreign relations and matters of war and peace. Moreover, they could refer to the Roman distinction between a *sponsio*, a less formal treaty which could be made by the commander on the battlefield, and a formal *foedus* which was made by the priests of the college of *fetiales*, directly committing the Roman people, and later by the emperor.[30]

Among the medieval jurists, there had been no consent whether a commander could enter an armistice. Whereas Bartolus of Saxoferrato (1314–1357) had affirmed this, others such as Alexander de Tartagna (c. 1423–1477) rejected it. The 14th-century commentator Raphael Fulgosius accepted the right of a commander to sign a short-term armistice, but rejected that he held the right to enter a long-term truce.[31] There thus was broad consent that a commander could not enter a long-term truce. While he did not really volunteer a clear opinion on truces, Belli accepted that commanders held a right to make short-term armistices, referring to Greek practice and citing several recent

28 Jörg Fisch, *Krieg und Frieden im Friedensvertrag. Eine universalgeschichtliche Studie über Grundlagen und Formelemente des Friedensschlusses* (Stuttgart, 1979), 349–359; Randall Lesaffer, 'Peace Treaties from Lodi to Westphalia' in Randall Lesaffer (ed.), *Peace Treaties and International Law in European History: From the End of the Middle Ages to World War One* (Cambridge, 2004), 20–22.

29 An important example thereof, apart from the Twelve Years Truce, is the Truce of Nice of 18 June 1538, in Dumont, *Corps universel*, vol. 4.2, 169–172.

30 Christian Baldus, '*Vestigia pacis.* The Roman peace treaty: structure or event?' in Lesaffer, *Peace Treaties and International Law*, 120–122; David Bederman, *International Law in Antiquity* (Cambridge, 2001), 194–202; Coleman Philippson, *The International Law and Custom of Ancient Greece and Rome* (London, 1911), vol. 1, 375–404; Karl-Heinz Ziegler, 'Friedensverträge im römischen Altertum', *Archiv des Völkerrechts*, 27 (1989) 53–54.

31 All ad D. 2.14.5.

examples.[32] Ayala shared Belli's opinion regarding short armistices – which he referred to as *cessatio pugnae* –, quoting examples from Roman history. He held firm, however, to the opinion that they could not enter into truces, here again with reference to Roman practice. Ayala also argued for the difference because short armistices 'do not put an end to the war' whereas long truces 'are rather by way of putting an end to the war'. In this respect, truces were, like peace, considered the preserve of the sovereign.[33]

The second problem pertained to the question whether the belligerents needed to formally declare war at the end of a truce if they wanted to resume hostilities, as of course was necessary after a peace treaty. Among the medieval jurists, the general opinion was that no new declaration of war was necessary. The commentator Baldus de Ubaldis (1327–1400) had defended this position, but confounded it by adding that one needed a declaration of war if there had been no war before the truce, contradicting himself on the main question at some point.[34] The question became of greater interest to the jurists of the 16th and 17th centuries, as the significance of declarations of war grew. Due to the Military Revolution and the growing monopoly of central governments over the business of war, over the 16th and 17th centuries, wars became ever more encompassing and disruptive of peace, involving the whole 'state' and not just the prince and his retinue and armies. Whereas Grotius would be the first to articulate it in those terms, contemporary writers on the laws of war started to think in terms of a state of war as opposed to a state of peace.[35] Whereas during peacetime, the laws of peace applied, during war normal peaceful relations and the laws that applied to them were suspended. To the state of war, the laws of war applied. In this context, formal declarations of war gained in importance. They did not only serve to appraise the enemy of the fact that one intended to wage war, they also served to appraise their own subjects of that fact. Moreover, declarations of war often stipulated a series of measures taken against the enemy, his subjects and property, thus suspending the laws of peace. As such, the declaration served to indicate the point in time at which the state of peace ended and the state of war commenced.[36]

Belli applied the distinction between armistices and truces to the matter. According to the Italian jurist, a declaration of war was necessary after a truce

32 Belli, *De re militari* 5.1.3.

33 Ayala, *De jure et officiis bellicis* 1.7.6.

34 De pace Constantiae, 9 and Ad D. 29.2.77.

35 Grotius, *De jure belli ac pacis* 1.1.2.1.

36 Randall Lesaffer, 'Alberico Gentili's *ius post bellum* and Early Modern Peace Treaties' in Benedict Kingsbury and Benjamin Strauman (eds.), *The Roman Foundations of the Law of Nations. Alberico Gentili and the Justice of Empire* (Oxford, 2010), 210–214.

for a long period.[37] Gentili touched upon the issue when he discussed an opinion rendered by the humanist jurist Andrea Alciato (c. 1492–1550) in which the latter seemed to hold that a war interrupted by a truce actually constituted two wars.[38] This implied that the truce had ended the war, not suspended it. Gentili rejected this, stating as proof that it was not necessary to declare war after a truce, but he conceded that the case might be different for 'very long truces which partake of the nature of peace and therefore are not granted by the military officers'.[39] Grotius held firmly to the opinion that a new declaration of war was not necessary as the state of war had only been suspended and not ended. He acknowledged that the Romans had sometimes acted differently, but that was because of their love of peace, not because it was necessary.[40]

The third problem related to the second. It was the question whether a truce constituted peace, war or something in between? Which laws applied during the time of truce, those of war or those of peace? What actions could be condoned during the truce? Or in the terms of the Grotian distinction between the state of war and peace, did a truce restore the same conditions as under the state of peace, or only partially so? Did it reach further than a mere prohibition to use force? Did it, among others, mean that reprisals or contributions were suspended too or that sequestered property had to be returned, or not? Several medieval civilians and canonists made statements to the effect that a truce equalled a peace, but there was no consent. In the *Glossa Lacessant* at D. 49.15.19.1, Accursius stated that a long-term *treuga* was a *foedus*. In his *Glossa Foederati* at D. 48.15.7 he held that a *foedus* made the partners into *foederati*. This amounted up to saying that they were true treaty partners who lived in peace and friendship and that a truce was thus a peace limited in time.[41] The 14/15th-century canonist Petrus de Ancharano distinguished three conditions – war, peace and truce – with truce as an intermediary category.[42] Sometimes medieval jurists would go into questions relating to particular rights, often because they had been asked to render a learned opinion in a pending dispute. Belli applied the distinction between short and long suspensions of war. According to him, a short armistice was more akin to war, whereas a long one was more akin to peace.[43] Gentili did not come much further than

37 Belli, *De re militari* 5.2.3 and 5.3.21-2.

38 Alciato, *Consilia* 5.17.

39 Gentili, *De jure belli* 2.12.305-6.

40 Grotius, *De jure belli ac pacis* 3.21.3.

41 Karl-Heinz Ziegler, 'The influence of medieval Roman Law on peace treaties' in Lesaffer, *Peace Treaties and International Law*, 155.

42 *Consilia* 88.

43 Belli, *De re militari* 5.2.

stating that long truces seemed 'to be a kind of peace', but were in fact not the same as a peace. But he neither went into the particular consequences of these statements, except in relation to the former question of declaration of war.[44] Grotius' line of argument came close to the one he had held on the issue of the declaration of war. He started by quoting the Roman writer Aulus Gellius (2nd century) who held 'nam neque pax est indutiae – bellum enim manet, pugna cessat'.[45] According to Grotius, this implied that everything valid during war would also be valid under the suspension of hostilities – that is, in so far as the armistice agreement did not derogate from it. But somewhat further, Grotius recognised that parties to a long-term truce may have had the intention to equal the state of affairs during the truce to the state of peace. In short, the early modern writers did not offer much clarification on the question what rights the parties had during the time of truce. They did not move much beyond the statement that while a truce did not constitute a full state of peace, it might in reality come close to it. Yet, a general rule underlying all these musings can be gleaned, namely that, as a truce only suspended war and did not constitute a full return to the state of peace, the state of war endured *insofar* as it was not – according to Grotius, expressly or intentionally (tacitly) – suspended by the truce treaty. Or, *a contrario*, that the state of peace was only restored to the extent that the parties expressly decided on. In the end, it was up to the parties to decide what the effect of the truce on the state of war was. The effects had thus to be gleaned for each truce from the stipulations of the treaty or the actions of the treaty partners during the time of the truce.

The fourth and final main question about the relative character of truce and peace related to the eternal or permanent character of peace. Over the Middle Ages and the Early Modern Age, in peace treaties it was generally said that the peace would be 'perpetual' or 'eternal'.[46] Rather than being a mere and seemingly naïve expression of the desire of the former belligerents never to resort to war again, the notion of (perpetual) peace had a quite specific legal implication. Baldus de Ubaldis, among many others, defined peace as 'discordiae ultimis finis, et perpetua et inviolabilis concordia'.[47] The words 'discordiae finis' or 'discordiae ultimis finis' were used by many canonists and jurists. This meant to imply, as Gentili stated clearly, that a peace agreement had to

44 Gentili, *De jure belli* 2.12.302-4.

45 *Noctes Atticae* 1.25.1. 'Because an armistice is not peace – for the war endures, but the fighting stops'. (My translation)

46 Fisch, *Krieg und Frieden*, 349–361.

47 Baldus, *Commentaria in Decretalium*, De Treuga et pace. Peace is the end of discord and perpetual and inviolable concord (my transl.).

definitely settle all the disputes underlying the war.[48] By consequence, the peace exhausted the right of the treaty partners to resort to war over the disputes settled in the peace. However, none of the medieval or early-modern writers stated this latter conclusion straightforwardly before the 18th century.[49] The late medieval and Renaissance authors did however expressly state the reverse, from which *a contrario* this rule could be deduced. They stated that if a new war broke out between the treaty partners for a new cause which had not been settled in the peace treaty, the peace (treaty) was not considered to be broken.[50] As Gentili had it, a peace agreement which did not exhaustively settle the controversies that had given rise to the war, was nothing but a truce.[51]

It is indeed the, albeit qualified, perpetual character of peace that makes for its fundamental distinctiveness from a truce. However long the period of a truce may be and however encompassing the abolition of the state of war and the return to the state of peace, a truce remains fundamentally different from a peace in that the peace exhausts the right of the parties to resort to war for the causes the war has been fought over,[52] while a truce does not.

Truce and Peace in Antwerp and Munster

In this section, we will try to asses what distinguished the Antwerp Truce of 1609 from a peace treaty. On the first two questions which were discussed above, the answer can easily be given. First, the Twelve Years Truce did not differ from a peace treaty as far as the involvement of the sovereign was concerned. It was negotiated and made under the same procedure as a peace

48 Gentili, *De jure belli*, 3.14.590-1, see also 3.24.708-11.

49 Christian Wolff (1679–1754) and Emer de Vattel (1714–1767) would do so. Christian Wolff, *Jus gentium method scientifica pertractatum* (1749, text of 1764 and translation, Classics of International Law; Oxford 1934, 2 vols.), 8.987 and Emer de Vattel, *Le droit des gens ou principles de la loi naturelle* (1758, text and translation, Classics of International Law; Washington, 1916, 3 vols.), 4.2.19.

50 Baldus, *Consilia* 2.195; Ludovicus Romanus, *Consilia*: 'Pacem rumpere non dicitur ille qui offensam insert ex nova causa superveniente et non ex antecendenti propter quam prius inimicus fierat simile de sententiae et transactione (...)'; Belli, *De re militari*, 10.2.27-8, 35 and 53, 5.2.3.

51 Gentili, *De jure belli* 3.14.591.

52 Generally speaking, because either they have been settled in the peace or because the parties declare that they will resolve their disputes about them through the use of peaceable means alone.

treaty, whereby a sovereign empowered his diplomatic representatives to negotiate and sign a treaty which he subsequently ratified.[53] Second, when at the end of the Twelve Years Truce war was resumed, no new declaration of war ensued.[54] For the latter two questions, a comparison will be made between three main and two additional texts. The main texts are those of the Twelve Years Truce of 9 April 1609, the draft for a new twelve years truce tabled by the Dutch delegation at Munster on 17 May 1646 and the Peace Treaty of Munster of 30 January 1648.[55] The two additional texts are the two interpretative Treaties of 7 January and 24 June 1610.[56]

Generally, one can distinguish three categories of clauses in early-modern peace treaties. First, there are the political concessions made and won by the signatories. In these, the claims for which the war has been waged are settled or reserved for future settlement by peaceful means. The second group brings the state of war to an end and settles all claims arising out of it. The third group regulates future relations between the former belligerents and restores and defines the state of peace. Under this last category, there are also provisions to stabilise and safeguard the peace. We will use this triple division to structure the comparison between the three texts and assess the Antwerp Truce for its resemblance to a peace treaty.

First, there is the political settlement of the disputes and conflicts between the belligerents. Here is not the time and the place to go into the political clauses of the Antwerp and Munster Treaties and compare them. It is clear that

53 Lesaffer, 'Peace Treaties from Lodi to Westphalia', 22–24.

54 On the resumption of the war in 1621, Jonathan Israel, *The Dutch Republic and the Hispanic World 1606–1661* (Oxford, 1982), 66–98.

55 For the Antwerp Truce, the official Dutch text of 24 April 1609 as published in Simon Groenveld, *Unie-Bestand-Vrede. Drie fundamentele wetten van de Republiek der Verenigde Nederlanden* (Hilversum, 2009), 115–127, will be used, as well as the English version from 1609, *Articles of a Treatie of Truce, Made and concluded in the Towne and Citie of Antwerp, the 9. of April 1609* (...) (G. Potter and N. Bourne, London, 1609). For the 1646 draft, the text in Van Aitzema, *Vreede-Handeling*, vol. 2, 54–78 will be used. For the Munster Peace Treaty, the Latin and Dutch editions published in 1648 and printed in Gerd Dethlefs (ed.), *Der Frieden von Münster/De Vrede van Munster 1648. Der Vertragstext nach eineme zeitgenössischen Druck und die Beschreibungen der Ratifikationsfeiern/De verdragstekst naar een contemporaine druk en de beschrijvingen van de ratificatievieringen* (Munster, 1998), 70–118 and 119–143.

56 For these, we use the following editions: *Verdrach ghemaeckt ende besloten inden Hage in Hollandt, den sevenden Januarii sesthien hondert ende thien* (...) (Hillebrandt Jacobsz., The Hague, 1610) and *Puncten ende Articulen verdraghen ende geaccordeert inden Hage in Hollandt, den xxiiii Junii inden Jare sesthien-hondert ende thien* (...) (Hillebrant Jacobsz., The Hague, 1610).

the main issues which concerned the belligerents and the negotiators in 1607–1609 and 1646–1648 were fairly similar. Next to the question of the freedom or sovereignty of the United Provinces, which was settled as a precondition to further negotiations, these covered territorial issues, trade rights and related tax issues, the rights of Catholics in the United Provinces and the Dutch navigation and trade in the Indies. Of course, on some points the outcome of the negotiations differed, but this had mostly to do with the political process as an outcome of the military and diplomatic situation, rather than with the distinction between truce and peace. The main question which interests us here is whether the political settlement of 1609, according to the treaty partners exhausted their right to go to war again over the same issues. It is quite clear that this was not the case. The whole purpose behind the option to make a long-term truce and not a perpetual peace was precisely to reserve the right to return to war over issues over which the belligerents could not reach a satisfactory, definite understanding. The fact that after 1621, the parties *did* resume war and that the same issues were at the centre of negotiations at Munster as they had been almost three decades before sufficiently proves the point.

This was also the case for the all-important point of the Spanish recognition of the freedom of the Republic. From the earliest stages of the negotiations before the Truce, the recognition of their freedom had been a precondition of the Dutch to open talks with Brussels and Madrid. In the armistice of 24 April 1607, the Archdukes had declared that they treated with the United Provinces 'as free States, to which [they] held no pretentions'.[57] In his ratification, the Spanish King Philip III had confirmed these words but had expressly added that his ratification would be null and void if no peace or truce would follow the armistice as it was intended.[58] The recognition of their freedom was not only a precondition for the States General to open negotiations on a peace or truce in 1607, they also demanded that a similar recognition would be included at the inception of the treaty. The negotiations about the text and its implications – mainly in relation to religion – continued well into the phase where the peace negotiations had broken down and a long-term truce had become the goal of the negotiations. The final treaty text held that the Archdukes were pleased to enter into the treaty, in their own names as well as in the name of the King, with the United Provinces in their quality 'and as holding, accounting and esteeming them to be free Countryes, Provinces and Estates, wereunto they pretend not any Right and Title of Soveraignty'.[59] At least to the Spanish,

57 Dumont, *Corps universel*, vol. 5.2, 83–84, my transl.

58 Ratification of 18 September 1607, see Dumont, *Corps universel*, vol. 5.2, 84.

59 Art. 1.

this did not in any way mean a definite cession of their rights and pretences. In the understanding of King Philip and his ministers, the recognition of freedom would only last as long as the truce would.[60] The text of the royal ratification of 7 July 1609 stressed that the stipulations of the Treaty would last for the term of the truce.[61] At Munster, the point of the freedom of the United Provinces was quickly ceded by the Spanish, but from a legal perspective the important element is that it still needed to be ceded.[62] In the end, whereas Article 1 of the Truce stated that the Archdukes were pleased to enter into the Truce with the United Provinces as being free states, Article 1 of the Munster Treaty stated that the Spanish King recognised them as free and sovereign states to which neither he nor his successors and descendents pretended anything or would ever pretend. Remarkably, Article 1 of the draft truce of May 1646 contained already more or less the same text, adding that this would also be so after the expiration of the treaty. In other words, if the Munster negotiations had led to a truce, the fundamental difference between peace and truce would have been blurred on the issue of the sovereignty of the Republic.

Second, there are the clauses which pertain to the state of war. Most early-modern peace treaties open with a general article which states that a perpetual peace is made between the signatories and that all (acts of) hostilities will cease between them.[63] Article 2 of the Antwerp Truce was clearly inspired by these traditional peace clauses, but was adapted to the occasion. It stated that there would be a truce for twelve years, during which all acts of hostility between the signatories would cease, either on land or sea, in all their territories and for all their subjects and inhabitants. The 1646 draft reiterated the same text. For the Munster Peace Treaty, the text was hardly rewritten. The word 'truce' was replaced by 'peace' and the twelve years term was barred from the text. For the rest, the wording was not amended. The peace was called 'goet, vast, ghetrouw en onverbreeckelijck' as the Antwerp text had it. The negotiators to the Munster Peace did not take the trouble of adding the word 'perpetual' or referring to 'friendship' between the sovereign parties to the treaty as was normally done in peace treaties. The fact that the Munster Peace was

60 See Chapter 2.

61 *Copie van de Agreatie ghesonden by de Mayesteyt des Conincx van Spaghnien* (...) (Johannes Moretus, Antwerp, 1609).

62 Israel, *Dutch Republic*, 360.

63 For all references to early-modern peace treaty practice, see Fisch, *Krieg und* Frieden; Lesaffer, 'Peace treaties from Lodi to Westphalia'; 9–44; Idem, 'Gentili's *ius post bellum*', 210–240; Idem, 'Peace Treaties and the Formation of International Law', in Bardo Fassbender and Anne Peters (eds.), *The Oxford Handbook of the History of International Law* (Oxford, 2012), 71–94.

based on a draft for a truce also spoke in another way. Contrary to what was the case for the vast majority of early-modern peace treaties, the Munster Peace lacked an amnesty clause. Such a clause normally stipulated that the signatories would not seek retribution or compensation, either through forcible or amiable means, for all acts and damages pursuant to the war. But the three texts did contain two stipulations, which at least covered part of what an amnesty normally would extend to. Article 4 of the Antwerp Truce dealt in general terms with the rights of the subjects of the belligerents to travel and trade in one another's territories. The article opened with a general undertaking that the subjects and inhabitants would forthwith and for the duration of the truce live in friendship, 'without calling to mind, or remembring any of the offences, hurts, and damnages, that they or any of them have received; had and endured in the forepassed Warres, and troublesome times'. The same phrases returned in the other two texts (Art. 4/4). Article 28 of the Antwerp Truce (Art. 55/57) stated that those people who had left for neutral countries had a right to return and could not be disturbed in their possessions.[64]

Generally, peace treaties dealt in quite some detail with concrete consequences of the cessation of hostilities and the end of the state of war. As was often the case in 17th-century peace treaties, the three texts of 1609 to 1648 contained a clause on the release of prisoners of war. Article 34 of the Antwerp Truce provided for the general release of all prisoners of war, without ransom. The text of the Truce was literally taken over in the 1646 draft and the 1648 Peace Treaty (Arts. 61/63), but in the Munster Peace Treaty it was expressly added that this clause also applied to prisoners who had served outside the Netherlands or had served in other armies than that of the States General. This was a telling extension as the measure would now benefit Dutch subjects who fought the Spanish in foreign lands and in foreign armies.

Peace treaties sometimes included provisions regarding the levying of contributions on enemy territory. The term 'contributions' is used to refer to two distinct practices from early-modern warfare. The term can refer to taxes levied by the authorities of the enemy in occupied territories, but also to the extortion of money payments by armed forces from local communities and land owners to spare them from attack or plunder. The latter interpretation is meant here. The Antwerp Truce did not contain a separate article on contributions, but it was clear from the negotiations that the cessation of hostilities of Article 2 and the express reference to 'subject and inhabitants' was meant to imply a stop to all contributions. After the Truce went into force, disputes arose

64 The 1646 draft contained an amnesty for all acts committed against the emperor and Empire vice versa (Art. 51).

between The Hague and Brussels over the arrears that some Flemish and Brabant villages owed to the Republic. With the second additional Treaty of 24 June 1610, a compromise was reached in the matter.[65] The draft of 1646 contained an article dealing with the arrears of contributions that were due at the inception of the truce (Art. 62). In a somewhat amended form, the article found its way into the Munster Treaty (Art. 64).

The Antwerp and Munster treaties were extraordinarily elaborate on the issue of private property and rights which had been affected by the war. This does not come as a surprise. The confiscation of enemy property, mainly property belonging to the subjects of the enemy found within one's territory, had by the early 17th century become a common aspect of war. Because the war between the Northern Netherlands and the Spanish Monarchy was in fact a rebellion and a civil war, confiscations had been a weapon of choice during the conflict and the amount of seized enemy property was far greater than in regular wars.

In the three texts of 1609–1648, the main provisions regarding enemy property came down to a general restitution of all seized and confiscated property, with the exception of personal or movables. This general solution was common to most peace treaties. The theoretical rationale behind this general restitution was to be found in the just war doctrine. Under this doctrine, war was an instrument for the just belligerent to enforce his rights upon the unjust belligerent. Moreover, the doctrine was discriminatory in that it held that only the just side had a right to be in the war and could thus benefit from the laws of war. By consequence, the unjust belligerent was liable for all the damages and costs inflicted upon the just belligerent. Therefore, the seizure of the enemy's goods and property was justified as a surety for his concession of the rights over which the war was fought to the just belligerent and his payment of compensation for war costs and damages to the just belligerent. As in reality, both sides claimed to fight a just war, they both claimed a right of seizure and confiscation. But as in peace treaties, no judgment was rendered on the justice or injustice of the belligerents' cause, these claims were released and the legal grounds upon which the right of confiscation was vested fell through. Therefore, a general restitution was called for.[66]

Article 13 of the Truce granted the original owners, their heirs and successors in law, the right to repossess all property that had been seized or confiscated because of the war, without the need for recourse to justice. All official acts of seizure and all subsequent transactions to third partners were thereby voided. However, the Antwerp Truce was not a definite peace treaty leading to

65 See Chapter 7 by Tim Piceu in this volume.

66 Lesaffer and Broers, 'Private Property', 182–195.

a full and final restoration of the state of peace, but a temporary suspension of the state of war. Consequently, Article 13 stipulated that the restored owners could not sell or mortgage their goods without consent of the enemy sovereign. This restriction indicated that the original owners only regained possession of their seized property for the duration of the truce, and that the title to the property remained in the balance. It was an implicit recognition that upon the resumption of the war, the goods could and probably would be seized again. It rested on the clear understanding that the truce suspended, but did not end the (state of) war. However, the Agreement of 7 January 1610 amended this. Article 6 of that Treaty lifted the prohibition to sell returned property, restoring thus for all practical purposes full ownership of the goods to the original holders. This relaxation of the prohibition to sell returned property during the truce was contrary to the essence of the temporary character of truce, but it was also a pragmatic concession to it. It allowed the repossessed owners to sell off their property before the war resumed and thus escape new confiscations.[67] Article 15 of the Truce provided for the occurrence in which the confiscated property had been sold by the enemy authorities. In that case, the original owners had to satisfy themselves with an annuity for the duration of the truce. Article 6 of the January 1610 Treaty sustained the prohibition to sell that annuity. The draft truce of 1646 reiterated the general restitution of seized and confiscated property in the same wording as the 1609 Truce. But it was expressly stipulated that the repossessed owners ('proprietarissen') could sell their goods without the need for permission. The prohibition to sell substitute annuities was repeated (Art. 23). This article found its way into the Munster Peace Treaty, but the exception of annuities was lifted (Art. 24). The exception of personal or movables was to be found in Article 25 of the Truce. It not only applied to movables, but also to all income gained from realty. The text was taken over, word for word, in Article 52 of the draft truce of 1646 and Article 54 of the Peace Treaty.

The Antwerp and Munster texts contained numerous more articles on private property and rights, including ecclesiastical goods. In the Munster Peace Treaty, 20 articles dealt with aspects of the restitution of private property. These were all literally or almost literally taken from the Antwerp Truce or the two additional treaties and had made their way into the Munster Peace Treaty by way of the draft truce of 1646.[68] The same went for the article dealing with

67 H.K.F. van Nierop, *Van ridder tot regenten: De Hollandse adel in de zestiende en de eerste helft van de zeventiende eeuw* (Amsterdam, 1990), 109 and 169–170.

68 Lesaffer and Broers, 'Private Property', 177–179. It concerns Articles 15, 16, 17, 18, 19, 20, 21, 22, 23, 24, 26, 27 and 32 of the Truce and Articles 7, 8, 9, 11, 12, 14 and 15 of the Treaty of 7 January 1610.

wartime trials. Article 10 provided that the sentences rendered in criminal or civil trials, which had involved subjects from both parties and where the defendant had not been able to defend his case, would not be executed during the term of the truce. The text was taken over in the draft and the Munster Peace Treaty. In these latter instruments, the text of Article 11 of the Truce which prohibited letters of marque or reprisal to be given out was inserted. A clause on wartime trials was quite common in early-modern peace treaties, but normally the sentences were declared null and void. The fact that the Antwerp and Munster treaties did not void the sentences, but only provided that they would not be executed, was consequential to the temporary character of the truce. Remarkably, the text of the final Peace Treaty had not been suitably adapted.

Except for the articles relating to private property and rights in general, the treaties also contained some articles on property rights and claims of the House of Orange. The incorporation of stipulations in peace treaties regarding important nobles had been a common occurrence during the Late Middle Ages and the 16th century, but it became far less customary during the first half of the 17th century. The House of Orange was, however, a case on its own. At Antwerp, and later at Munster, the matter turned around the extensive landholdings and other possessions of William the Silent (1533–1584) who had fled the Netherlands in 1567 and whose possessions had been confiscated by the Spanish. At the time of the Truce, his inheritance had not yet been divided amongst his heirs, chiefly his sons, Philip William (1554–1618), who lived in Spanish captivity, the Stadholder Maurice and his future successor Frederick Henry (1584–1647). At Antwerp, the issue was thus the undivided inheritance of William the Silent, giving it more cloud. During the negotiations leading up to the Antwerp Truce, the French mediators in particular were very keen on reaching satisfaction for Maurice of Nassau as a means of urging him to overcome his resistance against the truce.[69] In the end, Maurice's concerns about his financial position during the truce were for the most part allayed by the Republic itself. The 1609 Truce held two articles expressly dealing with the Orange inheritance. Article 14 extended the general restitution from Article 13 explicitly to the heirs and inheritance of William the Silent, including the possessions in the Counties of Burgundy (Franche-Comté) and Charolles.[70]

69 Instruction particulière audit sieur de Preaux, fait par ledit Jeannin, in Buchon, *Négociations diplomatiques et politiques du Président Jeannin*, 17–18 and Letter of Jeannin to King Henry IV, 1 May 1609, 669.

70 Article 19 of the Treaty of 7 January 1610 extended the restitution in general to these counties, thus not only for the property of the Oranges.

The same article also stipulated that the trial about Châteaubelin in Luxemburg before the Grand Council of Malines – the Supreme Court of the Southern Netherlands – would be pursued and that a verdict should be reached within a year. The general restitutions and the inclusion of the Oranges' property in Burgundy and Charolles found its way into the draft treaty of 1646 (Arts. 24–5) and the Peace of Munster (Arts. 25–6). Both the draft as well as the Munster Treaty provided for the immediate restitution of Châteaubelin to the House of Orange and the cession of all Spanish claims to the fief (Art. 27/28). The text pointed out that no verdict had been rendered by the Grand Council within a year as Article 14 of the Antwerp Truce had stipulated. Article 30 explicitly stipulated that the members of the House of Nassau could not be held accountable for neither the debts incurred by William the Silent after the beginning of the war in 1567, nor for any arrears related to these. This article was inserted in the 1646 and 1648 texts (Art. 57/59). The settlement on the Orange goods was supplemented at Munster by two separate agreements from 27 December 1647 and 8 January 1648. Article 45 of the Munster Peace stated that these treaties were to be executed as if they had been inserted word for word. In general, the differences between the three texts on the subject of the Orange inheritance are not relevant for the distinction between truce and peace.

As was common in early-modern peace treaties, the three texts held an article (Art. 27/54/56) which suspended all prescription between persons from the two sides for the whole duration of the war, which was said to have run since 1567. The 1646 and 1648 texts added that this suspension did not run during the truce period.

A third category of articles dealt with future relations between the signatories and their subjects. Most early-modern peace treaties held a clause 'de non offendendo', sometimes in the form of a separate article, sometimes as part of the general peace clause or sometimes combined with the amnesty clause. This clause entailed the promise not to do harm or cause damages, neither to suffer anybody to do harm or cause damage to the former belligerent, his lands, subjects and adherents. There was no traditional general clause 'de non offendendo' in the Antwerp and Munster texts, just as there was no general amnesty clause. The closest the texts come to a clause 'de non offendendo' was a promise by the parties that they would not neither act nor suffer anybody to act against the treaty (Art. 36/67/76) as well as the promise that subjects would henceforth live in good correspondence and friendship (Art. 4/4/4). As most early-modern peace treaties, the three texts held a provision for the case of an infringement against the treaty by a subject not acting under authority of his sovereign. As was customary, it held that the perpetrator would be liable for compensation. The injured party had no right to use force and the infringement did not cause the truce or peace to end. In case the lessee was denied justice by the former enemy, it was allowed to grant him a right of particular reprisal (Art. 30/58/60). Article 36 of the Truce, which returned in both the Munster texts (Art. 67/76) imposed the duty on the parties of immediate reparation in case they committed or suffered somebody to commit an injury against the treaty.

The Antwerp Truce and the Munster texts elaborated on the right of travel, navigation and trade of the subjects of the treaty parties. Article 4 of the three texts restored their peacetime rights to dwell and trade in the lands of the other party. The Antwerp and Munster texts differed in relation to trading outside Europe, but this did not pertain to the legal difference between truce and peace. This rather reflected the fact that in 1609 a definite settlement on Indian trade was yet unattainable, itself the main reason why the outcome was a truce and not a definite peace. The settlement of the Indian trade should not concern us here any further.[71] Article 6 was a 'most favoured nation clause' as it forbade the parties to levy any higher taxes or impositions upon the subjects of the treaty partner than upon the subjects of their allies and friends which were burdened the least. In Article 7 of the Munster draft, which returned as Article 8 in the final Peace Treaty, the clause had been changed to a prohibition to tax the subjects of the treaty partner more than one's own subjects. The new article also expressly excluded the 20% tax Spain had levied on Dutch subjects during the Twelve Years Truce. Article 7 of the Antwerp Truce, which was copied into the Munster texts (Art. 15/17) accorded the same trade rights in the Southern Netherlands and all lands of the Spanish Monarchy as the ones granted by Philip III and the Archdukes to the subjects of King James I (1603–1625) of England, Scotland and Ireland in the Treaty of London of 1604. Article 8 of the Truce protected the subjects of both parties against arrest and their property against confiscation – except of course in the context of a regular legal procedure. Of course, this protection was limited for the duration of the truce. The same article returned into the two Munster texts (Art. 19/20). As opposed to many other peace treaties, Article 20 of the Munster Peace did not provide for an extension of the immunity against arrest or confiscation for a certain period of time after an eventual rupture of the peace. This lapse seemed to be consequential to the fact that the Munster Peace Treaty was based on a draft for a truce. In case of truce, foreign subjects could of course calculate the date on which hostilities might be resumed. In Article 9, it was stated that disputes about some trade impositions would be referred to commissaries from

71 Art. 4 of the Antwerp Truce and the Separate Article to the Truce; Arts. 4–6 of the Munster draft and Peace Treaty; Israel, *Dutch Republic and the Hispanic World*, 367–370; Poelhekke, *Vrede van Munster*, 359–360; Van Ittersum, *Profit and Principle*, 343–346.

both sides who would arbitrate the matter. The article had disappeared from the Munster texts, but the matter returned in the article instituted the *Chambre mi-partie*, a chamber of arbitrators or commissaries from both sides with more extensive competence for disputes arising out of the interpretation or execution of the treaty (Art. 20/21). The Munster Peace Treaty contained several more articles on trade impositions, but these were already present in the 1646 draft, so again, did not reflect upon the distinction between truce and peace.[72]

A clause common to peace treaties between maritime powers was the one from Article 12 from the Truce (Art. 22/23), which prevented warships to enter the harbours and lands of the treaty party without permission, except in case of necessity. Article 29 forbade the building of new fortresses during the truce. This was an article that was clearly more natural for a truce than a peace treaty. The question whether it was allowed to build fortresses in the Low Countries during a truce was one which was often discussed in doctrine.[73] The Article was rehearsed in the 1646 draft, extending the prohibition to trenches and canals for defensive purposes (Art. 56) and, as such, copied into the peace (Art. 58). The latter is remarkable as it made the prohibition permanent. In Article 35, the signatories to the Antwerp Truce undertook to keep land and maritime routes open and to keep them free from robbers and pirates. This article too was copied into the Munster texts (Arts. 66 and 75).

Finally, Article 33 of the Truce, which was taken over in the two Munster texts (Art. 60/62) expressly stated that subjects from both sides could inherit from one another. Hereby all measures and actions which had prevented this during the war were implicitly lifted.

Conclusion

The Antwerp Truce of 1609 clearly proves that indeed, as many doctrinal writers had it, there existed a type of treaty somewhere in between an armistice and a permanent peace treaty, and that this type was referred to as truce. The comparative study of the Antwerp Truce of 1609, the draft for a new truce of 1646 and the Peace Treaty of 1648 furthermore indicates that early-modern doctrine captured practice rather well. As doctrine had it, the essential difference between a truce and a peace was not much related to the question to what extent the truce restored the state of peace, but lay in the fact that a peace exhausted the right to return to war for the same issues, and a truce did not.

72 Arts. 9–12 and 14 from the draft, 10–13 and 15 from the Peace Treaty.

73 Already Baldus, *Consilia* 2.295.

This difference appears clearly from the Antwerp/Munster case. The clearest indication lies in the choice itself for a long-term truce, which was made in 1608. Precisely because the parties could and would not reach a final settlement on some of the main and/or sensitive issues, they chose to make a truce knowing full well that this left open the possibility to resort to war sometime in the future. Moreover, one of the most striking differences in the legal-technical clauses of the Antwerp and Munster texts – even if it was lifted by the first additional Treaty of 1610 – clearly indicated the temporary character of the suspension of hostilities and of the right to use force to pursue the claims underlying the war. In the Antwerp Truce, the restitution of seized property was limited to repossession and not to a full restitution of ownership, thus indicating that the final decision on title and ownership was still in the open. It implied that the final verdict on the causes underlying the war had not been rendered and that new confiscations after the resumption of war were rightful and likely. The consequence of this essential difference was that whereas after a peace treaty, a new declaration of war was necessary before hostilities could be opened, this was not the case for a truce. In answer to the question whether or to what extent a truce restored the state of peace, the common answer given by the early-modern writers of the laws of war and peace was that a truce did not (temporarily) restore the state of peace by itself and thus did not go beyond a suspension of actual hostilities, but that treaty partners could and often would agree to suspend the laws of war and restore the state of peace in more general terms. The Antwerp Truce and the 1646 draft did just that, expanding the suspension of the laws of war and restoration of normal peaceful relations to such an extent that hardly any change or addition was deemed necessary to turn the draft truce into a final peace settlement. This left the Munster Peace Treaty to be somewhat peculiar in some of its wordings and clauses in relation to other peace treaties, but it did not detract in any way of its character as a permanent peace. Certainly after the Treaty of 7 January 1607 had lifted the most important restriction upon the restitution of seized property, the state of affairs under the Twelve Years Truce resembled the state of peace almost to the maximum. It was for all practical purposes, to turn the tables on Gentili's quote, nothing but a temporary peace.

Finally, we will briefly glance at the main other long-term truces from the 16th- and 17th-century from intra-European practice.[74] The Treaty of Nice

74 This excludes a comparison to the peace settlements between the Ottoman Turks and other Muslim powers on one side and Christian princes on the other hand, which until the 18th century were always temporary because of the dictates of traditional Muslim doctrine to that extent and pertained to a very different tradition of peace settlements.

signed between the Emperor Charles V (1519–1558) and Francis I of France (1515–1547) of 18 June 1538, while much less elaborate and shorter, also amounted to a temporary peace, in this case for ten years. It contained a general clause 'de non offendendo', suspended all letters of marque, restored rights of trade and stipulated a general and unrestricted restitution of seized property.[75] From the 17th century, three long-term truces are worth referring to. All of these were different from the Antwerp Truce to the extent that they provided for negotiations on a definite peace settlement and thus anticipated a future peace settlement. They did not, however, amount to preliminary peace treaties because no general outline for the future settlement was hammered out in these treaties. The Truce of Altmark of 25 September 1625 between Poland and Sweden was elaborate on the attribution of territories for the duration of the truce and the sequestration of disputed lands and rights. It contained an amnesty clause as well as several clauses on trade rights and restitution, stipulated the mutual release of prisoners and provided for the peaceful settlements of disputes arising out of breaches of the treaty by the signatories or their subjects.[76] The Thirteen Years Truce of Andrussov between Poland and Russia of 30 January 1667 was also most elaborate on the division of lands and territories during the truce. It contained clauses on trade rights, the release of prisoners and the peaceful settlement of disputes arising out of violations of the treaty.[77] The Truce of Regenburg of 15 August 1684, apart from offering a provisional settlement for disputed territories, contained a clause 'de non offendendo', a general restitution clause, the restoration of trade, a stipulation on the law applicable in trials between subjects from different treaty partners and a provision for the peaceful settlement of disputes arising out of the treaty or during the truce.[78]

From this brief comparison, the conclusion can be drawn that the Truce of Antwerp stands out among its kind. Not only was it the most elaborate truce in terms of legal detail, but above all it became closer than any to being a full, if temporary, peace. It was, after all, a failed peace waiting to be transformed into a full peace. That transformation would be another three decades in the making, but once it was decided upon, it only demanded minimal legal and textual adjustments.

See Karl-Heinz Ziegler, 'The peace treaties of the Ottoman Empire with European Christian powers', in Lesaffer, *Peace Treaties and International Law*, 338–364.

75 Dumont, *Corps universel*, vol. 4.1, 169.

76 Dumont, *Corps universel*, vol. 5.2, 494–496.

77 Clive Parry (ed.), *The Consolidated Treaty Series* (Dobbs Ferry, 1969–1986), vol. 9, 399–428.

78 Parry, *Consolidated Treaty Series*, vol. 17, 127–149.

CHAPTER 12

'La dernière ancre de leur finesse'

Truce and Peace Treaties as Criteria of bellum justum *in Early Modern Europe*

Bernd Klesmann

Introduction

King Henry IV of France had been corresponding for several years with his ambassador to The Hague, Pierre Jeannin, when he learnt in early 1609 that peace negotiations between the Archdukes, the King of Spain and the United Provinces were about to come to an end. A resulting treaty would settle a conflict reaching back to the time of his first marriage and would, in acknowledging Dutch freedom, be a decisive victory in a struggle that had influenced every move in European politics for decades, involving quite a French commitment even after the Peace of Vervins of 1598. However, the French monarch knew too much about the vicissitudes of the cabinets from Edinburgh to Turin to allow himself any enthusiasm. His central interest was to be involved in the elaboration of a favourable treaty by imposing, through a role of mediation, political recompensation for the considerable amount of subsidies that had been paid to the young Republic during his reign.[1] In several letters to Jeannin and Élie de La Place de Russy (fl. 1595–1610), Henry IV urged his diplomats to achieve a solid truce for twelve years including an explicit acknowledgement of free trade on all seas and warned them not to accept a mere prolongation of the current armistice (in vigour since April 1607) for another year, which in the plans of Madrid (and the mediators from London) would be '[…] la dernière ancre de leur finesse à laquelle ils auront recours, s'ils voient ne pouvoir obtenir mieux de vous, afin de gagner cette année, parce que les Espagnols véritablement n'ont argent ni forces préparées pour la guerre sitôt'.[2] Rumours about

1 Jan Den Tex, *Oldenbarnevelt* (Cambridge, 1973), vol. 2, 359; Geoffrey Parker, *The Dutch Revolt* (2nd edn., Harmondsworth, 1985), 235–240; Jonathan Israel, *The Dutch Republic. Its Rise, Greatness, and Fall 1477–1806* (Oxford, 1995), 421.

2 Henry IV to Jeannin and Russy, Paris 24 February 1609, in *Collection des Mémoires relatifs à l'histoire de France*, 2nd series (ed. M. Petitot, Paris 1819–1824), vol. 25, 226; four days later already, details of the Treaty were discussed: Ibid., 233–236; the financial situation of the Spanish monarchy was disastrous indeed, bankruptcy having been declared in November 1607, cf. Patrick Williams, *The Great Favourite. The Duke of Lerma and the Court and*

 | DOI 10.1163/9789004274921_014

Spanish diplomats trying to avoid any formal implication of King Philip III in a truce that should instead be ratified only by the United Provinces and the Archdukes made Henry assume that his opponents' intention was to preserve Spanish reputation and to create a sufficient number of pretexts to return to war in the years to come.[3] Mistrust and scepticism in this field, of course, were not unique to the King of France. His well-informed assumptions mirrored widely accepted notions of a general fragility of peace treaties and their political affinity to the legitimation of public warfare.[4]

After a brief outline of the main issues in early modern juridical discussions of peace and truce treaties in general, I would like to analyse several ways of using treaties in declarations of war before introducing some ideas about their impact on the Eighty Years War. While the importance accorded to the work of Hugo Grotius is partly due to the many innovative aspects of his writings, it is foremost the logical consequence of his eminent position in Dutch politics and literature that made him one of the most instructive observers and interpreters of the 1609 truce treaty.

'Induciae' – Juridical and Historical Implications of a Humanist Concept

Terminology

In the theory of international law of the 16th and 17th centuries, a truce is referred to as a 'treuga', 'tregua' or, more currently in humanist tradition, as 'induciae'.[5] The most concise definition has been given by Grotius in 1625: 'Truces are conventions, by which, even during the continuance of war, hostilities on

---

Government of Philip III of Spain, 1598–1621 (Manchester, 2006), 144–146; the diplomatic context, especially the circumstances of Peckius' pragmatic rendering to French pressure is explained by Patrick Claeys, 'De wijze Nederlander: ambassadeur Petrus Peckius te Parijs, 1607–1611', *Tijdschrift voor geschiedenis*, 105 (1992) 203–205.

3 Ibid., 223.

4 The Truce seriously altered Franco-Spanish relations, cf. Janine Garrisson, *Henri IV* (2nd edn., Paris, 2008), 306–307; on French arbitration in 1608/09 see Jean-Pierre Babelon, *Henri IV* (2nd edn., Paris, 2009), 927–928; Christoph Kampmann, *Arbiter und Friedensstiftung. Die Auseinandersetzung um den politischen Schiedsrichter im Europa der Frühen Neuzeit* (Quellen und Forschungen aus dem Gebiet der Geschichten, N.F. 21; Paderborn, 2001), 92–107.

5 'Indutiae' in classical latin; Hugo Grotius, *De jure belli ac pacis libri tres* 3.21.2 (1625, original text of 1646 and English translation, Classics of International Law; Oxford/Londen, 1925, 2 vols.), identified 'inde otium' as the correct etymology, reproduced as a possible origin in *Lexicon Totius Latinitatis* (ed. Francesco Corradini, Padova, 1864), vol. 2, 813; more probable

each side cease for a time'.[6] Taking into account the numerous attempts to deconstruct a 'grotiocentric' vision of early modern international law,[7] it still may be worth noting that this definition differs considerably from what Grotius must have read in the writings of his well-known precursors and intellectual models, Balthazar Ayala and Alberico Gentili. In his *De jure et officiis bellicis*, first published in 1582, Ayala had made a fundamental difference between two kinds of truce, according to the extent of their duration. While a short truce does not affect the validity of the state of war, a long truce – the alleged example is two years – 'seems to end the war'.[8] Gentili, in *De jure belli* (1597) had emphasized, just like Grotius was to do several years later, that 'induciae' were not synonymous with peace, but rather with an enduring state of war without acts of hostility, which Grotius named a 'sleeping' war.[9] While Gentili, however, had placed the phenomenon of truce somewhere between war and peace, Grotius insisted on Cicero's affirmation (*Philippica*, 8) that there was no such intermediary status in human affairs.[10] His explicit conclusion was that what had been said about war in previous chapters, could equally apply to 'induciae'.[11]

Nevertheless, it is clear that the cessation of hostilities during a period of truce from war made a considerable difference, especially regarding the

seems 'in-dutiae', i.e. 'tempus indutum' < 'induo', 'intermediate/supplementary time', cf. Karl Ernst Georges, *Ausführliches lateinisch-deutsches Handwörterbuch* (Basel/Stuttgart, 1958), vol. 2, 214; *Thesaurus Linguae Latinae* (Leipzig, 1900ss.), vol. 7/1, 1277.

6 *De jure belli ac pacis* 3.21.1: 'Induciae sunt conventio, per quam, bello manente, ad tempus bellicis actibus abstinendum est'. The English translation quoted from David J. Hill (ed.) *The Rights of War and Peace Including the Law of Nature and of Nations, translated from the Original Latin of Grotius* [...] *by A.C. Campbell* (Washington/London, 1901), 403.

7 Cf. the summay of several studies published after the 1983 anniversary, Antonio Truyol y Serra, *La Conception de la Paix chez Vitoria* (Paris, 1987), 241–274; Dominique Gaurier, *Histoire du droit international. Auteurs, doctrines et développement de l'Antiquité à l'aube de la période contemporaine* (Rennes, 2005), 164–165.

8 Balthazar Ayala, *De jure et officiis bellicis* 1.7 (Antwerp, 1597) 141–142; '[...] bello finem imponere videntur'; dimensions of time in peace treaties are explained by Randall Lesaffer, 'Peace Treaties from Lodi to Westphalia', in Idem (ed.), *Peace Treaties and International Law in European History* (Cambridge, 2004), 37–38.

9 Alberico Gentili, *De jure belli libri tres* 2.12 (1597, original text from 1612 and English translation, Classics of International Law; Oxford/London, 1933, 2 vols.): '[...] Induciae sunt belli feriae'; Grotius, *De jure belli ac pacis* 3.21.3 '[...] sublato impedimento temporali, ipso jure se exserit status belli, non mortuus, sed sopitus [...]'.

10 Grotius, *De jure belli ac pacis* 3.21.1: '[...] inter bellum et pacem nihil est medium: et bellum status est nomen, qui potest esse etiam cum operationes suas non exserit'.

11 Grotius, *De jure belli ac pacis* 3.21.1.

belligerents' rights and property. This is explained already in Grotius' famous earlier work *Mare liberum*, written in direct reaction to the war against the Portuguese in the East Indies. The young scholar, after having demonstrated that no state or power could claim any exclusive privilege to maritime trade and traffic, stated in his conclusion that these universal rights of free trade had to be equally respected in times of peace, truce and war.[12] The underlying argument was simple and ingenious: as a truce is by definition a temporary cessation of all acts of hostility, it includes a mutual guarantee of possessions, because any spoliation of possessions would constitute an act of hostility. As free trade and its benefits have to be considered as a kind of possession, no truce can alter trade arrangements.[13] Consistently, Grotius insisted on the point of view that the denial of traffic and trade by a political opponent constituted a legitimate ground for war.[14] A similar argument is to be found in *De jure belli ac pacis*, where the possessions of the concluding parties are declared untouchable in periods of truce.[15]

It is obvious that these terminological outlines perfectly served the Dutch point of view during the Eighty Years War. If the Antwerp agreement of 1609 was to be considered as a lawful truce, there could be no doubt that the United Provinces, constituting free states could make use of their right to wage war and to conclude treaties to end or suspend this war. Equally, according to the same theoretical framework, Dutch possessions in the East Indies, a major object of diplomatic controversy, were rightfully sustained and, by the universal law of nations, did not have to be abandoned. We shall see later how much these elements were crucial to the political context.

---

12 Grotius, *Mare liberum* (1609, Amsterdam, 1720), Ch. 13, p. 33; this last chapter of *Mare liberum*, probably meant to point out the importance of the treatise in the specific situation of 1609, does not figure in the earlier *De jure praedae* manuscript, Grotius' implication in the political negotiations of 1608/9 is well-known, cf. Martine Julia van Ittersum, *Profit and principle. Hugo Grotius, Natural Rights Theories and the Rise of Dutch Power in the East Indies, 1595–1615* (Leyden/Boston, 2006), lvi–lviii. For a recent critical edition with English translation: Robert Feenstra and Jeroen Vervliet (eds.), *Hugo Grotius. Mare Liberum (1609–2009)* (Leyden/Boston, 2009).

13 John Selden's famous *Mare clausum* (1635) in reaction to this position, stating that it was indeed the sea itself and not seaborne trade that had become inviolable property of the State, has recently been contextualised by Helen Thornton, 'John Selden's response to Hugo Grotius: the argument for closed seas', *International Journal of Maritime History*, 18 (2006) 105–127.

14 Grotius, *Mare liberum*, Ch. 13, p. 34.

15 Grotius, *De jure belli ac pacis* 3.21.6.

The subsequent development of international law widely respected the distinctions and definitions given by Grotius. While it is almost impossible to give a survey of the pan-European reception of his work in the 17th and 18th centuries, a number of examples might illustrate some of its main directions.

The German jurist Heinrich von Cocceji (1644–1719), who had studied law at Leyden and Oxford before teaching in Heidelberg and writing a compendium in three folio volumes dedicated to Grotius' main work, gave priority to correct interpretation without critical discussion. His comments on the important chapters from Grotius's *De jure belli ac pacis* are affirmative and limited to terminological explanations.[16] The Grotian assumption that the state of war continues during a truce, is contextualised by the preceding distinction between a state of war (status belli) and acts of war (actus belli).[17] Johann Gottlieb Heineccius (1681–1741), professor in Halle/Saale and, from 1723 to 1725, in Franeker (Frisia), the United Provinces' second university after Leyden, founded in 1585, published a voluminous commentary on *De jure belli ac pacis*.[18] Regarding the nature of truce, Heineccius puts the accent on a dual definition of war that includes two states fighting out a legal dissent (1) by armed force and (2) while abstaining from armed force, by upholding the intention to fight out the dissent. Truce is thus a convention during wartime. Heineccius made a distinction, however, regarding the bellicose or pacific character of this convention. This depended on its duration and the maintenance of warlike instruments such as armies, fortresses etc., and comes closer to Gentili's two-truce-theory. Though not discussing trade explicitly, it becomes clear from the permission of perfect freedom of traffic, that trade is not considered illegal.[19]

There have been, however, modifications of this quasi-canonical, exegetical approach. Samuel von Pufendorf (1632–1694), whose writings on natural law became important for the early Enlightenment through the French translations of the exiled Huguenot Jean Barbeyrac (1674–1744), professor at Groningen, adopted a critical point of view regarding the Grotian assumption

16 Heinrich von Cocceji, *Grotius illustratus seu commentarii ad Hugonis Grotii De jure belli ac pacis libros tres* (Wrocław, 1747), vol. 3, 434–478.

17 Ibid., vol. 3, 434, according to *De jure belli ac pacis* 1.1.

18 Johann Gottlieb Heineccius, *Praelectiones academicae in Hugonis Grotii De jure belli ac pacis libros iii* (Berlin, 1744); Roderich von Stintzing, 'Johann Gottlieb Heineccius', in *Allgemeine Deutsche Biographie* (Leipzig, 1880), vol. 11, 361–363.

19 General methodological disagreements between Grotius and Heineccius are analysed by Ernst Reibstein, 'J.G. Heineccius als Kritiker des grotianischen Systems', *Zeitschrift für ausländisches öffentliches Recht und Völkerrecht*, 24 (1964) 236–264.

of inviolability of wartime conventions, with truce being the most important one.[20] Particularly interesting is the point of view of Grotius' fellow Dutchman Cornelius van Bynkershoek (1673–1743), who may be considered as a prominent author of the early Enlightenment, and who frequently argued against the weight of formal tradition, referring to 'ratio' as the main orientation. In his *Quaestiones juris publici* (1737), he gave a rather critical account of the Grotian definitions. Although he was not primarily concerned with the problem of truce, it becomes clear from his statements about the nature of justice and fraud in times of war that he regarded formal elements of war, not unlike Pufendorf, as being part of 'generosity' rather than of actual 'justice'.[21] Although he insisted on the point of view that promises had to be kept even in times of war, because they had been pledged in situations where the actual war had been suspended, he generally considered fraud and arbitrary violence as legitimate means of pursuing the armed conflict in times of war.

Emer de Vattel (1714–1767), one of the major theorists of *jus gentium* in the Age of Enlightenment, adopted current doctrines about a desirable equilibrium of European powers and allowed war against universal hegemony, explicitly the wars of Henry IV against Philip II.[22] Besides, his system of international law is generally described as being more inclined to peace and justice than to the pursuit of dominance. Concerning treaties of truce, he recognised, for example, that not only are they apparently similar to peace, but that they are like a first step to a lasting peace agreement or a substitute for it. Truces between Christian powers and the Ottoman Empire had frequently been concluded out of unnecessary religious scrupulousness forbidding full-scale peace treaties with non-Christian sovereigns.[23] The conclusion of 'general' truces, i.e. of truces not limited to certain places or areas, remained clearly associated to supreme sovereignty.[24] Violation of a truce, however, provides, according to Vattel, the right to consider the treaty broken and to retaliate immediately. This vision of the truce thus proves to be developed in

20 Samuel von Pufendorf, *Le droit de la nature et des gens* 8.7 (transl. Jean Barbeyrac, Basel, 1732) vol. 2, 475–480.

21 Peter Stephen Du Ponceau (ed.), *Cornelius van Bynkershoek, A Treatise on the Law of War* (Phildadelphia, 1810), 3–4.

22 Richard Tuck, *The Rights of War and Peace. Political Thought and International Order from Grotius to Kant* (Oxford, 1999), 193; on Vattel's impact on 18th century theories cf. Gaurier, *Histoire du droit international*, 172–176.

23 Vattel, *Le droit des gens ou principes de la loi naturelle, Appliqués à la conduite et aux affaires des Nations et des Souverains* 3.16 (London, 1768), vol. 2, 207.

24 Vattel, *Le droit des gens*, 3.16.237, 209.

the classic age of international law with its emphasis on independent sovereignty.[25]

The 20th century atrocities and the general reconfiguration of international law after the creation of the United Nations reopened discussions about the required qualities of a lawful truce, the word being close to the similar terms of 'armistice' and 'cease-fire' that have been employed alternatively. After several modifications which take into account the new contexts of the post-colonial world order and the normative role of the UN Security Council, the emergence of the political hierarchy 'cease-fire', 'truce', 'armistice', concerning the extent of multilateral negotiation and legitimacy, illustrates the fundamental difference from the early modern system with its dual definition of 'general' and 'limited' truce, to be distinguished only by temporal and geographical extent.[26]

Political Validity

Political theorists since Machiavelli (1469–1527) have amply treated the possible ways of one-sided revision or non-observance of peace treaties.[27] In a famous and frequently quoted chapter of his *De Principatibus*, Machiavelli had compared the wise statesman to a lion terrifying his opponents, but at the same time to a fox whose intelligence and prudence allowed him to avoid the hidden traps of diplomacy:

> Since a ruler, then, must know how to act like a beast, he should imitate both the fox and the lion, for the lion is liable to be trapped, whereas the fox cannot ward off wolves. One needs, then, to be a fox to recognise traps, and a lion to frighten away wolves. Those who rely merely upon a

---

25 Cf. the bilateral definition of 'armistice' without any third power or arbitration involved in the 1899 declaration of The Hague Peace Conference, obviously incorporating traditional elements of 'induciae', e.g. the suspensive character, the distinction between 'general' and 'local' etc., James Brown Scott (ed.), *The Proceedings of the Hague Peace Conferences. Translation of the Official Texts. The Conference of 1899* (New York, 1920), 577–578.

26 Sydney D. Bailey, 'Cease-fires, Truces and Armistices in the Practice of the UN Security Council', *American Journal of International Law*, 71 (1977) 461–473.

27 I had the opportunity to present several aspects of the following outline at a meeting at the Herzog August Bibliothek Wolfenbüttel in 2005, cf. Bernd Klesmann, 'Der Friedensvertrag als Kriegsgrund. Politische Instrumentalisierung zwischenstaatlicher Abkommen in europäischen Kriegsmanifesten der Frühen Neuzeit', in Heinz Duchhardt and Martin Peters (eds.), *Kalkül – Transfer – Symbol. Europäische Friedensverträge der Vormoderne* (Veröffentlichungen des Instituts für Europäische Geschichte, Beihefte online 1; Mainz, 2006-11-02), 109–121; I wish to thank the conveners and participants for their helpful comments.

> lion's strength do not understand matters. Therefore, a prudent ruler cannot keep his word, nor should he, when such fidelity would damage him, and when the reasons that made him promise are no longer relevant.[28]

Even critical early modern interpreters of Machiavelli's work, like Hermann Conring (1606–1681), professor at the Duke of Braunschweig-Wolfenbüttel's university in Helmstedt, had to admit that the Florentine thinker had a point in advising the Princes not to clutch at the very letter of every treaty. After fundamental changes in the circumstances that had determined its conclusion, distance must be allowed to develop between the sovereign and the treaty.[29]

Political realities were of course trespassing systematic rigidity. On the other hand, the many faces of diplomatic controversies continued sharpening respective differentiations and juridical distinctions, as it has been shown that some important direct precursors of Grotius have drawn solid inspiration from close observation of political practice.[30]

---

28 *Machiavelli: The Prince* (ed. and transl. Quentin Skinner and Russell Price, Cambridge Texts in the History of Political Thought; Cambridge, 1988), 61–62; historical context and the anti-Ciceronian verve of Chapter 18 are discussed Ibid., xix–xx; *Machiavel, De principatibus. Le Prince* (ed. and transl. Jean-Louis Fournel et Jean-Claude Zancarini, Fondements de la politique; Paris, 2000), 150: 'Sendo dunque necessitato uno principe sapere bene usare la bestia, debbe di quelle pigliare la volpe et il lione: perché el lione non si difende da 'lacci, la volpe non si difende da' lupi; bisogna adunque essere volpe a conoscere e lacci, e lione a sbigottire e lupi: coloro che stanno semplicemente in sul lione, non se ne intendono. Non può pertanto uno signore prudente, ne debbe, observare la fede quando tale observanzia gli torni contro e che sono spente le cagioni che la feciono promettere'.

29 Hermann Conring, *Animadversiones politicae in Nicolai Machiavelli Librum De Principe* (Helmstedt, 1661), 167: 'Ad hoc, non Romani tantum civilis, sed etiam naturalis jus est, in contractibus bonae fidei si dolus malus commissus, aut si quis laesus fuerit ultra dimidium, aut si quod praeter omnem exspectationem ex stricta contractus observatione grande incommodum acciderit, aut denique si altra contrahentium pars contractum violaverit: licere tunc summae cuique potestati, ac proinde etiam Principibus, et rescindere contractus, et in integrum sese ac res suas restituere'. The fundamental debates about the philosophical figure of the 'righteous fool' and the existence of natural justice in the early 17th century, as inherited from the Melian dialogue in Thucydides and the arguments of Karneades in the writings of Cicero and Lactantius have been amply studied by Benjamin Straumann, *Hugo Grotius und die Antike. Römisches Recht und römische Ethik im frühneuzeitlichen Naturrecht* (Studien zur Geschichte des Völkerrechts 14; Baden-Baden, 2007), 96–127.

30 Randall Lesaffer, 'An Early Treatise on Peace Treaties: Petrus Gudelinus between Roman Law and Modern Practice', *The Journal of Legal History*, 23 (2002) 245.

Grotius' contribution to the notion of 'truce' seems even more interesting in another field: throughout his life as a scholar, politician and diplomat, the son of a Delft patrician family devoted himself to the foundation of Dutch historiography. While his early work *De antiquitate Reipublicae Batavicae* (1610) may be less famous for its historical accuracy and impartiality than for its rather free, sometimes arbitrary application of humanist erudition, it operated with all the essential technical terms of international law.[31] We can read about the Treaty of 1609:

> Finally [...], negotiations were started, [...] and when great difficulties hindered the conclusion of a peace-treaty, in the end a truce was made for twelve years, in the year 1609; at the opening of which a declaration in the Archdukes' own name and in Philip's name – from whom they had received their power – was included, in which they acknowledged that they signed this truce with the States General as being the States of free nations and cities, and declared that they would regard them as such, and that they would deny them no rights whatsoever.[32]

His posthumous text *Annales et historiae de rebus Belgicis*, first published in 1657 by his two eldest sons Corneel (1613–1663) and Pieter (1615–1678, at the time ambassador to the States General for the Elector Palatine), and in French translation in 1662, is a masterpiece of 17th-century historical writing.[33] The

31 The patriotic and aristocratic implications of this work are explained by Henk Nellen, *Hugo de Groot. Een leven in strijd om de vrede, 1583–1645* (Amsterdam, 2007), 97–99; cf. J.L. Price, *Holland and the Dutch Republic in the Seventeenth Century. The Politics of Particularism* (Oxford, 1994), 13; Johan Huizinga, *Holländische Kultur des siebzehnten Jahrhunderts. Ihre sozialen Grundlagen und nationale Eigenart* (Schriften des Deutsch-Niederländischen Instituts Köln 1; Jena, 1932), 26–27.

32 Hugo Grotius, *The Antiquity of the Batavian Republic* [...] (ed. and transl. Jan Waszink, Assen, 2000), 107; Ibid., 106 (ch. 7): 'Tandem [...] coepta colloquia: et cum pacem difficultates magnae morarentur, ad ultimum, anno mdcix factae in duodecim annos induciae; praeposita testatione ab Archiducibus tum suo, tum Philippi, a quo id mandati acceperant, nomine, qua se pacisci eas inducias cum Ordinibus Federatis, ut cum liberarum nationum ac civitatum Ordinibus, profitebantur, talesque eos a se haberi, et nihil a se in ipsos iuris obtendi'.

33 Hugo Grotius, *Annales et historiae de rebus Belgicis* (Amsterdam, 1658); Idem, *Annales et histoires des troubles des Pays-bas* (Amsterdam, 1662); historical research on this text may usefully be intensified, cf. Jan Waszink, 'Hugo Grotius' "Annales et Historiae de rebus Belgicis" from the evidence in his correspondence, 1604–1644', *Lias: sources and documents relating to the early modern history of ideas*, 31 (2004) 249–269; Henk Nellen identifies Tacit and Auguste de Thou as stylistic models, cf. Nellen, *Hugo de Groot*, 101.

narration in 18 books covers the period from the departure of Philip II to the conclusion of the Twelve Years Truce. The negotiations that led to the Antwerp Treaty have been amply described in this work, thereby underlining the diplomatic skills and patriotic righteousness of Oldenbarnevelt and his Arminian colleagues, who, with Grotius himself, were so violently attacked in 1618/19. Along with a detailed report on the circumstances of diplomatic meetings and court ceremony, the historian and renowned expert on *jus gentium* emphasised the fact that at the beginning of the negotiations in 1608, Ambrogio Spinola hid his desire to conclude a truce instead of a peace treaty, respecting the fact that Spanish King's reputation would be compromised by every renunciation of any rights of sovereignty over the Dutch rebels.[34] According to Grotius, the French and English mediators opposed the Spaniards' attempt to hinder and forbid Dutch trade in the Indies, stating that no such treaty, forbidding something that was allowed by the laws of nature, could ever be concluded. When finally the truce was about to be agreed upon, Maurice of Nassau warned his compatriots that this could be even more dangerous than open war, because it gave the Spanish the opportunity to rebuild their power and strike back in the years to come.[35]

On the other hand, authors familiar with European politics celebrated the Truce as the keystone of the late William of Orange's work, the architect of Dutch independence. Dominicus Baudius (1561–1613), a poet and historian familiar with French and English literature, devoted his last years to the praise of the 1609 Treaty and the historical account of its origins and miraculous fulfilment. His narration in three books, as he explained in its dedication to the States General, aimed at glorifying public virtue by giving a reliable account of the recent proceedings, including the reasons of the war against Spanish tyranny and the just cause finally prevailing by forcing Philip III to acknowledge the freedom of the Netherlands.[36] The speech of Jeannin, central part of the 3rd book, trying to convince the States General that the Truce offered by the Archdukes was sincere, discussed suspicions of fraud and the threat of a resuming of hostilities by Spanish forces, explicitly referring to several documents of the political controversy.[37]

34 Grotius, *Annales et historiae*, vol. 17, 533–534: 'Pacem vel inducias obtulerat Hispanus, presso diu arcano quod sero erupit, pacem se aequis conditionibus ferre non posse, inducias posse'.

35 Grotius, *Annales et historiae*, vol. 17, 543: '[...] nec pax hosti cupita, sed ut suo magis quam nostro tempore bellum gerat, aut bello gravius per discordias ac dona afflictet Rempublicam. Brevi reviviscent illi opes, nuper exhaustae [...]'.

36 Dominicus Baudius, *Libri tres de induciis belli Belgici* (2nd edn., Leyden, 1617), i–xxxv.

37 Ibid., 280–327.

The same ambivalence is to be found in iconographic representations of the truce, as has been thoroughly demonstrated by Martina Dlugaiczyk. The Twelve Years Truce was indeed one of the major inspirations for artists throughout Europe to conceive a specific allegory of truce, combining elements of a conventional glorification of peace like the olive branch or the 'kiss of peace and justice' with the traditional attributes of war like armour and weapons hinting at the possible renewal of war.[38] The magnificent painting *The prophecy of Isaiah*[39] shows the same alternation of irenic and bellicose symbolism. Without entering into the delicate question of the justice of war or the juridical state of the belligerents, the innumerable representations of this kind aimed at creating ways of celebrating peace, using the contrast with the threat of war to provide a glorious and dramatic framing.

The threat of a renewal of combat was, at the same time, the fundamental argument of the truce's opponents. Thus, in the opinion of an important political group in the United Provinces, a truce would lead to final defeat by means of postponed but unavoidable war. This popular thinking was backed by the re-publication of a letter of Justus Lipsius (1547–1606), the former glory of the Leyden, then Louvain universities. In this letter, Lipsius had allegedly advised the Archdukes in January 1595 to conclude a truce with the United Provinces. According to this text, a truce would be the safest possible way of assuring a strategic hold of the Netherlands without being bound by a definite obligation which a peace treaty would bring about. The truce itself is referred to as a 'golden hook' that could be useful to fish with in the pond of Dutch riches.[40]

38 Martina Dlugaiczyk, *Der Waffenstillstand (1609–1621) als Medienereignis. Politische Bildpropaganda in den Niederlanden* (Niederlande-Studien 39; Munster, 2005), 48–89.

39 Munich, Alte Pinakothek, cf. Rainer Wohlfeil, Trudl Wohlfeil, 'Pflugscharen statt Waffen? "Die Weissagungen des Propheten Jesaias" und der Waffenstillstand von Antwerpen 1609', *Journal Geschichte* 3(1989) 24–33.

40 *Justi Lipsii Epistola qua respondet cuidam viro principi deliberanti bellumne an pax an potius induciae expediant regi Hispaniarum cum Gallo, Anglo, Batavo, scritpa 3 januarij mdxcv* (s.l., 1608); the text was first published in 1595; Lipsius seems to have felt uncomfortable about public interest in this text, without completely denying authorship. G.H.M. Delprat, 'Lettres inédites de Juste Lipse concernant ses relations avec les hommes d'état des Provinces-Unies des Pays-bas, principalement pendant les années 1580–1597', *Verhandelingen der Koninklijke Akademie van Wetenschappen. Afdeeling Letterkunde* (Amsterdam, 1858), vol. 1, 26–27; Lipsius' correspondant was Franciso San Vitores y de la Portilla, author of the treatise *El mal de Flandes y su remedio*, cf. Antoine Coron, 'Juste Lipse, juge des pouvoirs politiques européens à la lumière de sa correspondance', in *Théorie et pratique politiques à la Renaissance. XVIIe colloque international de Tours* (Paris, 1977), 445–457 at 452; Alois Gerlo and Hendrik D.L. Vervliet (eds.), *Inventaire de la correspondance de Juste Lipse 1564–1606* (Anvers, 1968), 191.

Making use of Lipsius' academic and political authority, the pamphlet issued by the Dutch war party, failed to stop truce negotiations. The document may be regarded, however, as an indicator of powerful currents in public opinion seriously contesting any possibility of a valuable peace settlement.

Let us now examine the general context and political manifestations of this theoretical causality between truce and war.

Peace Treaties as Political Argument in War Manifestos

The form and substance of treaties of peace or truce have found their way into different rhetorical patterns of justifying public warfare. Authors of war manifestos in early modern Europe used three main types of argument to legitimise an official decision of taking up arms by establishing a 'justa causa', a core concept of the 'just war' doctrine.

Justa causa: *Violation of Treaties*

The early-modern theory of *jus gentium* was built on the traditional assumption that the legitimacy of war depended entirely on the necessity to restore a general state of justice. Just war required a just cause, i.e. the defence of justice threatened or attacked, therefore liberating the state from obligations of previous peace treaties that had lost their binding force. Grotius distinguished three types of cases: peace could be considered broken by acts (1) against what is inherent to every peace (2) against what is explicitly stipulated in the peace treaty (3) against what has to be clear from every peace treaty.[41]

The problem of the geographical extent of a possible treaty was crucial to any negotiation about ending the Spanish-Dutch war. Contrary to the broadly accepted assumption that European peace treaties by their very nature categorically excluded all areas outside Europe, especially the oceans 'beyond the line' of the tropic of cancer, war manifestos of nearly all European powers included grievances referring to extra-European events. The rise of Dutch colonial power during the Eighty Years War soon brought about many documents of this kind. When in 1672, for example, Charles II of England (1661–1685) declared war on the United Provinces, he made use of troubles in South America that had followed the Peace Treaty of Breda between England and the Netherlands in 1667 as an excuse. The transfer of colonists and goods from

41 Grotius, *De jure belli ac pacis* 3.20.27: 'Rumpitur pax tribus modis, aut faciendo contra id quod omni paci inest, aut contra id quod in pace dictum est aperte, aut contra id quod ex pacis cujusque natura debet intelligi'.

formerly English Surinam, now restituted to the Netherlands, had been slowed down or even stopped by the Dutch with the intention to hold back and steal English property. The declaration of 1672 finally made clear that none of the new alliances that Charles II would be forced to conclude in the course of the incipient war would aim at annulling the Peace Treaty of Aix-la-Chapelle (1668) which was, quite to the contrary, to be scrupulously respected.[42]

While the idea of 'no peace beyond the line' was irrelevant to official declarations, it was of the utmost importance for political and commercial reality throughout the 17th and 18th centuries. During the negotiations of 1608/09, the idea of a truce formally prohibiting trade and privateering in the Indies frightened the merchant cities of Holland and Zeeland who feared severe losses to their trade revenues.[43] Any treaty project thus had to face massive opposition, and future non-observance contributed to make it an active part of inter-state conflict.[44] It can also be noticed that truces did not differ from peace treaties regarding their interpretations in declarations of war.[45]

Justa causa: *Avoiding and Preventing Treaties*

Another way of using the general weight of peace treaties to discredit political opponents was the allegation of these opponents hindering the conclusion of such a treaty. The Swedish King Gustavus Adolphus (1611–1632), to cite another example from the contexts of war against Habsburg supremacy in European affairs, justified his invasion of the Northern parts of the Holy Roman Empire in the summer of 1630 by recapitulating his previous wars against the King of Poland who had received illegal support from the Emperor's troops. Finally,

---

42 Jean Dumont, *Corps Universel Diplomatique du Droit des Gens* (Amsterdam, 1726–1731), vol. 7.1, 164; significance *de jure* and *de facto* of 'no peace beyond the line' have to be distinguished, the latter being far more important, cf. Jörg Fisch, *Die europäische Expansion und das Völkerrecht. Die Auseinandersetzungen um den Status der überseeischen Gebiete vom 15. Jahrhundert bis zur Gegenwart* (Beiträge zur Kolonial- und Überseegeschichte 26; Stuttgart, 1984), 141–152.

43 Den Tex, *Oldenbarnevelt*, vol. 2, 369.

44 Opposition to the truce was broadly founded on Calvinist enthusiasm for the Dutch cause, cf. Sherrin Marshall, *The Dutch Gentry, 1500–1650. Family, faith and fortune* (Contributions in Family Studies 11, New York/Westport/London, 1987), 152–153.

45 Cf. the declarations of Louis XIV and Leopold I following the outbreak of the Nine Years 'War in 1688, only four years after the conclusion of a truce treaty in Regensburg: Dumont, *Corps Universel*, vol. 7.2, 170–173, 175–179; the example is quoted in different ways in contemporary literature on international law, cf. Frank-Steffen Schmidt, *Praktisches Naturrecht zwischen Thomasius und Wolff: Der Völkerrechtler Adam Friedrich Glafey, 1692–1753* (Studien zur Geschichte des Völkerrechts 12; Baden-Baden, 2007), 268.

several attempts to enter in peace negotiations with Poland had been prevented by Habsburg diplomacy, in order to act with more safety against the Protestant towns and Princes of Germany. Throughout his Manifesto, Gustavus Adolphus, whose appreciation of Grotius' writings is well known, addresses his opponents as 'the enemies of peace'. The Swedish participation in the Thirty Years War was justified as the defence of peace and justice against Vienna and Madrid striving at universal monarchy.[46]

The accusation of non-willingness to conclude peace can be found in the discussions about the Twelve Years Truce as well. In the eyes of the Truce's opponents, Spanish politics was fundamentally unwilling to reach a peace settlement, using the 1609 Truce only as a camouflage to prepare future warfare.

Justa causa: *Unjust Foundation of Treaties*

A third major argument in inter-state conflict was the statement that existing peace treaties had been concluded on foundations contrary to general notions of justice. We can observe this argument in Cardinal Richelieu's (1585–1642) text for Louis XIII's (1610–1643) declaration of war to the King of Spain in May 1635, inaugurating the final stage of the Eighty Years War. As the Emperor was just about to conclude a peace treaty (Prague) with a number of the German princes, France feared severe reverses for its strategy in Central Europe and Italy. As Richelieu pursued a more solidly European concept of peace, he attacked the Prague Treaty as a source of future dissent because of its one-sided tendencies in favour of the Habsburg powers.[47] Not unlike some of the Dutch leaders in 1609, France was aware of the risk of her enemies recovering from the pressure of war by a convenient treaty that would only favourably postpone the decisive war into an uncertain future. The peace treaty itself, although it had been proposed by the opponents as a first step to peace for all of Europe, in this perspective had more of a threatening war alliance, a league of enemies, than of a sincere settlement. Even the Treaties of Westphalia, emblematic examples of a historical achievement in European diplomacy, were used as an argument in times of war immediately following their

46 Sigmund Goetze, *Die Politik des schwedischen Reichskanzlers Axel Oxenstierna gegenüber Kaiser und Reich* (Kiel, 1971), 349–365.

47 *Lettres des manifestes du Roy de France, contenant les justes causes que sa majesté a eues de déclarer la guerre au Roy d'Espagne* (Paris, 1635), 7: '[...] autrement ce seroit fomenter une semence perpetuelle de discorde, et au lieu d'éteindre le feu, ce seroit le cacher sous les cendres pour le r'alumer de nouveau, avec d'autant plus de danger qu'il surprendroit à l'impourveu'.

ratification, as we know from the letters of Louis XIV (1643–1715) to several German princes, where he complained about the hypocritical manoeuvres of the Habsburg rulers who maintained their permanent alliance, making use of the Empire's soldiers, now at 'peace' with France, to simply send them to fight the French once more, under Spanish flags.[48] In terms of modern international law, the discussed patterns of one-sided non-acknowledgement of existing treaties are to be compared with the legal conditions of 'non-application of treaties'.[49] The most interesting similarities exist within the problematic areas of 'fraud', 'breach of a peremptory rule' and 'fundamental change of circumstance', all of them familiar to the observer of early modern discussions about the justice of war. The last area, coming close to the example quoted from Machiavelli, may be considered as the most general example, allowing manifold ways of contesting a treaty's lawfulness. Authors dealing with contemporary international law have required five conditions: the change of circumstances has to be (1) fundamental, (2) unpredictable, (3) essential to the original consentment, (4) seriously aggravating the obligations resulting from the treaty and (5) of primary importance for the future, not for obligations already fulfilled in the past.[50] It is difficult to make an assessment about the applicability of these criteria to 17th-century Europe. What might be considered as a desirable, albeit inexistent accomplishment of modern international law[51] is, of course, far from being a politically relevant factor for historical examination of the Early Modern Age. We might, however, gain some insights into the functioning and the controversial structure of 17th-century debates. Let us return to the analysis of the implementation and expiration of the Twelve Years Truce.

---

48 Vienna, HHStA, Frankreich Varia, K 6, Fasz. 9, Aktenstücke den Frieden von Münster und Osnabrück betreffend, Louis XIV to the Duke of Sachsen-Weimar and the Fürstbischof of Osnabrück, 1-14; 8r: „Vous n'auez pas oublié, que la principale condition qui me regarde, est compris dans l'article troisiesme, qui porte en termes expres, que L'Empereur, ni aucun Prince de L'Empire, ne pourra se mesler de la guerre que Je suis presentement obligé de soustenir contre le Roy d'Espagne [...]. On a pris quelque soing de sauuer les apparences, en faisant semblant de licentier les troupes, qui estoient au seruice de l'Empereur, lors qu'on les a uoulu faire passer à celuy d'Espagne."

49 Paul Reuter, *Introduction to the Law of Treaties* (2nd edn., London/New York, 1995), 163–209.

50 Robert Kolb, *Les cours généraux de droit international public de l'Académie de La Haye* (Brussels, 2003), 594, based on conceptualisations by Eduardo Jiménez de Aréchaga (1918–1994).

51 Reuter, *Law of Treaties*, 188–189.

The Truce of 1609 and the Legal Consolidation of the Dutch Republic

While discussing the formal context of the 1609 Treaty, it has to be observed that at the end of the truce, no explicit declarations of war were issued by the parties involved. As is clear from the legal doctrine of the time, declarations of this kind were not considered necessary after the regular expiration of a truce. At the same time, pamphlets discussing the possibility of a continuation of the truce were published throughout Germany, where the long-term conflict between the Habsburg powers and their Protestant opponents had reached a new stage after the rebellion of Bohemia and the expulsion of the Elector Palatine.[52] The *de facto* war between Spain and the Netherlands outside Europe finally seemed to make an arrangement impossible.[53] The diplomatic mission of Petrus Peckius (1562–1622), who had already been one of the Archdukes' negotiators of the truce in 1608/09, failed to save peace.[54] The documents of the decisive conferences in March 1621 reveal that besides a general consensus on the desirability of peace for all of the Netherlands, the question of sovereignty made an arrangement impossible: while the Archdukes made clear that the conclusion of the truce had been the result of their enduring desire for peace, they nevertheless proposed a political reunification under their rule. The Dutch answer, not surprisingly, as supported by Prince Maurice,[55] insisted on sovereign rights for the United Provinces which the 1609 Treaty had guaranteed without any equivocation.[56]

A lack of official declarations in 1621/22 may not be very surprising, considering the controversial status of the United Provinces between rebellion and inter-state war. At the outset of the conflict after the first waves of uprising in the Netherlands, several documents illustrated the violence of antagonism, without constituting a declaration of war in the terms of international law. Neither the King of Spain, who considered the incipient war a mere rebellion, nor the signatory states of the Union of Utrecht, who in the first stages of the conflict kept affirming loyalty to Philip II, were in the legal position to issue a

52 Johannes Arndt, *Das Heilige Römische Reich und die Niederlande 1566 bis 1648* (Münstersche Historische Forschungen 13; Cologne/Weimar/Vienna, 1998), 309.

53 Jonathan Israel, *The Dutch Republic and the Hsipanic World 1606–1661* (2nd edn., Oxford, 1986), 66–74.

54 According to Pieter Johannes Blok, *Geschichte der Niederlande* (transl. O.G. Houtrouw, Gotha, 1902–1918), vol. 4, 9, Burgundian tradition contributed to Peckius' abilities.

55 Israel, *Hispanic World*, 76–77.

56 Cf. Lieuwe van Aitzema, *Historie of Verhael van Saken van Staet en Oorlogh* (The Hague, 1657), vol. 1, 82–90.

declaration of war. The document that may come closest to this would be the Act of Abjuration of July 1581.[57] As the German historian Erich Angermann has proposed in very different contexts, the Declaration of Independence by the United States of America in 1776 offered a number of similarities to the 'Absage-Brief' or 'diffidatio' of the late Middle Ages, precursors of early modern declarations of war. According to Angermann, it could be interpreted as a specific rearrangement of the traditional discourses of grievances and complaint, proving the necessity to establish a new kind of political consensus without the ruler who had become a 'tyrant'.[58] Maybe some of these aspects might apply to the Act of Abjuration, for example by referring itself to the Pacification of Ghent (November 1576), which had not been respected by Spain, a pattern of argumentation familiar, as we have seen, to the early modern justification of war.

Just as there had not been an official declaration of war at the beginning of the conflict in the 16th century, it was omitted, in perfect accordance with the European political practice, after the truce had expired. After Peckius' departure from the States General and the unexpected death of King Philip III (31 March 1621), negotiations continued secretly between Maurice and Brussels, while measures of economic hostility such as the blockades of the Flemish seaports Dunkirk and Ostend were already in place in April.[59] A major signal was issued by creating the West Indian Company (3 June 1621), something that had been postponed in the decades before. Oldenbarnevelt, who had feared a renewal of disputes with Spain, had tried to prevent the creation of a Dutch West Indian Company even before the conclusion of the 1609 Treaty.[60] He was soon accused of conducting secret negotiations with Spain, an accusation that was to be repeated throughout the last years of his activities, and which contributed, among other factors, to his imprisonment and execution by the leaders of the counter-remonstrant party in 1618/19.

Pieter Johannes Blok has pointed out how the rise of Dutch trade activities was favourable to the creation of the West Indian Company, now that the risk of unilaterally breaking the Truce was no longer an impediment.[61] Considering the political and military context, however, one could raise the question if the creation of the company was the essential *point of no return* in the process of

57 Israel, *Dutch Republic*, 209–211.

58 Karl Vocelka, 'Fehderechtliche "Absagen" als völkerrechtliche Kriegserklärungen in der Propaganda der frühen Neuzeit', *Mitteilungen des Instituts für Österreichische Geschichtsforschung*, 84 (1976) 380.

59 Israel, *Hispanic World*, 83–87.

60 Blok, *Geschichte*, vol. 4, 20–21.

61 Blok, *Geschichte*, vol. 4, 296–297.

ending the truce: at the borders of the Republic, as no hostilities had yet occurred between Spanish and Dutch troops, negotiations still seemed possible, while the death of Archduke Albert (15 July) blurred political priorities. Until the end of summer, no major military action was taken to conquer one of the many important fortresses in the lower Rhineland.[62] Only in late autumn, the siege of Jülich was taken up by Spanish troops, severely limiting political options. Contemporary observers were of course aware of this lapse of time. Among numerous examples in pamphlet literature, a well-known engraving by Claes Jansz. Visscher (1586–1652) is quite revealing in this area:[63] A symbolic funeral procession of the treaty shows twelve monk-like individuals dressed in long coats carrying the coffin of the truce, of Peckius and the Archdukes. One of these individuals is wearing six zodiac symbols on his habit, reaching from Aries (the truce actually expired in April) to Virgo, thus emblematically illustrating the ultimate end of hope for a prolongation of the truce or an agreement on peace in autumn 1621.[64]

The *de facto* subsisting and somewhat lingering truce was, however, of no comfort to the Dutch war party in the months following its expiration. The situation of lasting non-war in the Low Countries stimulated the publication of pamphlets stirring up the fear of Spanish attacks. A collection of poetry by Jan van Foreest (1586–1651), one of the leaders of the new West Indian Company, recalled the terrifying details of the Spaniards' violence throughout the last decades and constituted an outstanding example of what was to be called the 'black legend'. From the edicts of Charles V up to the present day, Spanish tyranny and cruelty had been raging all over the Netherlands and the Americas alike. A particularly interesting series of verses was aimed at dissuading the Dutch from concluding peace on the conditions imposed by Brussels. Accepting peace on Spanish terms would be, according to the author, a mere capitulation and a trade of liberty for serfdom.[65] In the preface to his collection dedicated to the United Provinces, Foreest exhorted his compatriots to wake

62 Cf. the detailed accont of Jan Joseph Poelhekke, *'t Uytgaen van den Treves: Spanje en de Nederlanden in 1621* (Groningen, 1960); Israel, *Hispanic World*, 96–100.

63 Claes Jansz. Visscher, *Ende des Treves*, Wolfenbüttel, Herzog August Bibliothek, IH 133, reprod.: Dlugaiczyk, *Waffenstillstand*, Kat. 18.

64 Cf. the rather clumsy German explanation, probably in translation from Dutch or French: 'So viel Jahr der Treues gestandn/So mancher tregt am Sarck zu handn/Das meldt jede Kapp eben/Ihr Sechse gehn auf jeder seit/Der letzte thut noch eine zeit/ Sechs Monat drüber geben'.

65 Ioannes Forestus, *Hispanus Redux sive Exitus Induciarum Belgicarum. Ad Foederatos Belgas* (Hornae [Hoorn], 1622), 73–75.

up and remember Spanish tyranny that had apparently vanished into oblivion during the truce, the pernicious 'holidays from war'.[66]

Debates about the justice and political opportunity of war, peace or truce continued throughout the Eighty Years War. As is well-known, the final settlement of 1648 had its roots in the truce negotiations of the 1630s, when the memory of the Antwerp Treaty was still fresh. The controversial discussions about diplomatic decisions once more involved the United Provinces as well as the Southern Netherlands. Erycius Puteanus (1574–1646), one of Lipsius' most prominent former pupils at Louvain university, attempted to give a balanced survey of pro and contra arguments in his *Statera Pacis et Belli*, i.e. The Balance of Peace and War. It becomes clear from the polemical responses to this publication how much the political character of truce was still disputed among contemporary scholars. Puteanus had glorified the spirit of the truce and underlined that the only regrettable thing about it had been its limited duration. According to his point of view, the truce had only revealed the desirability of permanent peace, most noble goal of human society. As a truce of several years was nearly as welcome as peace, why not conclude a truce if it was easier to have than peace?[67] The sarcastic commentary of the anonymous critic, identified – unjustly as it seems – with Caspar Barlaeus (1584–1648), professor at the recently founded Amsterdam Athenaeum,[68] recalled the necessary complementarity of

66 Ibid. iii: 'Quis crederet tam breves belli ferias ita vos facere potuisse, ut principia reipublicae et hostis ille, cum quo tot annos vobis res fuit, omnino animis exciderint? Iam status cum hoste dies praeteriit. Si et hoc nescitis; ille vobis cum triplici exercitu venit id denuntiandum'.

67 Eryicius Puteanus, *De Induciis aut Pace Belgarum Dissertationes Variae* (Eleutheropoli [Amsterdam], 1633), 31.

68 Cf. A.J.E. Harmsen, E. Hofland, *Bibliografie van Caspar Barlaeus of Caspar van Baerle (1584–1648)*, Leyden University, Department of Dutch Language and Literature: http://www.let.leidenuniv.nl/Dutch/Latijn/BarlaeusBibliografie.html (Last update: 4 February 2009); Blok, *Geschichte*, vol. 4, 481; Louis D. Petit, *Bibliographische lijst der werken van de Leidsche hoogleeraren van de oprichting der hoogeschool tot op onze dagen* (Leyden/Leipzig, 1894), vol. 1, 203–204, did not attribute it to Barlaeus, but to an anonymous author probably from the Southern Netherlands. The anti-heretic invectives of the actual text are much more in harmony with this last assumption. In his letter to Puteanus (24 June 1633 according to the datation given by K. Van der Horst, *Inventaire de la correspondance de Caspar Barlaeus, 1602–1648* (Assen, 1978), 67, with reference to the manuscript in Brussels, Bibliothèque Royale), Barlaeus expressed consent and gratitude: 'Legi Stateram tuam, qua Pacis et belli momenta rigide ponderas. In ea nescio, an pietatem magis tuam, an facundiam, an prudentiam mirari debeam. [...] Ego vir summe tuis votis subscribo, et subscribunt omnes, qui togam tubae [the trumpet of war, B.K.] praeferunt'. *Casparis Barlaei Epistolarum Liber* (Amsterdam, 1667), vol. 1, 438–439; when Barlaeus took his

peace and justice that had to exist simultaneously in order to allow society to lay down its arms. 'Induciae' were undoubtedly better than war, and the best thing indeed would be peace. There were situations, however, which demanded a common defence against injustice, rebellion and heresy. If peace was the highest priority, why not simply render the whole of the Netherlands to the rebels without even fighting?[69] The ambiguity of a truce thus allowed different kinds of appropriation of the term; closer to war for its opponents preferring to fight out this war which would continue anyway during the truce; closer to peace for its defenders considering a truce as the first step towards peace.[70]

This political dichotomy, similar to the one of 1609, makes it even more clear how Grotius' association of truce and war was not aimed at surrendering to the Archdukes or having peace at any price, but was aimed at continuing trade and a 'sleeping' war in the Indies to assure a final victory and the complete sovereignty of the Republic.

On the other hand, early modern literature since Erasmus has presented the assumption that even full-scale peace treaties between sovereign states were in reality nothing more than a temporarily limited cessation of hostilities that would allow the belligerents to recreate their forces in order to continue fighting.[71] If we listen once more – for the last time – to what Grotius said about the circumstances and meaning of the 1609 Treaty, we might grasp another aspect of political reality, tempered, it is true, by lyrical sentiment and, more importantly maybe, as we have seen, by political partiality in favour of the agreement. In three different parts of his compendium of selected poetry of his early years, published by his brother Willem in 1617, the Antwerp Treaty is celebrated, highlighting several aspects:[72] While the epic *Induciae Batavicae*, among many other ideas, evoked the suggested etymological connection with 'otium' and gave a poetic illustration of the fixed duration of twelve years,[73] the

---

distances from the truce project, he apparently was led by his strong belief in Dutch victory, cf. Judith Pollmann, *Religious choice in the Dutch Republic. The reformation of Arnoldus Buchelius, 1565–1641* (Studies in Early Modern European History; Manchester/New York, 1999), 189–190.

69 *De Induciis aut Pace Belgarum*, 32.

70 *De Induciis aut Pace Belgarum*: 'Sed ego, ut omni sermone bellum excludam, Pacem Inducias vocare amo, Inducias Pacem'.

71 Dlugaiczyk, *Waffenstillstand*, 44–45.

72 Hugo Grotius, *Poemata, collecta et magnam partem nunc primum edita a fratre Guilelmo Grotio* (Leyden, 1617); the *Bibliothèque nationale de France* conserves Pieter Grotius' copy with personal annotations: Yc 9327.

73 Grotius, *Poemata*, 116: 'Otiaque in populos totidem promissa per annos,/Annua quot menses complectita orbita Phoebi'.

more elegiac *De induciis* aimed at warning the young Republic of internal dissent: God had deliberately created the constant threat of returning warfare to encourage prudence and civility.[74] Above all, the Sapphic *Ode pro Induciis* in its final stanza emphasized the central message of political obligation and legacy of the 1609 Treaty by insisting on the idea of dearly paid freedom which had to be passed on to the grandchildren of the Netherlands as a precious and glorious gift from their ancestors.[75]

74 Ibid., 406: 'Ne tamen insidijs marcentia corda paterent,/Bella cupit metui ceu reditura Deus,/Convenit, o, nobis haec quam bene regula, quae nos/Esse jubet cautos, et vetat esse feros'.

75 Ibid., 27: 'Omnis ut mundi meritura famam,/Cladibus multis, totidem triumphis/Emta libertas, eat in nepotes/Munus avitum'.

CHAPTER 13

The Treaty of London, the Twelve Years Truce and Religious Toleration in Spain and the Netherlands (1598–1621)

Werner Thomas

Introduction

In European historiography since the 17th century, Spain has always been seen as the ultimate defender of Catholicism against Protestantism. The Black Legend created an image of a country that was ruled by the Holy Inquisition, and in which even the King could not escape the orders of the inquisitors.[1] A regime of terror, dominated by auto-da-fé, torture and the stake kept the Spaniards within the boundaries of orthodoxy. Bartolomé Bennassar even refers to it as a *pédagogie de la peur*.[2] Religious tolerance was not exactly a concept that was and is related to the Spanish Monarchy. Benjamin Kaplan's latest book on the practise of toleration in Early Modern Europe, for example, omits Spain completely, except when discussing intolerance.[3]

1 On the Black Legend, see Sverker Arnoldsson, *La leyenda negra. Estudios sobre sus orígenes* (Goteborg, 1960); William S. Maltby, *The Black Legend in England* (Durham, 1971); Koenraad W. Swart, 'The Black Legend during the Eighty Years' War' in John S. Bromley and Ernst H. Kossmann (eds.), *Britain and the Netherlands*, vol. 5: *Some Political Mythologies* (The Hague, 1975), 36–57; Julián Juderías, *La Leyenda Negra* (2nd edn., Madrid, 1986); Miguel Molina Martínez, *La leyenda negra* (Madrid, 1991); Ricardo García Cárcel, *La Leyenda Negra. Historia y opinión* (Madrid, 1992); Alain Barsacq and Bernardo J. García García (eds.), *Hazañas bélicas y leyenda negra. Argumentos escénicos entre España y los Países Bajos* (Madrid, 2004); Rómulo Carbia, *Historia de la leyenda negra hispano-americana* (Madrid, 2005); Werner Thomas, 'De mythe van de Spaanse inquisitie in de Nederlanden van de zestiende eeuw', *Bijdragen en mededelingen betreffende de geschiedenis der Nederlanden*, 105 (1990) 325–353.

2 Bartolomé Bennassar, 'L'inquisition ou la pédagogie de la peur' in idem, *L'Inquisition espagnole, XVe–XIXe siècle* (Paris, 1979), 105–141.

3 Benjamin Kaplan, *Divided by Faith. Religious Conflict and the Practice of Toleration in Early Modern Europe* (Cambridge, Mass./London, 2007). On the contrary, in his latest book, *All Can Be Saved. Religious Tolerance and Salvation in the Iberian Atlantic World* (New Haven/London, 2008), Stuart B. Schwartz analyses in a masterly way tolerant attitudes among ordinary people in Spain, Portugal and their overseas territories.

 | DOI 10.1163/9789004274921_015

A similar image still exists of the Southern Netherlands governed by the Archdukes Albert of Austria and Isabella Clara Eugenia. Both sovereigns are seen as creatures of the Spanish King and slaves of their religious bigotry. Albert even received the nickname of 'grave digger of Protestants'. In contrast to the religious climate in the United Provinces, their country was a bastion of intolerance, and it was this lack of openness towards dissenters that led to its economic and political decline.[4]

In reality, since the reign of Charles V (1516–1558), the Spanish Monarchy pursued a two-track policy towards religious dissidents. So did even Philip II. Towards the subjects of *other* sovereigns, the Spanish King made the political interests of the Crown prevail over any religious considerations whatsoever. Thus, he allowed the so-called Alba-Cobham Agreement of 1575, concluded between the Duke of Alba and Henry Cobham,[5] that granted the subjects of the Queen of England religious toleration in Spain and the Netherlands, and in 1597 he came to an arrangement with the merchants of the Hanseatic League, allowing them the same rights as their English colleagues.[6] In both cases, Philip's forbearance was mainly inspired by commercial and political motives. In other words, in 1575 as well as in 1597, arguments of *raison d'état* more than religious fanaticism shaped the Monarchy's religious policy.

Towards *his own* subjects, on the contrary, Philip defended the principle of *cuius regio, eius religio*. He was of the opinion that as the sovereign of the Netherlands, he was entitled to determine the religion in his northern provinces. No subject of the King was allowed to practise any other religion but Catholicism. Religious dissidence was considered as the first step to

4 Cf. Roland Baetens, *De nazomer van Antwerpens welvaart. De diaspora en het handelshuis De Groote tijdens de eerste helft der 17de eeuw* (Brussels, 1976), vol. 1, 230, where the author describes the Merchant Adventurers's call for toleration as an 'insuperable barrier' for the Spanish authorities in Brussels. See also Denis Diagre, 'L'Archiduc Albert, souverain-modèle ou ange exterminateur?' in Anne Morelli (ed.), *Les grands mythes de l'histoire de Belgique, de Flandre et de Wallonie* (Brussels, 1995), 117–128. On the historiography of the Archdukes, see Werner Thomas, 'La Corte de los archiduques Alberto de Austria y la Infanta Isabel Clara Eugenia en Bruselas (1598–1633). Una revisión historiográfica' in Ana Crespo Solana and Manuel Herrero Sánchez (eds.), *España y las 17 provincias de los Países Bajos. Una revisión historiográfica (XVI–XVIII)* (Cordoba, 2002), vol. 1, 355–386.

5 Julio Retamal Favereau, *Diplomacia anglo-española durante la Contrarreforma* ([Santiago de Chile], 1981), 31, 46–52; Carlos Gómez-Centurión, *Felipe II, la empresa de Inglaterra y el comercio septentrional (1566–1609)* (Madrid, 1988), 71 ff.; Werner Thomas, *La represión del protestantismo en España, 1517–1648* (Leuven, 2001), 271–276.

6 Antonio Domínguez Ortiz, 'El primer esbozo de tolerancia religiosa en la España de los Austrias' in idem, *Instituciones y sociedad en la España de los Austrias* (Barcelona, 1985), 184–191 at 185.

(civil) disobedience, and liberty of conscience as a way to free oneself of royal authority. Any agreement on this point would therefore restrict royal power.[7]

In practice, religious toleration towards the subjects of other sovereigns was only pursued during peacetime. Moreover, the Spanish Inquisition clearly disapproved the Alba-Cobham Agreement and never stopped persecuting English Protestants, in spite of the complaints of the English ambassadors in Madrid.[8] In reality, the politics of repression of the Spanish Monarchy in Spain and the Netherlands did not change until the beginning of the 17th century, when religious tolerance was implemented in order to make international peace – Philip III's so called *Pax Hispanica* – possible.[9]

The mechanisms that led to this adjustment were two international treaties between the Spanish Monarchy and its most important Protestant enemies: the Treaty of London of 1604 and the Twelve Years Truce of 1609. Apart from the cease-fire and the end of military hostilities, their attention was mainly focused on commerce, that is, on the re-establishment of commercial relations and the conditions they had to comply with. Religious matters were hardly mentioned. Nevertheless, both treaties exercised a favourable influence on the religious policy of the Monarchy and eventually shaped a climate of what in Spanish is called – although in relation to the situation in the Middle Ages – *convivencia*, religious cohabitation.

Spain and the Treaty of London

The motives of the Spanish and English government to start the negotiations that led to the Treaty of London, signed on 29 August 1604, have already been studied intensively.[10] I therefore will not go into the political circumstances in

7 See my article 'Alva and Religion' in Maurits Ebben, Margriet Lacy-Bruijn and Rolof van Hövell tot Westerflier (eds.), *Alba. General and Servant to the Crown* (Rotterdam, 2013), 116–135, 398–402.

8 Gary M. Bell, 'John Man: The Last Elizabethan Resident Ambassador in Spain', *The Sixteenth Century Journal*, 7/2 (1976) 75–93; Thomas, *La represión*, 276–280.

9 On the *Pax Hispanica*, see Bernardo J. García García, *La Pax Hispanica. Política exterior del Duque de Lerma* (Leuven, 1996); Paul Allen, *Philip III and the Pax Hispanica, 1598–1621. The Failure of Grand Strategy* (New Haven, 2000); Antonio Feros, *Kingship and Favoritism in the Spain of Philip III, 1598–1621* (Cambridge, 2000); Jesús María Usunáriz, *España y sus tratados internacionales: 1516–1700* (Pamplona, 2006), 233–272; Patrick Williams, *The Great Favourite. The Duke of Lerma and the Court and Government of Philip III of Spain, 1598–1621* (Manchester, 2006).

10 Léopold Willaert, 'L'Angleterre et les Pays-Bas catholiques', *Revue Générale*, 6 (1905) 47–54, 566–581, 811–826; 7 (1906) 585–607; 8 (1907) 81–101, 305–311, 514–532; 9 (1908) 52–61,

which the Treaty was concluded, but I will strictly limit myself to the religious consequences in Spain and the Netherlands.

The Treaty of London offered British subjects in Spain and the Netherlands guarantees for tolerance without any reciprocity for Catholicism in Great Britain. Based almost literally on the Alba-Cobham Agreement, Article 23 of the London Treaty stipulated that English merchants in Spain or the Southern Netherlands were not to be molested for religious motives – that is, for being Protestants – if they did not cause any public scandal. Three secret articles gave more details about the final arrangement. The first secret article guaranteed that the subjects of the King of Great Britain would not be persecuted for crimes of heresy committed outside the territory of the Spanish Monarchy. The second established that they did not have the obligation to attend Mass in Spain or the Southern Netherlands, and that they could not be forced to confess or to take Holy Communion. However, when they entered a Catholic church or when they crossed the Holy Sacrament in the streets, they were obliged to kneel and render honour to it, or to hide in a side-street. The third article stipulated that when there were reasons to detain an English merchant, sailor or captain, the Inquisition would only confiscate the property of the accused, and not the whole ship or cargo, as had frequently happened in the past.[11]

737–745; Joseph Cuvelier, *Les préliminaires du traité de Londres, 29 août 1604* (Brussels/Paris, 1923); Albert J. Loomie, *Toleration and Diplomacy. The Religious Issue in Anglo-Spanish Relations, 1603–1605* (Philadelphia, 1963); Pauline Croft, 'England and the Peace with Spain, 1604. Pauline Croft Analyses the Causes and Traces the Consequences of a Momentous Treaty', *History Review*, 49 (2004) 18–23; Porfirio Sanz Camanes, 'España ante las paces del Norte a comienzos del siglo XVII. Del Tratado de Londres a la Tregua de Amberes', *Cuadernos de Historia de España*, 81 (2007) 113–134; Bernardo J. García García, 'Peace with England, from Convenience to Necessity, 1596–1604' in Anne J. Cruz (ed.), *Material and Symbolic Circulation between England and Spain, 1554–1604* (Aldershot, 2008), 136–150.

11 Antonis Anselmus (ed.), *Placcaeten, ordonnantien, landt-chartres, blyde-incomsten, privilegien ende instruction by de Princen van dese Neder-Landen, aen de Inghesetenen van Brabandt, Vlaenderen, ende andere Provincien, 't sedert 't iaer 1220* (Antwerp, 1648), vol. 1, 621–632. The text was also published in Jean Dumont, *Corps universel diplomatique du droit des gens* (Amsterdam/The Hague, 1728), vol. 6.1, 625 ff.; Stephen Whatley (ed.), *A General Collection of Treatys, Manifest's Contracts of Marriage, Renunciations, and other Public Papers, from the Year 1495, to the Year 1712* (London, 1732), vol. 2, 131–146; Joseph Antonio de Abreu y Bertodano (ed.), *Colección de los Tratados de Paz, Neutralidad, Garantía, Protección, Tregua, Mediación, Accesión, Reglamento de Límites, Comercio, Navegación, etc., hechos por los Pueblos, Reyes y Príncipes de España Con los Pueblos, Reyes, Príncipes, Repúblicas, y demás Potencias de Europa y de otras partes del Mundo* (Madrid, 1740), vol. 1, 243, 285 and 354.

The Treaty of London did not establish a regime of religious liberty, not even of freedom of cult for the English. It was a commercial agreement, and therefore only applicable to the merchant class, and by extension, to travellers: English subjects who decided to stay permanently – that is, longer than one year and one day – in Spain or the Netherlands still had to convert to Catholicism.[12] Also, public worship of any other religion than Catholicism was prohibited. With the exception of the English ambassadors in Madrid and Brussels, English subjects were not permitted to organise private religious ceremonies. Any conversation or debate with Spanish or Flemish subjects on religious matter was prohibited. Protestant literature was not to be brought into the territory of the Monarchy, even if it was only for personal use.

Once the negotiations ended, but before the ratification, Madrid took the necessary measures to avoid that the activity of the Spanish Inquisition would abort the Treaty, as had happened in 1575, when Grand Inquisitor Gaspar de Quiroga refused to implement religious tolerance towards subjects of Queen Elizabeth I.[13] In 1599, the Duke of Lerma had removed Grand Inquisitor Pedro de Portocarrero from office, and in the next ten years he appointed four different Grand Inquisitors, thus hollowing out their power and influence. In 1608, he even designated his uncle, Bernardo de Sandoval y Rojas. At the same time, he filled the Council of the Inquisition, also called *Suprema*, with his creatures, so that he could easily influence the religious policy of the Inquisition. In order to avoid that the actions of the relatively independent local tribunals would affect Spain's international politics, he stipulated that any sentence passed on English subjects had to be confirmed by the *Suprema* before its execution. In this way, any inconvenient conviction made by local inquisitors could always be overruled by Madrid. At least the Spanish government seemed to be ready to implement religious tolerance.[14]

However limited the concessions to Protestantism might have been, Spanish public opinion, and especially the orthodox sector of it, condemned the Treaty almost immediately. Since 1595, various Jesuit theologians had written treatises against religious freedom, and in his quite successful *De origine et progressu Officii Sanctae Inquisitionis* of 1598, the Inquisitor of Sicily, Luis de

12 Madrid, Archivo Histórico Nacional, *Inquisición*, reg. 2042–2054: case of Pedro Delarnodi, Santiago de Compostela 1612–1613.

13 Thomas, *La represión*, 276–281.

14 José Martínez Millán, 'Los inquisidores generales durante el reinado de Felipe III' in Joaquín Pérez Villanueva and Bartolomé Escandell Bonet (eds.), *Historia de la Inquisición en España y América* (Madrid, 1984), vol. 1, 887–892.

Páramo, argued the need for extirpation of all religious heterodoxy.[15] When in the spring of 1605 the Earl of Nottingham, Charles Howard, travelled to the Iberian Peninsula in order to attend the ratification ceremony, his diplomatic mission provoked very negative reactions. The famous poet Luis de Góngora noted bitterly:

> The Queen gave birth; the Lutheran came
> With six hundred heretics and heresies;
> We spent a million in a fortnight
> Giving him jewels, accommodation and wine.[16]

The London Treaty got through its first difficult moments when the English legation arrived at La Coruña. One of the English sailors almost immediately got into a fight with a Spanish priest and slapped him in the face. The opponents of the Treaty could not have dreamed of a better argument: the English had not been in Spain for a week, and there had already been a first incident with a heretic showing disrespect for Catholicism. However, the incident did not have major consequences: while the English admiral offered to hang the sailor, the Governor of Galicia gave him a meal and set him free.[17] The second incident occurred when the commissioners of the Inquisition found Protestant bibles in Spanish, printed in the Northern Netherlands, in the luggage of some members of the legation. They had to promise not to take the books with them.[18]

Although the first contact with the English delegation was somewhat difficult, in the days and weeks following their arrival there were no more incidents. On the contrary, Tomé Pinheiro da Veiga, a Portuguese at the Spanish court in Valladolid, wrote in his diary that the English 'behaved with much modesty, respect and courtesy towards statues and sacraments'.[19] The English

15 Apart from Páramo, see also Pedro de Ribadeneira, *Tratado de la religión y virtudes que debe tener el príncipe cristiano para gobernar y conservar sus estados, contra lo que Nicolás Maquiavelo y los políticos deste tiempo enseñan* (Madrid, 1595) and Juan de Mariana, *De rege et regis institutione* (Toledo, 1599).

16 'Parió la Reina; el luterano vino/Con seiscientos herejes y herejías;/Gastamos un millón en quince días/En darles joyas, hospedaje y vino', cited in Miguel Herrero García, *Ideas de los españoles del siglo XVII* (Madrid, 1966), 475.

17 John Stoye, *English Travellers Abroad, 1604–1667. Their Influence in English Society and Politics* (2nd edn., New Haven, 1989), 236.

18 Marcelino Menéndez Pelayo, *Historia de los heterodoxos españoles* (4th edn., Madrid, 1986), vol. 2, 123–124.

19 '[…] procedieron con mucha modestia, respeto y cortesía a todos los imágenes y sacramentos', Tomé Pinheiro da Veiga, *Fastiginia. Vida cotidiana en la Corte de Valladolid* (transl. Narciso Alonso Cortés, Valladolid, 1989), 161.

diplomats who were invited to the presentation of Prince Philip in the church of Our Lady of San Llorente left the church when Mass began. English members of the ambassador's suite were seen in Catholic churches, probably out of curiosity, but never caused any scandal.[20] Apparently, Spaniards gradually lost their mistrust.

Nevertheless, in the weeks and months following the ratification of the Treaty, the embassy in Valladolid and the court in London received many complaints about the non-application of the secret articles by Spanish authorities. Royal functionaries still confiscated English merchandise in Spanish harbours and the Inquisition still proceeded against subjects of the King of Great Britain as if the secret articles did not exist. In January 1605, Thomas Wilson, secretary to Sir Robert Cecil, described the sentiments of the Spanish people quite negatively:

> (...) for although Englishmen were so discreet to give noe scandale yet will the Spaniards both men and wemen be continually urging them, yea some of the cheefest of them in the port townes have said unto my self, yt lett ther Kinge doe what he will in other matters, but for the religion they will lose life and goodes and abandon their contry and goe dwell in the Indies rather then they will suffer heresye.[21]

Wilson's words clearly contradict Pinheiro da Veiga's description.

The reason for this potentially dangerous policy – Madrid was risking the rupture of the Treaty – lies in the slowness with which the secret articles were applied. While the English Crown informed the merchant community in London of the new situation already in September 1604, the Spanish Council of State waited until October before ordering the Inquisition not to start new trials on minor accusations, and to inspect English merchandise with less rigour than before.[22] The *Suprema*, in its turn, did not communicate the new policy to the local tribunals until October 1605.[23] But once the new guidelines had arrived in the districts, all subjects of the King of Great Britain were released, although not before the inquisitors reminded them of the conditions of the Treaty.[24]

---

20 Pinheiro da Veiga, *Fastiginia*, 83, 101 and 109.

21 Cited in Stoye, *English Travellers Abroad*, 357, note 40.

22 Loomie, *Toleration and Diplomacy*, 37 and 43.

23 Henry Charles Lea, *Historia de la Inquisición española* (transl. Ángel Alcalá and Jesús Tobío, Madrid, 1983), vol. 3, 265.

24 Madrid, Archivo Histórico Nacional, *Inquisición*, reg. 2075-15B (case of Jerónimo Alarde); reg. 1829-2ª (case of Duarte Monox). Cf. Henry Charles Lea, *The Inquisition in the Spanish Dependencies* (New York/London, 1908), 171. The Tribunal of Palermo also released all

This did not mean the end of all inquisitorial activity against the English. At least during the first years of the Treaty, local inquisitors were determined to strictly apply the secret articles and to punish English subjects that had been denounced. In almost all cases, they argued that the accused had occasioned public scandal. The concept of 'public scandal' was vague enough to permit such interpretation. Answering questions made by Spaniards on one's religion was already considered as 'scandalous', even if the Protestant did not start the conversation himself, but only responded to the curiosity of the local population. On several occasions the tribunals tried to punish these heretics severely. Time and time again their sentence was overruled by the *Suprema*, who defended more and more the Crown's interests of international policy rather than those of Catholicism in Spain.[25] And when the inquisitors seemed to have forgotten what these interests were, the English ambassador in Madrid did not hesitate to remind them. On several occasions, he intervened actively in order to stop inquisitorial persecution of subjects that did not respect the secret articles of the Treaty, reminding the King that any conviction could have negative consequences on the Anglo-Spanish trade and on the treatment of Catholics in Great Britain.[26]

The embassy itself converted into a real bastion of Protestantism in Madrid. Anglican services were held twice a day. In theory, only the members of the diplomatic staff had access to the chapel, but soon English and other Protestants residing in Madrid, mostly German Lutherans and French Huguenots attended the services. At the same time, it was a place of refuge for anybody who wanted to avoid Catholic Fasting Days. The Inquisition kept strict watch on the visitors of the building, but barely intervened. As time went on, the English ambassador felt so untouchable, that he began to organise a group of heavies to 'convince' British subjects not to convert to Catholicism. In some cases it even used nocturnal violence in order to prevent conversions, mostly of Irishmen. The *Suprema* was always informed about the incidents and was eager to punish the culprits, but had to limit its intervention, urging upon the ambassador to have a better control over the members of his 'family'.[27]

English prisoners, William Monter, *Frontiers of Heresy. The Spanish Inquisition from the Basque Lands to Sicily* (Cambridge, 1990), 247.

25 See cases in Thomas, *La represión*, 321–325.

26 Thomas, *La represión*, 325–333. For an exemplary case of diplomatic intervention on behalf of English prisoners of the Inquisition, see: Madrid, Archivo Histórico Nacional, *Inquisición*, reg. 108–110 (trial of Richard Scott).

27 Werner Thomas, 'Diplomatieke cultuur tussen religieuze verdeeldheid en staatsraison. De Spaanse inquisitie en de Engelse ambassade in Madrid in tijden van Reformatie en Contrareformatie' in Peter Van Kemseke (ed.), *Diplomatieke cultuur* (Leuven, 2000), 71–86.

It is therefore no surprise that very soon after 1604, persecution of British subjects diminished considerably. The number of Englishmen arrested by the Inquisition dropped from 142 between 1559 and 1604 to 37 between 1604 and 1648. While during the twenty years before 1604 the Holy Tribunal condemned more than eighty British Protestants, between 1604 and 1624 it received only 29 denunciations, of which seven ended in absolution *ad cautelam* and five were suspended.[28] Three more were reprehended in the presence of only the inquisitors, that is, not in a public auto-da-fé. Among the absolved, there were perpetrators of crimes that in other circumstances would have received a much more severe punishment. One of these was the sailor Tetos Cult, who spat at an image of a saint in a tavern in Sanlúcar de Barrameda at the beginning of 1605.[29] The worst offenders were simply banished from the country, as happened in 1609 to another sailor, Nicolas Rahen, who insulted two priests and mocked a statue of the Virgin in public.[30] No one was burned at the stake.

In spite of occasional local resistance, the climate of toleration created by the Treaty of London was never turned back. Although the Treaty was suppressed during the Anglo-Spanish war from 1624 to 1630, the *Suprema* waited two years before informing the local tribunals that they should treat the English as any other heretics. When it finally did, there were no obvious changes in the religious policy of the Monarchy. Only eight Englishmen were arrested; four of them were merchants who had not obeyed the command of expulsion. The Treaty of Madrid of 1630 confirmed the secret articles of the Treaty of London and ended *de facto* the persecution of Anglicans in Spain.[31]

The Netherlands and the Twelve Years Truce

While in Spain times were changing, Habsburg policy in the Netherlands remained almost the same. This was more or less the result of the arrangements Philip II had made at the end of his life. The King considered the Dutch rebels as his subjects, in spite of the Act of Abjuration of 1581, and it is therefore no surprise that when ceding the Netherlands – including the insurgent

28 Absolution 'for safety's sake', due to the doubt whether the suspect did or did not commit acts of heresy. If there was not enough basis for a formal accusation, the case was simply suspended.

29 Thomas, *La represión*, 315–317.

30 Madrid, Archivo Histórico Nacional, *Inquisición*, book 835, f° 372.

31 Thomas, *La represión*, 319–320.

provinces – to his daughter Isabella Clara Eugenia in order to resolve the Dutch problem in a peaceful way, Philip made her promise not only to maintain Catholicism, but also to persecute heresy by all means.[32] Moreover, the choice of Albert of Austria as her husband and co-sovereign made a change in religious policy in the Netherlands very unlikely. As former Cardinal of Toledo and Grand Inquisitor of Portugal, the Archduke had always defended religious orthodoxy against Protestantism.[33] And in the years that he was Governor General of the Netherlands, from 1596 to 1598, he had already shown what his plans with the Protestants in the country were, by condemning to death by burying alive the Brussels Anabaptist Anneke Utenhove.[34] Only a storm of protest from different sectors of society, with the exception of the Jesuits and the high clergy, prevented him from starting new religious persecutions. This setback did not mean that he altered his ideas about the fate of Protestantism in his country. Soon, he supported the proposal of the Antwerp vicar general to burn at the stake every reconciled heretic who relapsed.[35] Later on, in 1610, he even declared to the papal nuncio Ottavio Mirto Frangipani that, rather than having to allow Protestants in his country, he preferred not to have subjects at all.[36] This statement reflects a way of thinking very similar to that of Philip II.[37]

32 See the Act of Cession in Victor Brants (ed.), *Recueil des ordonnances des Pays-Bas: Règne d'Albert et Isabelle, 1597–1621* (Brussels, 1909), vol. 1, 7–13, especially the secret articles on 12–13.

33 Francisco Caeiro, *O Arquiduque Alberto de Austria. Vice-rei e Inquisidor-mor de Portugal, Cardeal Legado do papa, Governador e depois soberano dos Países Baxos. História e arte* (Lisbon, 1961).

34 F. Van Dijk, 'Het laatste ketterproces in de Nederlanden (19 juli 1597, Anneke Emelt buiten Brussel levend begraven)', *Gereformeerd Theologisch Tijdschrift*, 49 (1949) 219–231.

35 Marie-Juliette Marinus, 'De protestanten te Antwerpen (1585–1700)', *Trajecta*, 2/4 (1993) 327–343 at 328–329.

36 Alexandre Pasture, 'Le placard d'hérésie du 31 décembre 1609: sa portée juridique et son application pendant le règne des archiducs Albert et Isabelle (1609–1633)' in M.M.F. Béthune and Alfred Cauchie (eds.), *Mélanges d'histoire offerts à Charles Moeller* (Leuven, 1914), 301–310 at 304: 'A chi proponera in consideratione all' archiduca serenissimo che l'editto promulgato contra gli heretici per occasione delle prediche di Lillo havrebbe potuto far diminiure notabilmente il numero di vassali, fu data per sua Altezza pia et generosa risposta dicendo che più tosto desiderava di non havere sudditi che haverne di quella sorte'.

37 Dutch Protestants even reminded in their Beggar's songs that the entourage of the King had declared the same: 'Want de Inquisicy seyt/Thegens zijne Majesteyt/Liever gheen Lant dan Luthrianen', P. Leendertz, *Het geuzenliedboek naar de oude drukken uit de nalatenschap van E. Kuiper* (Zutphen, 1924), vol. 2, 53–55 (1597). At the occasion of one of the 1559 auto-da-fé, Philip II is said to have declared that he would prefer to hand over his own

Once installed as sovereign rulers of the Netherlands, the Archdukes made plans to continue the Habsburg anti-Protestant policy. During the meeting of the States General in Brussels in 1600, Albert hesitated to confirm the privileges of the different provinces because he thought that this would lead to the suppression of the edicts Charles V and Philip II had promulgated against Protestantism.[38] In fact, until 1606 the Archduke tried several times to renew the so called Blood Edict of Charles V. This edict of 1550 condemned to death not only all Protestants, but also everybody else who possessed, read or discussed forbidden books, attended Protestant sermons or lodged Protestants. At the same time, Albert wanted to re-enact some edicts concerning censorship and Protestant literature, and most of all, the 1556 edict promulgated by Philip II to confirm the anti-Protestant legislation of his father. Both the 1550 and 1556 edict had fallen into disuse since the time of Alexander Farnese. Indeed, in 1603 and again in 1606, Albert urged the governors of the different provinces to 'the immediate and severe execution' ('la prompte et rigoureuse execution') of the Caroline legislation on heresy.[39]

On the other hand, Albert continued the Habsburg policy regarding the presence of Protestants in newly conquered territory: they were simply expelled. At Ostend, all inhabitants had to take an oath of allegiance to the Archdukes and the Catholic religion. Protestants who did not want to convert were given three months to settle their affairs.[40] The same conditions were imposed on the population of the towns that were taken in 1605 and 1606. In Grol, for example, inhabitants were given two months to consider whether they would stay as Catholics or would remain Protestant and thus choose to leave the city.[41]

The Treaty of London did not force the Archduke – who did not approve the secret articles and held the opinion that Philip III made too many concessions

son to the Inquisition, rather than to tolerate that he would become a Protestant. Cf. Jesús Alonso Burgos, *El luteranismo en Castilla durante el siglo XVI. Autos de fe de Valladolid de 21 de mayo y de 8 de octubre de 1559* (San Lorenzo de El Escorial, 1983), 115.

38 Hendrik J. Elias, 'De ketterij in de Nederlanden onder Albrecht en Isabella. Een eigenaardig geval te Brugge in 1618', *Annales de la Société d'émulation de Bruges pour l'étude de l'histoire et des antiquités de la Flandre,* 68–69 (1925–1926) 370–387 at 370.

39 Aline Goosens, *Les inquisitions modernes dans les Pays-Bas Méridionaux, 1520–1633* (Brussels, 1997–1998), vol. 1, 126–127.

40 Brants, *Recueil des Ordonnances*, vol. 1, 256: 'vivant catholiquement soubs nostre obeyssance et dont ils seront tenus de prester le serment ès mains de nostre-dit officier et gens de loy que establirons en icelle ville'.

41 Emanuel Van Meteren, *Historie der Neder-landscher ende haerder na-buren oorlogen ende geschiedenissen tot den iare M.VI^C.XII.* (The Hague, 1614), f° 555v.

on the point of religion – to adopt major changes in his religious policy. In contrast with the situation on the Iberian Peninsula, very few subjects of the Queen of England had been persecuted in the Netherlands in the years before the Treaty.[42] Therefore, its religious arrangements were mostly theoretical. Apart from the English and Scottish regiments at Ostend, which constituted half of the garrison defending the town, the number of British Protestants in the Southern Netherlands was very limited. Although the Archduke had already in 1605 discussed the re-establishment of trade relations with England, the Brussels court was still considering its final decision until 1616.[43] Thus, many years passed before English merchants returned to the Southern Netherlands.[44]

The situation in the Netherlands changed when in the spring of 1607 peace talks started between Madrid, Brussels and The Hague. Religious toleration was one of the major subjects of discussion. At the beginning, the Spanish King and the Archdukes required religious freedom for Catholics in the United Provinces without reciprocity in the Southern Netherlands or Spain. Only then they would recognise the sovereignty of the Dutch provinces. On the other hand, the States General considered any demands of that type as interferences in its internal affairs and, thus, infringements upon its sovereignty. Therefore, and in spite of Philip's and Albert's instructions to their representatives that religion was to be the first matter that ought to be discussed, the head of the Spanish delegation, Ambrogio Spinola, almost immediately decided to give

42 Goosens, *Les inquisitions modernes*, vol. 2, 176–177.

43 Henri Lonchay, Joseph Cuvelier and Joseph Lefèvre (eds.), *Correspondance de la cour d'Espagne sur les affaires des Pays-Bas au XVIIième siècle* (Brussels, 1923), vol. 1, 442, n° 1075; 448, n° 1098; 452, n° 1113; 478–479, n° 1207.

44 It was only in 1615, for example, that about forty English families of clothiers from Middelburg asked for permission to establish themselves in Antwerp. This request occasioned a lively discussion between supporters and opponents at the archducal court that went on until at least the summer of 1618 and during which the danger of Protestant infection was the most important argument against the proposal, cf. Petrus F.X. De Ram, 'Un document sur la décadence commerciale d'Anvers au commencement du XVIIe siècle', *Bulletin de la Commission Royale d'Histoire*, 2nd series, 8 (1856) 296–312; Hendrik J. Elias, *Kerk en Staat in de Zuidelijke Nederlanden onder de regeering der aartshertogen Albrecht en Isabella (1598–1621)* (Antwerp, 1931), 26–28. Others argued that the risk of the spread of heresy was minimal, as most Flemish did not understand English: Lonchay, Cuvelier and Lefèvre, *Correspondance de la cour d'Espagne*, 486–487, n° 1233: letter of Iñigo Borja to Philip II, Antwerp 6 October 1616. Finally, in 1619 the families were allowed to come to Antwerp on the condition that no public scandal should arise, and that the English would not practice their religion in public: Elias, *Kerk en Staat*, 28.

preference to less explosive topics. Nevertheless, this could not prevent religion, together with disagreement on free navigation to the Indies, finally wrecking the peace talks.[45]

Once the negotiations for a truce had started, religion was, curiously enough, no major topic anymore. The final result was an arrangement that gave Protestant subjects of the States General the same rights in Spain and the Southern Netherlands as the Treaty of London did to British subjects, but without mentioning religion once. Article 7 of the Truce only refers to the clauses of the 1604 London Treaty:

> And the subjects and inhabitants of the lands of the States General will have the same security and liberty in the lands of the King and the Archdukes as have been granted to the subjects of the King of Great Britain, by the latest treaty of peace and by the secret articles concluded with the Constable of Castile.[46]

These secret articles, as we have seen, included regulations for the presence of British Protestants in Spain and the Netherlands.

Like the Treaty of London, the Twelve Years Truce procured to avoid Spanish and archducal subjects from being exposed to Protestantism. Nevertheless, its proclamation occasioned in the Southern Netherlands the same problems as the application of the Treaty of London had done in Spain, but on a much bigger scale. Dutch Protestants living under archducal rule felt protected enough to show their faith openly. In fact, they had already started to do so during the negotiations. At the beginning of 1608, Bishop Aubertus Miraeus wrote to the Archdukes that the shamelessness of the Protestants in Antwerp grew every day. From February 1609 on, more than fifty Calvinists attended the sermons at the residence of the States General's delegates in the city. This infuriated Miraeus, but he could not convince the city magistrate to take action against

---

45 Willem J.M. Van Eysinga, *De wording van het Twaalfjarig Bestand van 9 april 1609* (Verhandelingen der Koninklijke Nederlandse Akademie van Wetenschappen, afdeling Letterkunde N.S. 66.3; Amsterdam 1959), 114–115; Peter Brightwell, 'The Spanish System and the Twelve Years' Truce', *English Historical Review*, 89 (1974) 270–292; Simon Groenveld, *Het Twaalfjarig Bestand, 1609–1621. De jongelingsjaren van de Republiek der Verenigde Nederlanden* (The Hague, 2009), 33–48.

46 'Oock sullen d'ondersaten ende inwoonders van de Landen der Heeren Staaten de selve versekertheyt en vryheyt in de Landen van den voorseyde Heeren Koninck ende Erts-Hertoghen, die men toeghelaten heeft den ondersaten des Koninckx van Groot Bretanien, by het Leste Tractaet van Peys, ende de secrete Artijckelen ghemaeckt met den Connestabel van Castilien'. cf. Brants, *Recueil des Ordonnances*, vol. 1, 402–409 at 403.

them.[47] Once the Treaty was signed, a weekly transport service by boat between Antwerp and the Dutch town of Lillo was organised. Three of the twelve boats were collectively paid for by the richer members of the Protestant community in order to give their poorer coreligionists the opportunity to attend the sermons. On days with fine weather, local authorities counted more than six hundred Calvinists who embarked at the Antwerp wharf. On board, they sang Protestant psalms, raising their voice when they passed by the Spanish fortifications. Protestant literature was distributed among the participants, and many of them took it home once the sermons had ended. This even surprised the English ambassador William Trumbull, who in a letter to Sir Thomas Edmondes wrote: 'Such is the liberty which the Protestants of Antwerp do assume unto themselves since the making of the truce as they do every Sunday repair to the sermons at Lillo in great numbers'.[48] Moreover, Bishop Miraeus soon discovered that the Calvinist community of Lillo had started the construction of a much larger church building, which was financed by the contributions of the Antwerp Calvinists. He also found out that they got married in Lillo and baptised their children there. Back in Antwerp, they did not even bother to hide their religious conviction from the Catholic priests of the city.[49]

The Antwerp Protestants were not the only ones to take advantage of the new situation. At the same time, Dutch merchants, who were allowed to travel freely in the Southern Netherlands, were behaving without respect for Catholic religion and ceremonies. Already in May 1609, the Archdukes had to send instructions to the bishops, the governors and the Provincial Councils, urging them to vigorous application of the new legislation concerning Protestants in their country: every act or word that scandalised Catholics was to be punished; Catholic subjects were not allowed to abandon their faith; and Protestants that took up residence in the Southern Netherlands were to convert to Catholicism.[50] In July, the papal nuncio in Brussels, Guido Bentivoglio, did the same.[51] Nevertheless, daily contact between Catholics and Protestants produced

47 Marinus, 'De protestanten te Antwerpen', 329.

48 William Trumbull to Sir Thomas Edmondes, Antwerp 15 November 1609, published in: *Calendar of the Manuscripts of the Marquess of Downshire* (London, 1924), vol. 2, 179–181. I would like to thank Dr Paul Arblaster for this information. J.M.G. Leune, *Lillo en Liefkenshoek* (Brussels, 2006), vol. 1, 534 and 549, argues that these numbers are highly exaggerated.

49 Marinus, 'De protestanten te Antwerpen', 329.

50 Brants, *Recueil des ordonnances*, vol. 2, 1–2.

51 Alexandre Pasture, *La restauration religieuse aux Pays-Bas Catholiques sous les archiducs Albert et Isabelle (1596–1633) principalement d'après les Archives de la Nonciature et de la Visite ad Limina* (Leuven, 1925), 304, footnote.

continuous disputes and even violence. In an attempt to diminish or even eliminate religious friction and the consequent problems of public order, Albert issued an edict in July 1609, prohibiting

> from now on to set people against each other, or to conduct any disputation or conversation on whatever religious topic, or on what has happened during the Rebellion, [...] but all are obliged to put up with each other in silence, peace and concord, without causing scandal.[52]

It seemed like a somewhat naive attempt to remedy the situation. During the autumn, things got out of hand. The Antwerp Catholics felt more and more offended by the Lillo sermons and reacted violently. On 1 November, they assembled on the banks of the river Scheldt awaiting the arrival of the boats. Once the Protestants got ashore, they were insulted and threatened by this 'concourse of tumultuous people', as Trumbull called them.[53] In turn, the Calvinists shouted slogans such as 'down with papists and monks'. During the night, some of them destroyed a statue of the Holy Virgin at the entrance of the college of the Jesuit order, the members of which they held responsible for the anti-Protestant climate in the city.[54] Bishop Miraeus urged the Archdukes to intervene. Although Albert and Isabella could not directly forbid the construction of the church, they insisted that the city authorities finally prohibit the Lillo trips and punish subjects that had participated in the Lillo sermons.[55]

Philip III was almost immediately informed about the disturbances in Antwerp and other Flemish towns.[56] At the end of November, he ordered his ambassador in Brussels, the Marques of Guadaleste, to confront Albert with the inconveniences of the Lillo sermons and of the archducal policy towards Calvinists in general.[57] Under heavy pressure from Madrid, the Archduke promulgated on the last day of 1609 a severe edict that was to put an end to the

52 Brants, *Recueil des ordonnances*, vol. 2, 10: 'voortaen d'eene teghen den anderen op te worpen, oft van t'ghene des gheduerende de voorschreven voorleden troublen mach ghepasseert zijn, [...] maerdat sy sullen schuldich zyn, met malcanderen te draghen in alle stilte, vrede ende eendrachticheyt, sonder voorts te stellen eenich schandaal'.

53 William Trumbull to Sir Thomas Edmondes, Antwerp 15 November 1609, published in: *Calendar of the Manuscripts of the Marquess of Downshire* (London, 1924), vol. 2, 179–181.

54 Marinus, 'De protestanten te Antwerpen', 329.

55 Marinus, 'De protestanten te Antwerpen', 328–329.

56 Lonchay, Cuvelier and Lefèvre, *Correspondance de la Cour d'Espagne*, vol. 1, 343, n° 769.

57 Lonchay, Cuvelier and Lefèvre, *Correspondance de la Cour d'Espagne*, vol. 1, 343–345; Maurice Van Durme, *Les Archives générales de Simancas et l'histoire de la Belgique IXe–XIXe siècles* (Brussels, 1966), vol. 2, 570.

religious friction. In its introduction, he described the problems that had led to this measure: Dutch as well as Flemish subjects provoked Catholics in the Southern Netherlands by teaching their errors in public and by organising sermons and 'improper meetings at night' ('onbehoorlycke vergaderynghen by nachten; conventicles nocturnes'), thus committing 'scandalous deeds' ('schandaleuse feyten; actes et paroles scandaleuses') to incite and 'seduce' the local population. The new law prohibited every public or secret Protestant meeting, and the participation in it of any archducal subject. Dutch travellers were to behave with respect for Catholic religion and ceremonies, and Dutch subjects who took up residence in the Southern Netherlands were reminded that they had to convert to Catholicism, just as the Treaty of London stipulated.[58] At the same time, the provincial councils issued complementary measures. In order to prevent the importation and spreading of 'booklets, treatises and songs full of blasphemy and false doctrines' ('diversche boecxkens, tractaten, refereynen ende liedekens vol blasphemien ende valse leeringhe'), Dutch merchants were to allow inspection of the books they imported for personal use.[59] The Marques of Guadaleste as well as Albert's confessor Fray Iñigo de Brizuela, were satisfied with the measures that were taken and were fully convinced that they would stop Protestant infiltration.[60]

However, the situation in the Southern Netherlands did not improve at all. In September 1612, a Dutch Calvinist refused to kneel when the Holy Sacrament made its way through the streets of Brussels, probably motivating a third proclamation of the 1609 edict in November.[61] Two years later, the Archduke bitterly noted that 'several strangers, coming to our land, have done acts and held very scandalous discourses to the prejudice of our religion; some of them secretly imported prohibited books and distributed them among the people in order to divert it from its old religion'.[62] Spanish observers in Brussels noted a significant deterioration of the religious situation in the country. Fray Jerónimo Gracián de la Madre de Dios, a Spanish Carmelite monk residing in Brussels,

58 Brants, *Recueil des Ordonnances*, vol. 2, 26–28; Dutch version: *Tweeden Placaet-Bovck inhoudende diversche Ordonnancien, Edicten, ende Placaeten* [...] *van Vlaenderen* (Ghent, 1629), 30–32.

59 Brants, *Recueil des Ordonnances*, vol. 2, 33–35.

60 Lonchay, Cuvelier and Lefèvre, *Correspondance de la Cour d'Espagne*, vol. 1, 347; Van Durme, *Les Archives générales de Simancas*, vol. 1, 571.

61 Lonchay, Cuvelier and Lefèvre, *Correspondance de la Cour d'Espagne*, vol. 1, 395–396.

62 Brants, *Recueil des Ordonnances*, vol. 2, 221: 'plusieurs estrangers venans a nosdits pays, s'advancent de faire actes, et tenir discours fort schandaleux, au prejudice de nostre religion, aucuns y apportans secretement livres defenduz, et les divulgans entre le peuple pour le divertir de son ancienne religion'.

even wrote a treatise bearing the significant title 'Sparks of heresy that may fly from Flanders to Spain' (*Centellas de fuego de herejía que pueden saltar de Flandes a España*), in which he argued that, precisely because Spanish soldiers in the Netherlands were more and more exposed to Protestantism, they could mean a threat to Spanish Catholicism when returning to their homes.[63] Madrid was alarmed by the spread of new heresies in the Southern Netherlands, and the Spanish Council of State even dedicated some meetings to the problem.[64]

Apart from the attitude of the Dutch merchants, the Nicodemism of Flemish subjects was another growing problem. Many Protestants residing in the Southern Netherlands participated in Calvinist sermons in the south of the United Provinces – Cadzand, Sluis, IJzendijk, Aardenburg, Breda, Bergen-op-Zoom – or the north of France – Calais.[65] In 1610, the magistrate of Valenciennes arrested two Calvinists that had organised Protestant meetings in their houses.[66] The apprehension of one Alard Roulof two years later revealed the existence of a Protestant community in Lille. In at least eight houses in the city, some fifty Protestants met on a regular base.[67] In 1613 and 1614 similar communities were discovered in Arras and Douai.[68] From 1611 on, Bishop Johannes Malderus mentions different clandestine meetings in the city of Antwerp, probably a consequence of the prohibition of attending the Lillo sermons. Dutch preachers visited the Antwerp community and religious instruction was given to the children. Both activities show a certain level of organisation that alarmed the local authorities.[69] In Luxemburg, there was growing evidence

63 Werner Thomas, 'Jerónimo Gracián de la Madre de Dios, la corte de Bruselas y la política religiosa en los Países Bajos meridionales, 1609–1614' in René Vermeir, Raymond Fagel and Maurits Ebben (eds.), *España y los Países Bajos, siglos XVI–XVIII. Agentes e identidades en movimiento* (Madrid, 2011), 289–312.

64 Lonchay, Cuvelier and Lefèvre, *Correspondance de la Cour d'Espagne*, vol. 1, 432; Van Durme, *Les Archives générales de Simancas*, vol. 2, 14 and 443.

65 Arnold de Jonge, *De geuzenhoek te Sint-Maria-Hoorebeke* (Horebeke, 1979), 11; Brussels, Archives Générales du Royaume, *Conseil Privé – époque espagnole*, n° 1117: letter from the Privy Council to the authorities of Saint-Omer (1611); trial of Anthoine Le Candle and Franchoise Beccu (1613).

66 Brussels, Archives Générales du Royaume, *Conseil Privé – époque espagnole*, n° 1117: trial of Almbard and Hughes du Boon (1610).

67 Brussels, Archives Générales du Royaume, *Conseil Privé – époque espagnole*, n° 1117: trial of Alard Roulof (1612–1613).

68 Brussels, Archives Générales du Royaume, *Conseil Privé – époque espagnole*, n° 1117: trial of Maximiliaan Joyel (1613–1614); trial of Jehan Le Maire (1614).

69 Marinus, 'De protestanten te Antwerpen', 337.

that the Count of Manderscheid protected Protestants in his lands. In 1613, after a second trial, he and his wife were banished from the country and his possessions were confiscated.[70]

The Archdukes tried to remedy the situation. During the whole period of the truce, they insisted on the application of the measures taken to protect the Catholic population from Protestant influences. Already in April 1611, the Archduke had to repeat the 1609 edict.[71] When in August 1612, Rodrigo Calderón informed Philip III on the rapid spread of Calvinism in the South, the King subsequently insisted on more rigorous action against the former rebels, because he was convinced that if local authorities did not intervene immediately, Flanders would end up in the same way as the German Empire.[72] To prevent this, Madrid even thought about asking the Queen of France's mediation in order to convince the United Provinces of the necessity of respecting the arrangements made in the Twelve Years Truce.[73] The Brussels Council of State also insisted on severe punishment of Calvinist provocations, but in the end the Archduke only proceeded to a fourth proclamation of the edict on 4 March 1614. Three years later, on 25 March 1617, he was forced to do the same.[74]

The instauration of new heresy laws might lead to the conclusion that repression of Protestantism was intensified during the truce, especially in the cases permitted by the Treaty, that is, when involving Flemish subjects, Dutch Protestants residing in the Southern Netherlands, or Dutch merchants and travellers provoking 'scandal'. In reality, the truce led to a situation of *de facto* toleration towards foreigners *and* locals, in which only the most 'scandalous' cases were persecuted, that is: public worship of and propaganda for Protestant religions, and public insults to Catholicism, the Catholic Church and its ministers. Low profile Protestants – Dutch as well as Flemish – were generally left in peace. As early as 1610, Iñigo de Brizuela wrote in a letter to Philip III that heretics would no longer be molested if they did not profess their religion openly.[75] Moreover, when in 1617 Bishop Malderus decided to track down and punish

70 Brussels, Archives Générales du Royaume, *Conseil Privé – époque espagnole*, n° 1117 (for the 1603 case); Goosens, *Les inquisitions modernes*, vol. 2, 171–172 (for the 1613 trial).

71 Brants, *Recueil des Ordonnances*, vol. 2, 79–80.

72 Lonchay, Cuvelier and Lefèvre, *Correspondance de la Cour d'Espagne*, vol. 1, 344, n° 774, and 345, n° 775.

73 Lonchay, Cuvelier and Lefèvre, *Correspondance de la Cour d'Espagne*, vol. 1, 388; Elias, *Kerk en Staat*, 13.

74 Brants, *Recueil des Ordonnances*, vol. 2, 318–319.

75 Lonchay, Cuvelier and Lefèvre, *Correspondance de la Cour d'Espagne*, vol. 1, 347, n° 784.

Flemish Protestants, they protested, arguing that they were discriminated by comparison with their fellow believers from the North, and they threatened to abandon the city. The Archduke as well as the city authorities restrained Malderus from carrying out his plans, thus reaffirming this climate of relative toleration towards all inhabitants of the Southern Netherlands. The absence of centrally organised campaigns to eradicate Protestantism in the Southern Netherlands, in spite of the re-enactments of the 1609 edict, only confirms this new policy.

An example of religious toleration was the establishment, from 1618 on, of several Arminian pastors in Antwerp and Waalwijk with the approval of the Archdukes. The Privy Council even advised that nothing could prevent their presence in the Southern Netherlands if they respected the Twelve Years Truce. During their stay in Antwerp, they were not bothered at all. One of the Arminians even stated that in religious matters he felt more free than in Holland, and that the Antwerp magistrate favoured their presence.[76] Nevertheless, an official request of the Arminians to reside permanently in the South was refused because Albert hoped that their presence in the United Provinces would contribute to the restoration of Catholicism. In 1620 they were asked to leave the country, although more for political than for religious motives.[77] The return of the Merchant Adventurers to Antwerp in 1619, that brought hundreds of Protestants into the city, was also an example of this climate of relative toleration. In this case, the Antwerp authorities explicitly argued that the English could very well be granted free exercise of their religion, as was already the case with 'naturals', that is, the Flemish subjects.[78]

This situation did not change in 1621, when war broke out. Most subjects of the States General left the country. Inquisitorial persecution in Spain increased only very slightly. Although a few Dutchmen were condemned to the stake, this generally occurred because of political reasons, as the case of Hans Avontroot in 1633 demonstrates. Avontroot was officially burned because he had tried to convert the King of Spain to Calvinism. In reality, his execution was a not very subtle way of scuppering the peace negotiations with the United Provinces that had started in 1632.[79] Although in the Netherlands the Flemish bishops

76 Marinus, 'De protestanten te Antwerpen', 332.

77 Elias, *Kerk en Staat*, 28–30.

78 Lonchay, Cuvelier and Lefèvre, *Correspondance de la Cour d'Espagne*, vol. 1, 486, n° 1233: letter of Iñigo de Borja to Philip III.

79 Werner Thomas, 'El hombre que intentó convertir al Rey de España: Hans Avontroot (1559–1633)', *Foro Hispánico*, 3 (1992) 43–64.

intended to recommence religious persecution, they were not supported by local or central authorities. In the spirit of the Council of Trent, a good shepherd did not destroy his disobedient sheep anymore, but tried to bring them back to the flock by arguments. Episcopal visitations reports from the second quarter of the 17th century show the presence of several Protestant communities in different Flemish towns, who managed to survive until the Peace Treaties of 1648. And when in 1657 the Brussels government decided to promulgate one more time the 1609 edict, the Privy Council wrote to the vicar of the Bishopric of Ghent that 'nevertheless you will apply the law discreetly and with caution, and you will not bring into use inquiries that are more severe than those that were used during the years of the Truce and the following war, thus allowing toleration and coexistence, as was allowed then'.[80]

Conclusion

The Treaty of London and the Twelve Years Truce led to a change in the attitude of the Spanish Habsburg towards Protestantism in their lands. The need for peace and commercial interests imposed a regime in which a general persecution of Protestants no longer formed part of Habsburg religious policy. In part, repressive action was made impossible by the international situation. Madrid and Brussels feared for the fate of Catholics in Great Britain and the United Provinces, an element that was cleverly used by the English and Dutch governments. In fact, the agreements concerning the Catholics living in those parishes that belonged to southern bishoprics – Roermond, 's-Hertogenbosch, Bruges, Ghent and Antwerp, which included the parishes of Bergen-op-Zoom and Breda – but were military occupied by the Dutch, were almost never respected.[81]

But there was another reason that forced Madrid and Brussels to abandon religious repression, particularly in the Netherlands. From 1609 on, the Spanish King started to organise the reincorporation of the Southern Netherlands into the Spanish Monarchy, due to the childlessness of the Archdukes. Repression of Protestantism clashed with the effort of the Crown

80 '[...] que néantmoins pour eviter aux remuemens desdits estats vous aurez a vous en servir avec la plus grande modestie et retenue que faire se pourra, et n'user des recherches plus rigoureuses qu'on a faict au temps de ladite tresve et de la guerre en suivie, ains sera faicte pareille tollerance et convivence comme au mesme temps'. Cited in Elias, *Kerk en Staat*, 25.

81 Brants, *Recueil des Ordonnances des Pays-Bas*, vol. 1, 350.

to gain the hearts of the Flemish subjects. Instead, they reached for other weapons in order to limit the impact of Protestantism. In the Netherlands, the Antwerp Truce allowed the Archdukes to finally rebuild the Flemish Church and to implement the Tridentine Reform, including the implementation of mechanisms of social control. They thus created a type of religiosity that was strong and combative enough to resist Protestantism without any need for repression. The image of burning heretics belonged almost completely to the past. From being intransigent countries, the Southern Netherlands as well as Spain changed into more open societies, where religious tolerance was practised up to a certain point.

www.ingramcontent.com/pod-product-compliance
Lightning Source LLC
LaVergne TN
LVHW010555300926
849162LV00002B/336
9789004274914